D0742156

IDEOLOGY
AND
UTOPIA
IN THE
UNITED STATES
1956–1976

IDEOLOGY AND UTOPIA IN THE UNITED STATES 1956–1976

Irving Louis Horowitz

New York
Oxford University Press
1977

To Scott

Contents

Foreword

Over the years, Irving Louis Horowitz has established himself as an exceptionally prolific and significant practitioner of the sociologist's craft. A most important part of his work has been devoted to the study of power relationships in a number of major contexts—for example, in Latin America, the developing countries, the United States, and the linkages between the first two and the last. The present book is a collection of essays and articles on American politics which Professor Horowitz has written over the past two decades; about half of these have appeared during the 1970s. These essays are rich in insight and very often are models of penetrating analysis of the subject matter. Their range has the exceptional breadth which we have come to associate with their author himself. Here we may read and reflect upon topical matters of their time, such as the scholarly implications of the Pentagon Papers affair or J. Edgar Hoover's remarkable success in converting himself and his agency into apparently unassailable American institutions. Essays like this—shaped as they are by the author's drive to develop generally applicable propositions about the workings of this political system from highly concrete and dramatic cases—have a permanent value for students of this polity, a value extending beyond the specific circumstances which occasioned them. One may then turn to Horowitz's analyses of conservatism, liberalism and radicalism in contemporary America. It might be thought that all of this is well-trodden ground; but it doesn't take a great deal of perusal to convince the reader that the author is equally at home in the realm of political theory, and that the reading is well worth the effort.

Unlike many collections of occasional pieces by a single author, this book has a common theme, one which can be found on nearly every page. This theme, as I read it, is that of *contradictions,* and the fruits of these contradictions: the movement of American politics into a twilight zone of officially committed illegalities, mass apathy and Hobbesian struggles among radically polarized ethnic, racial and other interest groups. Such a *leitmotif,* in modern intellectual circumstances, is usually associated with a leftist critical perspective. And indeed, Professor Horowitz is a man of the left in the sense that his analyses are informed by a critical confrontation with the existing order and by a commitment to democratic values and to humanism. But the leftism here is neither cast-iron Marxism nor Con III egotism. It seems to me, instead, to rest on an uncompromisingly intellectual foundation, one which refuses to surrender either to dogma or to orgasm. Such major thinkers as Karl Kautsky and C. Wright Mills would, I think, be regarded by Horowitz himself as both his mentors and his co-workers in the endlessly difficult task of human liberation in which they have been engaged.

It is this perspective which has made Professor Horowitz a more trenchant and effective analyst of American politics than the large majority of pluralist political scientists on the one hand or of conventional Marxists on the other. As to the latter, for instance, Horowitz quite correctly notes that any "betrayal of the working class" in the United States has been very largely "self-betrayal," and arises from the overwhelming acceptance of the country's dominant social, economic and political institutions—and its "political formula" or dominant political myth—by the population at large. But as to the former, Horowitz penetratingly analyzes the extent to which pluralism is ideology at least as much as it is social science; and also the extent to which it, along with its parent liberalism, has collapsed as guide either to analysis or action in the present period. Finally, his radical commitment to human freedom in a manipulative and repressive context of Big Organization is perhaps best captured at the end of his essay on the condition of the working class in America. After giving us one of the most realistic discussions of the scope and limits of labor politics in America which has thus far been written, he notes the importance of maintaining the kernel of moral truth in socialist rhetoric: "Men who work also deserve to be men who rule."

A collection of thematic essays such as this is not the place to expect a single, worked-out statement of the author's theory of American politics. He does not, for example, attempt a systematic analysis of the contradictions which so massively penetrate American politics in the last quarter of the twentieth century. If I were to attempt to delineate the master or underlying contradiction which undergirds the system, I would begin from a position very close to that of James O'Connor. In the modern political economy, the state is a steering mechanism whose primary job is to do two potentially (and, increasingly, actually) incompatible things: to make the existing order of economic and social domination legitimate, and to maintain that legitimacy; and to be a centrally important vehicle for capital accumulation. To the extent that the economic upheaval of the mid-1970s turns out to be a *Konjunktur* rather than a temporary disorder, as Barraclough and others have argued, the incompatibility will very likely become much more visible in the years ahead. A detailed analysis of the New York fiscal crisis and its *political* implications is a most promising place to begin mapping out such old-new terrain. Be that as it may, Horowitz's vision is once more accurate when he argues—against both vulgar Marxists and the cash-register school of American pluralist political science—that the state is not a passive element in the processes of politics, the official role-holders who manage it have wills of their own, and that there is more than something to the notion of a *political* base and a *socioeconomic* superstructure.

But now, let Professor Horowitz tell his own story. It is well worth the reading.

Walter Dean Brunham

Massachusetts Institute of Technology
Cambridge, Massachusetts, 1976

Preface

IDEOLOGY AND UTOPIA IN THE UNITED STATES is a volume that is based largely on materials written over the past twenty years. Nonetheless, in deciding which pieces to include and which to leave out, I recognized that what was important, even imperative, to the integrity and usefulness of the work was the proper emphasis on what was must current among my writings within the confines of the theme. The purpose of this collection then is not to chart the rise or fall of personal consciousness, but, much more important, to illumine the current state of my work as it relates to the American society and polity, and, only secondarily, to present the state of the art known as social science.

As a result, I have written special new essays for both the opening and closing chapters of the book: essays that bring the story of ideology and utopia in America up to the present. In addition, in such chapters as "The American Way of Spying," previously published sections have been augmented by new materials bringing to bear on this particular subject new situations and events that have helped sharpen the focus of these articles.

I am not unmindful that a title as august and austere as IDEOLOGY AND UTOPIA, even as part of my own book's title, imposes grave responsibilities on me. It invites comparison and begs for trouble. In this case, comparison with Mannheim's classic study of the European scene prior to World War Two, and trouble to all who think that the words tradition and worship are identical in meaning. Nonetheless, this is the best title I could devise; most in keeping with the spirit and content of the essays.

Despite the diversity of themes and topics included in this volume, I have sought to select materials that will create an integrated work and not simply a potpourri of observations over time. Toward that end I have kept out time-bound pieces—such as immediate threats of atomic conflagration in the late fifties, or the unbridled big-power rivalry of the early sixties—that simply reflect an earlier phase of national concerns. International war has been replaced by internal conflict, and Cold War has given way to Détente—although I daresay big-power rivalry and the fear of international war remain very much in evidence.

Despite this careful screening out of obsolete, irrelevant, and at times even mistaken judgements, this remains a big book, perhaps longer than it need be or might have been had I started twenty years ago to write in a systematic fashion on ideology and utopia in the United States. On the other hand, I am surprised by the constancy of my preoccupation with those problems of values and interest that still polarize American society today. If the route is more circuitous, thereby demanding of the reader a somewhat greater commitment, the present format also has the advantages of an intellectual journey. It does not gloss over the reality of the moment for the sake of an arbitrary unity; nor does it avoid crucial issues that are lost as a consequence of a fading memory rather than real change in the American society.

One caveat is in order: my decision to limit the work to the time frame 1956 to 1976 does not place upon this period a unique historic significance. Rather, it is a way of denoting the period during which these materials were initially prepared for publication. As a matter of record, most of the essays herein included were written during the past ten- rather than twenty-year period of the work. An even larger number were prepared in the 1970s. Insofar as my earlier interests—conservative politics, industrial reconversion, mass employment and strategy, and managing global conflicts—still remain vital areas of investigation, these earlier items have been included. To this extent, then, this approach and further justification for the publication of these essays is therefore no more than superfluous rationalization. In my "world view," sentiments and systems are much closer in life than they are conventionally permitted to be in orthodox social science tradition. I would hope that a sense of social structure no less than the substance of the social process is herein conveyed.

It remains only to register my acknowledgments to the copyright holders of the pieces from which much of this volume has been drawn. These are listed in the following paragraphs. At the same time, it is a near hopeless task to acknowledge the help of others in this twenty-year sojourn. The world of ideas, like the world of human beings themselves, is interlocked. I submit this volume as a possible key to open one or more of these linkage issues—those particular issues that entered or became more tightly locked into American society during the third quarter of the twentieth century.

Most chapters in this volume have been previously published, often in considerably different form. I wish to acknowledge the publications in which the chapters made their prior appearance. The number in parenthesis following the publication indicates the pertinent chapters in this volume. When a chapter appeared in a book edited by a person other than myself, their names are listed with the title of the work. All other materials in this volume have never before appeared in print. Again, I would add that changes were made, and either additions or deletions provided, in order to strengthen the sense of narrative continuity. Finally, my appreciation to the original copyright holders for permission to reprint the articles and essays in this work.

Transaction/Society (1); *Social Science Quarterly* (2); Jerome H. Skolnick and Elliott Curries eds., *Crisis in American Institutions* (3); *Commonweal* (4); *Worldview* (5); *Social Problems* (6); *New Politics* (7); *The Bulletin of the Atomic Scientists* (8); *Science and Society* (9); *Foundations of Political Sociology* (10); *Radicalism and the Revolt Against Reason* (11); Abdul A. Said and Luiz R. Simmons, ed., *The New Sovereigns: Multinational Corporations as World Powers* (12); *The Rise and Fall of Project Camelot* (13); *The American Scholar* (17); *The Nation* (18); *Annals of the American Academy of Political and Social Science* (19); *Diogenes:* International Council for Philosophic and Humanistic Studies (20); *Journal of Applied Behavioral Science* (22); *Social Theory and Practice* (23). To all of the people in the past and present who have helped with the editing, copy editing, and typing of these essays, and to those who have shared with me that most precious of possessions, their ideas, goes my lasting gratitude.

IDEOLOGY
AND
UTOPIA
IN THE
UNITED STATES
1956–1976

Introduction:
The American Experience
with
Political Tragedy

My friend and fellow commentator on the American scene, Arnold A. Rogow, has expressed a frustration one commonly experiences when trying to identify categorically a large panorama: "The supreme difficulty facing any interpreter of life in America is that almost any statement he wishes to make about the United States he can show to be at least half-true." Knowing then that one can defend the position that the American experience is getting better, for instance, simply by maximizing the importance of equity and the preservation of liberty or employing a minimizing scenario to argue that the American core is rotting, citing racial violence and progressive involvement in imperial warfare, how does one go about doing one's job honestly?

One can make the confident wager that both scenarios are correct; or use a clever rubric and insist that objective scenarios are chimeric and what we really deal with are subjective expectations. If the vocabulary of motives is infinite, so too are the shadings of interpretation. Without wishing to foreclose on academic strategies for coping with the problems of interpreting America, I would like to state my own position, namely, that what is necessary is for one to move beyond the whole into the parts. Perhaps in the process an accurate whole will be described, but just as likely we will be left with parts. The choice then becomes whether we want limited revelations that deal with limited truths or cosmic revelations that may be largely unlimited speculation. I opt for the former, with the strong belief that a meaningful picture does emerge: a condition extending for two decades of tragedy.

3

Although there is no determinism that can demonstrate that the system is on the verge of collapse, there is also no current poll that fails to record a mood of economic pessimism, no theorem that dares ignore mass disaffiliation from the political party process. The behavior of elites and masses alike requires no nihilism to occasion present feelings of malaise. Assassinations that changed the course of political leadership, conspiracies to prevent the proper functioning of the electoral process, misinformation that prolonged the duration of hopeless wars—these are the legacies of the past several decades. The American experience with national defeat, the highest form of tragedy, is what this collection of essays is about.

Rather than explain the book in an introduction that would render the volume itself superfluous, I have decided that it might be more pointed to explain briefly how each of these essays came about and how they link up to the American experience with political tragedy. The volume is divided into six parts. There are a total of twenty-four essays, written over two decades. While all editing arrangements strike a note of arbitrariness, it is also true that the work of an individual has a singular quality as well, and hence a sense of continuity. I have done my best to enhance that sense of continuity by the formal arrangement offered.

The first section, "Presidential Politics," begins with two brief statements on the assassination of Robert Kennedy, which along with the previous assassinations of President John F. Kennedy and Martin Luther King, Jr., seemed to spell the death of the classical liberal model of twentieth-century presidential politics. Henceforth politics would no longer be normal in the sense of reflecting the popular will, but would itself be part of the sense of terror brought to American shores by the general malaise of unsponsored wars abroad. Probably because I participated in the Kennedy campaign in California at the time (the Spring of 1968), this particular assassination had an emotional as well as objective impact for me that I have always believed to be shared in some strange way by many other people. This abortive campaign also pointed up for me the fragility not simply of democratic politics, but of politics by famous names. The very theatricality of the campaign signaled the absence of mass participation in the political process.

The second essay in this section discusses the presidential terms of Lyndon Johnson, and attempts to show how America in the grips not so much of the imperial presidency as of the military presidency. President Johnson could run an integrated administration based upon populist premises within the country, while Commander-in-Chief Johnson based his foreign-policy considerations strictly on elitist premises. This bifurcated situation tore apart his presidential pretenses. Johnson was the epitome of mainstream America: convinced of the absolute worthiness of the American dream and equally convinced that all others must likewise share in that dream whether they wished to or not. Presidential militarism turned dreams of equality into nightmares of warfare. Finally, it transformed a President into a confused and bewildered private citizen.

The essay entitled "Reactionary Immortality" is a play on the efforts of some to characterize Mao Tse-tung, the Chinese revolutionary leader, as endowed with revolutionary immortality. I have grave doubts that politics can ever make immortals. Living politicians, more often than not, are rudely reminded just how "mortal" their political careers are. In the case of J. Edgar Hoover and the Federal Bureau of Investigation, we had that strange anomaly of the appointed official whom no one dared to dismiss. Hoover reflected an earlier pristine era when law enforcement was considered to be 180 degrees removed from political activities. Hoover's very administrative prowess, his denial of political biases as he cracked down on presumed enemies of the state, made him an exemplary case study in reactionary immortality. He was an untouchable in a world of crumbling political allegiances and ideologies. He represented a bureaucratic truth in a universe of political fantasies. Hoover's career pointed out not simply the limits of bureaucratic politics, but its absolute threat to the democratic process.

The final essay in this section represents a retrospective look at Nixon and Watergate. President Richard Nixon's presidency was more like a European premiership. He was never viewed as someone who could live out his term in office unwatched. From the early posters of the first campaign: "Would you buy a used car from this man?" to the very last cartoons in Punch: "Jump, jump!" there remained a suspicion that here was a plebeian politician and not a patriarchal President. This in turn led to a strong shift away from the presidentialist syndrome. For the first time in the twentieth century, the legislative branch exercised control or at least established parity with the executive branch. Congress now behaves like a European parliament rather than a rubber stamp as it does in authoritarian systems. If this creates an intense degree of chaos, it also has restorative power with respect to the nature of the democratic system. It converts a rather arid theory of checks and balances into the practice of checking some leader who had gotten out of balance. That is the key to understanding the impact of the Watergate episode.

The second section is entitled "Class-Race Politics." Quite frankly, I do not know what the singular, crucial variable is. I doubt that any unicausal explanation will suffice. If matters are to be settled in class terms, then the seeming bourgeoisification of blacks would lead to a breakdown of racial struggle. It should also lead to making those things such as bureaucracies superfluous. But if the nationalist argument is sound, and the amount of class mobility does not uniquely determine penetration of the American mainstream—if, in short, being black cancels out being wealthy—then one can expect an increase in racial struggles and perhaps a corresponding decline in class struggles. For the moment this is a great unknown and a problem yet to be answered by the great "unwashed."

The first essay in this section concerns "Race, Class, and the New Ethnicity." It shows how the ethnic factor, while legitimate, does not carry nearly the clout of either the race or class factors. It represents in part imitation of and adaptation to the model of interest groups originating in the federal government, rather than interclass rivalry in factories or racial confrontation in neighborhoods. The new ethnicity is not simply a celebration of old-country virtues and values, but, much more profoundly, the acceptance and even enthusiastic support of interest-group politics as a new style of getting ahead.

The chapter "Revolution and Counterrevolution in American Cities" was written at the peak of urban warfare between blacks and whites in the late 1960s. It became very clear even then that a settlement, at least a temporary settlement, of the struggle at the street level would be the surrendering of the cities to black and white poor, while blocking them from suburban areas, which would in turn remain the preserve of middle and upper classes. Equity would once more be conceived in terms of separate but equal: the traditional Southern approach of keeping the races apart but giving them equal access was transposed from regional rhetoric to national ideology. As subsequent events have shown, to be separate is already to be unequal. It presupposes not simply being apart, but being above and being below, a bitter lesson learned by nationalists and racists alike, albeit painfully and slowly.

The penultimate chapter in this section is an attempt to re-evaluate the condition of the working class, a working class that ironically reflects upward mobility and yet not much increase in trade-union participation. The gap between organized and unorganized working classes, between proletarians and marginals, becomes itself a bitter focus of struggle in the 1970s. And the American world hinges more on the struggle between those who work with their heads and those who work with their hands, between white collar and blue collar, between organized and unorganized, than between working classes and owning classes. In this sense, America has become a Hobbesian rather than a Marxian nation, a place where the war of all against all is conducted with a ferocity that makes nineteenth-century class warfare seem tame in comparison. It is pointless to say that this is the wrong war at the wrong time since this is in fact a war and this is the time. The task of anlysis remains as to how the present condition of the working class affects the structure of economic life in America as a whole.

The final essay in the second section, "American Futurology and the Pursuit of the Millennium," attempts to take up not so much the question of the year 2000, but rather what has taken place in the first seventy-five years of the twentieth century that permits us to disregard so casually the upcoming quarter-century in favor of analysis of the twenty-first century. It is a perplexing aspect of the American character that in the midst of troubles, optimism evolves. The social-science community is also working on problems of the twenty-first century. The purpose of my essay is not simply to defuse the futurology phenomenon, but, more pointedly, to examine the decennial characteristics of American politics, the framing of events in ten-year cycles that almost demand counterpoints to what occurred in previous decades. Beyond that, the essay tries to show that much less has happened than meets the eye. The same overall transcendentalism noticeable at the turn of the twentieth century remains very much present in the current decade. And while people might be surprised by the technological innovations of automobiles vis-a-vis the horse and buggy, or electricity in relation to gaslight, they would be far less surprised by the continuing structure of power balance in the nation and throughout the world. Technology moves rapidly, politics moves rather slowly, and morality hardly at all.

The third section, "Ideological Politics," derives from a belief that the United States is not exempt from iron-law tripartite politics, namely, politics between Right, Left, and Center. Even that iron law brings with it a unique and rich content, on these shores different from that in Europe or elsewhere. The essay "The New Conservatism in America" is the oldest one in the volume. It was written and prepared in 1955 and published in 1956. It represents a response to the first postwar wave of conservative attack on liberalism; prepared at a time when McCarthyism was no longer a thundering noise on the American scene, but had nonetheless left in its wake bitter disillusionment with the liberal management of the postwar world. It was out of this new conservatism as an ideology that a new conservatism as a practical reality emerged in the fertile crescent, extending from the southwest to the California Basin into the northwest. The essay was written prior to the renewed burst of military technology which followed the launching of Sputnik. The concentration of this "military-technological complex" in a "Southern rim" gave succor and sustenance to the new conservatism. Geography and demography conspired with the war footing of the American economy of the 1950s in providing the essential content and contours of that new conservatism, and hence led to the restoration rather than the elimination of ideology in America.

The essay on liberalism in part is a response to a troubled feeling that liberalism, contrary to what Lowi and Mills had written, is no longer a triumphant theology. Liberalism no longer either satisfies mass needs or represents elite persuasions in an unqualified manner. Something had been missed. Liberalism itself has undergone huge changes and is faced not so much with challenge on the Right as thunder from the Left. Beyond that, liberalism's pragmatic and pluralistic character only serves to polarize further the ideological framework in American life. Liberalism, far from being the accepted foundation of all political rhetoric, has now entered a stage where it is fighting for its life, and where the majority of the people are well contented with identifying with the word *conservatism* even if they do not accept its contents. It was only in the sense in which American liberalism identified itself with the overall concepts of progress and evolution that it became crucial, since when other concepts of progress were questioned, when evolution itself came to mean little other than change, the contents of liberalism were no longer identified with the manifest destiny of America. At this later stage of liberalism, *engagé* rather than triumphant, the paper was prepared.

The essay "American Radicalism and the Revolt Against Reason" came about with the publication of a second edition of my volume on Georges Sorel entitled *Radicalism and Revolt Against Reason.* The American 1960s have much in common with the French 1890s—a radicalism of immediacy, of sensuousness and gratification, of personal communion rather than overarching ideology. The two periods elicited similar expressions of disbelief in national models. Just as the radical socialism of Marx has worn thin, so the Bolshevism of Lenin has become threadbare. It is radicalism divested of national impulse that we have witnessed throughout the 1970s in the United States. In *The Struggle is the Message: The Organization and Ideology of the Anti-War Movement,* I attempted to take up the question in detail, but for the present volume, the opening sketch comparing the American New Left with *fin de siècle* France is sufficient.

The final chapter in this section, "Capitalism, Communism, and Multinationalism," is perhaps a bow in the direction of colleagues such as Seymour Martin Lipset and Daniel Bell. The end of ideology was indeed very much in the cards, not solely as an American experience, but as an international experience in *Realpolitik* as well. The end of ideology was announced with the shared vision of capitalist society in the United States and communist society in the Soviet Union in the faith and future of multinationalism. Wheat deals replace ideological rhetoric, and banking arrangements between the superpowers replace military arrangements in Southeast Asia. Détente has become a commercial way of life in America despite the fact that ideological rhetoric continues in full force from the cold-war period. What we are witnessing is not so much the end of ideology as the end of politics. The global nature of conflict will change and move away from the realm of economic systems to that of world empires; a showdown better appreciated by the likes of Sorokin and Toynbee than the structural functional social science we have grown up with.

The fourth section, "Sociological Politics," might be subtitled: "Abuses and Misuses of Sociological Performance in the Political Arena." What we have is a situation of social scientists performing services in the absence of a national consensus and ignoring that very fact in their decision-making processes. In a later work, *Social Science and Public Policy in the United States,* I discovered that where a prior consensus exists, one can seek authoritative and positive social-science inputs. Where a disagreement exists, as in American foreign policy in the 1960s, social science, like everything else, becomes subject to laws of behavior far beyond the scope of meliorative management. When the tail wags the dog, there may be a temporary increase in excitement and curious behavior, but in the long run, the dog will end up turning in circles and aimlessly wandering about. In some measure that was the case with social science in its policy-making role during the 1960s. Instead of cautioning as to the limits of policy-making, it entered the spirit of the national game and itself became victim and vanquished much as did the military establishment serviced by this sort of social science.

Project Camelot deals with what is perhaps the most well-known program involving social-science participation and promotion of civic action in Third World contexts. The tragedy is that a program that offered social scientists a golden opportunity to rise to the occasion and destroy the myths of American intervention in the rights of poor nations and poor people fell precisely on this count. It elevated the notion of civic action into social welfare and in this way disguised not only the in-effectiveness of social science, but also the disequilibrium it is dedicated to correcting.

Project Themis had the same basic purview as Project Camelot, only its concerns were more domestic than foreign in its effort to militarize the educational process internally. Perhaps it was too close to Camelot, or for that matter, too remote, but it illustrates well the point that what first appears on the scene of history as tragedy often returns as comedy. Project Themis, in its ambitions and attitudes, merely reflects what Project Camelot and its failures should already have alerted the social-science community to: the fact that the task of social science is to come up with a complete picture, one that recognizes what is impossible and not simply what is possible, what is unpredictable rather than the assurance that everything is subject to predictability.

The essay on the Pentagon Papers completes the package by showing that the involvement of social scientists in the Vietnam War occurred at the upper echelon, and not merely as a managerial input, that social scientists were involved with the manufacture of policy, not simply its evaluation. It is all too easy to see social science in a ludicrous light as a result of these projects. More important, these projects roused the social-science community to a level of opposition and struggle it had hitherto not known. These projects and the wars they justified provided a great divide between those who saw social science as simply a marginal celebration of the American experience and those social scientists who understood that the American experience itself was tinged, indeed saturated, with tragedy. Social science is not simply policy-making or policy evaluation. It is constant criticism and production of constructive alternatives to policies already entered into and programs the political machinery considers sacrosanct.

The essay "The American Way of Spying" was written somewhat more recently, in relation to the whole problem and process of covert versus open federal operations and renewed demands that information be distinguished from propaganda and research separated from counter-intelligence. "The American Way of Spying" illustrates how far social scientists have come in a decade, for no longer are they seen as innocent handmaidens of policies they do not set or create, but as the most articulate and forthright critics of such policies. If politics is a struggle, so too is science, and this conclusion indicates that mistakes have been made in that struggle involving nothing short of the nature of the social-science process itself, and beyond that, the democratic process.

The section "Military Politics" largely stems from an earlier period when scholars headed by David Riesman gathered around a journal called *The Correspondent* "in the tradition of Samuel Adams" and the Committees of Correspondence of the American Revolutionary War who alerted the citizenry that all was not well. Indeed, all was again not well. At the very time we were told about the end of ideology, the impossibility of racial strife, America as a unique new civilization, in point of fact the military and technological orders superseded *laissez-faire* marketplace considerations. Radical political discontent became dominant in an unprecedented manner, and from disenchanted sectors of the population that were far from impoverished. The United States, which had always prided itself on its tradition of professionalism with regard to the armed forces, for the first time witnessed the sort of politicization typical of so-called underdeveloped countries. The military rose to a crescendo of power unimaginable prior to World War II. It kept alive its impulse from that conflict. The World War II military generated World War III industries. The arts and crafts of warfare were not dismantled, nor were its artisans sent back to the barracks. They became the political kernel. It is hard to recall at this point how close to the actual management of American society the military came. The Vietnam defeat forestalled the very process of American militarization. It is hard to imagine what new triumphs and tragedies we might have gone on to if we had been successful in Vietnam, or just what boundaries would have brought the military to much higher levels of penetration of the political system.

The essay "Arms, Policies, and War Games" derived from the beginning of the McNamara-Kennedy era. It involved the entire concept of war as a game involving high stakes, fright, and all sorts of one-upmanships in which the world is reduced to a gambling table rather than a historical timetable. The entire paradigm of the 1960s was involved with gaming. Whether intellectually licit or illicit, the game was the thing. The Cuban missile crisis was conducted in an atmosphere of showdown poker, with the same sense of a gambler's instinct for victory, quite apart from long-range consequences. My purpose in this essay is to show the range of disequilibriums and misconceptions possible within the framework of game theory. War games have a place in the American political cosmos. They should not take place, however, without full knowledge of the potential enemy's perception of the world, particularly since in our time, diplomatic initiatives and lower stakes have come to be viewed as naive. For where the worth of wars is measured by the tens of millions rather than by each individual person in such a world, the war game becomes a way of life for the political system rather than simply one of its many tools. If war games prevail in these crude ways they will inevitably bring us to new conflicts. In fact, the profundity of a defeat such as Vietnam was needed to make everyone aware that beyond the game is the system, and beyond the system is the need for a pacific world in which other games and systems can be played out.

The tragedy is that the world of military politics is not simply elitist activity carried on by military and social-science mandarins, but one that the American population as a whole already participates in. The burden of my study on "Noneconomic Factors in the Institutionalization of War," which was prepared in connection with Senator George McGovern's first activities on assuming his Senate role, was to show what kinds of mechanisms were available to reduce tension and end the conditions imposed on America since World War II without bringing about economic collapse or calamity. It was my sad duty to report that the institutionalization of war was an accepted fact among Americans at every rank and level. Dismantling of even a single military base was likely to arouse outcries of sectional preference, unemployment, and a host of anguished appeals to the federal regime. Every factory producing aircraft, every firm producing armaments for the Third World, develops ground swells of concern from masses of proletarians who come to believe that no options are available and that civic authority is the threat to their economic well-being. The winding down of the cold war has not yet produced a decrease in arms production: regulations, yes, stable equilibrium between nations, yes; but reductions in arms come much more slowly and painfully. It would be a profound mistake to think that the "military-industrial complex" is simply imposed from the top. Militarism has saturated American life. It expresses the cultural proclivities of society no less than its economic characteristics: from it sportive interests to the instinct for violence. But above all, military politics spells security; pacific politics spells insecurity. Only now, with the crisis in economics reaching out in all directions, is the folly of such an approach beginning to be recognized by masses and elites alike.

The essay on the organization and ideology of the antiwar movement was written in connection with the Presidential Commission on the Causes and Prevention of Violence. The burden of the work is to demonstrate the exact correlation between antiwar sentiments and antiwar demonstrations and to show that the crescendo of antiwar participation followed hard on the heels of disenchantment and disillusionment with the war itself. Beyond that, I try to show that there was rank confusion between antiwar and radical sentiments, and that in fact they are not interchangeable. The assault on the war did not mean an assault on the American system; and the absence of such a simple understanding by the American New Left led to its increasing isolation and alienation from the midstream of American life. It confused the profoundly hostile feelings Americans had for a nakedly aggressive conflict with the repudiation of all things American, including qualities of the democratic process everyone has grown very attached to. As a result, the movement collapsed even before the war, and the war had to be fought out in a political vacuum during its last few years. Increasingly, radicals either fell back into mainstream American life or were totally removed from political realities. Perhaps this is always the fate and fortune of radicals: to provide a vanguard for a mass movement, followed by a period of participation in that mass movement, which in turn leads to another period of disaffection once the reason for the initial mobilization ends. The attempt to recreate in the 1970s the feeling of the antiwar spirit emerging in the 1960s collapsed: the Middle East turned out to be very different from the Far East; the Third World turned out to be much less pleasant than imagined—more nationalistic than revolutionary. The fervor generated by the war was vitiated by the consequences of that war, and the people marginally involved as well as the central actors turned their attentions elsewhere. America is a land of movements, not of parties, a land where the ebb and flow of movements leads to episodic politics rather than continuing politics. Episodes have a tendency to become theatrical, and drama turns to melodrama.

The chapter "The Politics of Détente" was written over a decade ago. It is ironic that détente is now put on the agenda of history as if it were a new discovery. Far from being a new discovery, it was opposed by people like Secretary of State Kissinger, who in the early 1960s were much more concerned with confrontation than with détente, and with the necessity for choice rather than the choice of necessities. It was in that context that the principles of bilateral and multinational settlements were prepared. The main point now, as then, and one that relates to the theme of "Capitalism, Communism, and Multinationalism," is that the bilateral context in which the politics of détente takes place serves to limit debate and discussions. It makes of détente very little other than big-power settlement, and stimulates a new kind of equilibrium, one that will be based not so much on Pax Americana or Pax Sovietica as on a peace grounded in power as such, quite independent of economic systems. Thus the subject of détente becomes one more form of closure, one more way of avoiding a further expansion of democratic horizons to the rest of the world.

The last group of essays can best be described as an attempt to show how old forms are crumbling in the face of new challenges. Distinctions that we have lived with are no longer valid and no longer offer security. It is not that the world is more inscrutable than before. It is rather that the artifices and boundaries we maintain have finally become too pronounced to overlook. We can no longer deal with a world in which everything is known in nineteenth-century philosophical terms. Perhaps the ultimate tragedy of America is its restlessness, its efforts to provide models for others that are in themselves not well understood as even being innovative. The American system has always prided itself on generating morality and innovation, but it has never known quite what to do with either. The four essays in this section are an attempt to show not simply the dissolution of the old, but the shape of the new.

The essay "Social Deviance and Political Marginality" attempts to confront a world in which everyone always knew what was good and what was evil, who was normative and who was deviant, a world of politics where everyone knew who was central and who was marginal, who was Republican and who was Democrat. Each of these distinctions crumbled in the crucible of actual struggles. The political nature of stealing and even violence is matched only by the social nature of marginal politics. What one ends up with is a gnarled bundle of twine, hard but unraveled because the human spirit sees things in much more integrated terms than the boundaries puritan America set for itself. Sex and politics, technology and economics, violence and pacifism, protest and anomie, each of these reified expressions is experienced by each of the actors in the American drama to a greater or lesser degree. The purpose of this essay is to work toward a political sociology that realizes the selective nature of deviance and the tactical nature of political marginality. Norms have crumbled, but so too have political allegiances and alliances. Conservatives might bemoan the loss of norms, and radicals be terribly upset that politics has been infiltrated by personal misbehavior. That is exactly the dilemma, namely, separation of politics from morality itself: the end of the Aristotelian premise that one moves inexorably from the political to the moral realm. There is no such automaticity of motion. If the line between the social and the political becomes less clear, the line between both the social and political over and against the moral becomes even more clear, since the acts of people, whatever their realm, suddenly become acts neither moral nor immoral —simply acts.

The essay "Social Science and Policy-Makers" is an indication that there is also an end of politics not only at the boundary-maintenance level, but at the operational level as well. For whoever is in power, it seems that the world of policy triumphs over politics. The need for exact information and the pursuit of that information takes precedence over various ideological or political persuasions. There is an interchange-ability of policy-making parts. The Secretary of State can service Democratic and Republican administrations; ambassadors to the United Nations can service Presidents from all parties. The policy-makers move in and out of government without much regard to function or role. The quality of being a kingpin has a reality over and above the political process. In this sense, the tragedy of American politics is the breakdown of representational democracy as such. There is a remoteness between those who rule and those who are ruled that can no longer be bridged by the voting act. The quest for community is not simply a demand for restoration, but a strange recognition that politics at the top cannot really be controlled by people at the bottom. In this world of political alienation the political process itself as a democratic act is thwarted.

The study "Ecological Movements vs. Economic Necessities" is yet another part of the unresolved antinomies which plague American society. Demands of ecological renovation come hard upon parallel demands for economic growth. To keep neighborhoods nice, at some levels means keeping people out, not just having a beautiful park. To keep industry at maximum output levels is not merely a matter of gross national product, but a decision to burn coke when coal is not available. There is a huge, perhaps unreconcilable struggle between those who are interested in a model of zero growth and those who are interested in a model of economic equity. The zero-growth model is an effort to freeze the relationships that obtain at present levels of income and opportunity. The equity model involves the redistribution of what wealth does exist by generating new forms of production if required. This is not so much a struggle between zero growth and full growth as between balances to be maintained and equities to be established. The suspicion that the environment movement in America is concerned with keeping in place the advantages of some, rather than extending the benefits of democracy to all, is what this study is about. This too indicates a note of consensus politics, and the tragedy here is between perfectly decent people lining up on two sides of a metaphysical fence that cannot be bridged without a real loss, either environmental or economic. Who is to make that decision?

The final statement, like the introductory essay, is concerned with a new element in American life, and I daresay in advanced Western societies generally: making do with less. For so long we have occupied a practical world of opulence and a corresponding intellectual world of influence and power that the international redistribution of wealth has taken place almost behind our collective backs. Neither the liberalism of Keynesian economics nor the radicalism of Marxian politics has equipped us for nasty, brutish survival struggles. Food and fuel become "weapons" and not simply commodities in abundance. Problems multiply and intensify because the distribution and allocation of scarce goods is a far cry from the distribution and allocation of easily available natural resources. But at the very point in time when a "Revolution of Falling

Expectations" is required, demands for greater equity within American society exert themselves. Freezing growth at present levels of production and consumption is one thing; guaranteeing the continuing demands of blacks, women, children, and minorities of all kinds is quite another. This then becomes the central contradiction of the mid-1970s; one that must be decided no less than addressed if this nation is to continue one and indivisible, and not just many and divided in goals and means. New political styles will inspire us to move from tragedy to triumph only if these present schisms and cleavages are both removed and resolved.

1976

Princeton, New Jersey

I

PRESIDENTIAL POLITICS

1

Politics
of
Assassination

Robert F. Kennedy, speaking in Cleveland on April 5, 1968—the day
following the assassination of Martin Luther King—attempted to match
the reality of regicide with the necessity for political mobilization. Little
did Americans realize that this eulogy would soon serve as epitaph.

> What has violence ever accomplished? What has it ever created? No
> martyr's cause has even been stilled by his assassin's bullet. And whenever
> we tear at the fabric of life which another man has built the whole nation is
> degraded. . . . There is another kind of violence, slower but just as deadly,
> destructive as the shot or the bomb in the night. This is the violence of
> institutions; indifference and inaction and slow decay. This is the violence
> that afflicts the poor, that poisons relations between men because their
> skin has different colors. . . . But we can perhaps remember, even if only
> for a time, that those who live with us are our brothers, that they share
> with us the same short movement of life, that they seek, as we do, nothing
> in purpose and happiness, winning what satisfaction and fulfillment they
> can.

In times of special crisis, Americans react with a sense of guilt by
acclamation. And not unexpectedly, this guilt prompts us to respond to
political assassination with moral outrage, not with political action. The
answer to terror, however, is not tears, but in this situation, the immediate restatement of the essential principles of legitimation upon which
this nation, or any other democratic society, is either to survive or to
perish.

The myths that were circulated by major political figures immediately following the assassination of Senator Kennedy can be categorized into five types. The routinization of the assassination of leading political figures compels us all to attempt to move beyond a state of shock to a statement of principles

MYTH: Assassination has become an infectious and contagious American style.

REALITY: While it is true that major political figures are periodically subjected to assassination attempts, these attempts are usually restricted to the top leadership, and this has been constant throughout the century. Hardly a President has not had attempts made on his life. More significantly, the murder of Senator Kennedy is only distantly related to earlier native efforts. When Sirhan Bishara Sirhan was captured, he said: "I did it for my country. I love my country." But his country turned out to be Jordan, not the United States. In his mind, apparently, there was a fevered, imaginary relationship between an adolescent experience of his and Kennedy's acceptance of the principle of foreign aid for Israel. What is involved, therefore, is a political pathology more than a psychopathology. And although this prosaic fact may take the vigor out of the demands of oracles and pundits for greater social controls, it shows the need for a response relevant to the role of prevalent ideologies of Middle East nationalism. Although the Jordanian ambassador may sincerely repudiate this assassination, the fact remains that the ideology that promoted such an attempt remains intact. The blunt truth is that assassination far more common in Middle East antipolitics than in United States politics.

MYTH: Violence has increased as the propensity of the society to accept change has accelerated.

REALITY: The propensity to violence is, unfortunately, far more constant than current rhetoric would have it. At least there is as much evidence that accelerated social change directs aggressive impulses into acceptable frameworks as there is that "social order" permits a greater degree of social cohesiveness. What is new has little to do with matters relating to "human nature," whatever that amorphous beast may turn out to be. Rather, the novel elements are, first, the incredibly easy access to weaponry of all sorts for all kinds of people; and second, the extent to which nonentities can become part of universal history by an act of regicide—an act linked to the publicity provided an event. Easy access to weapons plus total network coverage equals instant history. With weapons, impulses formerly bottled up or redirected along constructive lines can be quickly let loose to do damage. Impulse action is given ideological support in modern American society: one wing of the New Politics perceives the role of the individual or the conspiratorial group in terms of its ability to tear up established political continuities.

MYTH: Madmen and criminal elements will always be able to avail themselves of weapons, and therefore legislation against gun-toting penalizes only the innocent interested in self-protection.

REALITY: Admittedly, laws against gun purchases, like laws against discrimination, will not result in the elimination of crime, any more than civil-rights legislation does away with racism. But there is no evidence that gun-toting is a basic human appetite. More important, laws would make purchases more difficult and registration-tightening would make tracking down ownership easier. At the heart of the problem is not the lobbying of the National Rifle Association, but the fears of the police that laws against free distribution of weapons would eventually affect police departments—since the militarization of the police would also have to be curbed if registration is developed to increase the pacification of the civilian population.

MYTH: Since there is no evidence that there is a conspiracy in most political assassinations, as in the murder of Robert Kennedy, individual responsibility should be assigned; and when captured, the guilty person should be treated as demented and deranged.

REALITY: There are several fallacies in this line of reasoning. A premature dismissal of possible conspiracies, at least as a starting point in explaining political murder, is absurd. Conspiracies are empirical events. One can have a conspiracy, in fact, without a theory of conspiracy to guide the search for the source of a crime. Further, conspiracies—when they do take place—are extremely difficult to detect or uncover. But again, this is a problem of empirical barriers, not of assumptions. The idea that an assassination is an idiosyncratic matter, while perhaps reassuring to the general populace, returns the problem of regicide to the field of personal pathology. In a thoroughly unconvincing way, it disposes of those acts of fanaticism that may be linked to reinforced nationalist claims or ethnic affiliations. By broadening the interpretation of conspiracy, and by treating the Sirhan attempt, for example, as having precisely such a collective source, society could possibly have used the assassination of Senator Kennedy to bring about renewed efforts to obtain a Middle East settlement. The assassination of Martin Luther King clearly triggered such action in regard to relevant issues, namely, settlement of labor disputes in Memphis and a more positive congressional response to the Washington Poor Peoples' March. There is a pragmatic advantage then in making the fewest possible assumptions about assasination attempts, but when assumptions are made, there is little justification and a smaller payoff in choosing individual over collective modalities of explanation.

MYTH: The assassination attempts on men of stature, such as Senator Kennedy, drastically affect the course of history.

REALITY: Let it be said that this myth is hard to combat or overcome directly. It is always difficult to assess the historic importance of an individual to the course of future events. Such an assessment entails an estimate of the degree to which individuals in politics are autonomous or at least free to maneuver the ship of state as they wish. It is quite as difficult to judge how new events might change old leaders as it is to estimate how old leaders might shape new events. But there is no need to become excessively metaphysical in such a discussion. Attention might simply be drawn to the fact that the same social and political problems exist in 1968 as existed at the time of President John F. Kennedy's assasination in 1963. The war in Vietnam remains. Racial violence is increasing. On the other hand, the thawing of the cold war between the United States and the Soviet Union has continued at roughly the same pace under President Johnson. This is not to deny that changes in substance as well as style are brought about by an assassination; it is to say that problems of social structure and historical determination remain intact. However important the role of leadership in political organization may be, the role of total populations is, after all, far greater and more pervasive. Politics in America is still a game of large numbers. No political assassination can alter that fact without destroying American democracy.

As there is guilt, so too is there guilt alleviation. And the basic form this has taken under the Johnson administration has been the commission. We get riot commissions in place of urban renewal; crime commissions instead of full employment; and now a commission to investigate "violence in American life" in place of full political participation. It might be said that the candidacy of Robert F. Kennedy was dedicated to the overthrow of the bureaucratization and Washington-centered nature of current administration efforts. By a quirk of events, his death has led to a new commission—to the very phenomenon Kennedy found such an abomination. Sentimentality and brutality are first cousins—which is why they appear to coalesce so well in the present administrative "style."

The formation of a commission on violence makes only more remote resolution of the political dilemmas besetting the American nation. These dilemmas have been eloquently described in the Democratic primaries. The remarkable showings of both Kennedy and McCarthy indicate that the votes against the Vietnam War and the mishandling of the present urban crisis reflect a deep appreciation by the electorate of the nature of violence.

Throughout the California primaries it was clear that Kennedy's strength and survival depended upon a large outpouring of poor people and their spokesmen. Black Americans, Mexican-Americans, and the other ethnic and religious minorities that comprise a large segment of the California population demonstrated by their vote that Kennedy's tactic was also a principle. An estimated 80 percent of the Negro voters and 85 percent of the Mexican-American voters cast their ballots for Kennedy. Less than one week later, on Friday, June 7, at Saint Patrick's Cathedral in New York, the eastern brothers of these minority-group citizens— with the Puerto Ricans displacing the Mexicans—also symbolically cast their ballots. The remarkable gathering of hundreds of thousands of people throughout the night was more than a celebration of mystical martyrdom. Every man, woman, and child who placed his or her hand on the casket was registering a vote, a vote denied to them by the assasination.

A society that can still feel political tragedy has a great reservoir of political health and sophistication. The underprivileged sector of society must suffer the consequences of this latest political murder, since in this way the poor have been effectively disenfranchised. The assassination creates a situation of political desocialization at the very moment when Kennedy working for the minorities and McCarthy for the students and other disaffected citizens were revitalizaing the mainsprings of political socialization. In this sense the appointment of a commission on violence is a fruitless as well as thankless task, since the very act of depoliticalization is the source of further violence. The assassination of Robert Kennedy was an act of terrorism. To convert it into the basis for a feeling of collective guilt for increased violence is to ignore a basic fact of our times not only in the United States but throughout the world. Violence can and often is a political act, the first mature step beyond egotistic resolution of social problems. Terrorism is the opposite and negation of violence, since it frustrates and makes impossible the fruits of these very activities.

In his own way, Kennedy not only supported but drew sustenance from the "participatory democracy" advocates. Leaders of social-protest movements, new agrarian unions, and community racial and ethnic societies formed an urban backbone for Kennedy with which to take on the "party regulars." He was hardly the favorite politician of Washington insiders. His audacious attempt to use mass media to break the stranglehold of locked-in party organization was not to be dismissed lightly. The attacks on the Kennedy wealth were, in fact, in response not to the economic "oligarchical" tendencies of this wealth, but to the populist goals to which this wealth was being oriented. The Kennedy "coalition" of urban poor, ethnic and racial minorities, and a section of college and university personnel made the Democratic Party the natural home for these people. The assassination has changed the alignments but not the needs. In this sense, populism must readjust its vision of the politicians, estimating the short- and long-run damage occasioned by Kennedy's death, and considering if organization rather than charismatic channels may now be required.

Social scientists will feel a special loss, too, for Kennedy made use of social-science personnel to explore programs extending from Latin American aid to urban rehabilitation and renewal. As he wrote to me on June 3: "I have always believed that it is crucial to be assisted by social scientists in their particular fields in forming domestic and foreign policy."

The urgency of the age demands a movement, not a monument; confrontation, not conformity. The time for demonstrations of public sorrow passes quickly—despite the monstrous fact that within two months our nation has lost two of its staunchest fighters against current policies guiding the war in Vietnam and the war in the ghettos at home. It is now time to translate sentiments into politics. When all participate equally, the loss of a leader such as Robert F. Kennedy will be seen as the brutal price that men often pay in the struggle for a democratic society.

II

The single most important event of the 1968 electoral process was the assassination of Robert F. Kennedy, for from that event followed a number of political consequences that have thoroughly disrupted the pattern of American politics.

First: the assassination wiped out any possibility of mass participation in and eventual integration into the political life of their society by poor urban whites, the black masses, the Spanish-speaking minorities on both coasts, and many sectors of the middle class still committed to social welfare and social reform.

Second: the assassination of Kennedy served to polarize the Democratic Party and to cut off arbitrarily, and prior to the normal time allotted in the dynamics of convention-year politics, the debate concerning the issues of war and the ghetto. The assassination represented the abrupt termination rather than the resolution of various debates raging within the Democratic Party and within the nation itself.

Third: in effect, the elimination of Kennedy from the campaign profoundly affected the Republican Party, since it was no longer required to present a challenge to the Left and could in turn focus its energies on both galvanizing its own Right wing and capturing a portion of the Right wing of the Democratic Party. The nomination of Richard M. Nixon was a foregone conclusion the day Kennedy died, but not one day earlier.

Fourth: with the Democratic Party polarized and itself responding to the urgings of the party apparatus rather than the mass base of the Democratic voters, whatever popular resentment existed was easily matched by George Wallace and the American Independence Party. The working class, historically and congenitally unable to accept the Republican Party as an option, did see in the Wallace movement a form of moral integrity and a responsiveness to localist passions that were unreflected either in the welfare ideology of the Democratic Party or in the bourgeois ideology of the Republican Party.

As for the relevance of the present election to the future of American social and political change, this is a matter for obvious speculation. One view is that the Republican Party victory insures the integrity of a two-party system. Another view is that the massive defeat of Humphrey insures the final demise of the Democratic Party. My own personal feeling is that the form of party life in America is less important than the content, and what we witnessed both in the Miami and Chicago conventions is a rising tide of party populism reflected just as much in the struggle over party platforms and vice-presidential choices as in the overall struggle for the presidential nominee. The primary lesson to be derived is that one should not build a party base on the narrow shoulders of any one individual; nor should we allow the assassination of any one figure to so determine the course of American political history as to immobilize radical and liberal sentiment for years to come. If there were twenty Robert F. Kennedys—if there were even two Robert F. Kennedys—maybe the situation could have been saved. The fact is there was only one. And the McCarthy movement, based as it was on the middle-class antipolitique, could not sustain the momentum gathered in the current antiwar and black protest movements.

Customarily in American life political leadership has been far in the vanguard of mass sentiment. The tragedy of the electoral processes during the current period is that mass sentiments exist without political leadership to channel and give voice to basic urgings.

1968

2

The Rise
of
Presidential Militarism

Lyndon Baines Johnson is the perfect embodiment, if not justification, of role theory. Obviously any national leader, any President, must perform a multitude of tasks in the conduct of his duties. But in *The Vantage Point* we are presented with nothing less than a gigantic unresolved dualism. On one side is Johnson the President, dedicated to national cohesion through the liberal credo; while on the other side is the Commander-in-Chief, dedicated to international pacification through the military credo. To take this work seriously is to appreciate that Lyndon B. Johnson was dedicated to both roles and performed both with equal sincerity and tenacity. The tragedy—and his is a tragic book—is that he seems, at least in this *apologia pro vita sua,* to fail to appreciate the degree to which this duality of roles tore at the flesh of his administration, ultimately rendering him ineffective both individually as the nation's President and as its Commander-in-Chief.

The vantage point of the presidency—with its seemingly limitless opportunity to survey all and know all—ultimately became for Johnson an escape from reality, a hiding place in a world of bureaucratic obligations. But for Presidents, even more than for ordinary people generally, there is no place to hide. No amount of emphasis on duty, obligation, or national prestige would give Johnson a respite from tragedy. The Vietnam War serves as a silk thread running through the texture of his other policies and decisions. But it was more than just the effect of this one thread that ultimately ensnared the man who held fast to the design he had woven: the design itself became a tangle of broken dreams.

President Lyndon Baines Johnson

First, let us consider Lyndon Baines Johnson, President. We find a ferocious liberal cut from the mold of Roosevelt and the New Deal period. Although Johnson had often been accused of not realizing that the 1960s were different from the 1930s, my feeling is that he has not been given proper credit for understanding that they were indeed similar in one respect: that the one-third of the nation that was underprivileged, undernourished, and underrepresented during the Great Depression still existed one World War and three decades later; and this gave his national effort a nobility of character that sings out in his writings. President Johnson waxed elegiac about these tasks:

> Before me now was a call for action, a call for a revolutionary new program to attack one of the most stubbornly entrenched social ills in America. Like most social change, such a revolution would not come without a struggle. My perceptions of America persuaded me that three separate conditions were required before social change could take root and flourish in our national life—a recognition of need, a willingness to act, and someone to lead the effort. In 1963 I saw those three conditions coming together in historic harmony.

This "historic harmony" was in fact profoundly realized: the Civil Rights Act of 1964, the Voting Rights Act of 1965, the Fair Housing Act of 1968, the Federal Jury Reform Act of 1968, and other measures entitled Johnson to point out that during his administration legislation was enacted that extended to many more people the promises of equality at the ballot box, the employment center, the jury room, the public schools, and the private housing market.

It is important to note that Johnson understood not only his debts to the Roosevelt program, but also his differences with it. Above all, he recognized the profound shifts in American ideology from the 1930s' urban celebration to the 1960s' urban crisis; and from the intimacy of aristocratic faith in federalism to the depersonalization of life in the post-industrial age. Johnson's description of the urban malaise in the mid-1960s is certainly as sharp as that of any social scientist; and indeed it is precisely the social-science community that gave him the imagination necessary to cope with the new problems:

> The cities were on the brink of crisis. Their physical decay was accelerating. The slums were crowded with people untrained for jobs, many of

whom were lost even to the census count. The tax base of cities was shrinking as a result of the persistent flight of industry and middle class families to the suburbs. The cities were being choked by the congestion of their own traffic arteries. People were unable to walk the streets at night, because of the rising rate of crime. Across the entire country the problems of urban America were spilling beyond the borders of the cities into the fast-growing suburbs, and beyond them into the rural heartland. Consumers were being systematically deceived and bilked by unscrupulous elements in the marketplace. Air and water were being steadily poisoned by the uncontrollable wastes of our wealth. New housing was not being constructed rapidly enough to cope with our population growth. The landscape of our beautiful continent was being marred by junk heaps and litter and scarred by the bulldozer. These were the perplexing problems that could not be put off. In considering what legislative proposals I would make to the new Congress, I asked my staff to develop a program that would deal with the country's highest-priority needs.

The distinctive characteristic of Johnson as President was a sense of humanity that extended to small intimate details and that revealed the populist side of the man. He fought as hard for the Rat Extermination and Control Act of 1967 as for any major piece of legislation. Indeed, something within him permitted an emphatic response precisely at this level. The idea of the politician helping the poor had a special appeal to President Johnson. Whatever the potential for self-serving might be, still, the vocabulary of motives aside, it would be difficult to imagine President Eisenhower quite as upset with the problem of urban decay or quite as determined to have a Rat Control Bill passed.

The emphasis on social structure was more than concern for the intimacies of impoverishment; it was a remarkable self-critical capacity that one does not always associate with President Johnson; and in fact is completely absent in Commander-in-Chief Johnson. After the defeat of the Rat Bill, Johnson bitterly condemned the Republican-conservative Democratic coalition and went on to say: "I was ashamed of myself for not having prepared the House of Representatives and the nation to approach this issue more intelligently and with a proper sense of urgency. I thought I had done everything I could; I thought the logic of exterminating rats was self-evident. But I was wrong. This was a case where I left undone something that I should have done." A Rat Control amendment was attached to another piece of legislation, so the President won out on that one. But it is that spirit of engagement and that capacity for self-criticism that I found most remarkable.

Another area in which this self-critical spirit manifested itself was in his changing response to the social conditions of blacks and the growing grimness with which their condition pervaded urban domestic life. We have had no President, at least not in my memory, who has spoken so eloquently and forcefully to the question of black power; and it would be an outrageous falsification of history to deny President Johnson the force of his democratic fury:

> I am not interested in black power or white power. What I am concerned with is democratic power, with a small "d." As I look back now, that answer seems totally insufficient. It is easy for a white man to say he is "not interested in black power or white power." Black power had a different meaning to the black man, who until recently had had to seek the white world's approval and for whom success had come largely on white people's terms. To such a man, black power meant a great deal in areas that mattered the most—dignity, pride, and self-awareness.

Through all his activities at the level of domestic struggles, one had the feeling that he was keenly sensitive to the gyrations of national politics; to a tradition of persuasion, argumentation, and bargaining with legislative bodies, state gubernatorial bodies, mayors, and community leaders. In short, the President was not only in his métier in the bargaining situation; he was involved with what he knew best—with the kind of exchange system that is the essence of the American political system. As President, Johnson could express bitterness and even be acrimonious at losing. The fact of the matter is, however, that he had enough victories at the domestic level to permit him a certain tranquility and to allow him to transmit an ever deepening appreciation of the role of democratic processes in the formation of legislation. He was, in short, a good President.

Commander-in-Chief Lyndon Baines Johnson

The tragedy is that the qualities that made Johnson a good President made him a catastrophe as Commander-in-Chief. Here we turn from Dr. Jekyll to Mr. Hyde: to a foreign policy of conservatism, to a self-righteous priggishness in decision-making and, and to a faith in government by administrative fiat, all of which made him the butt of nasty jokes as well as the terror of those who dared to oppose him. As for any useful definition of conservatism in this specific context, we have the sacred text of Robert S. McNamara himself, who in 1965 outlined with remarkable precision the choices before the United States in Vietnam. The paragraph is worth citing for its remarkable exactitude in laying bare not only the choices of the 1960s, but also the decisions of the 1970s:

> We must choose among three courses of action with respect to Vietnam all of which involve different probabilities, outcomes and costs:

(a) Cut our losses and withdraw under the best conditions that can be arranged—almost certainly conditions humiliating the United States and very damaging to our future effectiveness on the world scene.

(b) Continue at about the present level, with the U.S. forces limited to say 75,000, holding on and playing for the breaks—a course of action which, because our position would grow weaker, almost certainly would confront us later with a choice between withdrawal and an emergency expansion of forces, perhaps too late to do any good.

(c) Expand promptly and substantially the U.S. military pressure a-gainst the Viet Cong in the South and maintain the military pressure against the North Vietnamese in the North while launching a vigorous effort on the political side to lay the groundwork for a favorable outcome by clarifying our objectives and establishing channels of com-munication. This alternative would stave off defeat in the short run and offer a good chance of producing a favorable settlement in the long run; at the same time, it would imply a commitment to see a fighting war clear through at considerable cost in casualties and ma-terial and would make any later decision to withdraw even more difficult and even more costly than would be the case today.

The first option was, of course, the position taken by the doves Fulbright, McCarthy, and Kennedy. And with the exception of one feeble attempt by George Ball, it was ruled out with precious little effort to analyze the consequences of an automatic negation or rejection of a peaceful Southeast Asia based on an autonomous communist regime in South Vietnam. There was complete understanding that without massive United States aid, the country called South Vietnam would collapse; but no understanding that military artificial insemination might not work either. The second option is curiously very much what the Nixon policy has been all about and just as curiously was rejected by the Johnson administration with a similar lack of detailed discussion. That left the third option of escalation, and the justification was as crude and as cheap as any made by any President in American history. And here it was Dean Rusk who set forth the presidential guidelines: "If the Communist world finds out that we will not pursue our commitments to the end," he said, "I don't know where they will stay their hand." Thus the domino theory became the dominant theory; we had the spectacle of the Department of State becoming even more hawkish and super-rabid than the Department of Defense. Here one cannot help but interject a piece of political history. I have always felt that the Department of State was close to being extinguished during the period dominated by Senator Joseph McCarthy. The attacks on the absence of quality in State Department leaders included frequent if often subterranean charges of homosexuality and the equally inane charges of communist infiltration. These led to an era of presidential personal advisors. It was Dean Rusk's self-appointed mission to resurrect the Department of State and eliminate the presidential advisory system—or at least to weaken its role. But as any perusal of the relative power of Henry Kissinger and William Rogers will attest, Mr. Rusk did not quite realize his institutional ambitions.

Lyndon Johnson continually faced a choice between the technological vigor of the new civilian militarism in the Department of Defense and the old-fashioned, romantic anticommunism of the Department of State. But like so many choices related to Vietnam, neither one was sound. And we have institutionalized neither the era of State Department leadership nor that of Defense Department hegemony. Rather the presidential advisory system was strengthened with McGeorge Bundy. Thus, even as a technique in the resurrection of the Department of State, the Vietnam War was a disaster—a small one, but symbolic of how the war was able to render federalism inept and civilian control inoperative.

It is curious that Commander-in-Chief Johnson rarely speaks for himself on the Vietnam War, even in his own book. We have already seen how McNamara formulated the policy, how Rusk rationalized the policy, and of course how McGeorge Bundy tragically showed how to execute the policy—a policy he called "sustained reprisal." Bundy was more than a leftover from the Kennedy administration; he was the presidential voice on the subject of the Vietnam War. He bore witness to the truth long ago stated by Karl von Clausewitz: "Notwithstanding the scientific character of contemporary military art, the leading outlines of the war are always determined by a political and not a military agency."

> The stakes in Vietnam are extremely high. The American investment is very large, and American responsibility is a fact of life which is palpable in the atmosphere of Asia, and even elsewhere. The international prestige of the United States, and a substantial part of our influence are directly at risk in Vietnam. There is no way of unloading the burden on the Vietnamese themselves, and there is no way of negotiating ourselves out of Vietnam which offers any serious promise at present. . . .

What was so amazing about Bundy was a ferocious determination (that lasted until he reached the Ford Foundation) to stay on in Vietnam no matter how long the military effort lasted and no matter what the consequences for the Republic.

The administrative capacity for self-delusion seemed endless. Perhaps General Westmoreland served President Johnson in quite the same way that General Creighton Abrams is presently serving President Nixon. Throughout, the American people were told of victories that were empty; of South Vietnamese determination and will to fight that were nonexistent; and of North Vietnamese and Viet Cong aggressions committed in their own homeland. President Johnson did not arrive at an understanding with his Vietnam adversaries in 1968; he simply assumed that understandings existed with the demilitarized zone as a border settlement between two alien nations, instead of a convenient division within one nation. He constantly assumed the existence of two Vietnams rather than one Vietnam, and the constant references to Hanoi and Saigon institutionalized an illusion, an illusion of course that the "other side" neither shared nor accepted.

On the subject of Vietnam the Commander-in-Chief proved to be constantly self-righteous and, above all, a man dedicated to administrative solutions of political problems. Congress, and the Senate in particular, appeared as part of the adversary camp—the obstructionist enemy within. After the Gulf of Tonkin resolution Congress no longer existed or no longer seemed to exist as part of presidential thinking about the Vietnam conflict. It was as if foreign policy were a purview reserved for executive authority only. The fanaticism of rule unchecked by law, those things that Johnson as President abhorred, were internalized by Johnson as Commander-in-Chief.

Nor was this simply a matter of Vietnam; one finds the same sort of presidential militarism at work in the Dominican crisis. "The last thing I wanted—and the last thing the American people wanted—was another Cuba on our doorstep." Apparently, the American people could accept another Bay of Pigs. Commander-in-Chief Johnson sent in the troops without reference to Congress, without reference to the Organization of American States (although the OAS was mentioned in terms of an antecedent determination reached in January 1962), and certainly without reference to the will of the people of the Dominican Republic.

It is appalling that the theory of the communist menace was used to provide a cover for the most naked act of intervention and aggression performed by the United States during Lyndon Johnson's tenure of office. This is outlined by the Commander-in-Chief himself:

> The decisions I made on April 29 were as follows: first, that the danger of a Communist takeover in the Dominican Republic was a real and present one: second, that a Communist regime in the Dominican Republic would be dangerous to the peace and safety of the hemisphere and the United States; third, that danger still existed, in the disintegrating situation, for both American and foreign civilians in Santo Domingo; fourth, that the United States would put in sufficient force to achieve two purposes: to create the international security zone recommended by the OAS and to

separate the rebels in the downtown area from the regular military forces; fifth, that we would seek a ceasefire, some kind of interim government, and the scheduling of orderly free elections in which all Dominican citizens, not just a minority with guns in their hands, would decide their political destiny.

The Johnson policy was based flatly on preventing another communist or socialist regime from arising in the hemisphere. One can only wonder in fear and trembling if Johnson would have sent the marines to Chile along its 2,000-mile coast line upon the assumption of power of President Allende in 1970. Indeed, neither the Commander-in-Chief nor his advisors seemed to have raised the question of whether or not this sort of gunboat militarism was itself a stimulant rather than a corrective; the poison rather than the medicine in inter-American relations.

The degree to which the Johnson period represented a turn in strategy away from massive United States aid, toward what the President described as a new age of regionalism, is most impressive. This attempt to develop a new sense of regionalism in Latin America was on inspection a way of forging a continental grouping in Latin America similar to that of the North Atlantic Treaty Organization (NATO), the Organization for Economic Cooperation and Development (OECD), the Southeast Asia Treaty Organization (SEATO), and the Australian, New Zealand, U.S. treaty (ANZUS). But this approach based on regionalism was in fact a cover for continued and even strengthened United States participation in hemispheric affairs at a much lower cost. It is interesting to note the degree to which the priorities shifted from economic aid to military support, even in the imagery used by the Commander-in-Chief. Thus, in effect, the presidential approach toward Latin America was economic integration of the hemisphere within a larger military interpenetration between hemispheres. And in this, one can only feel that the current policies of the United States, based on the new realities of multinational corporate activities, have continued in the same direction with a similar dreary series of results.

How and why was Lyndon B. Johnson permitted, in his role as Commander-in-Chief, to evolve a grand dualism that turned into a grand illusion? Several reasons suggest themselves. And while they are not entirely my creation, they deserve specific expression in terms of the Johnson period. First, foreign policy was simply beyond the limits of congressional domination by virtue of the absence of any clear juridical guidelines as to legislative controls other than sheer fiscal allocation. Second, as foreign affairs increasingly linked up with an advanced military technology, it became a private sector of experts and policy-makers speaking a language and demonstrating a rhetoric far beyond the pale of the usual elected official. There was the corollary assumption of technology as instaneous terror, a fear instilled by war gamers who argued that modern conflict requires and even demands a capacity for instant retaliation and anticipatory capacities to respond to military crises. In other words, Johnson as Commander-in-Chief became heir as well to the mantle of the technological system of political rule. Finally, it is clear that presidential militarism, as such, was legitimated throughout the postwar period; the rise of power in the executive branch superseding other branches of government had been insinuated from previous administrations from Roosevelt through Eisenhower and Kennedy. In this, Johnson was simply one in a line of succession of those who accepted the canons of presidential infallibility in the making of foreign policy; such infallibility went with the office, not with the party.

The fact of the matter is that presidential militarism, in the very act of breaking down the system of checks and balances guiding all domestic affairs, also served to rupture representational government itself. Ordinary people felt less secure and had less faith in the willingness of government as a whole to redress wrongs or correct mistakes. As a result, presidential militarism had the effect of stimulating mass movements on a scale unparalleled throughout the postwar era. For when a government is no longer responsive to the will of the people, then that will finds expression in unsanctioned and unceremonial fashion. It is no accident that the level of resistance and mass protest to the war in Vietnam follows closely behind every presidential decision to escalate. In short, the Achilles heel of the new style of presidential rule is that it stimulates a form of confrontation politics that is far more difficult to manage within conventional political terms.

That Johnson himself, at least in part, understood the demoniac consequences of his own bifurcation between the roles of President and Commnder-in-Chief—heir to the liberal throne of national policy and soldier of fortune in the conservative tradition of international policy—is made evident by his decision not to stand for reelection. This was, in my opinion, a necessary act; the act of an old soldier wearied of his command. There can be hardly a doubt that he would have won had he stood for reelection; without any question he certainly would have been nominated. In declining to run, he took seriously the problems of a Commander-in-Chief; namely, when the troops are divided, when loyalties are sundered, when ranks are thinned, it is time for another leader. It is a decision made by a Commander-in-Chief, and one very rarely made by a President.

Yet at the highest level he was unable to appreciate the fact that not to run for reelection as President implied a bankruptcy in the presidential political network; a breakdown in the very legitimacy of international politics insinuated by the gathering of experts in the National Security Council, the Department of Defense, and in the Department of State. This dualism that pressed on Lyndon B. Johnson is less evident in the world of Richard Milhous Nixon. That is because the world of Republicanism is more accommodating to the needs of domestic conservatives and international capitalists. If this gives the Republican administration a superficial air of having resolved the problems left behind by Johnson, then one need only examine the current state of affairs, both domestically and internationally, to see that in fact the party system has served more to disguise than to resolve the current outstanding contradictions within American society. This in itself perhaps should dispel the myth that the cat-bird seat of the Presidency is much of a vantage point in seeing, much less solving, American dilemmas. Finally, in the very act of renouncing state power, Lyndon B. Johnson himself probably understood and appreciated the disadvantages of vantage points better than any of his critics or crusaders.

1972

3

Reactionary
Immortality

The books of quotations from Lyndon Baines Johnson (*Quotations from Chairman L.B.J.*) and Richard Milhous Nixon (*Poor Richard's Almanack*) were collections done by critics in jest and in gibe. As such, the essential authenticity of these two men is left strangely intact. This contrasts markedly with the books of quotations from Chairman Mao Tse-tung and Director J. Edgar Hoover, which are in the different category of self-celebration. They are collections of sacred sayings selected by each author, each demonstrating an unabashed thirst for immortality.

Hoover's *On Communism* is a hoary collection of homiletics, polemics, and recollections. It must be judged in terms of the traditionalist American suspicion of those things alien, atheistic, or antagonistic to the American way. But rather than concentrate on some of the interesting theoretical points that could be extrapolated from Director Hoover's wisdom, it is perhaps more significant to examine the actual government documents under review that serve as the justification for the Director's ideologically transparent assumptions. For those who are deeply concerned with what Hoover himself considers to be his most important thought, *On Communism* will bring ample succor; but for those who are more concerned with the implications of his message, the testimonies provide solid evidence of the Director's reluctance or inability to come to terms with changes in the structure of American society, not to mention changes in the Soviet Union.

Obsolescence, intellectual as well as physical, is an affliction common to all organizations and all men. The three volumes of FBI budgetary requests before the House Appropriations Committee and excerpts from five decades of Hoover's speeches and writings make it perfectly clear that "waiting for the end" is a malady that overtakes the Right as well as the Left. Through these "works" one sees an almost comic spectacle of the old Right exhausting itself in symbolic battle with the very old Left. The hero is clearly John Edgar Hoover, defender of the American faith; while his nemesis is Gus Hall, the tenacious head of the Communist Party in the United States and the incarnation of the Soviet faith. Hoover now depends on Hall for his very *raison d'être;* the two men are the Abbott and Costello of American political life.

In these volumes, Communism emerges as an eternal oneness, endowed with the omnipotence as well as misguided interests generally characteristic of evil deities. This allegorical approach to the world has been winning the Director's increasing approval as more intricate models for explaining it are concocted. Hoover tells us that, "Although the names of the Soviet intelligence services differ today from what they were 20 years ago when Joseph Stalin was Premier, the objective of world conquest by Communism has never wavered. The change over the years has been not a change in objective, but a steady intensification of the effort to reach the objective, the destruction of a capitalistic country." By the simple substitution of the word "socialistic" for "capitalistic" in the latter sentence, we have the perfect summary statement of the goals of the FBI under Hoover's tutelage; he clearly thinks of capitalism as a moral movement rather than an economic system. But he is careful to rely on political allies, rather than his own agency, to execute such moral ambitions.

Communism is more than a malodorous vapor emitted by evil men to becloud the minds of good people. It settles and concentrates in geographical locales surrounding the dwelling places of the good and there awaits diabolical opportunities to do damage. Cuba is only 90 miles from Florida. The evil work of the Mexican Communists takes place in a "concentrated area . . . less than 150 miles from Laredo, Texas." Meetings of indigenous Leftists are not considered a part of the internal politics of sovereign nations but rather a ring of evil enveloping the American nation.

Lenin considered imperialism to be the last and highest stage of capitalism. In the same peculiar way, Hoover sees Communism as the last stage of moral deviance. Deviance comes from insidious exposure to Communism. We are told that (1) peaceful coexistence is not possible "with a country that every year has intensified its intelligence and espionage operations against this country"; and (2) "there are many gullible people who are against the policy in Vietnam as a result of the propaganda put out by some college professors who are naive and some students lacking in maturity and objectivity and who are constantly agitating and carrying on demonstrations in some of our largest universities." It does not occur to Hoover that the size and strength of the university may be related to the size and the strength of the student protest movement it harbors. Instead, he broadly hints that if only Communist speakers like the perennial Gus Hall and the inevitable Herbert Aptheker were prevented from keeping their lecture engagements on campuses, the innocence of American youth would be preserved.

This strange nature of moral deviationism appears repeatedly during Hoover's career. In the case of the black leader Bayard Rustin, Rustin's links with the entire antiwar movement were said to have arisen from his having been "convicted for sodomy" and for his violation of the Selective Service Act before World War II. Or again, when Hoover mentions that a Crime Prevention Commission has been set up in a California school, he also expresses regret that people like H. Rap Brown and Stokely Carmichael are allowed to speak to young students. The use of tax funds to support men whose positions he cannot accept is immoral. He speaks of these black leaders as "rabble-rousers," as men who live off, rather than in, the "so-called" ghettos, where presumably their children can be bitten by "so-called" rats. (Hoover is clever enough, however, to relate the radical protest movement in America to the behavior of black militants, for it is true that militants, in contrast to most black special-interest groups, oppose American foreign policy.)

Together with his fellow septuagenarians Harry Anslinger in the Federal Bureau of Narcotics and Lewis Hershey, head of the Selective Service Commission, Hoover is obsessed with the young. He relates a fundamentalist suspicion of the corrupting effects of secular education to a fearful awareness of the political volatility of university life. Drugs, military service, and radicalism are all loosely associated with certain members of the younger generation. For Hoover, it therefore follows that the universities have become enclaves of young radical opposition that must be broken.

At appropriations time, Hoover attempts to convince Congress—by offering a list of public appearances made by Communist Party leaders at various colleges throughout the United States—that the "corruption" of American youth may be attributable to political subversion. But Hoover's materials indicate that fewer than 70 appearances in all were made by Communist officals at American campuses during each of the three years reported in these hearings. This means that the collective position of the

Communist Party is probably heard less often on American campuses than the views of, say, Arthur Schlesinger, Jr., William F. Buckley, Jr., or any other major figure on the lecture circuit. Yet the persistence with which he presents his Communist speakers' chart at House and Senate Hearings makes clear that at least for Hoover this is, if not statistically meaningful, still an important indicator of what is wrong with American higher education. He emphatically states that although "We believe in academic freedom, this does not grant license to deliberately present distortions or falsehoods. Communists are not obligated morally or otherwise to seek for or to tell the truth. Some young people are capable of recognizing and exposing propaganda and propagandists. Others are not. This is the dangerous thing, particularly when it is recognized that the Communists in this country are conducting an energetic propaganda campaign to recruit young people to the Communist banner."

More recently, Hoover has extended his concern for education to the high school. Inviting black militants such as Brown and Carmichael to public schools is inexcusable: "They invite an individual of that kind to talk before a public high school composed of youth not at the age yet to properly evaluate what he has to say. He is enough of a rabble-rouser in the so-called ghettoes of the country where there are militant Negro elements that like to hear him expound; but to have him spew his venom in the schoolrooms is wrong."

Evidently Mr. Hoover considers the colleges and high schools the institutional framework through which the Communist ideology makes its deepest penetration. What is particularly absurd is that Gus Hall himself reinforces Hoover's charge by claiming that his Communist Party is indeed involved with the leadership of campus radical struggles. And in each year of testimony Hoover cites Hall to this effect without ever once questioning the validity, not to mention the blind conceit, of such a claim. At no point does Hoover challenge the veracity of Hall who, as the leading Communist menace, presumably would not be above lying and deception. Quite the contrary. The implicit contract between them is that neither shall challenge the fantasies of the other. One can confidently expect that an examination of the collective essays of Gus Hall would bear this out in reverse.

What enables the FBI to maintain its preeminent position as defender of American society? What are the ideological bases of its authority and prestige? To begin with, there is Hoover's legalism. In each of his pronouncements Hoover is careful to stay within the letter of the law. This emphasis on the legitimacy of the law has served to enhance rather than discredit his power. Nowhere in American literature may be found a clearer expression of that which separates an advocate of justice and a supporter of law. Hoover is a law-lover; there is no question of that. He always distinguishes the lines of responsibility between his offices and those of the Attorney General. However, and this too is a curious fact, these divisions of authority are drawn most sharply in matters of civil disorder involving black-white relations and least sharply in matters of civil rights involving political radicals. It would seem that demands for economic integration into the system are more acceptable to the FBI than demands for racial separation by lower-middle-class whites.

From the attempts of Attorney General William D. Mitchell in 1932 until the courageous efforts of Attorney General Ramsey Clark in 1968 to limit the scope of the Federal Bureau of Investigation, the philosophies of the Attorney General and the Director of the FBI have been at considerable variance. The Attorney General is usually guided by the belief that federal jurisdiction should yield to local and state regulations whenever possible. Hoover has always taken the position that, with the important exception of crimes violating the civil rights of blacks, federal policing of crime is made necessary by the ineptitude, bravura, and limited expertise of local officials. Thus, the peculiar anomaly arises that the principle of states' rights—one of the sacred cows of conservative doctrine—has nowhere been more violated and breached than in extensions of police power by conservative politicians who, following Hoover, are prepared to waive all constitutional objections in the name of efficiency.

The struggle between the Attorney General and the Bureau Director became openly ideological when Ramsey Clark and J. Edgar Hoover provided the first sets of public testimonies before the special Presidential National Commission on the Causes and Prevention of Violence. In what is now a classic presentation of different positions toward the "law and order" issue, the Attorney General saw the problem as the absence of equity in the distribution of law and warned against substitution of order for justice in processing criminal cases. Hoover, needless to say, presented the problem as a breakdown of order in the nation and the solution as the application of law without regard to the social causes of crime.

Underlying this extreme legalism is the question of Hoover's appropriations. As long as Congress continues to pass legislation granting the FBI jurisdiction in wide areas of national defense, kidnapping, extortion, robbery *et al.,* Hoover can demand and receive annual increases of funds for his agency, risking only the mildest quaver of protest. This extreme concern for formal law and equally strong disinterest in social expressions of discontent is one of the most characteristic features of Hoover's leadership of the Bureau. But it serves beautifully to make the actions of his Bureau appear above reproach.

Another issue, one closely related to the issue of legality, might be called bureaucratic competence or adherence to executive directives. The FBI is an agency that disseminates large volumes of information on Communism and crime, but it is never presented as a policy-making agency. Hoover speaks of acting under "Presidential directives requiring the F.B.I. to ascertain facts pertinent to the loyalty and security risk of employees and applications for positions in the Government service or in activities incident to which the Government has an official interest." These enable the FBI to justify its investigation of the private lives of all citizens who are in any way involved with the work of the Government. Since the directives are general in character, the manner in which they are interpreted becomes of central importance. Here too a significant distinction may be drawn between what is formally sanctioned and what is actually undertaken.

The same demand for bureaucratic competence underlies current calls for professionalization of police work. But Hoover, more clearly than other cops before and after him, understands the opportunities offered by the shift from elective to appointive power in government and the enlarged role of expertise in this shift. In his earlier work, *A Study of Communism* (1962), Hoover points out that there are many Communist activites "with which the average citizen cannot directly contend." But more: "nor would it be desirable for the average citizen to play a direct role in combating them." The struggle against Communism must be as professional an activity as "the science of espionage" necessitates. "To meet effectively the Communist subversive thrusts, it is essential to employ highly professional counterintelligence measures—measures for which the average citizen is neither equipped nor trained. Modern-day counterintelligence, with its emphasis on professional skills and training as well as its reliance on competent scientific aids, is a task for experts."

Like any other agency, the FBI has special access to knowledge. But Hoover chooses to "classify" his special knowledge, which puts him in a position to bludgeon any feeble opposition to his budgetary demands with the superior information at his disposal. The secrecy in which special knowledge is held enables the F.B.I. to claim that confidentiality is required for the effective operation of the department. Invariably, questions arise at these hearings concerning matters such as case loads per agent. Perhaps there are vague doubts about the need for an increase in the number of agents, but Hoover has the facts at his fingertips and the congressmen docilely respond to his information edge. Having accepted the presumptions of the Bureau, they can do little to deny the agency more money. Thus that special knowledge serves both as a weapon of organizational supremacy and an instrument of high government finance.

An additional FBI ploy, and again one not often recognized by congressmen, is to create and sustain an image of its impartiality. The agency is presented as equally harsh toward each enemy of the nation. But its claims to equal treatment are in fact nonsense. Hundreds of pages are offered on the "Communist conspiracy," while only passing references are made to right-wing organizations such as the Minutemen or the John Birch Society. Hoover's only real concern with the John Birch Society is that so many of his former agents openly work for it and indeed make their past affiliation with the FBI a featured selling point for leadership of the Right. Even under rather obvious prompting to have the FBI go on record with respect to Birch Society activities, Hoover can only work up enough steam to resent the Birchites' jeopardizing the organization's presumed "impartiality." "It is an improper attempt to capitalize on the name of the F.B.I."

But the agency's impartiality has been inadvertently discredited by Hoover himself in discussing where his *other* agents often wind up after leaving the Service. "Seventy per cent of our special agent personnel have been with us 10 years or longer. We do have a problem now and then, but I do not raise any obstacle to it, of large companies and corporations asking some very capable man in the Bureau to take a position in their organization, such as that of vice president. I lost one many years ago who became vice president of the Ford Motor Company. I lost a man just a few years ago who was agent in charge of my New York office and is now a vice president of American Airlines. There are nine Congressmen and one Senator who are former special agents of the Bureau." Just how service in the Bureau equips one for the vice-presidency of Ford Motors or American Airlines is not explained—although one might surmise that they are employed in connection with plant sabotage, record tampering, and union pressures. Thus far at least, vice-presidencies seem to be the upper limits of the F.B.I. as a quasi-official placement office.

Concerning impartiality, civilian rights and political rights are also confused. Hoover has lately been referring to the work of the enemy with respect to the rights of blacks in the South. The Ku Klux Klan is converted into a right-wing counterpart of the Communist Party. In point of fact, its specific modes of operation and its quasimilitary character distinguish it most sharply from the debating society that the American Communist Party now represents. This juxtaposition of Right and Left nonetheless provides precisely that aura of impartiality and equal treatment that permits the FBI to claim a nonideological base. Critics of the Bureau have overlooked the fact that what distinguishes the FBI from the Gestapo or the old GPU is precisely the faith in "law" to accomplish the essential tasks of preserving state authority. In this, in contrast to Himmler or Beria, Hoover is a giant.

These four points, turned into presumptions—legalism, bureaucratism, priestly wisdom, and political impartiality—coalesce to make possible the legitimacy of the FBI in both war and peace. We must now turn finally to the world as it is perceived by J. Edgar Hoover and to what could be called the four fears that the man has as a public figure—for it is clear that for Hoover the world is a perpetually frightening place. This fact comes through time and again in his discourses, or better, monologues, before the House Subcommittee on Appropriations.

First, there is his fear of not living up to the images of the FBI as presented by the mass media. Although it is clear that Hoover sincerely believes his own rhetoric, his notion of cleanliness and sound hygienic practices is less the outcome of an internalized Protestant ethic than it is a response to American hero-types generated by the mass media, particularly television. Hoover is so concerned with what he calls good character and personal appearance that he would "rather have vacancies than employees who do not measure up to those qualifications." He refers to the television program on the FBI and the model inspector as portrayed by Efrem Zimbalist, Jr. Young, well-groomed, cool under pressure, courteous to all friends of America, the FBI agent is strikingly liberated from inner turmoil, doubt, confusion, or sophistication. Mirror, mirror on the wall, how would I look, feel, and act if I were younger? "Like Efrem Zimbalist, Mr. Hoover," assures the captive mirror. For Hoover, self-image and organizational image are one, and "I want our agents to live up to that special image."

Related to this whole question of image and appearance is Hoover's second phobia, namely, sexuality—homo or hetero. The theme haunts the man in every report. Perhaps its most fascinating expression came in the statement he issued in response to Congressmen Charles S. Joelson's and John J. Rooney's promptings on the "appearance" of Bureau agents. "As regards appearance, Mr. Congressman, I certainly would not want to have any beatniks with long sideburns and beards as employees in the Bureau. . . . No member of the Mattachine Society or anyone else who is a sex deviate will ever be appointed to the F.B.I. If I find one in the F.B.I. he will be dismissed. As to appearance, our special agents in a broad sense are really salesmen. They interview the presidents of large banks, the chairmen of the boards of large corporations, long-shoremen, and laborers. They have to sell themselves to them to get their confidence to obtain the information they need."

What is fascinating, even puzzling, is that it is apparently perfectly permissible for agents to "sell themselves" in the line of duty but not to "give themselves" in their private experiences. The dialogue is a sobering indication that Hoover's traditionalist view of masculine behavior will, when integrated with other agent standards, presumably provide a bulwark against sexual and criminal deviance generally. Again, the Hoover hardline seems not so much linked to Protestant beliefs, but to the simple police notion of the dangers in sexual "deviance."

The third great fear is oppressive Communism, or better still, the Communist Party. Strangely, Hoover displays no ideological awareness or even concern with the structure of Communist Parties throughout the world. And in the 1969 report he reveals only the barest recognition of the pluralization of the radicalism in the United States. Hoover has a typical policeman's definition of a Communist, namely, a "dues-paying" member of the Communist Party. When asked if Herbert Aptheker was a Communist, Hoover quickly responded, saying, "Yes, and his daughter Bettina is just as much a Communist as he is"—a "dues-paying member," no doubt. Bettina Aptheker, Herbert Aptheker, Gus Hall, etc., the names keep recurring, indicating Hoover's need for a personal embodiment of the Communist evil rather than an analysis of the party structure. It is not the political role of these poor people (or perhaps their lack of a real political role) but rather their mere existence as "card carriers" that seems so painful and yet so fascinating for Hoover. And since the rhetoric of people changes at a slower rate than the reality of organizational decay, Hoover as political analyst has proved to be a failure.

The final fear, perhaps the most frightening, is that of criticism. Not that there has been much criticism in Congress. It is simply impossible for Hoover to accept the idea of being wrong, to acknowledge an improper understanding of an issue, or in any way to reveal a weakness in either his organization or his personal opinions. The testimony provided by Hoover stands as a veritable indictment of congressional timidity and insipidity. At no point in three years has anyone offered anything but the most sycophantic response to Hoover's testimony. Hoover is always being congratulated, and in turn the leader drops pleasantries on the home towns of the congressmen before whom he testifies. The city of Monrovia, California, is more frequently cited than any other city or town in

America simply because Congressman Glenard P. Lipscomb comes from Monrovia. This ludicrous conspiracy of mutual flattery serves to deflect criticism and transform the hearings into an annual celebration.

A hypothetical postelection activity has the President-elect in the year 2000 automatically reappointing John Edgar Hoover Director of the service and turning his attention to more problematic choices. This black humor points up the totalitarian essence of the organization. For whether Hoover is in fact the real leader or just a front man for other more dynamic figures is less important than an encrusted situation in which he can no more be replaced or be "permitted" to retire than can Mao Tse-tung. Indeed, few doubt that an organizational "crisis" would occur in the FBI were such a retirement to ensue by a means other than natural death. But what must also be realized is that the precipitating cause of such a crisis lies within an organizational situation in which one man alone has been permitted to embody the structure and sentiment of the entire force.

Hoover is one of America's few remaining "symbols" of the pristine age of primitive anti-Communism, a leftover from an age of simplicity, if not of purity. The death of Hoover would mean only the final passing of a policy based on coping with the Bolshevik Revolution as our chief internal menace. The file checks, wiretaps, security clearances would still remain. After all, they are part of the endemic features of a genteel totalitarianism. But without Hoover these interventions into the affairs of private souls would be deprived of their patriotic *telos* and be seen as crude impositions. President Nixon and his advisors also know this to be true. This is why the FBI's symbol without substance remains stubbornly entombed in his Washington office, while our political leadership hopes that nature disposes of what man seemingly cannot depose.

1969

4

The Europeanization
of
American Politics

Watergate is more than a historic event in American politics. It is an apocalyptic event in American morality. It represents a benchmark abruptly terminating 200 years of innocence, empirical confirmation that Providence has abandoned America for parts as yet unknown. Textbooks on law and political science have been filled with equilibrium models of how the United States works: checks and balances among executive, legislative, and judicial branches of government; an everlasting stasis between the two political parties; a firm belief in the responsiveness of federal authorities to *vox populi*. Indeed, the foresight of the founding fathers, the authors of the Federalist papers such as Madison, Jay, and Hamilton, was enough to make one believe in miracles. But there was one great premise taken for granted. The founding fathers of the Constitution predicated everything and staked everything on the belief that those who ruled, although chosen by the people and hence not always brilliant, would at the very least be honest. And it is the age of innocent belief in the politician as honest man in the Montesquieu sense of *L'Esprit des lois* that came crashing down with Watergate.

The Federalists were thoroughly aware of the dangers of concentrating power in the hands of a single charismatic leader. But in their writings and in their age it was the prospect of too much power in the hands of the legislative branch that was of paramount concern. They feared in this "first new nation" that a legislative majority would become unhinged and threaten the rights of the minority. And they had ample evidence from the inherited European systems of this sort of "mobocracy." Being men of property only reinforced this sensitivity to legislative constraint.

The issue was how to increase the powers of the presidency to counterbalance the presumed potency of the legislative branch. The idea of a single President rather than a plural presidency was debated. It prevailed on the basis of yet another assumption: the existence of a judicial electoral college comprised of leading citizens. What in effect took place was an early break with the utilitarian-enlightenment premise that major decisions should not be made by one man acting in isolation, but by a collective body of elected officials. Most institutions, from corporations to voluntary agencies, are run on the premise of checks and balances generated by plural executive leadership. The primary exception of note to this pluralism is the American presidency. And with the concomitant rise of experts replacing electoral officials in the decision-making roles, the presidency became not just largely independent of legislative or judicial controls, but insulated from such constraints. The growth of the "imperial presidency" coupled with the declining ability of the legislature to initiate or sustain autonomous action was thus the constitutional backdrop to unchecked power, otherwise known today as corruption in government.

It is not that American politics is any more corrupt or dishonest than it ever was; this is a debatable position. Rather, it is that the evidence of corruption has been so sharply presented by mass media that even the most duncelike devotee of American political mythology can no longer deny it. Instead of producing universal morality, mass politics has brought us down the slithering path of selective pragmatism, a word that has become a euphemism for collective immorality. But since this is a change in the perception rather than the reality of American politics, the real issue becomes: Why now? What has happened to compel a lifting of the shades, to reveal a cracked windowpane behind which the exercise of politics is conducted as the impromptu use of raw power, simply to retain government office?

One convenient fiction is that the senatorial hearings, and the subsequent revelations of the Cox review commission, reveal an auto-didactic learning and healing process. It is asked more in desperation than in certainty: Where else in the world would such revelations of corruption in high places have taken place, and beyond that, once revealed, not shaken the nation to its roots and foundations? Yet, presidential authorities fought these special senatorial hearings tooth and nail; withholding support, information and, finally, openly confronting and challenging the legitimacy of the Ervin subcommittee to hold public hearings altogether. The Archibald Cox commission, the executive counterpart of a congressional committee, once it got close to the connection between presidential policy and economic manipulation, was overthrown in a frightful *putsch,* a one-day takeover that involved a Federal Bureau of Investigation seal-off of the Cox commission offices that frightened even the more ardent supporters of the President.

The idea that the Watergate revelations are an unmixed blessing represents sophism. It assumes, somewhat grotesquely, that only when a state organ reaches a condition of total corruption can the real health of the body politic be brought to the aid of the organism. This is a sort of bourgeois equivalent to the vulgar Trotskyist "theory" that the worse that things are in the present, the better they must get in the future. Such forms of explanation as offered by the legion of presidential advisers and apologists are, in effect, not explanations at all, but panegyrics and hyperbolic nonsense. The plain truth, as now everyone recognizes with a sigh of relief, is that the fascist timetable, coming in the form of nervous nativism, has been seriously put back, if not permanently stalled by the Watergate hearings. At least in its elitist variety, the fascist threat to suspend civil liberties and to equate criticism with subversion and opposition with antipatriotism has been profoundly weakened. That this in turn has led to a serious lacuna, a state of suspended political animation in which power itself appears to be exercised in a vacuum—even foreign power, as is clearly demonstrated by the current paralysis characterising United States foreign policy from the Middle East to Southeast Asia—is a deeper outcome of the Watergate revelations.

To illustrate this paralysis, one might look at the current oil situation. It would be difficult to imagine a nation as powerful and imperial in its pretensions as the United States bowing so meekly to the wishes of Saudi Arabian oil ministers if there did not exist a real crisis in United States foreign policy. In this sense, the Arab oil embargo was fortuitous in its timing. It corresponded precisely with a paralysis in United States internal affairs. As a result, if for not other reason than to have breathing space to restore the confidence of its public, American foreign policy is at its lowest ebb with respect to bellicosity and belligerence. Whether this has happened as a result of Soviet-abetted Arab intransigence is less significant than the simple fact that under conditions of domestic unrest the imperial eagle has turned into an international pigeon. As a result, the United States may be compelled to deal harshly and even punitively with internal dissension. It is, after all, far simpler to manage internal threats from unemployed laborers or disenfranchised minority groups than to respond to overseas threats from "Third World" sheikdoms, which nonetheless have the freedom to call upon Second World bolsheviks.

Watergate has thus served to encourage already widening tendencies in the direction of neoisolationism; toward an intense turning within, no less than inward. The rise of spiritualism, psychologism, healing, and all sorts of other "superstitious" practices from palm-reading and astrology to devil worship is likewise indicative of a sure-sighted collapse of wills (assuming we ignore the question of capacity) by America's political rulers. They will not easily risk a world war on the say-so of a President who has proved himself to be less than candid. The recent congressional measure, approved over a presidential veto, limiting the war-making powers of the executive office, that is, of the Commander-in-Chief, is an indication, not only of a breakdown of confidence in the presidency of Richard M. Nixon, but in the overall ability of the United States to win wars, and not simply engage in them.

The principal consequence of Watergate is that it reflects the growing intensity of inner-party and intraparty conflict in the United States. In the past, the structure of American party politics was best described as a matter of shadings and nuances between fundamentally similar organizational types; whereas in the post-McGovern reform period, the gaps between the two parties have become much sharper, calling into question fundamental premises about who governs, the nature of state responsibility for the welfare of the poor, the obligations of the State to provide full-employment conditions, and even the racial, class, and sexual compostion of the party leadership itself. More than that, as the present halfway Keynesian house began to show its cracks, the need to move beyond welfarism became paramount. Hence, a polarization process commenced, with the dominant wing of the Republican Party embracing a doctrine of law, order, respect for leaders, continued high military expenditures; in short, the verities of what Lasswell long ago identified as the Garrison State. The Democrats, for their part, became acutely aware of the theme of social injustice: the rights of black minorities and the outrageous iniquities to which majorities like women are subject.

As we come into the 1970s, the competing philosophies of the two parties stand as follows: for the Republicans, the main purpose of citizenship is service to the state; for the Democrats, the main concern of the state is service to its citizens. This classic dichotomy, with roots deep in Western political thought, became the substance of the 1972 elections, although at times this was hardly apparent, disguised as it was by the personal styles of the candidates. As the party of power, the Republicans were not about to risk everything in exchange for an "alien" McGovern philosophy that must have seemed to the likes of Nixon, Ehrlichman,

Haldeman, Magruder, et al. a veritable assault on 200 years of the American way of life. In this sense, Watergate was but one incident in the ongoing struggle between conservatives and radicals, all of whom ostensibly accepted the restrictions of American social structure. But in the polarized party analysis of what is right and wrong with the American structure, a cleavage between Democrats and Republicans was revealed that was as deep, if not deeper, than exists throughout the European political system.

A major reason why Watergate has aroused worldwide interest is that it made apparent just how great was the extent to which American politics, in the past said to have been providentially guided toward eternal consensus, has become Europeanized. Europeans are familiar with crises in governmental confidence, dismissal of leading political officials for corruption and dishonesty in the conduct of duty, and the cynical manipulation of public office and public trust for private gain. The shock of recognition for the American public was that the American political system is likewise not exempt from the laws governing any other parliamentary regime. In fact, Providence took this moment to abandon America to its own devices, a condition of being adrift well known in Western European capitals long suffering under feeble traditions of parliamentary cretinism and executive corruption.

The reason why Watergate became a postelectoral rather than pre-electoral scandal is first and foremost the huge power of the Republican Party apparatus to delay any real investigation of the break-in of the Democratic Party headquarters until the elections were well out of the way. The clever if transparent rationale was that to have done otherwise would have turned the investigation into a political football. But a second factor, perhaps equally necessary for the scandal to have remained buried for so long, is the curious tendency of the Democratic Party to engage in self-deception. In part, this was a consequence of the bitterness of the conservative factions of the party who lost out to the radical wing. But even such an erstwhile figure as Gary Hart, Senator McGovern's campaign manager, barely mentions Watergate as a factor in his book-length review of the 1972 campaign. However, when the elections were held and the presidential landslide became apparent (even in the face of stiff popular resistance to Republican Party candidates at congressional and statewide levels), then the full investigation into how this landslide was manipulated and managed by the presidential advisers, if not the top man himself, could no longer be suppressed. Only then, in the aftermath of the dirty tricks campaign that isolated and defeated Muskie and Humphrey and took the full measure of Senator Eagleton, did the attitude of the

Republican high command to the Democratic Party—conceiving it as the Enemy and not simply the Opposition—become manifest. Only at this point, too late in time to reverse the Nixon landslide, did the Democratic Party mobilize and articulate its concern over the future of democracy, no less than the future of the party system as such.

A special tragedy of the Watergate aftermath is the inability of the American Left (presuming such an entity actually exists) to seize the moment to put a reasonable series of options before the American public. At a time when the need for fundamental political and economic reforms loomed large, when the American people could clearly see structural weaknesses in the American system of government, the literary Left is able to come up with only a series of empty and tendentious platitudes about the evils of American capitalism. Just as the Right saw Watergate as a purifying agent within the World's Greatest System, the Left saw the same event as evidence that this is the World's Worst System.

As one shrewd political scientist, Edward Schnier, remarked recently in *Transaction/Society,* the Watergate affair pointed up the weakness of a Left that was strictly ideological and lacking utopian capacities, that is, a Left that could criticize but not construct alternatives. If evidence for this judgment were needed it is the Left's tragic inability to mobilize a single demonstration, spark a single mass form of protest, or launch an impeachment movement. Instead, what occurred was the strange spectacle of a stranded Republican minority registering moral indignation while political capital was made by the frustrated Democratic Party majority. The Left remained outside and above the battle: taking two steps backward into abstraction as the American people struggled to take one step forward into specificity.

The Watergate hearings and their revelations on matters ranging from rage against isolated antiwar protestors to extremely shady and sharp tax practices have compelled Americans to confront the fact of political venality, a charge of malfeasance no longer tossed aside as the ravings of the radical fringe. In the light of the near-total silence of the Left, the impulse to reform gives way to the instinct of self-preservation. In this sense, Watergate is not a revolutionary spectacle of Marxian proportions, in which an exploiting economic class and its state machinery give way to mass uprisings and a new radical leadership as they did in the Bolshevik and Maoist revolutions. Rather, we witness a bizarre spectacle of Hobbesian proportions in which the ruling elite and state authority as such are rendered helpless by inner-party strife and intraparty rivalry.

Watergate has not elevated the Democratic Party to virtue or relegated the Republic Party to damnation. Yet there is a dangerous precedent set in which the holders of state power are unwilling to abide by the premises and principles that have governed the United States for nearly 200 years. The present circumstances seem attuned to the English and French revolutions, in which aristocratic elites displayed precisely the same collapse of class nerve and moral verve that created leadership vacuums then in which disenfranchised groups were compelled to seize power. The present unrest derives not so much from any doubt as to the authenticity of a crisis in the American Leviathan, but rather from how this crisis will be resolved in the long pull of time, and what social forces will be released able to move us beyond this malaise. The practical issue becomes: Will the United States talk Left and move Right and thus create a climate for a flourishing fascism, or will it be capable of restoring national confidence based upon a cleansing or purge (there are no pleasant palliatives to describe the question of impeachment or removal of a President from high office) of the present holders of authority. Only one fact is certain: the present politics of centrism cannot be sustained amidst a climate of corruption and crisis.

As a result of this desultory performance on the part of the ideological Left, we are threatened with the possibility that the Watergate affair will be reduced to a matter of Republican Party strategy, that is, conservative decision-making concerning the advisability or inadvisability of going with the President for the congressional and state elections of 1974 and the presidential elections of 1976, or moving toward a solid front behind Gerald Ford, the new Vice-President. The choice becomes a conservative one: to "brazen it out" with Nixon or to "ride the new wave" with Ford. But either decision leaves the Left at the starting gate, without a program and without a vision. Thus, no matter how important Watergate may be in relation to the structure of power in America, the absence of an organized Left with a historic vision and mission to capitalize on such an event means that this event becomes part of a deepening cycle of cynicism and antipolitics in America. It feeds rather than destroys the revolutionary myths. It leads to a Hobbesian rather than a Marxian series of responses to the political turmoil. This means that those who praise order when they really worship terror have the most to gain by a scandal that in its origins and evolution should have held out the promise of a democratic response to terror.

Events, even important ones, are not self-evident in their political consequences. The tragic inability of the Left to capitalize on Watergate means that, at best, the reform wing of the Democratic Party will emerge with a newly born strength; at worst, Watergate will lead to a new style of fascism—less Platonist, less elitist, but no less dangerous or virulent, since fascism also has been known to come in populist packages, wrapped in slogans celebrating integrity and integration. In short, Watergate does not alleviate the fear and trembling. Watergate proves that, even in America, politics does not stand still and constitutions are not made for eternity. However, Watergate also makes plain that the velocity of social change and political corruption may lead to something worse no less than something better. An era of turmoil may give birth to new beginnings, or it may also stir up ancient evils. This is a time for careful searching rather than careless celebrating, itself not a small lesson that Americans are finally beginning to learn.

1974

II

CLASS-RACE POLITICS

5

Race, Class, and the New Ethnicity

Recent attitudes and changes in behavior of working-class Americans, sometimes called "new ethnics," have deeply shocked and bewildered many sensitive commentators. The supposed return to militant self-identification has led one radical to claim that "the working-class white man is actually in revolt against taxes, joyless work, the double standards and short memories of professional politicians, hypocrisy and what he considers the debasement of the American dream" (Hamill, 1969). The same display of muscular working-class behavior has led an equally radical critic to assert that "the hard-hat labor unionists, and they are by no means limited to the building trades, have joined with the military elite and their political spokesmen. This suggests the great danger of the rise of a proto-fascist workers' movement in the United States. Whatever social and cultural forces may be invoked to explain this development, it is already manifesting itself in a variety of ways. The racist hard-hats from many unions are the potential street fighters of American fascism" (Hill, 1971). From the foregoing statements it is difficult to surmise who is in greater need of depolarization—the working class or its intellectual respondents.

Who is an Ethnic?

Whatever actual evidence we have is considerably more bland and nondescript than that required for either of these two projections to be valid. At the level of attitudes, several generalizations can be made: first, working-class ethnics are for the most part neither more nor less prejudiced against the black community than the wealthier classes (Hamilton, 1971:135). Second, classical aspirations for upward mobility and geographical relocation along class rather than ethnic lines still characterize working-class ambitions (Campbell, 1971:43–44). Third, working-class allegiances to the party system remain essentially as fluid or as fixed as they have been for ethnic and racial groupings (Mikulski, 1974:355–359). Fourth, it has been questioned whether feelings of alienation and anomie have affected the working class more than other social sectors. The working class continues to favor government welfare and income maintenance programs—especially those affecting them in particular (Greeley, 1969:45–55).

In a recent prestigious colloquium, it was asserted that even at this late date there remains no clear definition of the working class; no statement, even at a statistical level, of any special economic squeeze against the working class; and finally, there remains the highest doubt that a problem specific to blue-collar workers or to white ethnics as such exists. Problems seem universal, affecting blue-collar and white-collar people alike, affecting ethnics and blacks alike, and affecting different nationalities and religious groups alike. In short, economic problems are endemic to the United States of America, and the ethnic aspects of these problems are simply expressions of such universal class dilemmas (Levitan, 1971: 13–20).

Whether or not the foregoing summation is complete, the rise of a new literature on blue-collar ethnics does herald something novel in the social sciences. If nothing else, this literature gives the last blows to earlier analyses based on the end of class interests, class ideologies, and class politics, even if only to replace them with nothing more substantial then verbal celebrations of ethnic interests, ethnic ideologies, and ethnic politics (Krickus, 1969).

Any attempt to define ethnicity raises at least three sociological problems: (1) who is an ethnic; (2) how can ethnicity be distinquished from other social variables and character traits; and (3) what can ethnicity predict—what are its behavioral consequences? Before coming to terms with the current ideological and political uses of ethnicity, it may be worthwhile to describe the ideological sources of the current celebration of ethnicity.

The general characterization of ethnicity in the social-science literature can be summarized under seven headings:

1. It is frequently claimed that ethnics are neither very rich nor very poor, nor part of either the ruling class or the underclass. Rather, they are often identified with either the blue-collar working class or the lower-middle class.

2. The current literature presents highly selective idiosyncratic definitions of ethnicity. Jews and Japanese are often excluded by intellectual fiat from the ethnic category on the basis of their middle- or upper-middle-class positions and their upward mobilities through education; other times, they are included as a political category of an "anti-WASP" sort.

3. Ethnicity *within* lower-class groups or racial groups such as blacks seems to be excluded from discussion. Thus, for example, distinctions and differences between East African blacks and Jamaican blacks are very rarely spoken of by those defining or employing the term "ethnicity."

4. There is a strong tendency to describe ethnics in terms of whites living in the urban complex or the inner city, in contrast to whites living in suburban or nonurban regions.

5. A distinction is often made between nativists and ethnics, that is, between people who have Protestant and English-speaking backgrounds and those with Catholic and non-English-speaking backgrounds, although in some cases (for instance, the Irish) ethnics may be identified solely on the basis of religion.

6. Ethnics are said to have a vocational orientation toward education, in contrast to a liberal arts or humanities orientation. They tend to be nonacademic, anti-intellectual, and highly pragmatic. Interestingly, although blacks are perhaps the best illustration of a vocationally oriented subculture, they are not generally categorized as ethnics.

7. Ethnics are usually said to possess characteristics and attitudes identified with those on the political Right: strong patriotic fervor, religious fundamentalism, authoritarian family patterns, and so forth. Indeed, characterizations of ethnicity and conservatism show such a profound overlap that the only difference would appear to be the currently positive attitude toward ethnics on the part of learned observers (see, for example, Coles, 1971).

Determining who is an ethnic has more to do with sentiment than with science. The concept defines a new, positive attitude toward those who fit the model. One now hears "them" spoken of as middle class, lower-middle class, or working class in contrast to lower class. They are said to be part of a great new wave of populism: the struggle against opulence on one hand and welfare on the other. As such, the concept of ethnicity claims a political middle ground. It does not celebrate a national consensus nor does it accept the concept of a class struggle. Its ideologists perceive ethnics as an interest group rather than a social class. In this sense there is a kinship between classical liberalism and the ideology of ethnicity. It promotes the theme of cultural pluralism and cultural difference rather than social change or social action. Perhaps this explains why dedicated civil libertarians have moved their attentions and affections from the black underclass to the white ethnic class (Coles, 1971; Novak, 1971; Cottle, 1971a; Friedman, 1967).

One of the more customary ploys in refocusing attention away from blacks and towards ethnics is to point to quantitative parity. The new ethnics take note of the fact that there are nearly as many Americans of Italian and Irish extraction as there are of African extraction. The supreme difficulty in this sort of quantitative exercise is the absence of qualitative commonsense: the blacks have a unique and special history in America that provides them with a solidarity and a definition quite apart from other Americans; whereas the Italians and Irish, and other ethnic groupings as well, have a far weaker sense of delineation and definition. The blacks (and this they share uniquely with the Jews) represent a group apart; the new ethnics represent groups that would like the future payoffs, but not the historic penalities, of beoming a group apart.

The Roots of Ethnicity

The rise of ethnicity as a separate factor reflects the existence in America of what has been called a cross-cutting culture, that is, a culture that makes no particular effort to build a common identity among those who comprise the 80,000,000 members of the working class. A number of observers have discussed the persistence of ethnic identity from this vantage point. "Michael Parenti has observed that in a single weekend in New York separate dances for persons of Hungarian, Irish, Italian, German and Polish extractions are advertised in the neighborhood newspapers and the foreign language press. Herbert Gans and Gerald Shuttles have discussed the persistence of a tightly knit network of relationships among Italians living in Boston and in Chicago. Occupationally, the $5,000 to $10,000 category embraces secretaries and assembly line workers, senior clerks and cab drivers. Geographically workers spread out over the south with its racially dominated politics, the midwest where fear of communism is a serious sentiment, and the northeast where problems of traffic congestion and state financial support for parochial schools excite political passions" (cf. Howard, 1971:65–66).

Ethnicity refers to a cluster of cultural factors that define the socio-gram of the person beyond or apart from the racial or class connections of that person. It defines the binding impact of linguistic origins, geographic backgrounds, cultural and culinary tastes, and religious homogeneity. In this sense, the concept of ethnicity is not only distinguished from class but in a certain respect must be considered its operational counterpart. It provides the cultural and theological linkages that cut through class lines and form new sources of tension and definition of inclusionary-exclusionary relationships in an American society grown weary of class perspectives on social reality.

The renewed emphasis upon ethnicity signifies the decline of achievement orientation and the return to an ascriptive vision. Generational success can no longer be measured in terms of job performance or career satisfaction. Therefore, new definitions of group membership are sought in order to generate pride. These often take the form of a celebration of ethnic origins, and generate a feeling that such origins somehow are more significant than class to group cohesion.

The notion of ethnicity, like other barometers of disaffection, is indicative of problems in self-definition. Americans have long been known to have weak class identifications. Most studies have shown that class identification is weak because class conflict is thought foreign to American society; everyone claims to be a middle-class member (Centers, 1949). Few see themselves at either end of the class spectrum. As a result, class as a source of status distinction is strong, but as a source of economic mobilization it is weak (cf. Hodges, 1964:1016). In a sense, the concept of ethnicity closely emulates the concept of race; for race, unlike class, is based upon ascription rather than achievement. But ethnicity defines a community of peoples having language, religion, and race in common—if it does not imply a commonality of tastes, what Novak (1974:23) has termed "gut issues." For example, Poles and Italians share religious similarities, but they are not likely to share ethnic identities. The Church has long recognized ethnicity on the basis of linguistic and national origin rather than simply the universal ministerial claims of Catholicism.

The problem with determining the behavioral consequences of ethnicity is the difficulty of establishing whether there are common political demands or even common economic conditions that all national and linguistic minorities face. Aside from the fact that a bare majority of ethnics participate in Democratic Party politics, there is little evidence that ethnics do in fact share common political goals. There seem to be greater gaps between first- and second-generation Irish and Poles than Irish and Poles of the same generation (Greeley, 1969:46-48). Hence the actual power of ethnicity as an explanatory variable must be carefully evaluated.

In large measure, the new ethnicity reflects rather than shapes the new politics. The present era represents a new kind of emphasis. The collapse of federalism, the strain on the American national system, and the consequent termination of the melting-pot ideology have together led to a situation where ethnicity, in a sense, fulfills the thirst for community—a modest-sized community in which the values of rural America as well as rural Europe can be simulated in the context of a post-industrial world, without the implied criticism of America inherent in radical and youth movement communities.

Disillusionment with the American system and its inability to preserve a universal series of goals has led to a reemergence of community-centered parochial and particularistic doctrines. The sympathetic response of the American nation to the unmasking of historical injustices heaped upon the black people has made it seem that ethnicity could achieve the same results by using a similar model of social protest.

A notable shift in attitudes at the ideological level has emerged. What once appeared to be a minority problem with its attendant drives toward integration into the American mainstream has now become an ethnic problem with its attendant drives toward self-determination apart from the American mainstream. To be more precise, there has been an erosion of that mainstream. With the existence of 20 to 30 million first- and second-generation Italian-Americans, 9 to 10 million Spanish-speaking Americans, some 13 million Irish-Americans (these often overlapping with 48 million Catholics), who in turn share a country with 6 million Jews and 23 million blacks, the notion of majority status for white Protestant America has been seriously eroded. The notion of the WASP serves to identify a dominant economic group but no longer a uniquely gifted or uniquely destined-to-rule political or cultural group. Thus, ethnicity has served to express a genuine plurality of interests, without necessarily effecting a revolution in life styles or attitudes. Equality increasingly becomes the right to be different and to express such differences in language, customs, and habits, rather than the right to share in the white Anglo-Saxon Protestant ethos that dominated the United States up to and through the end of World War II and the Cold War period.

Ethnicity is also an expression of the coming into being of new nations throughout the Third World—African nations, Asian nations, Latin

American socialist states, Israel as a Jewish homeland, the reemergence of Irish nationalism. The international trend toward diversified power bases has had domestic repercussions on minority standing in the United States. The external reinforcement of internal minorities has changed the self-image of these internal minorities. The new ethnics are (in part at least) the old minorities in an era of postcolonialism, in an era of capitalism on the defensive at least as a cultural ideal if not as an economic reality. Thus, whether ethnicity takes revolutionary or reactionary forms internally, its rise to conceptual and ideological preeminence clearly represents the breakup of the old order in which Anglo-American dominance went uncontested.

Race, Religion, and Ethnicity

The concept of ethnicity not only has its origins in the successful strategy of blacks for gaining equality through struggle, it also harkens back to the earlier ethnic drive for acquiring equality through education. Whether these new ethnic struggles will be successful depends on whether ethnicity is an overriding concept or simply a word covering differences of a profound sort between linguistic and religious groups. The fact of being Irish may be of binding value, but the fact of being Protestant Irish or Catholic Irish certainly would take precedence over the ethnic unity. Similarly, being a Ukrainian may be a binding value as long as Ukrainians are defined exclusively in nonreligious terms, for the Ukrainian Jews certainly do not participate in the same ethnic goals despite a shared geographic and linguistic background. Hence, unless it can be demonstrated that the concept of ethnicity forms the basis of social solidarity and political action and is not simply a residual category, ethnicity may explain little in the way of behavior.

The new emphasis on ethnicity is distinguishable from the old emphasis on minority groups in the United States primarily because it represents repudiation of the "melting pot" ideology. More significantly, it represents a breakdown in what used to be known as the majority. It is very difficult to have minority studies in a world where the major impulse is weak, nonexistent, or defined as another minority. Hence, the rise of ethnicity as a rallying point seems to be in inverse proportion to the decline of white Anglo-Saxon Protestantism as a consensus framework. The latter, too, has turned ethnic. Ethnicity has become a relative concept instead of a subordinate concept.

All models are subject to limitations. The call for "Ethnic Power," modeled as it is upon the past decade of civil rights struggles, provides a perfect illustration of this fact; it involves a blurring of the special circumstances of blacks in the United States. It would not be entirely amiss to note that the black presence in the United States was largely involuntary, whereas the ethnic-minority presence was largely voluntary. Moreover, the black experience in America was linked to the plantation as a total institution and connected to the degradation of the blacks as people; white immigration (ethnic immigration) involved participation in the building of America and particularly in the building of its industrial life. Thus, while models for ethnic separatism are premised on the black movement, simultaneously they display little awareness of the different circumstances of black participation in American affairs throughout the last hundred years.

Few doubt that a latent function of current appeals to a new ethnicity are directly related to the Great White Hope, to the theme of ethnics preventing blacks from becoming the major power bloc in urban America. As such, ethnicity becomes a response not just to present superordinate traits of the dominant American sectors. Ethnicity becomes a euphemism for the fight against crime in the streets and for the fight to maintain a white foothold in the major urban centers. Support for the claims of ethnicity must also be viewed as a reaction to the flight of huge sectors of the middle class to suburban America, thus leaving the white working-class ethnics to absorb the full impact of black militants and black organizations in the American cities.

The celebration of ethnicity is not so much a recognition of the special contribution of Europeans to America as it is the manufacturing of a new conservatism. Ethnicity furnishes expression to goals and values of an organized group of white working-class Americans dedicated to the maintenance of their comparative class positions. As such, ethnicity becomes yet another hurdle for black Americans to jump in order to gain equal status in this society. An overt struggle between whites and blacks is intellectually unpalatable; hence ethnicity emerges to defuse racial tensions by shifting the struggle to the loftier plane of downtrodden blacks and denigrated ethnics.

At an entirely different level the celebration of ethnicity has either brought about strange new alliances or established the potential for such new coalitions. Most important in this connection has been the renewed effort in the Jewish community to reach an accommodation with other ethnic leaders. The informal pact between the Jewish Defense League and the Italian-American Club simply highlights tendencies in current ethnic politics to accept the current American value system and to reject claims of national or racial separation.

After years of struggle in support of black egalitarianism and in particular black institutions of higher learning, Jews are now being criticized as never before by their black colleagues. Whatever the roots of black nationalism, the first contact of the black is with the Jew as landlord, shopkeeper, and realtor. Whether the turn of the Jewish community to ethnics will resolve their problems with blacks is difficult to ascertain. In fact, what is being jeopardized is the special philanthropic relationship that has existed throughout the twentieth century between the black and Jewish communities and that perhaps is epitomized by such established black leaders as the late Reverend Martin Luther King and such Jewish leaders as the deceased Rabbi Stephen Wise.

The middle-class character of the alliance of blacks and Jews has long been understood. Its focus on education as the main avenue of upward mobility a priori ruled out the possibility of revolution. And as young blacks move more conscientiously toward revolutionary goals and an older generation of Jews moves with equal rapidity toward reformist goals, the historic alliance between these two peoples becomes more seriously jeopardized. The educational model proved less efficacious for the postwar blacks than had been anticipated; as a result, blacks turned toward a political model, operationally defined by a direct challenge to, and search for, a share in state power. Be that as it may, declarations of support by the Jewish community, or its self-declared representatives, on behalf of the ethnic urban working class, have little more than symbolic significance. The class barriers between people continue to be clearly more durable than the commonality of race.

Various organizational efforts to sensitize and depolarize, although well intentioned and intellectually sincere, start from a fundamentally erroneous premise; namely, that the key polarity is presently between black America and ethnic America (Levine and Herman, 1971:3–4). Such a formulation does permit various organizations, especially Jewish middle-class organizations, to perform their historic role of honest broker and friend at both courts. However, the likelihood is that, despite the differences between Poles and blacks in cities like Detroit or Gary, their problems arise from common sources—lack of steady jobs, poor upgrading procedures, lack of meaningful retraining programs, and a breakdown of urban development—each of which should (if the proper conclusions are drawn) create the basis for class solidarity rather than simple ethnic separation along racial or religious lines.

It can be understood why some organizational leaders of the Jewish community would seek rapprochment with ethnic groups. However, since the ethnics themselves often define the Jews as outside ethnicity and since the class formations that separate ethnic America from Jewish America continue unabated, the possibility of alliance seems remote and, when executed, tenuous. It may represent a tactical side bet in a specific community where Jewish-ethnic interaction is high, but little else. Again, the cross-cutting characteristics of race, class, and ethnicity tend to make nonpolitical coalitions exceptionally difficult to maintain over any period of time.

The special tactical relationships between blacks, Jews, and ethnics is really central to the future of the working class in the United States. Since the United States has become something of a three-track nation, the blacks are identified as being either on the goverment payroll or on the government dole. The Jews are identified as being entrepreneurial kingpins in America. The ethnics are seen, or perceive themselves, as the true heirs of the working-class spirit (Novak, 1971:44–50). The present tendency of Communist parties throughout the world is to accept, if not adopt outright, anti-Semitic postures. This is partially an opportunistic accomodation to its working-class and black constituencies—which see Jews more as exploiters than as exploited. The problem of "dual allegiance" seems to be real for the Communists only when Jews and Israel are involved, not when citizens of the United States pay allegiance to the Soviet Union.

Even the Executive Director of the National Association for the Advancement of Colored People has recognized that blacks subconsciously apply a higher standard in the evaluation of Jewish attitudes than that of any other group and hence become deeply disturbed when Jewish behavior is like that of other whites. Similarly, it is evident that the Jewish response to manifestations of black anti-Semitism is often in terms of the European holocaust rather than the American ghetto experience.

> There is a positive factor at work in Negro-Jewish relations—above and beyond the close and analytical scrutiny which both are accustomed to render to the issue of their relationship. This is the working partnership which has developed among professionals in the respective organizations and among officials and academicians, whose daily pursuits bring them into close and continual contaČt. The antennae of representatives in those categories are highly sensitive; they respond to warning signals with consultations; efforts to mediate tension spots; and attempts to achieve formulations, which will accomodate at either end.

This kind of "adaptive prophylaxis" offsets respective levels of apprehension, or irritation, in the different constituencies. Leading black and Jewish organizations have worked to reach agreement on equal employment opportunity: the troublesome issue is whether federally imposed guidelines and timetables would, and should, assume the aspect of preferential quotas. The type of racial and religious compromise that will be reached will clearly not only defuse the issue of employment for minorities but largely determine the ethnic posture (Morsell, 1973:91–92).

Black-Jewish competition has been defused among religious leaders in particular. Black Christians and more liberal Jewish organizations have taken the initiative in overcoming the intense racial-religious dichotomies of the past decade. To this extent the tactic of accommodating the new ethnicity will lose its impulse. The more traditional alignments of blacks and Jews on a liberal axis will confront the white ethnic on a conservative axis. It might be that such competition is merely illustrative of false consciousness; the "real" issue remains economic. However, such a point of view automatically and always assumes a primacy of the economic. This very unwillingness to take seriously the competition of race, ethnicity, and religious clusters is in part responsible for the renaissance of ethnicity.

Political Uses of Ethnicity

Ethnicity is at least as much a tactic as a definition. The new ethnicity is a statement of relatively deprived sectors seeking economic relief through political appeals. Traditionally, such relief was found through the trade union movement. However, the growing bureaucratization of trade unions has signified a parallel decline of faith in class warfare. To seek relief from factory owners or managers has come to seem less efficient than to appeal to or, if necessary, threaten the federal government. For example, during the 1973 energy-fuel crisis, the mass representatives of the Teamster Workers, over and above either trucking managers or unon officials, demanded directly from the government wage benefits corresponding to the new price hikes. The political apparatus provided for such fiscal compensation due to rises incurred from higher operating costs. Collective bargaining was transformed into state decision-making.

The idea of a direct bargaining process between an outside group and the federal administration is not new. The essential tactic of black organizational life, certainly since the New Deal, and intensified after World War Two, was precisely to negotiate directly with the political system; in this manner circumventing the economic subsystem. The efficacy of this newer political model is attested to by health and welfare legislation, civil rights rulings, Supreme Court decisions on educational opportunity, and presidential commissions on minority rights. Negotiations between mass outsider groups and state officialdom has clearly achieved more than the previous search for economic equality through class struggle was able to do. This shift from economic to political realms has come to be shared by ethnic representatives, by those who seek to obtain from the government for Americans of Polish, Italian, or Irish extraction similar rights to those obtained by the black leadership.

The dilemma of this approach arises not so much in the model; indeed, to extract promises and seek restitution from federal agencies does seem more promising than to achieve wage benefits from industry. Rather, the dilemma resides one step further back in time: in the differential histories of the black people vis-a-vis the ethnic groups who seek to emulate this racial style within American politics. Even the most ardent defenders of the new ethnicity admit to substantial differences between race and ethnicity on this score.

> The new ethnicity does *not* entail: (a) speaking a foreign language; (b) living in a subculture; (c) living in a "tight-knit" ethnic neighborhood; (d) belonging to fraternal organizations; (e) responding to "ethnic" appeals; (f) exalting one's own nationality or culture, narrowly construed. Neither does it entail a university education or the reading of writers on the new ethnicity. Rather, the new ethnicity entails: first, a growing sense of discomfort with the sense of identity one is supposed to have—universalist, "melted," "like everyone else"; then a growing appreciation for the potential wisdom of one's own gut reactions (especially on moral matters) and their historical roots; a growing self-confidence and social power; a sense of being discriminated against, condescended to, or carelessly misapprehended; a growing disaffection regarding those to whom one had always been taught to defer; and a sense of injustice regarding the response of liberal spokesmen to conflicts between various ethnic groups, especially between "legitimate" minorities and "illegitimate" ones. There is, in a word, an inner conflict between one's felt personal power and one's ascribed public power: a sense of outraged truth, justice, and equity (Novak, 1974:19).

The new ethnicity is thus a subjective matter of discomfort, dissatisfaction, and disaffection. It is not a question of oppression or subjugation. As a result, it is hard to avoid the conclusion arrived at by Myrdal that the new ethnicity is not a populist movement, but an elitist demand by a rootless third-generation intelligentsia.

> In addition to a missing urge to reach the masses for whom they pretend to speak, the writers on historical identity rather systematically avoid the problem of poverty and all that is related to it. To this also belong the limited horizons, the lack of rational perception of themselves and the nation, and a reluctance to organize with other groups having the same interests to press their demands through the means freely provided by a democratic America. It is poverty and all this, not the lack of historical

identity, that holds American ethnics down. At the same time, it permits the formation of policies that run counter to the American dream of a free and democratic society that creates happiness for all its people, from wherever they have come. . . .

The "enemy" the ethnic intellectuals commonly put up as a target—i.e., those people in America who believe in the perfection of the melting pot—is a straw man. For several decades I have been closely following events in this country, and I have seldom met any fairly well-educated American who subscribed to the melting pot with the naivete customarily attributed to those who supposedly held that idea. . . .

That America is a pluralistic society where people with different cultural backgrounds have to live together and mold a nation is an obvious fact. And that this creates problems and difficulties is also obvious. But America in general has shown great capacity to absorb cultural patterns from diverse sources (Myrdal, 1974:28–29).

This set of demands made by "voluntary ethnics" may very well not be representative of the wishes or desires of Americans of Polish, Italian, Irish, or other European extractions. Myrdal's summary of the distinction between problems of identity and problems of poverty indicates the essentially middle-class psychologism underlying at least one part of the new ethnicity.

In its most current and sophisticated form, the analysis of ethnicity is made in terms of the migration, absorption, and identification of new groups. In its celebrationist form it is said that America has been uniquely able to incorporate all new groups into its social life and political experience (Handlin, 1957). The current charge is that such integration and incorporation is largely chimeric in nature. The evidence for this is that the culture costs of immigration, as well as the class exploitation of ethnic groups, have been vastly understated.

> Lost in the ethnic interstices of the American social structure, the larger question of class is never engaged, nor is even at issue. This kind of ethnic reductionism forces us to accept as predetermined what society defines as truth. Only through ethnicity can identity be securely achieved. The result is that ethnic questions which could, in fact, further our understanding of the relationship of individuals to social structures are always raised in a way that serves to reconcile us to a common heritage of miserable inequities. Instead of realizing that the lack of a well-defined stratification structure, linked to a legitimated aristocratic tradition, led Americans to employ the language of ethnic pluralism in exchange for direct divisions by social class, we continue to ignore the real factors of class in our society (Greer, 1974:34).

The same problem in cross-cutting now exists in the current sophisticated expressions of ethnicity no less than in earlier forms. While blacks are included among the ethnics in the sophisticated version, the politics of ethnicity tends to counterpose its own needs over and above the racial requirements of blacks. Beyond that, the extent of the failure or success of culture pluralism to modify the culture modism of American industrialization is an empirical issue not easily decided in terms of the moral superiority of pluralism over monism.

The weighting of the ethnicity factor with respect to race, religion, and class remains an issue not only in terms of the identification that people have with ethnicity, but in its galvanizing impact. We have first the empirical question of the importance of ethnicity and, second, the strategic question of the ability of ethnicity to generate political action. Implicit in a great deal of literature on ethnicity is an automatic assumption that ethnicity and working-class membership are axiomatic, while the blacks are identified as lower class, or outside the system of the working class. In a sense, sociologists have exaggerated the idea of a lower-class culture (Rainwater, 1966:172-216; 1970:361-397). More to the point, there has been a profound misreading of the actual distribution of the blacks in American society—for if they have a distinctive culture, they nonetheless form an essential human core in the U.S. labor force, particularly in service industries, government work, and heavy-duty labor. They represent between 15 to 16 percent of the labor force, in contrast to 11 percent of the population as a whole. They are becoming unionized at a more rapid rate than their white ethnic colleagues (Brooks, 1970:169–170; Rustin, 1971:73–74). They also are a crucial factor in assembly-line industries such as steel and auto. What sets them apart is not that they are low class while the white ethnics are working class, but that the bulk of black labor (because of its historical marginality and nontechnological characteristics) remains nonunionized, while a larger percentage of white ethnic labor (also deriving from historical sources such as immigrant syndicalist backgrounds and specialized craft forms of labor) is and has been for some time largely unionized. Accentuating the gap between lower-class black culture and working-class white ethnicity is a profoundly conservative reading of actualities—one that disguises the acute responsibilities of an American labor force sharply divided between the one-fourth that is highly organized and the three-fourths that are poorly organized, if organized at all.

This concept of ethnic organization as a precondition for class solidarity is a theme struck by any number of commentators. Richard Krickus (1971:30) has summed up this sentiment with particular force:

With rising self-awareness, the appearance of vigorous leadership, and the evolution of organizational structures, many black communities can meet the minimum requirement necessary for coalitions. Because similar structures do not exist in most white ethnic communities, a coalition with blacks is not yet feasible. Until the white ethnics, through heightened group identity, generate new leaders and develop new organizational props, the precondition for coalition activities will not materialize in their communities.

But the author of these sentiments makes it clear that the purpose of such organizational pluralism is more ambitious.

If the white ethnics are to cooperate with and work toward common goals with their nonwhite neighbors, they must acquire the means to articulate their demands in a more effective fashion. Through this process of articulation a clear view of their own self-interest will surface. This in turn is a precondition to their working together with other groups that share many problems in common with them (Krickus, 1971:30).

The strategic nature of the concept of ethnicity is self-evident. The assumption is that there is a lock-step arrangement between ethnic identification and political activity; a confrontation will presumably create the basis for ethnic and racial harmony. The notion of collective self-interest or group self-interest, so important in the development of the black civil rights movement, thus becomes the model for ethnic self improvement. The dilemma exists nonetheless since it might well be that distinctions and differences between Catholics and Protestants, or for that matter, ethnic enclaves within Catholicism, will exert far more influence than the simple dichotomization required to make ethnicity a successful strategy and response to racial identity.

Ultimate class identities can readily become blurred by the immediate ethnic pluralities. The rhetoric of racial and ethnic antagonism may be heightened rather than lessened by the assumption that separate organizational forms are now required for both black and ethnic groupings. To define tensions between ethnics and blacks without clearly demarcating the similarity of their class interests, which might also involve an identification of class hostilities, serves to exacerbate rather than eliminate tensions. It is to assume that specialized interest groups and momentary tactical considerations must always prevail over long-run tendencies and trends in the class composition of American society. It is also to assume that Jews as ethnic types have a sameness that also makes them part of this solution based on ethnicity. It might be just as easily the case that Jews too reveal profound antagonism within their numbers based on considerations of class and religion. For example, there remains a considerable spread in the class and occupational ladder among Jews and perhaps an even wider disparity between orthodox, reformed, conservative, reconstructionist, and other varieties of Jewish religious practice. Further, on the grounds of national and ethnic backgrounds, Jews of East European and Asian or Middle Eastern origins show wide disparities. And of course beyond that are the gulfs of a more political sort, between Zionists, non-Zionists, and even anti-Zionists. To perceive Jews as one unified phalanx is thus to credit them with far greater unity than they in fact possess. It is also to assume that the world of Jews is necessarily forged exclusively by threat mechanisms from outside groups. It is to deprive them of that organic integrity said to be an identifying hallmark of other ethnics.

The new world of ethnicity is filled with premises and strategies based upon models largely derived from other groups. The selective and subjective method of defining membership in an ethnic group permits the concept to be employed in any number of political contexts. It might well be that however flawed the concept of ethnicity is at the theoretical level, it can nonetheless serve as a rallying cry for those groups who are dismayed and disturbed by the breakup of ethnic communities in American society. The Jews, in particular, were castigated for being the first to abandon the urban ship in favor of suburbia. Why ethnicity must, perforce, take an urban rather than suburban form is rarely examined, much less critically dealt with.

Within the political framework of American mass society, it might be that ethnicity functions as a conservative manifestation against the breakup of community. In substance, although clearly not in form, this is similar to left-wing radical and racial nationalist groups who likewise exhibit tendencies toward communal apartness, and racial and religious efforts at firm exclusionary-inclusionary relationships.

Patterns of disaffiliation have found expression in all sectors of American society. Those who identify with the past, like those who trust only in the future, have similar problems with the present system of affluence; but, quite clearly, they have posed different solutions. It is plain that forms of social change will be scarcely less painful in the United States than they have been elsewhere. Such forms involve coalitions and consolidations of a type that may, in the long run, lead to racial harmony and class unity. However, the more likely immediate outcome will be a forging of ethnic sensitivity that will tend to minimize and mitigate against such efforts at unification and national integration.

There are those who look forward to a great age of unification between lower-class blacks and working-class white; but unification, even on the basis of expediency and political coalition, seems remote. Not only is the social system unable to provide much hope for such a coalition, but the structures of unionism on one hand and racial separatism on the other conspire to frustrate race-class fusion (cf. Leggett, 1968:144–154). That the concept of ethnicity has created one more large-scale strain in the 200-year history of American society is a reflection of the growing intensity of separatist politics and industrialist economics. The ultimate fruit of a policy of racial supremacy has been the emergence of a politics of ethnicity. Both race and ethnicity have threatened the survival of the social system and yet neither seems prepared to offer an option for all other peoples living within the United States. In addition to class and race, ethnicity must now be seen as a measure of disintegration in the American sociopolitical system. Indeed, however weak this variable might be, the fact that it has moved from the sociology texts to the neighborhoods is indicative of the tragic ruptures in a nation unable to overcome the collapse of federalism at home and the shrinkage of imperialism abroad.

Ethnicity is a surrogate concept, an expression of disintegration and deterioration of the national economic system and national social priorities. Like other notions of a particularistic nature, its importance derives more from whom it excludes than whom it includes. It is a response to a collective anomie, an era in which the halcyon days of confident national priorities and arrogant international goals have become remote. Representative government has turned unrepresentative. Regulatory mechanisms have turned oppressive and bureaucratic. Large factory management and large factory unionism have joined forces to present the ordinary laborer with an unresponsive structure. The drive for economic rationalization has led to the multinational corporation and international cartelization at an accelerated rate. This conglomerate push has underscored the economic impotence of the ordinary person; and the tendency toward subsystemic approaches is reflected in the turn towards ethnicity.

The revival of ethnicity as a working-class value is paralleled by the middle-class return to race, sex, property, and other definitions for surmounting the vacuity and vapidity of postindustrial capitalist life. The weakness of the success ethic and the achievement orientation is revealed in middle-class youths' emphasis on rurality, fundamentalism, psychologism, and other forms of the *Gemeinschaft* community of fate that presumably was left behind with the Old World and its feudal relationships. Those groups identified with the blueing of America (see Berger, 1971) are no more content with the progress of this nation than are those who are part of the greening of America (see Reich, 1970). That expressions of discontent should take different forms in different classes is certainly not without precedent, but what is surprising is the uniformity of the demand to get beyond the present malaise, the widespread resentment that makes clear that the old sociological consensus and the old political checks and balances are no longer effective mechanisms against disaffection of large portions of American society.

If ethnicity is a surrogate concept, it is nonetheless necessary to make plain what it is a surrogate on behalf of. Politically, it represents a demand for larger participation in the federal bureaucracy; economically, it is a demand for higher rewards for physical "hand" labor, at the expense of mental "head" labor; and culturally, it is a statement of the rights of groups to their distinctive life styles. Beyond that, however, are the historical dimensions: the return to ethnicity, insofar as it is more than an intellectual pipe-dream, is also a return to community: a pristine era in American life, before the melting-pot ideology boiled out the impurities of the immigrant generation with a weird mixture of external pressure and internalized guilt.

The return to ethnicity is more than a restatement of ascribed values; it harkens back to a period in which family allegiances, patriarchal authority, foreign languages, and the meaning of work itself had a certain priority over occupational and monetary achievement. On this point there can be no question that the prime targets are the blacks, who have employed the welfare model in order to gain a measure of influence and even self-respect, and the Jews, especially those of the second and third generations, who have employed the educational model to create the basis for rapid upward mobility. The problem is that the new ethnics have a hard time thoroughly identifying with the former model, and an equally hard time gaining access through the latter model. Tragically enough, they lack a model of their own.

By extension, it might be claimed with justification that the Jews have largely used the concept of social class both to explain the American system and to live within it comfortably. The blacks have generally employed a concept of racial nationalism to explain why, despite the appearance of wealth, they have been kept out of the advantages of the class network. It is only natural, under the circumstances, that the rise of an ethnic consciousness would lead to a search for large-scale alternatives. Many people of Catholic faith, Polish-Italian-Irish-Ukrainian ancestry, and working-class membership, seem to be inexorably locked into the American system at its lower, but not lowest, points. As a result, this sector of the population, which has fallen behind in real economic terms with respect to the rest of America, becomes a potentially volatile force. Ethnicity provides the same sort of explanation without attempting to peddle a working-class analysis to a conservative set of workers, or a race analysis to a set of white people.

Ethnicity is a formula for linking people and classes who would otherwise tend to be more divided than united by matters of religion, country of origin, and linguistic affiliation. Whether in fact ethnicity can, in an operational sense, prove to be as potent a factor as class or race seems somehow to be less important than the fact that the American social-science community has moved beyond its old formulas of class, status, and power to a newer formulation of class, race, and ethnicity—in which questions of status and power become intervening variables in the larger matrix of primary human associations.

Tendencies toward individualization and privatization are evolving into a durable counterculture: on one side are students, blacks, and chicanos; while on the other are ethnics: Poles, Catholics, day laborers, and all the whites who have failed to milk or melt into the "system." Whether the response has been Left or Right is less important than the impulse to resist encroachments on the "little people"—the public turned ethnic with a missionary vengeance. The making of the new minorities points up the huge shift in the United States from a nation of factory workers to a nation of marginals, i.e., service-oriented personnel. The response, in some measure, whether put in terms of racial politics or ethnic politics, is a demand for a politics of scale, in which the possibility for the control of decision-making and policy-making would be restored to communities of responsibility. This impulse toward community control is a possible source of new coalitional efforts, whether under the label of populism or welfarism, that might provide some hope for a reinvigorated politics. The rise of ethnicity as a basic concern and a root concept should not be dismissed, nor should it be celebrated. But ethnicity certainly must be charged and ultimately channeled, if this nation is to transform its current marginality into a new level of centrality, that is, of mass participation in the democratic processes.

1972

6

Revolution
and
Counterrevolution
in American Cities

In the halcyon days of the New Deal, the National Resources Committee (1937) issued a report on *Our Cities,* a most enlightened description of what is wrong with the quality of urban life in America: unbridled exploitation of land by private owners, slums and blighted areas expanding more rapidly than rehabilitation programs, high taxes caused in imbalanced industrial structures. Looking through this 1937 document, one is struck by the realization that the magnitude of these problems has increased but their character has not changed. Even the demand in the New Deal report that industrial plants conform to the human needs of the city or else face restriction is roughly parallel to the antipollution restrictions now being placed on would-be industrial tenants of the inner city.

What then has happened in the interim to exacerbate the problem? It is this: thirty years ago the essential polarity was between what was called the "urban enterprise" and "rural life." The polarity that currently defines the situation is the inner city—or the city as enlarged ghetto on one hand, and suburban enterprise—or the county as industrial enterprise on the other. It might be said, from a socioeconomic perspective, that this is really the same problem writ large—since the problem of size only enlarges the scope of the urban malaise; it does not change things. Thirty years ago, the ghetto was within the larger entity—the borough of Manhattan or the borough of the Bronx—now the ghetto *is* the borough. But what is merely a matter of scale enlargement from an economic viewpoint is a qualitatively new dilemma for political men.

City Finances: From Affluence to Austerity

The political system of alderman, councilman, borough presidents, and mayors was laid out at a time when the city was a viable and growing community. Today, when the city must be considered anything but viable or expanding, these same political structures with their built-in constraints and mutual responsibilities have made of the mayor's post an office that is more readily described in psychological than political terms. As former Mayor Joseph Barr of Pittsburgh recently declared:"You are beat like a bag of sand all day. You leave the office and you really feel like you've been clubbed all day."

An old adage is that wealth breeds corruption. However, the corollary is rarely drawn: poverty breeds austerity. And in the history of the American city, corruption has been a vital input in getting essential tasks done from building bridges and highways to paying off racial and ethnic leaders to prevent ghetto explosions. But now the padding has gone out of city budgets. Apart from the fact that most of the financial obligations are ongoing in character, i.e., salaries to police, firemen, and other service personnel, little in the way of new money is entering the city treasury.

Increasing city taxes helps little, since those best able to pay such taxes have moved to the suburbs. Local debt per capita has quadrupled since 1946 while the per capita federal debt has declined substantially (Piven and Cloward, 1967). New York City provides a classic model. One out of five people now lives in poverty. Most of those living in poverty are members of minority groups, a condition suggesting that such trends will persist. These minority groups are pouring into the city, while the middle classes are leaving in almost equal numbers. From the 1960 census to 1966, Bronx median family income declined from $5,830 to $5,525, this in the face of an annual inflationary rate of three to four percent. Further, the number of families in the Bronx earning less than $3,000 per annum increased from 16 percent to 21 percent. To the economic data one must add the geographic problems. The total population in New York's chief ghettos, such as Central and East Harlem, has decreased by as much as 25 percent; however, at the same time the numbers of blacks and Puerto Ricans in these ghettos have increased—so that in Bedford-Stuyvesant, there are now 93-95 percent blacks, in contrast to 85 percent only six years earlier (cf. Lurie, 1963; Manso, 1969; Olson, 1969).

This brief capsule of economic and ecological information describes a situation that is already well known. What is not well appreciated, however, is that this condition deprives the cities of the necessary financial "fat" to do business as usual. The possibility of building low-rent housing, taking care of block mayors, or "fixing" the right people at the right time, is sharply reduced in this era of urban economic austerity. To this situation must be added the pressures created by the drive toward "clean government" that is perhaps enforced more by the desperate needs of a city for federal and state funds than by any alteration in the moral climate of the city. That the cities have become "cleaned up" may thus work to the disadvantage of the poor more than to their advantage. The cities, in effect, are more cleaned out than they are cleaned up (Hartman, 1967).

Strategies for running a city have not changed even among "newcomers" to political power. Certainly, nothing in the preelection statements of Hatcher in Gary or Stokes in Cleveland indicated an awareness that the old structure might no longer keep erect the decaying cities and their own political machines. Yet clearly the old is giving way: at the same time that the costs of education, welfare, and health are increasing, the local tax base has dissolved (Tax Foundation, 1969). The same payoffs no longer obtain for the mayor; and in turn, the mayor cannot guarantee the same network of rewards to party stalwarts or to personal cronies.

In the light of erosion of the fiscal foundations of most large American cities, the interesting question is: Will the simple act of electing black mayors serve to "keep the lid" on the black population? It has been suggested by black militants that the black mayor is the glorified "block captain" of yesteryear. The new mayor and the old block captain manage the crumbs by means of which the seething ghetto mass simmers down. But just as the black block captains had fewer jobs to dole out and less money to spread among friends and party stalwarts than did their white counterparts, the new black mayors find themselves with little but promises and hope to offer their constituents. It seems dubious that the tactic of employing black mayors in powderkeg cities can contain the sort of militancy prevalent in black ghettos—a militancy that perhaps has become as harsh in its condemnation of "Negroes" as it is of "Honkies."

The Flight of Talent

The first law of the political jungle is survival. Even electoral losses serve to test the mettle of those who enter politics with a soft skin versus those who enter with the will to win. The Jamesian dictum of the "tough minded" versus the "tender hearted" has traditionally applied in the American political arena. Yet despite such an obvious dictum of survival, the summer of 1969 witnessed the resignations and announcements of retirement of mayors of several major cities. Among the casualties were Joseph Barr of Pittsburgh, Jerome P. Cavanagh of Detroit, Arthur

Naftalin of Minneapolis, and Richard C. Lee of New Haven. The men were more than local figures. They were architects of national policies toward urban areas. Their activities ranged from holding office in the prestigious United States Conference of Mayors to framing the Federal Model Cities program.

Many factors may have contributed to their decisions: the ethnic and religious bases of support that put the special-appeal politician into office have largely turned suburban; the potential of the mayor's office to become a stepping stone to national fame and power has given way to gubernatorial and senatorial office holders—wielders of far greater power; being mayor is no longer a sinecure, but very hard, often unrewarded work; and with the loss of the city tax base there has been a corresponding loss of the patronage pile that in former eras kept disbelievers and dissidents in line. Finally, the loss of funds has exacerbated conditions to the point where the generally "civilized" forms of mayoral control—bribery and graft—have given way to increasingly "uncivilized" confrontations between police power and poor man's power.

Allied to the flight of funds has been the flight of talent available to urban elites. In an ealier age, political appointments had a certain strategic and status value; but now, these same positions are far less enticing. The options open to technically trained personnel in private enterprise are extensive, and the risks run are far fewer. Thus, even if and when a man of talent can be found for the mayor's post, the back-up posts are increasingly filled by semicompetent or even unqualified people. In the face of such a situation, generating public-spirited behavior at a citywide level is at least as difficult as it is at a statewide or federal level—without the rewards of these state and national offices.

Like major administrative posts in universities, the office of mayor is no longer a high-status, low workload position. It is usually a terminal post and rarely leads to higher political office. It is increasingly a post that demands the juridical skills of an eighteenth-century lawyer rather than the verbal skills of a turn-of-the-century ward heeler. The "fun" has gone out of the position almost as rapidly as the trough has been emptied of surplus.

Getting exact information on the qualifications of city experts is, to say the least, very difficult. A big-city mayor does have the supplemental support of federal and state agencies assigned to city affairs (often unwanted support, viewed as interference). Also the mayor's office can count on foundations and private organizations who provide free resources in small amounts, but resources that are relatively unencumbered with bureaucratic sloth. Ford Foundation programs in New York and

Cleveland during 1968 and 1969 are a good illustration of instances where experts made the difference between "hot" and "cool" summers. However, the foundation personnel remain only marginally linked to city administrations. Thus, the problem of getting high-level personnel into local city government remains.

In a perceptive essay on "The Mayors vs. the Cities" in the Focus on New York issue of *The Public Interest,* James Q. Wilson (1969:31) points out both the difficulties in getting needed expert help and the liberal liability they can become once acquired.

> For all the talk about cities being "where it's at," very few able administrators seek out employment in the low prestige, low-paying jobs that city hall has to offer. There are such people, but they are small in number and young in age. To get the best of them, or even any at all, every big-city mayor is in competition with every other one. The mayor that runs (however well advised) a busines-as-usual administration is at a profound disadvantage in this competition. Indeed, the would-be mayor must often start seeking them out when he decides to run for office so that they can give him the speeches, the position papers, and the "task force reports" that increasingly are the hallmark of a campaign that wins the sympathy of the media. The process of tuning the mayor to be responsive to the audience begins, therefore, even before he becomes mayor. And if he should ever entertain any thoughts about taking a "tough line" or going after the "backlash vote" (however rational such a strategy might be), he would immediately face a rebellion among his younger campaign and staff assistants.

In some sense, the problem of keeping middle-echelon appointees in local government is a reflection of the larger problem of keeping the office of the mayor nationally important. Very few mayors seem able to achieve higher offices, such as governorships or senatorial nominations. Since doing a good job as mayor becomes an impossible task, the use of the office to create a sound political image becomes similarly impossible. And as the office of the mayor becomes a political dead-end, the opportunities to build a sound cadre around the office diminish.

The City Divided

Another prime explanation of the problem of the urban governing malaise is to be found in an ecological pattern that concentrates black population in the cities, white population in the country, but white political systems in both areas, with relatively interlocking structures. Ethnic politics, particularly in the large eastern and midwestern cities, continues as usual: the mayoralty continues to be the plum of Irish

Catholics (Cavanagh in Detroit, Daley in Chicago, Yorty in Los Angeles, Collins in Boston, Tate in Philadelphia) and increasingly of Italian and Spanish Catholics (Alioto in San Francisco, Cervantes in St. Louis, Addonizio in Newark). By the time the blacks assume the mayoralty, the tax base of the inner cities is so eroded that the finances of these cities are drastically inadequate to permit the exercise of normal local corruption: patronage jobs from the local armory to newspaper delivery stands, smalltime graft guaranteeing rapid construction work and electrical and plumbing installations, the manipulation of the size of police and fire departments to guarantee jobs for overzealous and undertrained youth, and the satisfactory management of a welfare system to prevent starvation from within and looting from without. All these subrosa "services" collectively added up in the past to a political machine working effectively. The voting base, padded by these marginal personnel, thus reinforced the incumbent and his party apparatus.

Of the total population growth of cities in the last 20 years, nearly 80 percent of the nonwhite increase has been in the central cities, while approximately the same percentage of the white increase has been outside the inner-city regions. Nonetheless, these redistributions of population signify much more than simple ecological transformations. The gap between death rates for white and nonwhite infants has remained a constant ratio. In 1955, infant mortality for whites was 23.6 per thousand in contrast to 42.8 per thousand for nonwhites. In 1965, the aggregate figures declined somewhat, but in the same proportions—infant mortality for whites was 21.5 per thousand, while for nonwhites the figure remained considerably higher, 40.3 per thousand. Beyond that, living areas inhabited by blacks and Chicanos contained 3.5 times the proportion of substandard housing to that found in white areas. Nonwhite unemployment rates consistently run two to four times that of white rates, with rates among young males as high as 40 percent in some cities. As recently as 1964, a nonwhite American with four years of college education could expect to earn $6,000 less in his lifetime ($185,000) than a white who had completed only the eighth grade ($191,000). Black median income as a percentage of white median income has actually dropped to 53 percent from a previous figure of 57 percent (U.S. Dept. of Labor, 1966; U.S. Dept. of Commerce, 1966, 1967). These figures underscore the economic and social sources of political instability. They do not really explain this instability, for if some indicators are worse, others are better or at least getting better (Olson et al., 1969).

The exacerbation of racial tensions is further reinforced by the fact that efforts at racial balance, slum clearance, and urban improvements have a strong cleavage effect that underscores the intense racial separatism that has come to define urban affairs. The city is now two cities—divided not so much by educational and income levels as by racial clusters. Attempts to break down this separation have taken only certain forms, such as the Hemisfair in San Antonio, which displaced blacks and browns, but not middle-class whites, or magnificent baseball and football stadiums in the midst of still unrenewed black ghettos in cities such as Atlanta and St. Louis, or more subtly, racially "balanced" communities in areas formerly deep in the ghetto regions, which provide buffer zones under the guise of integrated living quarters. Whether such decisions are made consciously or otherwise, they still have the same consequence of dividing black and white citizens, and hence making "two cities" within a city, ungovernable by a single mayor (cf. Schrag, 1969).

"The process of polarization" is a pleasant phrase that disguises a very unpleasant situation. A great deal has been said of the militancy of the Black Panthers in Oakland, the Revolutionary Action Movement in New York, the Liberators of St. Louis, the Blackstone Rangers of Chicago, etc. But the fact is that the white working class has been mobilizing its own efforts in paramilitary defense. *The New York Magazine* of April 14, 1969 reports the following:

> The revolt involves the use of guns. In East Flatbush, and Corona, and all those other places where the white working class lives, people are forming gun clubs and self-defense leagues and talking about what they will do if real race rioting breaks out. It is a tragic situation, because the poor blacks and the working-class whites should be natural allies. Instead, the black man has become the symbol of the working-class white man's resentments. "I never had a gun in my life before," a 34-year-old Queens bartender named James Giuliano told me a couple of weeks ago. "But I got me a shotgun, license and all. I hate to have the thing in the house because of the kids. But the way things are goin', I might have to use it on someone. I really might. It's comin' to that. Believe me, it's comin' to that."

The task of making allies, "natural" or otherwise, out of enemies is exacerbated by the response of a white working class that cannot get beyond the bills of the week to reports about welfare mothers organizing for the purpose of getting credit cards. Even if community control does not guarantee economic equality, it would at least permit the emergence of countervailing pressure groups that would lessen the present age of urban anxiety.

The response from urban leaders has not exactly been illuminating. A marked note of architectural monumentalism has crept into the thinking of leaders of such cities as Philadelphia, Pittsburgh, and St. Louis. Each seems bent on making their cities major tourist attractions and in developing multimillion-dollar projects that lead to the creation of pavilions, malls, plazas, cultural centers, etc. that bring visitors for a week or suburbanites for an evening, but do next to nothing for the inner-city dweller, who continues to live in the interstices of the city. This architectural monumentalism has the support of real estate and banking interests and easily generates matching federal funds, but call it "Fun City," "The Iron Triangle," or "Gateway to the West," this monumentalism is itself a large part of the problem and hardly a solution to it. It too only reinforces the fact that one mayor is required to preside over two cities, or more to the point, two virtually sealed-off sets of racial and social classes.

Federal Programs versus Local Power

At the very moment that the city tax base is so severely eroding, there is also militant resistance by state and federal agencies to shouldering any new financial responsibility. The Pennsylvania legislature has repeatedly rejected requests for city payroll taxes that would obligate those who live in the suburbs but work in the cities to pay for the privilege; and the same fate has befallen efforts at indirect levies in New Jersey and elsewhere that call for a new tax on banks and lending institutions, a tax earmarked for use in programs to ease the plight of the urban poor. When this has been coupled with the cutback in federal programs sponsored by the Office of Economic Opportunity and its various training and welfare centers, the magnitude of resentment by the cities has been equaled by the magnitude of resistance by suburban regions to pay any increased tax. The war on poverty has come to look more like a war on the poor, as both federal and state bureaucracies remain unwilling to act, while suburban publics are unwilling to pay. Under the circumstances, the routes currently open to the cities are considerably fewer than those of even ten years ago. The riots and looting that have intimidated urban dwellers serve to reinforce the death wish of suburbanites to bottle up the cities, to put a cork on them economically and educationally, and permit them to become sources of warfare between blue-collar workers and welfare recipients (Gans, 1969).

The old protest that urban renewal means nigger removal has been borne out by the vivid and livid descriptions of federally sponsored housing projects in big centers like Harlem and Watts. James Baldwin has called such projects prison houses for poor blacks, and his descriptions only underscore the widespread feeling that such planning creates urban monstrosities: the constant failure to attract residents to these projects in such low-income areas as the Pruitt-Igoe district in St. Louis indicates the failure of bureaucracy, if not the failure of planning for, rather than by, people. That sociologists like Herbert Gans (1962) and Lee Rainwater (1967) have documented these charges many times over does nothing to erase a quarter-century of planning activities that took into account the political needs of the mayor's office, the economic needs of the federal authority, and the engineering needs of the housing authority—but not the human needs of the inhabitants.

The physical and social structures of virtually every large city in the nation have become increasingly unable to meet the needs of rapidly growing populations for jobs, housing, education, and other services. Urban elites are decreasingly in a position to cope with massive violence, population concentration, and postindustrial pollution (Boulding, 1963). But the trigger mechanism of these constants is the racial variable. The absolute rate of urban decline is important, but much less so than the relative living conditions of white and black, rich and poor, suburb and inner-city residents.

The solutions put forward under both Democratic and Republican welfare administrations accentuate federal support programs at the expense of local authorities. This has the dramatic effect of weakening still further the mayor's authority by creating a link between city welfare leaders and national directors that bypasses city government. The differences between the welfare program of Nixon vis-à-vis that of Johnson relate to the relative controls of welfare funds by local versus national figures, but they do not serve to restore the lost fiscal power of the urban mayor. The poverty gap is now roughly 10.8 billion dollars. By expending this amount, in addition to the 8 billion dollars already allotted to the welfare programs, all 30 million Americans now in the underclass can be brought above the poverty threshold. Such income maintenance programs have built-in levers for work incentives. Thus, even Nixon could not get away from increasing the urban poverty indebtedness, nor could he possibly restore the authority of the mayor—since the funding process continued to cycle in from the government to the neighborhood.

The difficulty here is that the enormous cost of the bureaucracy to maintain and establish this program would eat up most of these funds; it would reinforce precisely the sort of federal involvement that has worked so ineffectively in the past, and it would further weaken any sense of local autonomy or even mayoral control of the urban governed. What is so tragic is that the very people who advocate even greater expenditure of federal funds in income maintenance programs and guaranteed annual wages do appreciate more keenly than most that it is precisely these programs that in the past have accentuated rather than alleviated the income gap between the rich and the poor. One such person, Philip M. Klutznick, Board Chairman of the Urban Investment and Development Company of Chicago and the American Bank and Trust Company of New York, put the matter quite directly (even though he went on to support bigger and better bureaucratic programming).

> State and now Federal aid to education is meant to better educational opportunity for all. Actually, it has widened the gap between expenditures for education in the suburbs as against the inner city. Yet, the pressing and demanding need was the reverse. Likewise, in housing, the FHA and public housing programs were supposed to help everyone. Yet, the first worked to accelerate the white man's escape to the suburbs and the second increased the number of Negro ghettos in the inner city.

Under such circumstances to argue the case for an enlarged bureaucracy seems ingenuous if not worse.

The difficulties in the life of the city, or the life of the mayor for that matter, ought not to be confused with the character of the continuing impulse toward urbanization. By 1964 the portion of the population living in metropolitan regions had reached 65 percent, and 70 percent by 1970 is projected. But in 1900 over 60 percent of this metropolitan population lived within central cities; by 1965 the number had declined to under 50 percent. In short, the growth of suburbia has been staggering, ranging from New Orleans with a suburban increase of 109.0 percent in one decade (1950-60) to Dallas, where the suburbs increased by 30.7 percent. In the meantime, the inner cities of New York, Chicago, Philadelphia, Detroit, Baltimore, Cleveland, Washington, St. Louis, and Boston were undergoing varying degrees of economic decline and political polarization. An analysis of economic patterns yields some basic statistics. Residents of the inner city in 1950 earned roughly 88.5 percent of the income of their compatriots in the suburbs. This figure of median family income shows a widening gap; by 1960 the ratio was 86.2 percent—or for the average suburban family an income of $7,772 while the inner-city income median was $6,697. Thus economically as well as demographically, the gulf between the inner city and the suburban regions is widening in the same way as the gap between underdeveloped and properly developing regions (cf. Seligman, 1965; Laumann, 1966; Downes, 1968; Lockard, 1968). However, this problem takes place at the opposite end of the historical spectrum: it is the problem of overdevelopment, not underdevelopment that defines the inner city. We sometimes forget that the gulf between the properly developing society and the underdeveloped society is paralleled by a gulf between the former and the overdeveloped society. By overdeveloped society I mean: facilities available (like parks and malls) that are not used; factories that underemploy; subway stations and highways that break down as a result of overproduction and overuse of cars. The problems of too much, rather than too little, characterize the American city. And as such, the problem is not the search for avenues to "modernization" but for ways to curb the effects of modernization.

Mayors today often confront the same dilemma that rulers of underdeveloped nations face: they are responsible for the formulation of realistic planning objectives in difficult and treacherous circumstances. Rarely are there well-developed information sources about conditions; and hence, to distinguish between what would be and what should be becomes impossible. Furthermore, the distillation of common social goals at a high level of abstraction is easy enough—everyone wants to reduce crime, expand education, eliminate racial discrimination. But when it comes to the essence of these things, questions change from "principles" to "priorities": from what a society should provide in the way of services to which services deserve attention.

The crisis in our cities is perhaps best understood as part of the crisis in the federalist system of representative democracy. When one person represents one hundred people, the town-hall concept of direct responsibility can be maintained; when one person represents one hundred thousand, the representational concept of general-will responsibility can be maintained. But when one person represents one million people, any notion of democracy becomes strained and tenuous, and ultimately must break down. The political space between ruler and ruled becomes so great that the very notion of participation itself disintegrates. And this is precisely what seems to have happened in the large cities (Davidson, 1969; Slayton, 1969).

The big metropolis is the setting for bitter struggles among competing interest groups—ethnic, racial, class, etc.—and so planning mechanisms must solicit a consensus on what the problems are, what the causes are, and what kind of city is desired, each of which assumes an agreement between the very groups involved in a political fallout to begin with (cf. Smith and McGrail, 1969). The worth of community control is that it reduces the magnitude of the planning process and simultaneously makes possible more effective small-scale planning by bypassing the interaction of antagonistic interest groups—since these interest groups would themselves form the nucleus of the new community. Clearly this is an idea/vision—but at least it permits the creation of an urban policy of scale—something clearly lacking in the present competition of interest groups in a zero sum game.

It is not so much a question of the mayoralty changing, as of the quantitative ratios changing so drastically that the very concept of urban rule collapses. Neither in access nor in control do the people of a city like New York feel that they have a real part in the political apparatus. The political party system, itself an elitist inheritance, only serves to isolate further the political processes from the intimate social processes. This was the kernel of truth in the Norman Mailer campaign. He appreciated the degree to which alienation has become a fact of urban political life, affecting leaders no less than citizens (Manso, 1969). What he failed to realize is the next step—the need for New York to be broken down, not built up into a fifty-first State.

It has become fashionable to raise questions about the "price of community control" (Beck, 1969: 14-20). It is said that most serious programs for welfare or education require such high expenditures of risk capital that only citywide units can possibly manage such amounts rationally and economically. Another argument against community control is that "liberalism" itself would be sacrificed if the city was sacrificed. The size of the unit is equated with its politics, i.e., ghetto ideologies function at community levels and integrationist ideologies function at the macrolevels. Therefore, the city is said to be a bulwark against fanaticism of right and left, black and white. While both arguments have prima-facie merits, they overlook (or suppress) important parts of the community-control argument. Let us take each one separately.

While the costs of welfare and education programs are extremely high and growing higher (the cost of educating one child varies from $1,000 to $1,500 per annum), the ability and willingness to absorb such increased costs could more readily come from communities running a gamut of class elements than from racially sealed ghettos such as now exist. Behind the community-control approach is a threat not to present levels of federal support, but only to the arrogant control of these funds by outside agencies. In the long run, however, community control may indeed lessen federal support, as local communities discover they can better manage their own affairs and determine the long-run benefits and costs of federal and state aid programs.

This proposal for a polity of scale would parallel an economy of scale. I am not suggesting simple localism, that is, "neighborhood control" or "block participation." These schemes, similar in content if not in form to the community-participation programs in isolated areas of Latin America, fail to take into account the ineffectual and unmanageable nature of simple anarchism, not to mention the "colonizing" role of the metropolitan center. What I am suggesting is that areas such as Bedford-Stuyvesant with its 300,000 people and Harlem with its 500,000 represent quite large-scale cities—in fact they have comparable autonomy or political clout. The mechanical theory that people first associate themselves with blocks, then with neighborhoods, and only then with communities—and that social reorganization of urban affairs should move in parallel fashion—simply ignores the fact that social and political life has a reality of its own quite apart from the natural history of individual political socialization. In short, the needs of large groups do not necessarily have to move in the same cognitive grooves as the growing-up processes of individuals.

Those who argue that liberalism operates with unique worth at the urban level forget that the foundation of liberalism is not the size of federal work and welfare programs, but the fact that each person counts as one—not less than one and not more than one. Even if the cities could deal more adequately with problems of jobs and income and thereby minimize pressures for higher public support of education and welfare, it would not alter the fact that liberalism for many has come to be defined in terms of adequate living conditions. The character of liberalism, however, is uniquely linked to the quality of life—specifically of political life, because even the enfranchisement of the 40 percent or so of nonmobilized and nonparticipating citizens depends on a sense of community and a sense of mission. These sensibilities are much more easily nurtured by direct control at a community level than by indirect control at an impersonal bureaucratic level. The ploy that distinguishes community control from "administrative decentralization" is just a tactic—since the latter is a consequence of the former and not an option to community control. Thus, the argument that guarantees of adequate living standards—the "ends of liberalism"—would be frustrated by community control seems spurious and part of a general campaign to perpetuate a political party process that, whatever its worth at the gubernatorial or national levels, has proved woefully inadequate at the city level.

Economic and Political Elites

The relationship between size and governability of a city is only slightly less critical than the crisis of representational government as such. The movement toward community control is as powerful among the "left" as it is on the "right," as motivating a factor in the behavior of the black underclass as it is in the white working class. In New York City, the movement for "community control" of the educational system at the Ocean Hill District is but a forerunner of a citywide struggle of racial and ethnic minorities to decentralize the Board of Education—if not to dismantle it entirely. Given the bureaucratic, unresponsive, and notoriously undemocratic history of the Board, the only wonder is that demands for local control did not come sooner. The trouble is that the taxes from which the apportionment of funds for these school districts are drawn are collected on a citywide, statewide, and ultimately nationwide basis. Thus the search for political and educational control comes up against the hard facts of economic and financial "responsibility" being lodged in remote quarters. Here the mayor is caught in a crossfire, not simply of racial versus ethnic interests (largely spurious divisions, one might add), but the much more real bifurcation of powerful community political life and equally powerful economic interests—neither of which are particularly responsive or responsible to the mayor's office. Nor is this a New York phenomenon. The same sort of bind affects the mayor of St. Louis in relation to welfare and health services. Such services are provided by either local business elites or federal political elites, again neither of which is responsive or responsible to the mayor's office. Thus the political bases of power have become smaller and smaller—down to the community and block levels, while the economic bases of power have become larger and larger—up to the state and federal levels. At either end of the spectrum, the city mayor has become obsolete.

The Ocean Hill-Brownsville experiment in local control of education is simply the first indication that beyond local discontent is community control. That it will be a long, arduous task, that many good people will be hurt in the process, that exaggerations will arise along with innovations, all this should caution us in blueprinting the forms of community political life; but it certainly does not lead to any revision of my original premise: the collapse of the city as a viable insitution of social control or political participation.

In line with this, social planning has become extremely difficult. First, planning must be coordinated with federal commitments, established by bureaucrats who themselves are often hamstrung in making financial decisions. Second, social planning requires the kind of rezoning legislation that realty interests and banking interests jointly sabotage; and finally, the type of social planning done in the past has made the beneficiaries of such programs increasingly suspicious.

Dis-annexation

Urbanologists have a convenient fiction that people living in suburbs "need" the city — as a place to work and as a place to get away and play (Community Relations Service, 1969). This is, to say the least, highly problematic. The rise of industrial parks and the decentralization of industrial plants as such have led to an industrial exodus from the city at least as rapid as the population exodus. A city like New York, for instance, has lost a large share of its garment and clothing manufacturing—and did so long before the Jews, Italians, and Irish left the inner city. Further, as for the city providing recreation and enjoyment, these facilities too have been relocated. Theaters playing first-run films and performing live plays in earlier years could only be found in the inner city; now they exist in nearly every suburban region. Further, most new stadiums are built in suburban rather than urban regions—San Francisco's Candlestick Park and New York's Shea Stadium are more easily reached from the midpeninsula and Long Island, respectively, than by roads linked to the inner city.

A dilemma arises at two ends: first, new minicities are in fact able to provide a total network of services for counties that makes participation in the life of the inner city superfluous; and second, when urban renewal in the inner city is tried, it is usually in areas inhabited exclusively by black and minority groups, thus serving only to intensify an already raw racial separation. To speak of solutions, therefore, without questioning the very content of the city government and urban economics, is simply ludicrous. The problem of the mayoralty situation is in the final analysis the problem of urban viability itself.

A deep tragedy in this so-called new philosophy for cities is the fallacious assumption that the central city and the suburbs form a single unitary entity. According to Charles Abrams (1964, 1965), the able urbanologist, city and suburb depend upon each other for job opportunities, services, recreation, escape, variety, and progress. The plain fact is that this is decreasingly the case. The relative total autonomy of suburban regions is now a full fact if not a particularly full philosophy. In a recent television documentary, "Sixteen in Webster Groves," few of the youngsters interviewed had ever been to the inner St. Louis city—even though it is but a ten-mile car ride away! Only curiosity coupled with the impulse for social good led to their going to St. Louis even at age 16. Indeed, with the present superhighway system it is possible to get from the country to a destination within the center city without going through the urban interstices. Whatever else this implies, it is clear that the suburban regions do provide a total life package quite apart from the urban city, which perhaps explains why movements for amalgamation and fusion of city and county districts have failed so decisively (cf. Bollens and Schmandt, 1965: 491-524).

In each and every major industrial region there are now industrial parks of a size and scope that obviate further contact with the inner city. The industrial park is, to date, the most powerful development recruiting the blue-collar worker to the suburbs, following his white-collar brethren by one decade. Coupled with the movement of industry is the growth of huge shopping plazas providing everything from banking services to bowling tournaments. It is a tragic mistake to think that the excitement of the city, the lure of the inner loop, is irresistible. To the white-collar worker, the inner city represents as much an evil as the entire city once represented to the 19th-century rural Protestant. To the blue-collar worker, the suburbs represent an escape from ethnicity and proximity to the black population. To the offspring of both these major class sectors, the suburb is an uncontested way of life—and if anything, their impulses are for nostalgia and more retreatism—and not for involvement in urban affairs. Even though urban communities of the young sometimes display political concerns in demonstrations, marches, and vigils, they show negligible interest in traditional party or electoral politics.

The thunder on the racial left is well known. But no less ominous than black demands for community control are the increasing demands for community control and for "dis-annexation" coming from the white working class and ethnic blue-collar workers. The more the whites feel that they occupy "enclaves" in cities that they once dominated, the more they begin to react in terms of autonomous self-governing proposals. The situation in Mayor Richard Hatcher's Gary, Indiana, is probably typical of situations elsewhere. Indeed, the probability is that were Shaker Heights an incorporated part of Cleveland, Ohio, a similar opposition to Mayor Stokes would be exhibited.

Eugene Kirtland, head of the "secessionist" movement in Gary's quasifashionable Glen Park division, recently put the matter this way in a *Harper's* interview (Frady, 1969: 41-42):

> The small, middle-class property owners out here look on dis-annexation as a defense for their investments. Oh, there are many reasons—people feel we would have better economic development under our own government, for one thing. Gary's like every other middle-class community, I suppose: the good people don't say anything until it's almost too late—but then watch out!

Beneath the rhetoric of threatened mass violence is the antifederalist theme that has become the common demoninator for animus on the Right and Left.

> People just generally feel institutions are getting too big, too remote, and impersonal and unresponsive to individuals—that goes for business and government too. And now you've got all these taxes to finance social change, and it's the average Joe in the middle of the block who's having to pay them, but for what? He doesn't really know how they're spent, why they're spent, or how much is spent—-he just knows it's a lot, and he's paying it.

One might argue that this is just the black-white struggle being presented in covert fashion. But I suspect that whether or not this is the case, the fact that both blacks and whites are responding in an identical "anticivic" fashion indicates that the end of the city as a politically viable unit may fast be approaching.

The community level of politics is hardly limited to representational forms of struggle. It is beginning to characterize confrontational politics as well. Some of the smaller eastern cities, e.g., Plainfield and New Brunswick in New Jersey, have witnessed situations in which public officials, fearful of the cost in lives of trying to reassert control over the area, cordon it off but do not allow police to enter. Then for a period that may last from a day to a week, state authority over the embattled community is held in abeyance as militant armed youth exercise *de facto* control. Finally, the standoff is broken by negotiations between public officials and representatives of the rioters. H. Rap Brown has encouraged the development of what sociologist Martin Oppenheimer (1969) has called the urban guerilla.

> Look what the brothers did in Plainfield. The brothers got their stuff. They got 46 automatic weapons. Then they went back to their community . . . and they told that peckerwood cop: "Don't come in my community." He didn't come. And the only reason he didn't come was 'cause he didn't want to get killed. And the brothers had the material to do it. They had 46 carbines down there. That's what he respects—power. He respects that kind of power.

Under such circumstances, it is pointless to ask whether the community represents a viable alternative to politicization to the city. The more pointed question is how well the city fares when its officials are forced to deal with community "leaders" on a basis of parity. Confrontation politics may be the forward wedge in the legal redefinition of urban affairs.

The solution is *not* to make states out of our big cities. Indeed, this would only compound the dilemmas by further bureaucratizing urban regions and separating them from the rest of the country.

The solution is *not* to incorporate vast stretches of country into the big cities, first and foremost because such steps have been vigorously resisted by county dwellers, who fear the loss of their autonomy; and second, because like the plan for statehood, the incorporation of counties into cities only deepens the bureaucratic malaise by encouraging precisely the kind of giantism that is at the root of the problem to begin with.

The solution is *not* to increase the taxes people pay—either on income or on property. These are already at maximum figures and increases merely drive the much maligned middle sectors to the suburban regions faster. Furthermore, these taxes most often affect the city residents and leave relatively unaffected those who use urban facilities but do not live within the urban centers.

The solution is *not* to ban automobiles or other vehicular forms of transportation. To deprive the inner city of such transportation, that is, to "countrify" the city is precisely to deprive the city of the throb and vitality that made it great to begin with. The creation of "downtown malls" is furthermore not to touch the problem of the urban poor—it is only to make the life of middle-class shoppers more comfortable. A more rational and equitable form of transportation may be indicated, particularly public transportation programs such as the Bay Area Transit Authority. But this is no solution for cities like New York which have large, and largely underutilized, subway systems.

In the first stage, New York might be divided into five cities—with each borough becoming an incorporated, legal entity distinguishable in its administration from every other borough. After that, the boroughs themselves should be split into organic neighborhoods—something remarkably simple to accomplish in some cities and more difficult, but still not impossible, in others. Bensonhurst, Borough Park, Coney Island, Hamilton Parkway, Sea Beach, and Brighton Beach area; each of these already shows profound sociological commonalities, boundaries fixed by ethnic, racial, and religious conventions that supersede the recognized legal boundaries of the borough system.

I am suggesting that urban politics is a question of control and that, in turn, the quest for community is a thirst for politics (Greer and Minar, 1968). It is control that defines the extent and the limits of power. The present "controls" have clearly broken down. What is needed is not restorationism, not law and order, not bigger and better budgets, but the exercise of power, the establishment of intimacy between rulers and ruled. If this strikes some as restorationism of another variety, of the town-hall variety, then so be it. The fact that a model from an earlier age in American history exists is an argument neither for nor against this proposal. Indeed, the urban dweller does perceive himself as a resident of a neighborhood (not even a district) and often a block (where even the neighborhood may be the enemy).

This brings us to the more sophisticated position that community control and dis-annexation or decentralization in general are not necessarily mutually exclusive. Alan K. Campbell has recently made this point decisively.

> Although students of American federalism have for generations tried to divide the functions of government among the levels in a clear-cut and precise fashion, such a division is impossible. It is not functions which are assigned to parts of the governmental system, but rather power. It is quite possible to design a system where local communities are given substantial influence in the administration of functions, even though those functions must, for technological and economic reasons, be performed on an area-wide basis. . . .The desire for community involvement, the need for citizens to have a participating role in the system, goes far beyond disadvantaged blacks and discontented young people. Underlying, in part, the movement to suburbia by the white middle-class was a search for community (Campbell, 1970:208).

The struggle around "decentralization" is perhaps the opening wedge to what Saarinen (1943) long ago called the larger struggle for "organic integration." Every major city has "real" neighborhoods that can form the backbones of new organisms of authority relocated at the community level. People do their living in these smaller units—all the way from the block to the borough. In this form, the people have themselves already answered the question of the feasibility of community control of urban America (cf. Heilburn and Wellisz, 1968).

Natural divisions exist in San Francisco, with districts like Fillmore, Haight-Ashbury, Russian Hills. Similar divisions exist in New York: Greenwich Village, Sheepshead Bay, Bay Parkway, etc. What is lacking is not the existence of the community, but the juridical sanctions for the community. The present level of political struggle is thus centered on securing legal status. In this way the citizens move beyond professional sanctity toward community needs (cf. Gittell, 1968: 70-71).

The community or small city offers distinct advantages for all sectors of the urban population. It presents the first clear indication of the reduction, if not the end, of the welfare system; an end to the psychic state of anomie and impotence caused by living in "ungovernable" surroundings; an end to arbitrary and profoundly resented schemes for creating racial balance that never really touch the actual imbalances of income and housing; and it represents a real break with conventional party politics, which would permit new coalitional formations and new groupings along the interest lines that exist now in the third part of the twentieth century rather than those left over from the last part of the nineteenth century. But above all else, it creates a condition of proximate parity between the inner city and the suburban minicenters—by giving them similar structural forms and by granting the citizenry similar rights and obligations. The inner city will become desirable only when it incorporates the major positive features of suburban living; spacious housing, good highway systems, a public education network good enough to absorb all sectors of the population, etc. To maintain the city as an "amusement capital" or "leisure playland," or even as the "center of banking and commerce," is to perpetuate the artificial division between inner city and outer suburb—a division whose very existence makes a solution to our domestic ailments impossible.

What most holds back the breakup of the central city into various middle-sized cities is the failure of the city's inhabitants to learn how to execute their ideas and a larger and mostly unstated fear that they will lose federal funds for support of the poor. The principle of the urban poor is territoriality. The principle of the working class is expropriation. Thus the poor, despite their many deficits and disadvantges in the organization of political appeal, have a larger advantage: they are defending the neighborhood, a very real fact of geographic and ecological integrity. It needs no utopian programming or blueprinting; and it is largely capable of uniting diffuse class interests (i.e., the black poor and the white working class), and hence represents a healing revolution rather than an abrasive revolution.

The differences between centralized and community systems of governing obviously affect specific policies on everything from fluoridation to floating school bonds; the contradiction for most liberal-minded people is that they prefer the goals of big government but would like to see them brought about through community control. This is not to be. One has to accept a certain bridling of enlightened policies if one wants community control; whereas one has to accept the bureaucratic apparatus if one wants certain welfare programs. As the operations of the Community Action Program during its first four years indicate, a choice must be made in terms of a theory of government and also in terms of a set of specific policies (cf. Levitan, 1969).

What can be said is that the centralized approach has received a far greater trial run than decentralized approaches—perhaps because it squares better with the federalist ideology that has dominated American life since its constitutional fathers formulated it. But if the problem of police brutality is going to be resolved, community control is necessary. This will also mean an increase in segregated communities (on both black and white sides). Community control is not a panacea and is not without high risks. For instance, it may temporarily stimulate rather than settle inequalities in the distribution of material perquisites (cf. Greenstone and Peterson, 1968). But such risks seem eminently worth taking at a point when the struggle for improved services depends increasingly on the conscientiousness of citizens—and people will pay for what they can see is beneficial, not for what big government agencies say is beneficial. Big cities are big governments—and are so perceived by the people they rule. Because cities have not and cannot act against national interests, community control seems a necessary as well as feasible response to urbanized anomie.

The high irony of the present situation, viewed ideologically, is that the doctrine of pluralism in the hands of its prime advocates, such as Robert Dahl (1961) and Nelson Polsby (1963), represents a celebration of American democracy and the countervailing elite formations that add up to a *laissez-faire* polity. But it resolves itself in a quite different way in the current situation. For men like Nathan Hare (1969) and Charles Hamilton (1967), the same doctrine of pluralism is a justification for the breakdown of American democracy, a statement that pluralism is separatism and conflict politics and not the hidden hand of consensus politics. Aside from proving that any doctrine can be used in just about any way, it shows how the oligarchical potentials of separate principates do not quite die out in a democracy, but rather come back in the form of the local party boss or "block captain." The cry of pluralism in the hands of the decentralizers is a demand for making democracy viable at the expense of the national orchestration of politics that was envisioned by classical political pluralism with its veto effects and interest-group formations. But this too means that even the rhetoric of conventional liberal wisdom has been undermined by the new urban condition.

If the city is ungovernable in its death throes, then the community is governable in its resurgence. This in turn is but a particularistic manifestation of the decline of federalism at the political level and "mass society" at the economic level. Masses are turning into publics. The push toward bigness translates itself into a search for privacy and intimacy. The pluralism that saw its pinnacle in the play of interest groups within the city has increasingly become realized in the play of interest groups among communities. It is all too easy to dismiss Nathan Hare's assertion of his faith in the pluralistic ideal as simple demagoguery. Quite the contrary, his is indeed a touching faith precisely in the substance of liberalism: the system of political checks and balances that truthfully, accurately represents and reflects real interests in contrast to contrived interests. If the cities seem to have a bleak future, there is nevertheless no need for apprehension. The community, that clustering of human souls and ecological boundaries under direct supervision of the inhabitants of an area, has been revitalized—and with it, let us hope that the Greek ideal of democracy exercising its magic within the community can protect us from the worst excesses of anomic gigantism and bureaucratic planning.

1970

7

The Present Condition
of the
American Working Class

Even a casual perusal of the socialist and radical literature on the
contemporary condition of the working class and the likelihood of a
working-class revolution reveals a situation of towering confusion. The
workers have become a veritable inkblot test, confirming the faith of
"classicists" in their vision of a vanguard workers' movement and,
equally, confirming the belief of "revisionists" in their vision of workers
as authoritarian. And there is a whole cluster of academics uncertain of
the workers' political ideology but nonetheless convinced that workers
are better off unorganized lest they enlarge the size and scope of the
fascist thrust. In such circumstances it is perhaps easier to understand, if
not appreciate, the reticence of social scientists on the condition of the
working class in the United States.

Three Theories of the Working Class

Illustrative of the orthodox tendency is the work of Ernest Mandel. He
claims that "if we examine the long term trend, there is no doubt that the
basic process is one of growing homogeneity and not of growing heterogeneity of the proletariat" (Mandel, 1968: 165). Mandel still argues that
there is a "working-class vanguard" and that this said vanguard was
betrayed by a degenerate "classical labor movement" that "stopped
inculcating the working-class vanguard in any consistent manner against
the poison of bourgeois ideas" (pp. 168-169). But despite this pharmaceu-

tical description of betrayal from within and of the pernicious force of mass communications and bourgeois ideology from without, we are assured by Mandel that the contradictions grow sharper and that the very character of labor-union organization will eventually stimulate proletarian revolution (p. 169).

The difficulty is that when confronted with the need to present evidence for this classical position, Mandel must refer to the student movement in France. To be even remotely convincing in his argument, Mandel must convert the students into an arm of the proletariat. Further, although Mandel is apparently elated by the size of the 1968 "May revolution" in France, claiming it to be larger than past historic proletarian movements, he does not discuss why, given such numbers, the revolution petered out and the workers returned to Gaullist normality within a week. Only two years after it was written, the analysis reads like a sorry piece of black humor.

It is also necessary to raise forcefully, without shame or trepidation, the "American exceptionalism" thesis. The polarization of class and race in the United States, with its attendant movement of the unionized working class to the Right, makes it hard to maintain the doctrine of *trahison.* The working class has not been betrayed. It has done much of the betraying—and the failure of industrial unions like those in the construction and steel industries to integrate the races would indicate that labor conservatism is not the exclusive hallmark of craft unionism but likewise characterizes proletarian trends as a whole. But the point is not to criticize Mandel, since he illustrates only one tendency in contemporary neo-radical thinking. Let us turn to his opposite number, Seymour Martin Lipset, for another view.

According to Lipset, a rise in literacy and formal education should have brought about a lessening of working-class authoritarianism. In point of fact, using his own measures, a very different outcome occurred: the working classes have actively supported political candidates from Robert Kennedy to George Wallace. In short, they support precisely those candidates who support them on economic issues. The working class becomes neither more democratic nor more reactionary, but, instead, less political in general. Another major conceptual problem in Lipset's work is that he makes little serious effort to distinguish between working class and lower class. With the exception of those distinctions forced upon him by data others have collected, he makes no real distinction between types of working-class activities that might more readily account for variations in attitudes than conventional variables drawn from Weberian notions of social status.

At the time Lipset formulated his authoritarian hypothesis in the late 1950s, it was clearly intended as a buffer against a Communist interpretation of working-class behavior. It is also clear, as the steady stream of references to Marx, Engels, and Lenin reveals, that Lipset conceived of this essay, as Theodore Adorno before him had, as an exercise in revisionist Marxism, and not as anything resembling a Weberian formula for studying the masses. Lipset conceded that his data presented problems—activists can turn into retreatists overnight and authoritarianism in one situation does not necessarily lead to an authoritarian personality type, as Adorno (1950) postulated. Nonetheless, the same problems that plague Mandel, earlier had befallen Lipset—problems that arise from the assumption of a historic world mission for the proletariat, a belief that the mission of factory workers remains intrinsically and irrevocably revolutionary. And it is precisely this tenet of faith that has been most emphatically broken by the emergence of the trade-union movement.

If the proletariat is authoritarian and the middle class is the carrier of the libertarian faith, where does that leave the Marxist concept of working-class revolution? It is precisely this problem in Marxism, and not the problems of the proletariat, that informs Lipset's vision. Like Lenin, he must make the condition of the working class a cause for profound concern in the postrevolutionary period. But we have yet to compare the working class and the middle class in terms of revolution, marriage making, and home building. Crude measures of voter identification prove very little, since political parties in the West usually contain both authoritarian and democratic tendencies.

Lipset's position is more subtle and complex than his critics are usually willing to admit. In the first place, he draws a sharp distinction between economic and noneconomic issues; he declares that the poorer strata are everywhere more liberal or leftist on such economic issues as state support, graduated income taxes, and support of unionism. However, "when liberalism is defined in noneconomic terms—as support of civil liberties, internationalism, etc.—the correlation is reversed. The more well-to-do are more liberal, the poorer are more intolerant" (Lipset, 1960: 169).

Lipset adduces a number of variables to support his contention about authoritarian predispositions in lower-class individuals. Among them are fundamentalist religious beliefs, low education, low participation in political or voluntary organizations, little reading, isolated occupations, economic insecurity, and authoritarian family patterns. A major difficulty is that the data, drawn from Stouffer's work (1955), actually show very small political differences between well-defined manual workers and white-collar workers. Indeed, education seems to be a more important variable than class in determining "authoritarianism." Lipset is thus forced to equate, at least implicitly, know-nothingism and working-class authoritarianism. Furthermore, it is far from self-evident that the new working class is as inextricably committed to a Leninist notion of "economism" as Lipset believes.

In a recent article on new currents in labor, Bogdan Denitch (1970: 353) made the intriguing observation that in

> France in 1968 and Italy in 1970, the most militant strikers came from areas with the most advanced technology and the highest proportion of highly skilled or educated workers in electronics, chemistry, auto, aircraft, as well as from previously passive "middle class" professions—teaching and journalism. Characteristic of these strikes is a stress on democracy at the point of production rather than mere traditional wage demands.

In other words, the newer and more specialized elements in the working class, far from increasing authoritarian pressures, have raised anew the classic democratic issues. At the very least, this lends support to those who still maintain a certain faith in the open-endedness of working-class ideologies.

The difficulties in Lipset's appraisal are more apparent in retrospect. And while this evaluation is by no means intended to minimize the importance of his great insights, a catalog of the problems inherent in his perspective is necessary to move beyond them. First, he operates with an unstated, and I daresay, unexamined code of union democracy that is more typical of some old-fashioned craft unions than new-fashioned industrial unions. This is because craft unions approximate the professional standards of nonlaboring elites. Second, he operates with a theory of authoritarianism that fails to appreciate adequately the special non-political characteristics of labor organization and labor ideology among the members of the American working class. And third, he operates with a theory of status deprivation rather than one of class consciousness; hence, he better explains the behavior of a smaller militant wing of labor than he does the general labor force as such. The large bulk of labor remains committed to liberal ideology and electoral politics. The notion of working-class authoritarianism cannot help but disguise this ongoing central fact of American society.

Lipset has the same evidentiary problem as Mandel. He must prove that the mainline behavior of the middle class is somehow more democratic than that of any other sector. Since all definitions of authoritarian and democratic political behavior are relative, the question is, authoritarian in relation to whom? At that point it becomes quite apparent that the working class is neither more nor less authoritarian but increasingly like the middle class in its political ideology and voting patterns.

Labor is wedded to the ideology of American society and that means the politics of interest groups and the economics of state manipulation (if not state intervention). One might say, therefore, that labor has become pragmatically antirevolutionary, or at least antisocialist. But such developments, onerous as they may appear to advocates of socialism, are a far cry from authoritarianism. One gets the impression that Lipset, like Mandel, is deeply troubled by a labor movement that does not conform to socialist goals. Rather than accept this fact, Lipset labels the working class authoritarian, when in point of fact, this is simply a euphemism for the working class's rejection of European socialism.

In a sense, the works of John Leggett (1968), and before him, Ely Chinoy (1955) and Robert Blauner (1964), represent efforts to preserve the Marxist kernel, without falling into cliche-ridden ideas either of the Left or of the Right. Interestingly enough, each of these three researchers did his work among industrial workers and, in particular, among automobile workers. Their work represents an effort to link Marxism to sophisticated survey research and field techniques of investigation. Using Leggett as a prototype, we can say that the sociological Marxists have gone far beyond the abstracted empiricism of a Lipset or the grand theory of a Mandel.

Leggett's position is that two variables—uprootedness and ethnic-racial background—scored highest in explaining class consciousness. Those workers uprooted and fragmented by the Depression and its lengthy aftermath still harbor strong tendencies toward class definitions of reality; and ethnic groups consistently show greater class consciousness than do long-assimilated groups. Leggett tries to indicate that workers engaged in marginal activities, such as the California farm workers, reveal a higher degree of working-class identification than do others. The same is true for other marginal sectors that are unorganized. They tend to show a pattern of demand and identification sharply distinct from that of unionized laboring groups.

Counter to Mandel's claims, Leggett indicates that there is a growing heterogeneity in the working class. He discovered that the mainstream working class does not constitute a homogeneous mass of workmen undifferentiated in ethnic background and opinions on class matters. Ethnic subcultures exist and in certain ways reflect their class composition (Leggett, 1968: 62-75). But this heterogeneity may represent new forms of coalition politics having progressive payoffs—for instance, labor-black coalitions—and does not necessarily lead to simple fragmentation.

Although Leggett's research is consciously, almost self-consciously, "anti-Lipset," it probably does more damage to such orthodox Marxist notions of class as Mandel's than to the Lipset framework, since the latter has already clearly demarcated a realm of analysis that granted the continuing force of "progressive" ideas in the economic arena but documented the continuing impulse to democracy among unionists. Nevertheless, Leggett's data do not reveal any particularly strong authoritarian tendencies even in the more general questioning he engaged in. On the contrary, the workers tend to reveal not just a class consciousness but a relatively democratic value orientation as well.

What seems particularly relevant is the underlying implication in Leggett's work: the working class is basically a large-scale interest group, which may overlap at times with neighborhood organizations based on racial or ethnic interests, that has as its core the advancement of the needs and overall position of the working class in American society. Insofar as these needs and demands represent a vanguard frame of reference, socially and politically no less than economically, the interest patterns exhibited retain their progressive vitality. Leggett does grant the growing tendency toward violence that may vitiate and cancel older forms of nonviolent voting responses to political affairs. This does not necessarily represent authoritarianism, but rather a simple change of tactics necessitated by the continuing failure of American society to provide for the basic needs of workingmen—black and white, organized and unorganized.

While Leggett has sought to provide serious measures of working-class consciousness, like all other speculations about labor's unique role, his work is burdened with notions of the ultimate destiny of American labor. Since labor is very much like other groups in the United States and is becoming more so annually, a defense of its special democratic nature seems at least as difficult to sustain as Lipset's argument concerning its special authoritarian nature. Leggett is reduced to saying that some interest groups are really better and more progressive than others. This certainly may be the case, but it is a far cry from the higher promises of revolutionary action and ultimate democratic commitment. I therefore find Leggett's argument persuasive but his conclusions somewhat less than encouraging—at least from the standpoint of revolution-making.

From Class Politics to Interest-Group Economics

I have fewer objections to Leggett's approach than to the rigidity of a Mandel or a Lipset. And these objections rest upon a belief that Leggett's stratum of Detroit auto workers may be atypical, rather than typical, of certain national and international trends. After all, "Reuther's union" remained one of the few honest efforts to raise radical and liberal alternatives, and the auto union constantly worked to integrate black workers—particularly in the wake of the 1943 Detroit riots. Even so fertile an acorn as Leggett's studies is not by any means the whole forest. But before proceeding to trees and forests, it is instructive to take up one point that is implicitly rather than explicitly stated in Leggett's argument: namely, that interest-determined demands of the working class are somehow instinctively and intuitively more progressive than those of other sectors. In a sense, any large-scale disaffiliation on the part of workers, southerners, blacks, and so forth, creates a basis for undermining confidence in the United States; but it is really hard to see why labor is in a unique historical position on this score or why "militancy" is somehow galvanized toward Left-oriented mass politics. Indeed, the Wallace phenomenon occurred precisely after the death of Robert Kennedy—so that the formal designations of Right or Left seem less important than the central importance of interest demands among the working class. And it is hard to determine that working-class demands are peculiarly more noble or more radical than other demands. Leggett fails to investigate the possibility that labor demands may actually conflict with black demands, that coalition efforts may not occur. Indeed, the developments in such working-class cities as Gary and Cleveland indicate a rising polarization, rather than pluralization, and a distinction between kinds of consciousness, so that *black consciousness* becomes a veiled euphemism for "antihonky" attitudes and *union consciousness* a reference to racist attitudes among whites. Thus, heterogeneity ought not to be confused with democracy any more than homogeneity was confused with consciousness by Mandel.

Certain microscopic observations must be made if the subject of labor is to be discussed intelligently and if we are finally to reach some appreciation of the scientific rather than emotive aspects of the Marxist tradition. Because for so long we have been accustomed—in the social sciences at least—to speak of workers in terms of upper, middle, and lower sectors of the working class, we have forgotten that this designation is based on considerations of status rather than considerations of class. Also, since most of our statistics are in the form of occupations, the data we have on the labor force in the United States is limited to considerations of income and work performance, with little data on intraclass factors.

There is a range of factors with which present types of federally gathered statistics are unable to cope satisfactorily. Among the most prominent of these is the distinction between skilled workers and unskilled workers. Only a hairline separates managers from technicians, but a veritable millennium separates both from day laborers and more traditional types of factory labor. In a sense, we now have a portion of the labor movement that is not so much bourgeoisified as it is professionalized, with very high notions of craft and skills. I daresay there is at least as much pride in specialized knowledge among locksmiths as there is among lawyers, and this development, along with its attendant conferences, seminars, schools, congresses, and so forth, provides a new basis of security and safety for the working classes. Increasingly, working-class consciousness is not so much a matter of political activity as of professional skills.

It might be argued that this does not touch the problems of the assembly-line workers or manual laborers but, in point of fact, it touches them very directly since it is precisely this kind of labor that is increasingly automated and increasingly subject to obsolescence. In other words, that portion of the labor movement that conforms most closely to socialist imagery is losing its capacity for large-scale political clout.

It is also the case that among unskilled workers are found the sharpest group identifications in the United States. That is to say, the ranks of the unskilled laborers are filled with white ethnic Americans and black Americans who have only a vague and distant affiliation with trade-union ideology, so that working together simply reinforces ethnic and racial distinctions rather than builds any sense of common labor identity. In this respect, the American experience sharply diverges from the European, since in Europe one can count on a high degree of ethnic and national homogeneity, whereas in the United States these forms of identification become factors in minority self-consciousness.

The nature of work itself has changed. It is not that work is less important than it was in the past. This is a kind of holy myth held by technologists and hippies alike who somehow have the mistaken and misanthropic notion that we work less because we are more technological in orientation and skill. What has occurred is not a lessening of the work pattern—sometimes it is the work itself that has expanded rather than the nature of the work process that has changed, and work requirements have become extraordinarily complicated. This again is related to the rise of skilled workers and once more clearly separates the categories of labor from one another. There can be no common struggle unless there is a commonly felt need to struggle and this is precisely what we do not have in the United States. It is therefore absurd to expect a classical type of working class to emerge in American society. But, parenthetically, the rise of extreme right-wing groups is also unlikely, since professionalism is not so much anti-Left or anti-Right as it is antipolitical and anti-ideological.

What we are witnessing is a phenomenon quite common in American history: the decline of a social class. We have seen an agrarian class shrivel, in less than 70 years, from 60 percent to 6.5 percent of the American population. At the same time we need and grow more food than ever before. The same phenomenon is occurring in the ranks of the proletariat. The fact that workers are becoming proportionately fewer in numbers and at the same time more productive in their output produces the problems of a declining class and the fear and trembling attendant to such a decline. The muscular show of force on the part of the "hard-hats" is not so much the energized outburst of a revolutionary class as it is the fear-stricken response of a group dimly aware of the ebbing of its own importance, while it must witness the emergence of an educated sub-class that always seems victorious despite its supposed effeteness.

We now have the rise of a Hobbesian working class; that is to say, a class that calls for law and order and demands that the bourgeoisie behave itself: mind its manners, not to mention its morals. The political impact of this conservative response to American mobility and innovation has been vitiated by the rise of specialization and professionalization, by absorp-tion of the working classes into the ranks of mainstream America. Such parallel processes mitigate political sentiment among the working class and make them neither authoritarian nor democratic, neither fish nor fowl, but, like most Americans, interested in their own economic well-being and devoted to maximizing their own portion of the finite pie off which the whole system thrives.

A remarkable illustration of this turn from party politics and toward economics is contained in the recent interview of AFL-CIO president, George Meany. His assault on the leftist sectors in the Democratic Party, on the New Left directly and, no less, on the Wallace rightist movement, adds up to a disengagement from party identification. His belief that the Democratic Party is in "desperate shape," in a "shambles," echoes the be-lief of many elements in the white working class who see the political ap-paratus as such slipping out of their control and becoming the voice for other interest groups, particularly the black people. Meany's ideology is not classically conservative and hardly authoritarian, but rather status quo, pure and simple: "the more a person has of the world's goods, you know what I mean—for himself and his family—the more conservative he becomes in the sense that if he is moving along and he sees chances of moving further along, he doesn't want to upset the machinery. . . . I think he is going to fight for a greater share and that he is going to do it through the same instrumentalities that he used in the past" (Meany, 1970).

Raising the question, whither labor? is basically to ask if labor will rise again in a swell of more or less leftist militancy to give moral leadership to the "disadvantaged." It is clear that I do not believe a resurgence of the militant-moralistic unionism of the Left is likely in the foreseeable future. Indeed, given present tendencies, should a massive economic depression occur, the shape of labor organization is more likely to move it even further to the Right than to the Left—for a number of reasons.

American labor, at least after 1880, was not, in the main, of the Left in any classically socialist sense of the term. Its Left orientation has always been modest, if not peripheral, and thus has not suffered such a dramatic decline as is often made out. Since there is more continuity between past labor attitudes than is usually appreciated, it is not likely that leftist rejuvenation will be dramatic.

The acceptance of unionism has been too widespread and publicly legitimated by national legislation, especially since 1932, for the issue of union recognition to incite labor agitation. Earlier periods of militancy were chiefly the result of employer or government (though mainly the former) hostility to recognition of trade unions, to principles of collective bargaining representatives for the rest of the working class. Recognition, quite established now, cannot presently or in the near future stir labor unrest.

Organized labor is only a small minority of the U.S. population and considers itself dependent upon public sympathy, congressional benevolence, and, for various reasons too involved to go into here, the Democratic Party's good offices. It has, for this reason, always hesitated to press itself politically by building an independent labor party because such a party could not sustain a broad coalition of interests, and labor suspected that in the long run it would wind up isolated, alone, and a mere political sect. (There are many other reasons, of course, for resistance to an independent radical labor party but fear of isolation is a chief one.) This was not true in England and elsewhere, where the laboring class was a much larger portion of the population. The minority status of organized labor in the United States, combined with the fact that technological change did not multiply at a great enough rate the kind of jobs that could have vastly enlarged a labor constituency, makes it unlikely that labor would initiate "third" or radical party building. So, in addition to the fact that labor is not likely to revive moralistic union building in the name of industrial democracy, it is also not likely to build any labor or radical independent party in the name of political democracy (at least not unless all kinds of industrial jobs are "deprofessionalized" and become subject to union domain, thereby enlarging the organized labor force).

The organized worker is no longer likely to be a European immigrant struggling for citizenship as well as union status. He is "Americanized" and better integrated into U.S. society. He has fewer moments of indignation: he is far less frequently exlcuded or mistreated. Moreover, there are more legal channels through which he can act (such as labor relation boards), and, because he is no foreigner but a "native American," he is more aware of them and feels entitled to resort to them. His children are not learning about his trade. Instead, they are escaping, at his own insistence, to colleges and elsewhere, and the family no longer engenders militant union values.

Widespread publicity has been given to corrupt union practices, and so few intellectuals or youth look to unions as models of popular democracy. The worker has lost many of his ardent admirers and apologists and is in no position to entertain himself with illusions about the breadth and quality of the public support he could rely on if he were to get up, stretch his radical muscles, and carry on a bit. A favorable "climate of opinion" would have to be created to encourage him to think boldly, and no such radical trends are in the offing.

Like other people, workers suffer disadvantages and, at some point in time and in response to certain stimuli, they devise strategies for overcoming them. Once they have overcome the major part of their distress, they deal with their other grievances and problems by reliance on incremental adjustment; they organize to protect gains won and settle into the society to behave like other interest groups.

It would be a mistake to build an argument with this as its sum and substance no matter how elaborately stated. The implication is that once material gains are achieved, discontent generally simmers down. In fact, in the past, when workers' demands were met or limited objectives realized, they were often emboldened to define and press for new benefits. Therefore, precisely because workers' goals (union recognition, control of job dispensing, wage and material benefits, shorter hours, improved health and safety conditions on the job) were finally formulated in legislation, one could reasonably have expected that this success would have created the very preconditions today for demanding more, socially as well as economically.

The question then remains why workers have not carried the struggle further.

There are several reasons in addition to those mentioned at the outset. A demand for reconstitution of economic and political relationships to allow disadvantaged groups a high degree of control in public decision-making is not a claim or demand that timid men can make. Where could workers derive such a conception today? Socialists are sometimes interesting critics but unconvincing analysts of American society, or fail to be so because they are too preoccupied with concerns not closely related to industrial affairs. Moreover, creating a sense of being entitled to full "industrial citizenship," or even outright industrial control, is dependent on higher levels of education and technological ability, promoting a sense of competence among men who feel capable of wielding greater power and will not tolerate being deprived of it.

But worker technological and educational growth has not kept pace with industrial change and growth. Workers do not feel able to govern. In previous periods, their skills inspired them to demand recognition and bargaining power. Workers were especially emboldened by the fact that employee and employer expertise often approximated each other in business and technological matters. The working man, especially the craft worker (who frequently had supervisory or shop-owning experience in the late nineteenth century) had an idea of exactly what duties were involved in the greater role he sought. Nevertheless, he did not demand industrial control because even then industrial complexity was beginning to surpass his knowledge.

From Interest Group to Professional Caste

If late nineteenth-century industry was beginning to elude worker expertise, how much truer this is today. Today the working man would need massive doses of scientific, technological, and investment policy-training in order to think in grand terms, as a competitor for industrial control. Moreover, the working man is often too ill-equipped, without training in the rudiments of law and economics, to rise in union ranks; he is not likely to replace present union leadership with a more militant voice. In fact, as Chinoy demonstrates, the worker's comparatively diminished "expertise" destroys his interest in industrial affairs and causes him to dream of escaping from industrial discipline to a little farm or small business of his own, living as a consumer rather than as a producer. He fears groups like blacks or students who show signs of gaining sufficient political importance to outstrip his influence in society altogether. Pushed aside, peripheral, he is more likely to follow the blandishments of the Wallaces than those of the radicals. Burnham has pointed out that when men belong to class or ideological parties, they are much more "immunized" from political challenges than when they do not. In the United States, neither Democrats nor Republicans are receptive to populist class ideologies; they are thus less inhibited from moving to the Right. The American worker, not immunized by membership in a socialist or labor party, is more likely to drift to the Right when society makes him particularly uncomfortable or diminishes his importance. The union leadership, preying on workers' fears of loss of welfare benefits, is all that has stood between cementing an alliance of the workers and Wallace's movement.

A Left labor movement can emerge again (if, indeed, it can be said that it ever existed in the United States) among new workers in the labor movement—recent students, white-collar personnel, and blacks; that is, among sectors of the population already unionized. Higher educational attainments enable these new groups to compete for industrial control, while the blacks have motivations not unlike those of the old immigrants (granting all kinds of differences), that encourage mass participation. But these groups are not flocking to industry.

Without fresh recruits the labor movement loses its "movement" character and settles for interest-group status—incremental adjustment of economic demands and grievances—and rests uneasily in a politically polarizing environment, trying to make such economic gains as it can protect in lieu of an increase in participatory or decision-making rights. While blacks are now becoming a crucial factor in some industries, such as auto and rubber, they remain marginal to the general network of power in labor organizations.

It might be argued that it does not really matter if today's worker and the present labor movement are not likely to surge to the Left. What if the labor movement should "rise" and go so far as to dominate every industrial enterprise in sight? Is it not technology and not "interests" that determines decisions? Not entirely! Does construction of low-, middle- or high-income housing arise from technological necessity? Does it make a difference that military rather than civilian resources developed atomic energy and an "atomic technology"? It is true that state-owned enterprises allocate funds for cultivating certain technologies and not others, recognizing, of course, that domestic national arrangements are not the only framework within which technologies are developed. This does not mean that technology does not make demands on men for rationalization of production, accounting, and distribution methods. It does. It also does not mean that men are free to push technological evolution in any direction they please. They are not. But it does mean that technology and governance are related affairs. Technology is a bundle of possibilities at any given time. The direction any one of its parts takes in the course of time is, as much as it is anything else, a reflection of value choices, social needs, and policy arrangements. To rearrange industrial governance by changing the industrial governors, a change in priorities within a nation must be made, and this will find its technological reflection in the United States as a whole.

This does not negate the fact that, to a degree, labor must adjust to the character of technology. However, if men can consciously make something as elusive as "history," they can also consciously direct something as concrete as technology, although not strictly according to their own will. In a word, technology is not bound by "iron laws." If workers can press for industrial control and achieve it, technological development can be altered in important ways to make a difference.

The constant search for labor's Archimedean lever usually takes the form of coalition demands: Will it be a coalition of black people, students, and intellectuals that will pave the way for the future of labor? Blacks are clearly into a pattern of upward mobility leading to professional roles rather than union activities. The students represent a radical wing of their own and perhaps form a class unto themselves. While they may emulate and even absorb many trade-union features in the years to come, the fact that students perform head work rather than hand work and perform such activities in relatively nonprivate enterprise makes the possibility of unity between the working class and the student class remote.

Although labor intellectuals still exist in the ranks of the working class (indeed, they have begun new efforts at developing labor colleges and research projects geared to the historical, sociological efforts of labor), they have really lost out in any meaningful sense. After the fiasco of the 1948 C.I.O. Political Action Committee and with the further fragmentation of all pre-World War II coalitions, any chance of a Left-led intellectual faction within labor or between the labor movement and the intellectuals has just about vanished. This is not to say that intellectuals and the labor movement are polarized as such, only that any overt Left ideology finds scant support in the ranks of labor officialdom.

This is not to say that coalitions cannot occur or will not take place among all these groups. It is to say that the very subject of coalition illustrates the dilemma of the working class. It seems uniquely incapable any longer of functioning as a class in itself, much less for itself; thus the politics of interest-group behavior take over. It is important to take into account the fact that interest groups do not require massive size and massive mobilization. Labor does not require coalition of any kind because it does not, in fact, have ultimate demands to make upon society but rather ameliorative demands, which are being met.

The failure of labor politics in the United States largely flows from the new forms of work that increasingly revolve around the peculiar cross-fertilization of labor and management or, at the very least, of technical labor and professional occupations. As we move beyond the present era, we may well experience a renewed and vigorous critique of the bourgeoisie as a class of owners who work neither in management nor in production but simply absorb profits. A portion of the managerial class may join the ranks of organized labor in a renewed assault on the economic and moral opprobrium of ownership without operational control and without consent, thereby diminishing external dominion (cf. Oppenheimer, 1970:27–32).

If, in fact, managerial sectors move into labor and provoke corporate reaction, a left-wing thrust is more than possible. On the other hand, if labor cannot generate sufficient autonomy to provide dynamic leadership and must join the managerial ranks to gain any of its ends, it is likely that the thrust of labor will be toward some kind of industrial quasi-fascism in which technology and managerialism rule.

Such realignments and polarizations seem somewhat distant. Yet, they continue to present real, if limited, options available to the working class. And if we are able to begin to think in these terms, we will be in a postion to discard what is obviously dead in the socialist rhetoric about labor and perhaps to preserve its kernel of empirical and moral truth: men who work also deserve to be men who rule.

1971

8

American Futurology
and the
Pursuit of the Millennium

One of the pleasant fictions of orthodox sociologists is that science is modern, in contrast to journalism, which is backward. I suspect, however, that in this respect sociology, like all other persuasions touching upon the life and death of human beings, falls prey to its worst examples and conventions. The cult of futurism, not only in its sophisticated sociological expressions but also in its pedestrian ideological forms, exhibits many of these tendencies. We have Norman Vincent Peale desperately urging us into the future by demanding an end to social problems in the name of personal resolution (cf. Thomas, 1974: 30-31).

> As a nation we have a future, a real future. And one reason I believe this is that increasingly from people everywhere we are hearing a fresh, new, vital question. It is not that old helpless query, "Why doesn't somebody do something about things?" That is passe, a bygone question. Instead, lots of people nowadays are resolutely asking, "What can I do?"

Then we have Lowell Thomas revising the Panglossian Doctrine by locating the best of all worlds in the United States.

> After roaming the world for more than six decades, I am more convinced than ever that ours is the grandest country on earth, and so far as I know this is the best of all worlds. Why they are even getting ready to reopen the gold mines high in the Colorado Rockies. . . . Let's get ready for the best year we have ever had (Thomas, 1974:30-33).

113

With such universal pomp and circumstance, it is little wonder that the sociological response to demands for a better future has been quick in coming.

The Dangers of Oracular Sociology

A curious role sociologists play in contemporary America is that of oracle. It is understandable, if not entirely laudable, that in a secular society a group of professionals should perform ministerial functions. Sociologists have assumed this role not only because of the decline of faith in organized religion but also because a need continues to be felt for some kind of generalized wisdom about salvation as collective, terrestrial, imminent, total, and miraculous (Cohn, 1970:14–19). By default, or because of the modesty of others, sociologists become new theologians in a universe in which God has presumably been killed—sometimes by social scientists themselves.

The recently published papers of Daniel Bell (1973), Leo Cherne (1972), George Harris (1973), and the decennial thoughts of Daniel Patrick Moynihan (1973) are impressive in that they suggest the persistence of an oracular tradition, even among empirical social scientists. What might have formerly been an uncomfortable role becomes all of a sudden quite gratifying. Social scientists appear untroubled by the clerical role despite the fact that few claim theological license (though the American sociological ancestry is very much wrapped up with theology). They respond to a felt need for realistic yet comforting answers during a period in history in which theological tradition does not offer the kinds of answers that are presumably required by a highly industrialized and modernized society.

Unlike the theologian, futurologists tend to exaggerate differences with the past; they have an apparently insatiable need to distinguish our times from all others. We live only in the present moment in time and only in that moment in space. Therefore, it is little wonder that the futurologists want to see the present moment in special terms, even if those terms are cast in the dismal language of crisis and convulsion. Perhaps theologians, who deal in larger time spans, have greater wisdom than social scientists, for they suggest a continuity of present needs with past performances. An essay by Barbara W. Tuchman (1973:39–46) makes this same point most succinctly. She describes a "typical" century, the fourteenth century, and implies that the twentieth century might be very much like that century. After all, idiot kings and corrupt dynasties have much in common with corrupt executives and idiot advisors. The fourteenth century, she observes, was violent, bewildered, disintegrating, and calamitous; in brief, exciting but not especially distinguished.

Some sociologists share with futurologists that extraordinary enthusiasm for the present, an assumption that the period they are living through is somehow more fragile than any other, filled with tragedies not before felt, and accomplishments not before realized. One way we do this is by spurious arguments, by centennial analogies, by comparing ourselves with great epochs like the thirteenth-century City of God and the eighteenth-century City of Man. Tuchman well understands that our age may be a much more ordinary and prosaic period than we admit to ourselves. Indeed, our centennial accomplishments to date are more in the nature of destruction than construction. The fourteenth century had its Black Plagues, in which nature violated man; but what prior century could boast of three holocausts costing millions of lives: Nazi concentration camps, the atomic bombing of Japan by the United States, and the Gulag Archipelago in the Soviet Union? The plagues of our age are visited by people upon other people. Certainly, such criminal immolation has no comparison in any previous century. This was my purpose in comparing the fourteenth and twentieth centuries: an attempt not to avoid "real" history but to reach real understanding.

This sense of the ordinariness of the past might well be consoling and instructive, especially in the face of our own civil disarray. Reflections on ourselves from the perspective of 600 years might provide a more revealing, albeit more modest, image than the clutter of immediacies does. For that matter, simple comparison with a great era like that of ancient Athens or thirteenth-century Paris is gratuitous. Certain ways of behavior, certain reactions against fate, throw mutual light upon other epochs. Tuchman shrewdly notes that the fourteenth century was nondescript in terms of actual world historic achievement. Yet to the people who lived in the fourteenth century, like those of our twentieth century, it was a moment of truth. It is intriguing that, when we compare two epochs (any two epochs), we rarely treat an "ordinary" century like the fourteenth century in comparative terms because of our temporal self-centeredness. If one is Roman Catholic, the choice is usually the thirteenth-century City of God; if one is a secularist, the choice is usually the eighteenth-century City of Man. Ordinarily, we are not interested in dull centuries. We do not want to believe that our particular century is dull, that we are living through 100 years of relative uncreativity. Yet the possibility may well be that our century is not quite as exciting and not quite as precisely delineated an era as we should like to believe.

We are now going through a period that is somewhat different from former great epochs, but more like the "dull" fourteenth century: an antihistorical, superstitious era. In the past, the passion for truth was historical; the feeling throughout the nineteenth century, in the tradition of Michelet, Hegel, and Marx, was that to know history was somehow to know truth. In the twentieth century, with the decline of historiography and with the decline of faith in the veracity and accuracy of historical judgment, we have turned our passions upside down. We are now much more consumed by a presumed knowledge of the future. Futurology is as important in Eastern Europe as in the United States and Western Europe. Intellectuals now demand, not so much *past* confirmation of the present, but *future* confirmation of the present.

One cannot push the analogy with past centuries too far. There are specific characteristics of the twentieth century that distinguish it—unfortunately not so much in its creativity as in its crematoria. Ours is the century of total destruction. Hiroshima, Nagasaki, Auschwitz, and Belsen all have as their common denominator the capacity for technological totalitarianism; specifically, the genocidal destruction of select, sample populations. The existence of a psychological threshold, not a military or technological threshold, with respect to the use of atomic weapons and gas chambers, illustrates the enormous differences between the potential for total annihilation in our century and that of any previous epoch, much less the fourteenth century. The Black Plagues may have taken an equivalent number of lives, but they did so through providential anger and not political willfulness. And that makes a considerable difference.

The tentativeness of present-day social life has led to a veritable celebration of what past centuries thought of as negative personality traits: alienation, privatization, anomie, and so on. Beyond that, the huge concentration of destructive power in the hands of the very few has properly infused a feeling of powerlessness as well as aimlessness in the very many. Thus the very scientific discoveries that should have encouraged feelings of greatness and even grandeur have to the contrary encouraged the deepest feelings of collective and individual doubt about science, technology, and knowledge as such. In other words, every paradigm that defines the modern order of things now conjures up the deepest feelings of pessimism and returns us to the millennnarianism and salvationism that are likely to adopt the rhetoric and mannerisms of this supreme age of analysis and science.

Both sociology and futurology are a consequence of the same problem: namely, our own discomfort and disquiet with the present moment. What we really want to know about is ourselves; and what we want to elucidate under any criteria is how to live in this 24-hour period, followed by the next 24-hour period. From this point of view, futurology, or the "science" of looking into the future, is in fact based upon the same psychic feelings and needs as those of intellectuals who insist upon looking into the past to cope with the present.

Plunging into Oracular Sociology: Decennial Tendencies

Despite these lengthy prolegomena on the risks and dangers of oracular sociology, I shall tread the same murky waters. Knowledge of past errors scarcely prevents us from making similar mistakes in the present. My immodest goal is to characterize the 1970s in contrast to the 1960s; and hopefully, at the same time, to elucidate the enduring features of this century in contrast to past, and in all likelihood, more humane centuries.

An American paradox is that today's outrage may well turn into tomorrow's commonplace, while nearly every commonplace statement can with equal impunity become intensely suspect. This is a nation built upon polarities: brutality and sentimentality, nobility and infamy, philanthropy and high thievery. But these are not the sort of dialectical interactions that lead to regeneration and transformation; rather they are unyielding bifurcations that characterize American society. The forms of such polarizations constantly change, yet reconciliation remains as distant as ever. Perhaps this is why after 200 years Americans are still in nervous search for that elusive higher ground and remain as fascinated with their own past and future as any new nation in Africa or Asia, while being no more confident of the future than these new nations.

The first major transformation that distinguishes the 1970s from the 1960s is what might be called the decline of racial politics and the sublimation, although less pronouncedly because of its later start, of sexual politics. Despite the endless stream of outpourings, ravings, and mouthings about problems connected with race and sex in America, the fact of the matter is that the steam has gone out of many ascriptive sentiments. One need only note that the only potent organizational forces in American black life date from the 1950s and earlier: the NAACP, the Urban League, and the black churches. With the marginal exception of the Black Muslims, or Nation of Islam, practically every organizational form of the sixties has either been dissolved or has receded into obscure oblivion. The struggles that now take place are largely between the black bourgeoisie and the black proletariat, between blacks in the suburbs and blacks who remain behind in the hard-core poor areas of the city. These are as intense as and even more intimate than relations between blacks and whites. Issues dividing the races remain real enough, but the very selective and partial nature of their resolution has only highlighted intraracial strife between those who are "making it" and those who are not.

This same sort of fragmentation, though taking profoundly different shape, is now evident in the movements of sex and generation against being confined and defined by an ascribed status. Since the women's movement was largely amorphous to begin with, it has not suffered from a loss of what it never possessed: a coherent organizational form. Still, one senses a genuine polarization between demands of women for economic equality and those for sexual freedom. These demands need not be polarized. But given the different constituencies involved at each end of the ideological stick, economic and sexual needs tend to become disintegrated. It would seem that the higher the economic status of women, the greater is the demand for cultural forms to follow suit. Such demands, very often against the constraints of parenthood and household chores, share much in common with the general middle-class drives toward psychologism, privatization, and intensely personalistic explanations of worldly events.

There is a decline particularly in the confrontational aspects of politics and a pendulum swing back to what might best be termed achievement politics—i.e., "getting ahead in the system." "Getting ahead" politics can mean anything from policy-making in a corporate context, to rising within a trade-union hierarchy, to participating in working-class politics. The return of an achievement orientation in the economic and political life of America is a central reality of the 1970s, and this factor is highlighted by the renewed vigor of industrial unionism.

A great deal of American history makes sense in terms of this dichotomy between achievement and ascription. It explains the forms of mobility, not just the facts of mobility. Sociologists are much too cavalier about the words "class, sex, and race," not realizing the difference between possibilities of income mobility and the relative immobility of items such as race, religion, and sex. Certainly the deepest fear of the black community is that even with class mobility, and even with the possibility of socialism, they might still be confronted by profound racial bias in American society. Indeed, if the patterns of the socialist world are to be remotely taken seriously, one would have to say that such nationalist fears are considerably supported by the evidence. Socialists, like sociologists, have much to explain for their inability to take account of huge gaps between class mobility and relative racial immobility within advanced industrial nations.

The emergence of black consciousness was greatly enhanced by antiestablishment black organizations that emerged from the civil rights movements of the 1960s. Even as catalysts, such organizations as the Congress of Racial Equality and the National Welfare Rights Organization served an immense purpose in the sustained drive for increased black participation, representation, and equity. But it was an equity within the system rather than against the system. Likewise, the organizational expression for women's rights, from the National Organization of Women to the various splinter groups urging everything from lesbianism to abstinence, also served to redress major grievances within American society. And as long as high production and profitability were maintained, such demands by women could be met. The generational or student movement was simpler yet to accommodate, since for the most part its basic demands were for greater educational participation rather than any increased portion of the American pie.

The specific organizational forms that emerged in the 1960s quickly fulfilled their norms and ceased to exist. In place of these organizations, more broad-gauged and even conservative forms emerged that better suited the scope and magnitude of racial, sexual, and generational needs. It is a melancholic truth that radical expressions of protest, when anchored to real needs, find these same demands articulated—often in a diluted form, to be sure—by mainline social and political agencies. As a result, radicalism finds itself "subverted" as often by its successes as by its failures. This certainly seems to be the case for the 1960s, during which forms of repression, while real enough, were not nearly at the force level commensurate with the destruction of these new organizations. Such destruction came about as a result of the "inner contradictions" of a Left with a series of programs, but without the support of a mass base to carry them out. The price of ideological purity came high: insulation from working-class economic realities and isolation from mainline political reforms.

A new aspect is one I would refer to as the Hobbesian condition of working-class sentiments in contrast to their often presumed Marxian condition. The working class, especially its "vanguard" trade-union quartile, has become the bulwark of the established order, rather than its enemy. The tensions that have emerged in the 1970s are much more heavily weighted on the side of class politics, rather than race, generational, or sexual politics. Perhaps it is a tribute to the wisdom of traditionalists in the trade-union movement that they saw this coming more clearly than did most spokesmen for the New Left, who deprecated class economics in the name of a raucous, often non-existent mass politics.

The resurrection of trade-union movements came about in a politically conservative climate, in contrast to the racial, sexual, and generational politics of the last decade that took place (ostensibly at least) in a more radical antiwar environment. This is a crucial difference between the 1970s and the 1960s, because this *geist* helps to shape the character of class struggle and of something even more basic: how the social system and the political order are to be run, how they are to be altered, and by whom. The question of class has once again become a central consideration, whereas the question of ascription or caste has been reshelved. The consequences of this change are not easy to ascertain. But as long as there is serious, growing doubt in the public's mind that the American economic system may not be able to deliver high levels of goods and services to its citizenry, the pendulum will remain firmly on the side of achievement considerations. It is only when goods turn into goodies that the clamor for greater equity among contending ascriptive groups becomes central.

One serious consequence of this return to achievement and move away from ascriptive considerations in both politics and economics is polarization between the haves and the have-nots. This gap has markedly increased even in the few years that have elapsed in this decade. Have and have-not are defined not simply in terms of racial, generational, or sexual criteria, but in terms of clearly economic criteria. Class polarization results from inflationary economics; it is a consequence of less housing, less money for mortgages, fewer available morgages for existing housing, shortages and price increases in food, gasoline, and other goods. Those who continue to have a substantial stake in the system have the wherewithal to maintain a very high life style.

What seems to be happening in the 1970s, in contrast to the earlier decades of the twentieth century, is a distinct class polarization, as a result of an economic situation that is much different from the Depression years, but one that has nonetheless the same consequences: a widening gap between wealthy and poor, between opulence and impoverishment. There is a selective process of haves and have-nots, as there always has been. But curiously, there is also polarization even within black life: a slender majority of the black community can now be classified (and from their point of view must be classified) as middle class rather than lower class or working class. This is an enormous shift, not only in black life, but in the character, in the tenor, of the 1970s. It is no longer quite so easy for everyone to fit the category "middle American" (cf. Wattenberg and Scammon, 1973:35–44).

Along with this polarizing element is the depolitization of the young. Economic polarization, the resurgence of an achievement orientation, and the plain fear of working-class conservative power have reduced generational consciousness. Beyond that, the collapse of generational power is a response to something that is inevitable in almost every generation, but is extremely painful when it occurs: *la trahison des clercs,* the treason of intellectuals.

The leadership of the political generation of the young in the 1960s has become either quiescent or self-liquidating. Rennie Davis formerly urged the young to participate in civil disobedience; now he wants his dwindling constituency to crawl, if necessary, to serve the One Perfect Master. Others, like Abbie Hoffman, have "turned straight" (at least in appearance) and have been indicted for being heavily involved in illegal drug trafficking. Others have claimed leadership in nonexistent communist and radical organizations before fading into oblivion; still others have returned to the true and perfect church; and finally, some have become jet-set radicals. Such tendencies within the leadership of the youth generation of the 1960s have generated a disorientation that contributed enormously to quiesence.

In past generations, conservative, liberal, and radical organizational life shared a democratic code turned into fact: leadership emanated from the rank and file. In any organization, leadership was a function, in part of quality, of chance, of virtue, of opportunity, and of being in the right place. One way or another, leadership depended on membership. But the radical movement that emerged in the sixties had no membership. The movement existed only as an abstraction. The leadership, if you could call it that, was appointed by the United States government. When they indicted the Chicago Eight, they endowed, or perhaps bestowed, leadership status on people who were not leaders in any sense of the word—except, perhaps, in the McLuhan sense of being media celebrities, i.e., leaders in terms of knowing how to get television and press coverage.

What emerged in the 1960s, in retrospect, was a "leadership" fabricated by the United States government through a series of political trials. As a result of this singling-out process, ordinary people became self-appointed and self-anointed leaders. The strange leadership of the young, not being subject to normal organizational constraints, behaved without a sense of organization and discipline except that imposed by courtroom regimen and trial procedures. Their rampant individualism was an important factor in the rapid demise of generational politics. McLuhanism rather than Marxism prevailed. Cultural heroes emerged who were infrequently, if ever, tied to organizational requisites. Hence a high level of idiosyncratic behavior prevailed in dwindling left-wing politics (cf. Flacks, 1974:56–71).

In the larger perspectives of the present decade, we witness a progressive shift in the relationship between work and leisure. This has become a paramount issue in the 1970s. It is not simply that the work ethic is declining, but that people work at a leisure ethic. Concern is not so much focused on a 4-day, 32-hour week as it is on the maximization of leisure life or private life. In the 1970s we are not simply polarized in an *objective* sense, along class lines or have and have-not lines, but in a *subjective* sense, in our private lives. The private life is intensely isolated from the public life, and everyone works to maximize the amount of private space over and against public or civic obligation.

This is an inexorable and powerful tendency. It can be termed anomie, privatization, alienation—whatever fashionable language one wants to use. In its simplest atomic sense, the amount of time given to the production of social goods is constantly diminishing in relation to the amount of time given to the consumption of private enjoyment. Whether it takes the form of drug use, sex, or travel, the gap between the public work life and the private play life has become extremely intense in American life. It is an extraordinarily explosive aspect of the contemporary scene, since the ability of the society to produce continuing surpluses of goods at profitable margins is at stake. Moreover, the compartmentalization of work and leisure stimulates a Veblenesque world in which wealth and opulence are defined precisely in terms of the personal consumption and private time that you buy away from the public time or the public world. In this way, the subjective component in American life now holds together in mortarlike fashion our various polarizations and life styles: the desire to maximize leisure and minimize work cuts across racial, sexual, and generational boundaries. It is a common denominator of the American style and the American scene, working all the way from the top of the economic ladder down to the bottom. When it does not work, then one knows real poverty as subjective impoverishment. The definition of impoverishment and poverty in American life now is much more the amount of work one has to do to survive than the amount of money one has in the bank.

In this connection, one notices a theoretical shift in the decade as well: a movement from economism to intense psychologism. Definitions of the world are made less in terms of objective indicators of the gross national product than in terms of encounter groups, psychotherapeutic sessions, hallucinogenic drugs, astrological escapism, mind expansionism, religious mystification, and satanic mystery cults. There is a turning away from the social person or the socializing aspects of life to the private aspects of life George Harris calls "the search for the soul." It would be a mistake to ignore this side of futurology, i.e., as a movement for psychic gratification.

One notices the unmistakable linkage between leisure, the private life, and the intense psychologism of that life. The public consequences of all this are the dissolution of the family as the essential unit, the breakup of marriages (though not the idea of marriage), and the breakup of community life. In general, psychologism as an ideology reflects the intense personalism in current living. The result is not so much the rugged individualism of past efforts at social mobility as it is a not-so-rugged isolationism from mainstream society. Even people who in previous generations rarely had much concern or much use for this kind of psychologism now find themselves entwined in this perspective whether they like it or not, through wives and children or through relatives of one kind or another who have chosen "alternative" life styles. The world of leisure and the polarization of opulence and impoverishment are also linked to the return of class, because only class permits the life of leisure, which in turn makes possible a psychologistic point of view. The poor always live in terms of economic "realities." But for the affluent, the satisfaction of material needs has led to a lessened interest in greater wealth and a concerted effort to convert affluence into immediate gratification.

This polarization between work and leisure, hand work and head work, is just as evident in the Soviet Union as it is in the United States. The gap between working for the state and having fun is even deeper, broader, and more alienating in the so-called socialist world than it is in the capitalist world. Perhaps the problem is industrialization per se, rather than production in relation to capitalism. In any event, an essential task of the twentieth century has been to overcome this dichotomy in an effort to make work a genuinely creative activity and leisure a real contribution to the work life of society. In this respect the size of a society may turn out to be as significant as its structure; and hence, I would argue that small societies or small nations have a better opportunity to solve big problems than enormous nation states whose priorities are most often transhuman, if not categorically antihuman (cf. Dahl and Tufte, 1973).

Some Further Extrapolations: Centennial Tendencies

American society (in the past) has been remarkably stable at both its economic and political levels. One cannot help but admire Alexis de Tocqueville's *Democracy in America,* not only for its historical perspicacity, but also because it still seems to be such a clear and adequate description of the social psychology of Americans nearly 150 years after it was written. Likewise, one can hardly read Karl Marx's writings on the *Civil War in the United States* without feeling a similar sense of the unresolved nature of this country: North versus South, industrial versus agrarian, internationalist versus isolationist, and a host of issues raised but not necessarily resolved by the American Civil War. I am not suggesting that American life is static— far from it. Rather, the fundamental thrust of this country, its guiding value scheme, has remained remarkably vibrant throughout its 200-year history. This fact has been the bane of reformers and revolutionaries; for the very ability of the nation to absorb and co-opt new industries and ideologies alike depends on this valuational underwriting of the system by the people as an entity. It may well be that things are now falling apart or that huge transformations are in the works. From my point of view again, rather than emphasizing how dramatic and apocalyptic the year 2001 will be in contrast to the year 1974, I find it much more feasible and sociologically interesting to take into account the dialectic of discontinuities and continuities within American social life that have made possible the expression and subsequent absorption by the society of radical options without those radicals expressing them emerging victorious.

If one were to extrapolate further, the entire twentieth century embodies a remarkable turning away from the nineteenth-century focus on controlling modes of production to a more subtle struggle to dominate the mass media. Daniel Bell properly refers to a new scarcity, not of goods, but of information and coordination of time. He points out that time becomes in the end an economic calculus. This calculus, however, is not entirely cultural or superstructural; in part, it is a political calculus. But Bell misses the point of his own observations: information is a consequence of control and domination and not simply orchestration and coordination. The United States could not have had the kind of political movements that emerged in the 1960s without television and the entire information media. Likewise, one could not envision the kind of national political scene that exists in the 1970s in relation to Watergate without the existence of well-established apparatus to allow for the instantaneous dissemination of news. In fact, the Watergate television hearings have been referred to as "Sesame Street for adults." With the exception of the devastating Army-

McCarthy hearings, this is the first time in which the citizenry actually participated in senatorial hearings. The opportunity to participate, even symbolically, in the communication of ideas becomes even more important than the productive capability of the society. The struggle to dominate the informational system becomes itself a major source of social struggle often involving a major cleavage within political life.

In previous epochs the political subsystems in America were sufficiently separated from society as a whole to operate undisturbed, no matter what the immediate condition of the larger society might have been at any particular moment. Thus, in the past, those things that most closely affected ordinary people—transportation, communication, energy, power, commodities, foodstuffs—operated despite momentary and even endemic political crises or national tragedies. Indeed, the autonomous characteristics of the economy in past time is attested to by what used to be the relative imperviousness of the gross national product to political pressures. At present, this seems far less true. In the past, radical demands for greater equity were made and could be met with relative tranquility as a result of the ever-expanding profitability of the economy. Thus the sixties were superior in economic terms to the fifties, and radical politics took place more as a response to affluence than to poverty.

In the seventies, at a time of intense political crisis at both the presidential and congressional levels, we are also experiencing a serious failure of the economic subsystem to maintain its past level of peak efficiency. Not only is a strong undertow of economic inflation wiping out personal savings and the idea of saving itself, but we are also experiencing a series of minor calamities that approximate wartime conditions: fuel shortages, an energy crisis, food shortages, paper shortages. Whether such shortages are real or induced, their consequences are real enough. If life in the United States is not quite crisis-ridden, it is at least much more tentative; and the assumption that the good things will be abundantly available has gone by the boards. The automatic American faith that every need will be fulfilled and that every expectation will be realized has been severely jolted in the 1970s. What might be called the ordinary activities that go on at the subsystemic level have become problematic. Since this is occurring precisely when the rest of the system is being shaken to its foundations, the character of the present moment can be referred to as a crisis period, however terribly overworked and overburdened that word and the suggestion of apocalyptic change it evokes may be. The 1970s, unlike the 1960s, have made plainer than ever before the necessity to choose or, more exactly, the necessity to articulate the underlying premises of the political system as a whole, if there is to be any sense of direction in resolving the keenly felt problems in the social and economic subsystems.

In an international context, a clear point of departure from the 1960s is the conviviality, if not necessarily convergence, of the United States and the Soviet Union. This political and economic situation is, worldwide, the most decisive aspect of the 1970s. Why it came about is much less a matter of presidential initiative than of fundamental strategy. On the one hand, multinational corporate structures must maintain every sort of hegemony; on the other hand, multinationalism needs an international realignment to avoid adventurism between the small powers and confrontations between the major powers at an international level. Big-power doctrines of peaceful coexistence have been reduced to a rundown of brutal, hard, ungenerous, and unyielding variables (cf. Weisband and Franck, 1971:36–44). A climatic belt is shared by the United States and the Soviet Union. The peoples of both nations are basically of the same racial stock. Both peoples have nominally Christian traditions. Both are major industrial powers, sharing a faith in commodity affluence. Finally, both peoples have a powerful armed force and have in the past been militarily victorious. Under the circumstances, the showdown politics of the Cold War have yielded to the accommodation politics of multi-nationalism. The realignment was almost inevitable on the basis of these combinations and permutations of socioeconomic factors. This rapprochement is disastrous to the pretensions of parity by the Third World. It presents an uninviting framework for the needs of backward nations, for whom the struggle between the United States and the Soviet Union has provided a basic wedge, a basic foot into the development-aid door during the Cold War period of 1948-71. Now that wedge has vanished and with it the edge that derived from the big-power confrontation and competition.

A shattering aspect of the twentieth century is the severe limits to any fundamental structural changes in a century that was declared to have "shaken the world." Take as an example the Hobson and Lenin theories of imperialism in relation to both the first and current decade of the century. One finds at the beginning of this century that the United States, Russia, Japan, Western Europe, and England, the big five of imperialism, dominated the world. Now, as we draw toward the close of the century, after two world wars, countless numbers of miniwars, endless social confrontations, international realignments, and permanent cold wars, whatever changes may have taken place in "systemic" terms, the list of major powers is the same: the United States, Russia, Japan, Western Europe, and England.

Every major imperialist power at the end of the twentieth century remains in the forefront of both industrial production and mass consumption. But this is less disturbing than the continuing peripheral character of the Third World to both production and consumption. Admittedly, socialist nations like China and capitalist nations like Canada, Brazil, and Australia in all likelihood will emerge as major powers of the twenty-first century. It would be foolhardy to ignore such a probability. However, progress can be very slow. Even 75 years and two-and-a-half world wars later, the shift of real power and industry has barely begun to take place. My point here is not only an economic one concerning the relative stability of the dominant powers over time, but also a social-psychological one: futurologists have often promulgated exaggerated notions that somehow things are changing much more rapidly than in fact they are. My point is that fundamental economic controls exercised by political elites have been enhanced rather than destroyed by technology and invention in the twentieth century. Labels have changed with breathtaking suddenness, but systems have changed much more slowly. To be sure, even where systems have changed, mechanisms of domination and repression have remained intact and, at times, even been enlarged and enhanced in the name of the revolution.

One has to ask finally whether war ever really settles the question of power. The presumption, whatever the political persuasion, has almost always been that warfare in fact determines and defines national and international realignments as well as determing the winners and losers in the larger rational sense. But Germany and Japan, who presumably were losers in the classical game of imperialism, are in the 1970s now emerging as the most powerful nations in the world. Such a situation is hard to understand and even harder to respond to emotionally and intellectually. It is difficult to define enemies and friends when they change on a decennial basis. China was a friendly nation during World War II, an enemy in the 1950s and 1960s, and (for now) a friend in the 1970s. Similarly, Japan was the "enemy" in the 1940s and a friend since the 1950s. Russia was a friend in the 1940s, an enemy in the 1950s, a not-so-good friend in the 1960s, and a close friend in the 1970s.

The psychological feeling of the present period is the breakdown of parochialism and the rise of cosmopolitanism; a rise in a generic "goodwill" approach for people, for nations; a kind of pluralism in attitude; a breakdown of the idea of the church triumphant or the nation triumphant. National and other chauvinisms are collapsing not because of any new enlightenment or because people have become instantaneously virtuous, but because the world has become smaller. The tactics and strategies of the moment have changed so profoundly that no one believes in the intrinsic superiority or inferiority of anybody; or if they retain such beliefs, they can no longer put them into use on a grand scale. The result is what one might call democratization through strategy and tactics.

Another phenomenon, and one that obviously is of great concern and consequence, is the militarization of political life in the Third World. There are, in fact, few nations with civilian leadership in any part of Asia, Africa, or Latin America. Even in the poorest parts of Europe, such as Spain, Portugal, and Greece, the military has allied itself with elitism and expertise. The military as a political force (in contrast to its function as a professional force) is typified by nondemocratic politics or politics by expertise rather than by mass persuasion. In the 1970s, the military pressure on civilian forms of political rule has become precipitous, even in the United States and Western Europe. Whether or not the kind of democratic politics that we have known and that we are presently dedicated to preserving can withstand the impact of bureaucratic expertise and administrative collectivism will become a major test for democratic rule in the coming years. The impact of elitism, the impact of decision-making behind the scenes, keeping not history but a mass public in ignorance, is a problem that can no longer be dismissed. We have already seen the cracks in the democratic mirror in the United States and certainly in Europe. Thus one would have to say that a deep-rooted phenomenon of the 1970s is not simply the militarization of political life, but perhaps the very style of governance, even in the industrial nations of the West. Whether or not the democratic style and the democratic system can be maintained in the face of the ongoing, onrushing drive toward industrialism and the kind of nationalism that requires a military organization (if nothing else than as a symbol of relative power) is a moot point. The collapse of civilian leadership in many parts of the undeveloped and less-developed portions of the world has now spread to the more developed nations—with consequences yet to be understood.

Most American intellectuals tend to evaluate American realities in terms of Marxist categories, i.e., to see events in terms of class and revolution. Yet in America, the Hobbesian war of all against all, and the demand on the part of all contending groups, is not for revolution but for law and order; meaning, very concretely, a demand on the part of the "masses" that their "elites" rule—the Hobbesian paradigm. The working class has mounted an attack on effetism and privatization; it displays an anger and animosity toward a world of leisure and opulence that it fails to share. In previous decades, in previous centuries, we conceptualized the social sources of change as emanating from below. Now the impulse for change comes from the top, from political and economic elites. Innovative programming comes from the professional intelligentsia. As a result, from an unrequited fear that the bourgeois emphasis on innovation is risky, poorer people demand order, structure, and survival of the system. This certainly is a factor in the current strategy and tactics of Republican Party politics, no less than that of the Wallace wing of Democratic Party politics. We are witnessing a topsy-turvy phenomenon that in general overrides classical European Marxist notions of class interest: the Middle Americans want the system to survive, while the Middle Classes are much less certain about the matter. This is true in terms of the uneducated vis-à-vis the educated; the rank and file vis-à-vis the avant-garde; ordinary parishioners in contrast to church reformers and radicals. At every level one finds a similar polarization of class values.

This view has little in common with the fashionable concept of working-class authoritarianism. The insistence on legitimacy and law is a far cry from a demand for restoration and reaction. Indeed, what we are increasingly confronted with is a three-tier system: a working class concerned with legitimacy; a middle class with intensely reforming instincts concerned with social change, and when it cannot achieve that, a change in rhetoric and ideology; and finally, a ruling class made irresolute by competing and nearly balanced claims of the lower classes and the middle classes. What appears to be a wavering, unsteady characteristic of the ruling class is indeed a quality of American and Western life in general. This sense of political and moral ambiguity is a result of attempts by the ruling class to lean simultaneously in two directions: toward the political needs of a mass constituency and toward the sociological needs of a class constituency. This tension between mass and class in American life reflects itself in a ruling elite not nearly as sure of its goals as it was earlier in the century, but not quite as puttylike and amorphous as those who deny the existence of a ruling class entirely would have it.

As long as this three-tiered class system exists as an unresolved triadic dilemma, one is in the grips of a Hobbesian world. The "conservative" poor and the "liberal" rich may be transitory aspects of the 1970s, rather than symptomatic of a long-range revision in social reality. Yet, to start from Hobbes is to end with political analysis. And perhaps the very preeminence of political sociology rather than political economy is the essential touchstone of our age and a key reason why so much inherited wisdom has failed us when we need it most, in 1974.

This is an age of political sociology rather than political economy.

Problems of policy-making, fiscal distribution, energy allocation, and the like are determined by the political system. To be sure, this political system must operate within the parameters and limitations of the economic system. But the economic classes have become limited partners in this process. The survival of capitalism depends on the strength of the American state. And it is hardly a casual afterthought to note that the survival of socialism depends largely on the strength of the Soviet state. The present century has been a world of structural reversals, no less than role reversals: of political bases and economic superstructures. This has been the shattering lesson of twentieth-century capitalism, socialism, and fascism alike. To forsake this century morally for a utopian future that might be better or for a grandiose past that surely was better is a reasonable enough posture. But to falsify essential, overriding facts of this century is a risky proposition. Overcoming the two sides of false consciousness—ideology and utopia—is, after all, what the social sciences are pledged to do with all their might.

1974

III

IDEOLOGICAL POLITICS

9

New Conservatism in America

Conservatism was perhaps the first political movement directly involved with politics as such; Bernard Crick's (1962) *In Defense of Politics* makes this quite clear. That is to say, one of the important aspects of modern classical conservatism (that of the eighteenth and nineteenth centuries) is that it grew out of the very soil of politics. It was the product of political policy-making and of men who were directly involved in the making and breaking of nations. Examination of the elite backgrounds of the conservative movement indicates how radically different it was from that of more plebeian liberal forces: Edmund Burke, one of the shining lights of the English Parliament; Prince Metternich, the kingpin figure of the Congress of Vienna in 1815 and one of the most significant personages of that period; and in this country, John Adams and Alexander Hamilton—the Federalists. Yet, the conservative movement grew out of practical politics. It did not spring to life as an ideological movement with a plan to change the world. It did not begin with a design for the future: it came into being as a result of an effort to maintain the status quo, to maintain the order intact. In effect, conservatism was concerned primarily with order because the men who were identified as conservatives were concerned with order, a consequence of their functional position in the eighteenth and nineteenth centuries.

But one would have to say that the twentieth-century conservatives, or nonconservatives, are in a sense the very opposite of their classical predecessors. In its classical form, conservatism was a response to political involvement, but twentieth-century conservatism is a response to alienation from that involvement. Russell Kirk or Peter Viereck (as is evident in the literature they produce) are very much outsiders looking in. Twentieth-century conservatives, as an organized body, are outside the power system. The conservative rhetoric has not penetrated the halls of power, and furthermore the conservative point of view is no longer a consequence of holding power. In its classical form, conservatism represents a position of dominance; in its modern form, it is in a subordinate, external, alienated position. An analysis of conservatism shows that while in terms of doctrine there may be lines of continuity between its classical and modern forms, functionally and politically there is incredible discontinuity. This is the result of many events that have taken place in Western Europe and the United States—principally, the rise of liberalism, socialism, and communism. From 1848 until the present, the political mood has been within that framework. The breakup of the old aristocratic order upon which the conservative view is based, coupled with the collapse of visions of empire and the end of monarchy as a viable system, all helped to destroy conservatism as a political force; but it has lingered on as a political ideology.

In the United States, from 1775 (the period of the Revolution) until the Clay-Calhoun era (about 1840), conservatism, whether it be English-imported Toryism or Whiggism, was in a remarkably powerful position. Conservative strength is reflected in the character of the United States Constitution, in the division of government into three separate and equal branches, in the nature of who voted, and in monetary requirements for voting. It is reflected in the division of the legislative branch into two houses, one based on unequal representation, in the strict constructionism of the Supreme Court, and in the strong Hamiltonian money and banking policies. In other words, one could say that up to and perhaps including the age of Jackson, conservatism was not alienated from mainstream politics and so was very much an authoritative force. It is not that it lacked opposition, but that the opposition in the main was not quite so strong as the conservative forces.

Not until the Jacksonian period did the kind of populism that led to the breakup of conservatism as a movement emerge. The Jackson administration was especially important in this breakup—even more important than the Civil War—because it spearheaded a strong populist tradition. Later, with avowedly conservative Presidents, even with conservative Democrats and Republicans, there was an unshakable commitment to liberalism, which meant a commitment to rapid progress and national growth. During this long period of time, the early status quo proclivities declined, even with the most conservative writers. They were revived much later in the literary work of people like Irving Babbitt and in the political work of senators like William Borah. At the end of the nineteenth century and in the twentieth century they reemerged as a claim against the liberal society, but this time it was a sentiment of criticism rather than establishment. The power of conservatism in its new form, in contrast to classical conservatism, took root first in the period of Reconstruction, when conservatives criticized the way that the revolutionary aspect of the Civil War was handled—the fact that the black, once freed, was really more enslaved by the wage system than he had ever been by the aristocracy—and, furthermore, criticized the industrial system. Conservatism became a savage opponent to modernization as such. Over the long span of time the old conservatism became separated from the new conservatism by its functional posture with respect to the new order of things: it started as a majority doctrine and ended up as a minority one.

Several factors were involved in this reversal. First, conservatism is an ambiguous doctrine. Comparison of Peter Viereck's (1949) *Conservatism Revisited* with Russell Kirk's (1953) *The Conservative Mind* shows them to be very different. Both books are representative of the conservative movement, but they are so different in style and posture as to raise the question of whether a definition of conservatism is possible. Furthermore, even if we could arrive at a satisfactory settlement of the conservative ethos—such as mistrust of rapid change, faith in the binding qualities of religion, a concern for reason over the passions, a belief in natural law rather than social contract—we could not be quite sure whether a conservative thrust is possible without a conservative class. Conservatism is a movement, an ideology, but it has no class to give it support. The middle classes—this is especially true in the United States— are liberal. The labor classes are liberal. There is no need for a class to hold to a conservative rhetoric because the conservative ideology serves no class function (although it may, of course, render intellectual services). What happens to the conservative mood is that it tends to become very badly divided, with one wing moving very close to a kind of neofascism and the other wing moving toward a vague kind of liberalism. To a degree, there may even be an accommodation with left-wing ideology. In either case, there is a movement away from the conservative position, and the conservative movement rends itself by moving Right or Left. This does not happen within the speculative realm, within the realm of marginal men, but with men who have tradition, who have English ancestry, who have Episcopalian connections. But their relationships to each other are vague rather than powerful, and vague linkages do not make for satisfactory politics. The difficulty with conservatism is that as a political force it is not supported by class forces within either American or European life. At the same time, as an ideology of intellectuals, it must suffer the same criticisms that it launches against its opponents—namely, that it is abstract, vague, irrelevant, and not tied to the real issues. In other words, the very premises that move people toward the conservative view also tend at the same time to break their connection with the conservative style: the justification for entering a conservative framework is somehow made self-defeating by the fact that conservatism cannot escape its own criticism of other ideologies. All ideologies face dilemmas in America, but none more so than conservatism because it singularly makes a claim to political relevance yet has no real claim or relevance. It must accept the framework set by a cosmopolitan liberalism, while steering clear of the ultranationalism of nativistic reaction.

Every ideology seems to carry within itself a mass concept and an elite concept. Marxism, which is supposedly a doctrine for the masses, harbors the deepest kind of elitist assumptions. This is also true of socialism, anarchism, and every other kind of doctrine. There is no doubt that the rise of a class of bureaucratic experts is a kind of conservative triumph. But one should not confuse elitism in general with conservatism as an ideology. Conservatism is eschewed by almost every man of power. The Democratic Party, for instance, has rested its case on the popular classes and on the popular will. Concern about the popular will and the democratic majority has been so overwhelming in recent times that the government has determined from the results of the most recent survey whether a war should be escalated. So in a functional sense the conservative philosophy of Edmund Burke hardly governs present-day men of power. There is no open recognition of conservative ideology of any faction representing conservatism, only people who say "Slower" or "Faster" instead of "No." Ultimately, conservatism is reduced in political terms to a cry against minority groups, social welfare, and government involvement; yet, in the extreme, it verges toward neoanarchy—an attack on the state as such. The frenetic attacks by certain conservatives upon the so-called communists in government in large part stem from their feeling that all state power or state authority is intrinsically communistic. Insofar as there is pervasive government control, they argue, the state has been moved much closer toward a "communist" solution.

Too often, when examining conservatism, one develops a rhetorical definition instead of a useful one. The fundamental definition of conservatism is the minimization of state authority and the maximization of individual opportunity and autonomy. Every bona fide conservative takes the standpoint "that government that governs least governs best." But very few labor leaders or businessmen—whom one would expect to be committed also to free enterprise—will rest their case on that position. Quite the contrary. The liberal position dominates in most business circles; those who are making the dollar know better than to act against their own interests. Every stratum of business above that of petty shop-keeping is concerned with positive, affirmative government intervention in the struggle for government contracts, for grants from state institutions, and so forth. What has happened is that conservatism has collapsed as a movement; at best it is a posture. If one examines political funding in recent presidential elections (1948-1968), one will find that the major business organizations supported the Democratic Party at least as often, and to the same extent, as the Republican Party. Even organizations such as the National Association of Manufacturers, which is relatively to the right of the various chambers of commerce, were unable to support the idea that government intervention should be entirely eliminated. The idea of government intervention and state and federal supports has become so thoroughly institutionalized that the ideological cornerstones of conservatism have become an academic matter. Criticism of the rise of state authority is no longer justified, because in a historic sense the conflict of interests from a practical point of view is now a struggle between liberalism and socialism. Our own vision of the situation is distorted. Every chamber of commerce is committed to progress, not to the status quo. The argument to plan or not to plan is the argument between liberals and socialists; it is not an argument between conservatives and liberals. Fragmented planning is exactly what liberalism is about.

The irony is that some aspects of conservative criticism have a great deal of merit. Although it is rarely taken seriously, there is much to be said for the argument that federal governments have an incredible amount of power, that instead of states withering away, as Marx suggested, they become more powerful. That absolute power tends to corrupt absolutely is a more realistic formula than that the states will wither away when the classes wither away; it is certainly better supported by evidence. It seems unlikely that conservatism will die away. It will live on as other kinds of doctrines, such as anarchism, continue to live on: it will persist as a critique of the social order. The social origins of the conservative critique are different, perhaps, but it functions to call to mind the fact that the present order of things is not idyllic. State power is indeed a form of creeping socialism; but only in the special sense that socialism readily acknowledges the planning and programming of economic systems.

Conservatism has staying power because it is the only nonradical or nonsocialist way of handling certain problems. In the social sciences it provides an ideologically meaningful framework and avoids the demons of socialism; it is an important device for galvanizing people into action in response to the macroproblems in the social sciences. Large numbers of political scientists, economists, and sociologists, if not enamored of the conservative frame of reference, at least give it serious thought because it does provide a perspective on serious problems without a commitment to revolutionary thought. Thus conservatism's main modern function has been as a preliminary to important social-science research; movements such as that led by Leo Strauss in political science have at their core a desire to attack the most significant problems of the age without embracing radical points of view. For certain types of men the problem becomes how to criticize society and how to evaluate social systems without seeming to become radical and without making commitments to utopias. One might say of present-day conservatism, at least as it applies to social science, that it is a counterutopian response to the need for large-scale research. This is a far cry from its beginnings in the halls of power, from Metternich's settlement of European affairs, but, in all truth, this may be the necessary end of any doctrine that no longer has a social base.

There are roughly two ways to avoid being typed as a liberal or a member of liberal society. One can identify with the socialist or communist vision of social utopia, which defines an optimal end point. The other way is conservatism. Conservatives are in the awkward position of being without a viable social utopia, since the corporative state and system crumbled long ago, after the Burke era. As a result conservatism has substituted a kind of therapeutic politics, in which the state is rejected. It is this war on politics, if you will, that gives strength to the political society. There remains a rather marked interest in conservatism among college students and among intellectuals in general. The ideology fulfills urgent psychological requirements, and, from that point of view, is extremely important.

The conservative anticommunist posture, for instance, has as its deeper source the mistrust of any external power imposed on the individual. Its thrust and bite is not anticommunism, but the fear of being taken in. It is based on the fear that manliness will be destroyed by the state, that the value of work will be replaced by the desire to be taken care of. This indicates not simply an "anti" sentiment, but a profound feeling of disgust and revulsion with the possibility that men will be controlled by impersonal bureaucratic institutions. That is why present-day conservatism always emerges as critique. Of course it is negative; it should be negative, because the positive affirmations all come in the form of destruction of the personality, in dehumanization. The sentiment that conservatism appeals to and gives deep significance to is a sentiment that offers an idealization of the person. The grounds are relatively irrational —tradition, faith, religion, symbol systems—and they ostensibly enable the individual to come to terms with himself as a person and to become a defined personality. Conservatism in the present period is a form of therapy; as such, it is extremely important and not to be taken lightly.

Economically and socially, American society is moving in the direction of statism rather than toward an atomistic pure liberal society. This movement can be partially seen in the growth of bureaucracy. In the field of business, many areas are dominated by three or four huge corporations that seek to preserve themselves rather than compete in the free market-place. Individuals find their position within the market not simply by economic choice but by all sorts of status criteria. As the business world comes to depend increasingly upon government, it loses its power of autonomous decision-making. And this makes conservatism increasingly anachronistic, despite the weaknesses of liberalism.

There are those who argue the thesis of the end of ideology within the West. If this is true, it is the first time in history that a social system has presented no more conflicts. Certainly it is the case that traditional divisions no longer obtain. For example, the socialist party is now very much like the liberal in rhetoric, just as classical conservatives have the same problem of distinguishing themselves from liberals. The character of the competition and conflict is very different. For example, the struggle for power may well involve relatively few men who control relatively few machines; it may take on an international character between have and have-not nations. In truth, liberalism as an ideology has triumphed. It is difficult to accept that fact, however, so we say that all ideologies have been abolished, as Lipset claims, or we decry the bureaucratization of life. Liberalism's triumph is that its age is the twentieth century, not the eighteenth century. Everybody is a liberal. Everybody believes in the free exchange of ideas. Everybody believes in restricted planning, but not national planning. Everybody believes that democracy is a good thing, but not at the expense of social order. Everybody believes that the rich should be taxed, but not to the point of eliminating profit incentives. The eccentric solution is the conservative or socialist option. Ideology has not dissolved, nor is there any firm evidence for the dissolution of Western society. Rather, we are profoundly committed to the liberal point of view and we are genuinely outraged by the nonfulfillment of the goal of complete material satisfaction for all citizens. The liberal belief is so profoundly rooted that the interesting question is how the triumph of liberalism took place so thoroughly and what its long-range prospects are.

Why is the liberal formulation vague and the conservative formulation not; and why has liberalism nonetheless become the basic political style in the Western world? There are several possible reasons:

The middle classes form their own historical vantage point; in some deep measure, they incorporate the liberal policies of the French Revolution, German Englightenment, English Revolution, and American Revolution. The middle sectors have always been involved with liberalism as the justification of their behavior and point of view. Therefore, it is natural that once they did come into power their rhetoric would survive and triumph.

Activities in the world of science throughout the eighteenth and nineteenth centuries also gave support to liberalism instead of conservatism. For example, Darwinism, the idea of evolution, the entire notion of change in types and structures and their effects, became a rallying cry for all believers in the ultimate equality of men through equal opportunity. Inevitably, in the nineteenth century, Darwinism came to mean progress. Darwinism had the added advantage of describing a struggle for survival rather like a stock-market exchange system. Scientific activities also had the effect of supporting the liberal framework.

The challenge of the nineteenth century was no longer an aristocratic challenge. The working classes were interested in unionization and independence from the middle class, so that the center of interest became the extent to which liberalism could permeate the working class and prevent revolution. The biggest threat (to the middle class) was socialism, not conservatism, and therefore they offered up as much as possible without giving up their sovereignty and so tried to minimize class friction without encouraging revolutionary violence.

There is no mystery about why liberalism emerged victorious. The only mystery is how liberalism in the twentieth century was able to reconcile the uses of any degree of state power with its faith in individual freedom of action. Here one comes upon some very interesting possibilities—namely, the breakup of the hegemony and strength of the bourgeoisie to determine, without intervention, the goals of all social classes. Isolationism, which deepened in the United States in the twentieth century as manifest destiny and Pax Americana, supplied ideological continuation for the conservative framework. In postwar politics conservative wings crystallized within both parties. The domination of this conservatism doomed the Republican Party to minority status, but it also tended to make the Democratic Party centrist and nonideological in character. Present-day conservatism again has a practical concern with politics. It also has problems that go along with these concerns.

The most difficult thing for opponents of conservatism to understand is that underlying the antipathy to communism is the strong feeling that it is equivalent to total regulation. Conservatism is nostalgic rather than utopian; the past rather than the future holds the key to conservative solutions. There are, however, values to conservatism's nostalgic rural-ism and, whether ideal or otherwise, they are genuine in application. It is easy to dismiss nostalgia and ruralism only if one fails to consider how deeply we all are involved with nostalgia—both as a frame of reference and as a belief that the dim past was better than the present. Conserva-tism may not answer certain kinds of needs but one must take seriously its claims upon men, and consider why, without an undergirding social class, conservatism prevails among a large portion of minority groups. The answers given to these questions are all too often oversimplified. Furthermore, they tend to be based on liberal rather than scientific assumptions and take for granted that conservatism is absurd. I argue that conservatism is a serious position that will continue to be represented as American society matures. Twentieth-century conservatism demands a mature industrialized society. An underdeveloped or developing society cannot afford the time, the leisure, or the effort required to work within conservative frameworks. Conservatism is both a consequence and cri-tique of industrialism.

The New Conservatism and the Critique of Politics

One of the leaders of the conservative revival in America has admitted that "conservatism is among the most unpopular words in the American vocabulary" (Viereck, 1949: x). It is also one of the most persistent currents of thought. This unpopularity and persistence are not unrelated: the history of modern conservatism in large measure is the history of conscientious defiance of every major advance shaped by popular demo-cracy. The renewed popularity of the conservative philosophy of civilization is therefore of more than casual interest.

In recent intellectual history, conservatism's most effective prophets have been Russell Kirk and Peter Viereck. In educational theory, the conservative school is represented in its many facets by Arthur Bestor, Bernard Bell, and Gordon Chalmers. There is also the ascendancy of antinaturalist philosophies such as those of Eliseo Vivas, John Wild, and Jacques Maritain. And there is the school of history, propagated by Allan Nevins, which is attempting to rewrite American history in terms of the business class. Perhaps the high-water mark was the publication of a multivolumed study of the Standard Oil Company. This task, undertaken by the Harvard School of Business Administration, made the a priori decision that the Rockefeller portrayed by past historians never really existed, that instead he was a blameless hero who transformed the oil industry from anarchy to scientific organization.

The number of intellectual areas traversed by the new conservatism is as widespread and ramified as American society itself. It is my aim to explore the historic roots and essential premises of an outlook that is making a strong bid to replace pragmatism as the philosophy of American business civilization. Rossiter (1955) makes the best attempt, to my knowledge, to summarize conservatism's current status.

Ultimately, modern conservatism faces the same theoretical opposition that older conservatism did. Burke attempted to defeat the menacing principles of the French Enlightenment and Revolution and the hopes it aroused in the masses of men: complete social and political equality, a recognition of the right of man to economic well-being and happiness, the supreme authority of men to judge their mode of life independent of theological edict, and belief in the possibilities of the endless and inevitable advancement of society. Since these remain goals to be fought for, the conflict between conservatism as a theological posture and as a political program retains its vitality. What has drastically changed are the forms Enlightenment precepts have been taking throughout the world, the urgency of the conflict, and the classes that embody these contrary traditions.

Edmund Burke

The spiritual fountainhead of conservatism, as most writers agree, is the English statesman Edmund Burke. He serves the new conservatism well, for his age, like our own, was one of enlightenment and revolution. In large measure, modern conservatism attempts to apply to the Russian Revolution the stigma attached to the French Revolution. There was the pietism that held that since society was but a fragment in the cosmological hierarchy, the basis of human relations must be theological. The foundation of material prosperity should be the recognition and veneration of private property. It was Burke's intention to prove that eliminating firm social distinctions would be tantamount to flouting Providence. He also taught a moral absolutism, an eternal order of values that could never be experimentally verified, but only revealed. This moral hierarchy was graded from the highest religious ideals to the lowest leveling sentiments. And last in theory but first in actuality was Burke's social elitism, a stress on the inherent worth of socioeconomic stratification and the attendant duties and rights of class to class and man to man. All three aspects, pietism, absolutism, and elitism were said to be valuable in the promotion of social harmony and stability. And for the contemporary conservative, as for Burke, "Harmony, not struggle, is the ruling political objective" (Hogg, 1947: 32). Because Burke defined the various principles of conservatism so diligently, his "ideas did more than establish islands in the sea of radical thought: they provided the defense of conservatism" (Kirk, 1953: 61).

Burke's approach set the classic pattern of conservatism as a reaction to the main direction of social life. In his own time, he reacted to the French Revolution as any man of economic substance did but with greater eloquence and vituperation. The tendency has been to overlook the fact that it was not the "excesses" of the Revolution that Burke countered; the Revolution was itself an excess because it settled matters with the *ancien régime* outside the framework of tradition and convention. Burke was adamant on this point. For in the partnership of social forces, "all men have equal rights, but not to equal things. He that has but five shillings in the partnership, has as good a right to it, as he that has five hundred pounds has to his larger proportion" (Burke, 1854-57b: 331–332). Once this precept of the right of the rich to be rich and the poor to remain poor is accepted, revolution becomes a political equivalent of theft. The Enlightenment announced the doctrine of popular sovereignty as the inherent right of man in civil society. This was the excess that Burke (1854-57b: 335) could not forgive: "Men have no right to what is not reasonable, and to what is not for their benefit." Ordinary men being unable for want of the "leisure to read, to reflect, to conserve," only those who do, "what I should call a natural aristocracy," can properly judge what is reasonable and beneficent for the whole of society (Burke, 1854-57a: 85). For Burke, economic paternalism was the answer to popular revolution.

The quality of the French Revolution that was perhaps more disturbing to the natural aristocracy than even the event itself was that its ideas spread. British Jacobinism as represented by such sturdy democrats as J. B. Priestley, Thomas Paine, and William Godwin offered a serious challenge to the "great compromise" of 1688. The ideas of liberty and universal fraternity opened up the possibility that the exploited could act as a social force for themselves and not just remain an amorphous mass. Burke grasped the meaning of these international ramifications of the Revolution. The cry of anarchism was sent up as a flare in the night. Only obedience, sacred and profane, could save official society from the excesses of the masses. Burke's admonitions to the empowered classes were heeded.

The nineteenth century dawned with reaction triumphant throughout Europe. But the enthroned sat restlessly. The idea of the French Revolution remained potent, its canons strengthened rather than refuted by Schiller and Hegel. Hegel (1929: Preface), though a faithful servant of the Prussian state, perceived that "the spirit of the age has broken with the world as it has hitherto existed." He had a "foretelling that there is something else approaching." The emperor of Austria, the king of Prussia, and the czar moved swiftly to counteract this "something else"; and Metternich supervised the formation of the "Holy Alliance."

The transmission of Burke's ideas to Metternich was direct. Some of Metternich's most trusted advisers introduced English conservatism to central Europe. Metternich's Concert of Europe was an attempt to effect a "great European compromise" by the application of conservative doctrine designed to cement relations between a functionless aristocracy and peripheral portions of the professional and middle classes. But he was very much aware that the grand conservative concern was doomed (Viereck, 1949: 108).

The Revolution of 1848 brought down the aristocratic house of cards. The top elements of the middle class took command of the political machinery. At the same time, workers were undergoing a period of rapid maturation. From the time that Metternich's conservative synthesis collapsed, it became clear that future social events would no longer rest on aristocratic claims of legitimacy and law. The old conservatism became painfully aware that it was fighting for a losing cause. Its main economic props were collapsing. Theology, too, found itself unable to compete with the social and scientific revolutions of the period. In the latter half of the century, there was little left for conservatism to do but follow Cardinal Newman's lead in abandoning the world of material relations entirely and content itself with a pseudosacred realm of values and feelings.

The conservative philosophy came to consider itself the guardian of traditional values against the encroachments of science and industrialism and the bourgeoisie that promoted them both. "Let Benthamism reign, if men have no aspirations," Newman (1878: 280) said acidly. Newman presented the bourgeoisie with an impossible choice: "We must make our choice between risking Science, and risking Religion." Profits dictated that the middle class risk religion. For this, conservative philosophers have never forgiven industrial society. For as they warned, science and secularism, the rejection of belief and faith, would one day become an instrument of the propertyless mass. W.E.H. Lecky pointed an accusing finger at the bourgeoisie who acquired "vast wealth by shameful means."

It was they, the businessmen living by the utilitarian credo, who were laying the seeds for the destruction of society. "When triumphant robbery is found among the rich, subversive doctrines will grow among the poor. When democracy turns, as it often does, into a corrupt plutocracy, both national decadence and social revolution are being prepared" (Lecky, 1896: 501-502).

Having only memories, aristocratic conservatism became very historical minded, but it was a sterile historicism. It was not an effort to understand the processes of human societies, but an apologia for the continued existence of a whipped aristocracy. Conservatism, old style, revealed, as did Newman and Lord Acton, a desire to return to an "organic Christian society." But by the beginning of our century, this was all that was left to traditional conservatism. The conservative became a critic without portfolio. It remained for modern American conservatism to demonstrate the unexplored possibilities of this philosophy in making a forthright appeal to the new aristocracy of industrial wealth.

Conservatism in America

Historically, with the exception of its use by the southern slaveholding class, the conservative philosophy has always played a secondary role in American thought. This is not surprising when one recalls the absence of a feudal economic structure. Convention and status were concepts hardly calculated to fire the imagination of a civilization that had to be carved from the wilderness. When Alexis de Tocqueville (1900) in his *Democracy in America* noted that Americans were the most fully realized expression of Cartesian practicalism and yet managed to remain the least philosophic people, this is essentially what he meant. Nonetheless, conservatism has persisted in the form of an "aristocracy of mind." From the time of Jonathan Edwards (who argued that the rulers of society and theology should be those who have been granted divine grace with a "supernatural sense") to George Santayana (who would promote a society ruled by men able to transcend "animal faith" and lead the "life of reason"), American conservatism has been oriented toward an aristocracy of knowledge. Eighteenth- and nineteenth-century conservatism in America talked itself into believing that it had overcome the problems of its European counterparts by augmenting Burke with Harrington. The natural inequalities of man could not be touched by political reformers and philosophic radicals because, as John Adams (1850-56: 382) observed, no human legislator can ever eradicate inequalities implanted by Divine Providence. Natural inequality, for Adams and his successors, implied the existence of a natural aristocracy that could withstand social upheaval because it was presumed to be providential rather than social in character. This shrewd bifurcation of the ideal and the material enabled conservatism to thrive on American soil despite adverse conditions. But by the same token , its stress on an aristocracy of knowledge deprived it of the support of the great mass of Americans of all classes. In past centuries, the United States had little regard for contemplative pietism and elitism, approaches that in no way could be instrumental in the feverish effort to catch up to and then surpass European industrialization. Conservative philosophy, therefore, spent much time criticizing the expansive business civilization. Whatever was of value in this critique was unfortunately dissipated in conservatism's inability to measure the actual historical movements in American life. In substituting the formal values of the past for what such values represented in a new world, conservative philosophy reached a pinnacle of intellectual isolation.

Instead of succeeding in its aim of providing a stream of intellectual continuity to match the continuties in nature, conservatism championed a bifurcation of the past and present. The battleground of ideas assumed the character of the glorious past resisting the encroachments of a decadent present. This dualism was brought to full focus in Henry Adams' (1957) *Mont-Saint-Michel and Chartres.* In establishing the idol of the past as a sure way to protect the "harmony" of future generations, conservatism severed the real and the ideal, the material and the spiritual, the continuous and the novel elements in society. Such an alienation ultimately served to destroy an understanding of and respect for the achievements of the past. It fostered a utopianism lacking an essential democratic content.

It should not be strange to find the new conservative literature uncritically praising the admittedly minor tradition of John Adams, John Randolph, and Irving Babbitt. These figures shared a condemnation of the materialism of a modern industrial society that turned her back on heavenly values. Conservatism attempts a miraculous inversion of the historical process. The movement of life creates new problems demanding new solutions. The utility of previously defined theories is severely circumscribed by current needs. In its mistrust of the incessant movement of American life, conservatism has rejected the great fact that the world of man is not exempt from the process and progress of the universe. Adams opposed the inevitable broadening of the democratic base by pointing to the heavenly basis of social stratification. Randolph and Calhoun opposed any termination of Negro slavery by appealing in a platitudinous fashion to state sovereignty. Southern conservatism in the nineteenth century was barbed criticism of northern capitalism in a frenzied effort to prove that chattel slavery was not as brutal as wage slavery. Southern conservatism preferred to ignore the requirements of an American business economy. It paid for its ignorance in humiliating defeat. Early in this century, Babbitt opposed technological growth because he felt it destroyed the beauty of the labor process. In his case, as with prior conservative doctrinaires, what was being rejected was the forward movement of life itself.

The spark of the new conservatism is what Laski termed the business civilization in decline. Present conservative philosophy has meaning only if it is viewed in the context of a business class in search of some outlook less shapeless than pragmatism. Oscar Handlin (1954), in his preface to *Elihu Root and the Conservative Tradition,* notes that the twentieth century is a "critical juncture in American history," a period in which "the evolving industrial economy of the nation produced men of wealth who needed the support of a conservative tradition." It could not be otherwise. The lack of a rooted aristocracy made conservative doctrine distasteful to the earlier American middle class. It is only in the modern era that conservative thought has become politically significant because only in this period is there a middle class that finds comfort in looking backward. The significance of the current dearth of literature on the "new capitalist revolution" (see Berle, 1954) and the current attempts to write the history of business practice in adulatory terms lies in the linking of the middle class to an explicit conservative philosophy. It is hoped that from this class a new aristocracy can emerge, playing the same role in confounding revolutionary attitudes that the older conservatism attempted in a less favorable atmosphere. The remaining problem is to show the business class how to avoid the same dismal fate as the nobility.

The new conservatism is no less critical of middle-class morality than its historical counterparts. Its rapierlike criticism finds comparable expression only in the literature of American radicalism. The "Coca-Cola civilization" has been severely criticized by Brooks Adams and Robert Hutchins, two of the finest representatives of the conservative "Left." However, the critique of capitalism is made with an eye toward its preservation. As a biographer of Brooks Adams puts it, it is an attempt "to preserve as much as possible of the old way of life and at the same time to reconcile the velocity and extent of mechanized change with responsible administration for the general welfare" (Anderson, 1951: 200). It is this aspect of conservatism that drives many of its advocates to the precipice of fascism. In its frenzied efforts to preserve the old, conservatism may surrender to corporatism, ruralism, and ultimately to fascism.

The new conservatism has no desire to see the downfall of a business economy, but simply to make its board of directors more conscious of ultimate goals. In this way, it is hoped that the wealthy classes will be able to provide a world leadership that will insure American hegemony. The difficulties in the conservative position arise when in the name of tradition it attempts to dam up that very tide in human affairs that gives worth to the past.

The conservative revival in the United States may seem to appear to derive from two sources. One is the present aberration in the relationship between the capitalist and socialist worlds. The international struggle for the minds of men has produced on the national level mass fear of alterations in the socioeconomic structure. There is an almost patholo-gical identification of change with socialism. This has provided the proper soil for a conservative "renaissance." The new conservatism has transformed the nineteenth-century critique of socialism, to the effect that "socialism is slavery," into a twentieth-century first principle. The current labeling of all manner of reform tendencies, from abolitionism to the New Deal, with the "egalitarian" and "leveling" curse is adequate testimony of the extent to which the new conservatism attempts to satisfy the appetites and prejudices of a business civilization.

The other major source of contemporary conservatism's power issues from the widespread disillusionment engendered by bourgeois existence. While making it perfectly clear that they stand on the side of property rights, conservatives are nonetheless critical of those tendencies that produce excess corruption of the moral fiber of the people. The stress on the rural life as the good life, when considered in this way, is a sort of bourgeois asceticism calculated to engender a love rather than a revul-sion for societies built on private property. The following comment by Eliseo Vivas (1950: 314) is typical of the character of criticism launched by the new conservatism:

> I see no reason to assume that there is more love in this scientifically enlightened and humanitarian age of ours than there was in those ages which partisanship and historical ignorance dismiss as the days of the Inquisition. All the evidence points with some clarity the other way. Let us remember that it was left to our generation to invent the fact, no less than the term "genocide."

The new conservatism is a search for meaning, an attempt to anchor the middle class to something more fundamental than the shifting sands of

James's pragmatism, something more worthy than a philosophy of will that reduces moral righteousness to success. In this way, the new conservatism hopes to replace the pluralistic world of pragmatism, with its many truths, with a monistic world that charts an absolute and theologically sanctioned truth.

Because contemporary conservatism realizes that to go forward means to embrace the socialist ideal, it chooses to look backward to a more ethically stable climate—to the high point of thirteenth-century feudalism if possible, or if not that far back then to the England of the Great Reaction (1790-1832). These are specific historical directions that the new conservatism looks toward. The enormous theoretical issue this raises, that is, the maintenance of the past qua past in the face of steadily advancing material culture, is usually resolved by coming down on the side of the hoary past against the main currents charted by the natural and social sciences. If a portion of pragmatic doctrine rests upon resolving dilemmas through expediency, the new conservatism demonstrates the lengths to which it can carry the pragmatic method while revealing a profound disenchantment with its system.

Elitism

Elitism is not a modern innovation. It gained currency with the first definite political and economic divisions among men. In Greek antiquity it had already hardened. Plato presented elitism as being in the nature of biological reality, while Aristotle shifted the basis of his elitism to sociological grounds. With some justification, Aristotle noted that the growth of knowledge is stimulated by a leisure class that has time to think and rule. Elitism was, and remains, a theoretical justification for the existence of a society with ruling and ruled classes. In its philosophic pretensions, earlier American conservatism stands very close to Aristotle's social elitism, while the new conservatism has rediscovered the use of a biological fixing of status first developed by Plato. The new conservatism is in theory a series of footnotes to Platonist teachings. And it should not be overlooked that the present output of "defenses" of Platonism parallels efforts in other areas of thought to reduce the history of culture to the history of conservatism (see, for example, Wild, 1953; Levinson, 1953).

Contemporary conservatism is, like its ancestors, far more a negative reaction to continued social development than a positive enunciation of principles. In Burke, we find a violent reaction to the French Revolution; Henry Adams reacted with equal vigor to the expansion of American industry; Jacques Maritain and George Santayana react, each in his own way, to the heresies of socialism and secularism. This negativism is especially pronounced in conservative efforts to resurrect elitism as a fundamental social law. The "desperate naturalism" of Santayana attempted to resolve the contradictions of modern life by absolving the rational elite from its worldly dilemmas. The rational-intellectual life "is no fair reproduction of the universe, but the expression of man alone" (Santayana, 1953: 174). Reason exists in man alone because only man is conscious and ideal-forming. The life of reason is a life of contemplation, of harmony. This view bears a strong spiritual kinship to the dominant philosophy of the medieval age. Yet it is presented to contemporaries as a plausible solution to current affairs. This solution is achieved by making reason the exclusive preserve of the elite. In order to maintain the delicate balance of society, the aristocratic elite must be preserved— being the group that alone can rise above the contradictions of reality to rational contemplation. In his late work, Santayana (1951: chap. 42) made clear his hope that the American industrialists would one day form the backbone of a contemplative elite. Any effort to destroy an elitist society would mean a reversion to biological levels of existence that would involve men in a series of struggles for the progress of the "rabble." Santayana's elitism is a calculated reply to the Enlightenment faith in progress as the extension of equality. "Progress, far from consisting in change," insists Santayana (1953: 82), "depends on retentiveness." The spirit of order and law beat hard in Santayana. Rather immodestly, the new conservatism assumes that the destruction of elitism would automatically result in the destruction of society itself—because it identifies society with capitalism and itself with both.

It is both possible and desirable to develop social forms without either an elite or a leisured aristocracy. Nor does the absence of elitism logically imply the "leveling curse." The faith in radical democracy is not a desire for deadening uniformity. On the contrary, the extension of economic equality would make possible a genuine intellectual diversity, because it would allow for the development of the potentialities of the massive proletariat, what one conservative calls "an ugly modern word for an ugly thing" (Kirk, 1953: 392). In the analysis dealing with the machinery for preserving culture, the new conservative avoids discussing ways of extending this precious culture, for a new society of 30 million Shakespeares and Newtons, such as Saint-Simon envisioned, would only destroy elitism. Any admission that knowledge and action belong to the community of man in common undercuts the basis of conservative philosophy. In the choice between preserving either elitism or culture, the modern conservative faces a problem that cannot be resolved with platitudes. To those, like Peter Viereck, who identify conservatism with political stability, elitism becomes central, while for those, like Robert Hutchins, who identify conservatism with the preservation of cultural values, elitism is secondary. The change in attitude toward the issues of elitism and past traditions is one of the cornerstones separating the new from the old conservative.

The undifferentiated frontal attack on democracy and socialism generally takes the form of flaying the heresy of revolution. Cromwell, Robespierre, and Lenin, and the movements they led, are provided with a set of immutable qualities. "Impatience and ignorance are characteristic of democratic ages" (Kirk, 1953: 189). It is therefore no surprise to find a treatment of the differences between democracy in seventeenth-century England, eighteenth-century France, and modern Russia reducing itself to an examination of the extent to which "violence replaced law" and "barbarism replaced custom." If American democracy is gross and ignorant, Russian democracy can only be described as more gross and more ignorant. Abstract ethical dogma replaces factual analysis of the nature of social classes and the expansion of political democracy. Conservative social philosophy evaluates man's relationships with his fellow man in terms of its own unique moral commitments. The "life of reason" cannot be led by the majority because most people are regarded as animal-men. Democracy is held to be inferior to either theocracy or timocracy. The extent to which the new conservative is willing to gauge the worth of a political system by its treatment of the elite reveals the extent to which he holds a profound distaste for the democratic form of rule.

Since the American middle class has been sated with the antispeculative arguments of pragmatism, the new conservatism has had to manufacture its elitist aristocracy out of that portion of the middle class that can temper its acquisitive bent with contemplation. Its recruits are often found in the educated and professional elements. Because the new aristocracy is in large measure an *ersatz* group, modern conservatism has devoted great energy to developing a philosophy of education. It is through its educational strategy that the new conservatism attempts to define a set of postulates to appeal to those who may gain from being part of an American elite. Even here they must look backward. In Plato's categories of bronze, silver, and gold men, the new conservatism finds its "positive" outlook. Henry M. Magid offers Plato's elitism as the only realistic approach the rulers of society can take toward political and educational philosophy. First, for the mass of men "loyalty" is essential. In a dynamic society, loyalty cannot be taken for granted; it must be promoted. The young are taken in hand before they can achieve intellectual maturity and critical skill, and they are taught how to be loyal and what to be loyal to. This is achieved by indoctrination through carefully written histories, stories of heroes, and by example and enforced ritual. In educating an elite, we are urged to "get beyond the myths and stereotypes of education for loyalty to a presentation of the actual facts of political life, how our political institutions function"(Magid, 1955: 37). Hand in hand with the ruling elite march those granted an "education for understanding," individuals who have the task of searching for the "truth about the foundations, normative as well as factual, of political life itself" (Magid, 1955: 42). The philosopher in this way forms a superelite, the only group seriously allowed to conduct an inquiry into the basis of society. The stratification in this system of educational philosophy is, we are assured, a guarantee of harmony because it makes clear the bifurcation of the theoretical and the practical. Such political realism sounds peculiarly like the ideals advocated by extreme reaction. It canonizes the separation of head and hand fostered by every dominant class in history.

The elitism advocated by the new conservatism differs but quantitatively from the biological stratification preached by European fascism. It is of small consolation that the elitism of an intellectual aristocracy is said to be more benevolent than that of a "race" or "nation." The principal premise of man's natural inequality is challenged by neither. In any such arrangement, the schisms of humanity would be made permanent features of social existence, rooted in either "natural law" or "divine law." Thinking and doing, like rights and duties, would be severed. In theory, the conservative position flows evenly from the pursuit of knowledge, to the achievement of dynamic thinking, to the right of rule. In actuality, the procedure is somewhat different. Because the proletarian monolith is held incapable of anything greater than believing myths propagated by men of silver and gold, their efforts must remain confined to doing what they are told. With the great bulk of civilization conveniently eliminated politically, the right of rule falls naturally to those classes already ruling. Because the giants of thought are deemed by conservatism to be also the giants of industry, the elitist scheme becomes an elaborate justification of the status quo. We are presented with an eternal separation of men into fixed economic and intellectual molds, a large price indeed to pay for "harmony."

The recognition that inequality is an existing fact is no special insight into the new conservatism. It is equally clear to contemporary democratic philosophies that this is so. The essential difference is that the liberal and socialist traditions consider the inequality inherent in class stratification as something to be opposed. In this sense, they, too, struggle for harmony by pointing out that antagonistic industrial relationships prevent harmony. The new conservatism considers economic stratification to be necessary and beneficial to the public welfare. It would mitigate gradually whatever evils result from social disparagement, so as not to disrupt the basic composition of classes. "Conservatism derives its inspiration and seeks to base its policy on what conservatives believe to be the underlying unity of all class . . . their ultimate identity of interest, their profound similarity of outlook" (Hogg, 1947: 31). Having already rejected any view maintaining that class divisions at the productive base cannot yield a community of interests, it is a simple jump to the proposition that "the nation, not the so-called class struggle, is at the base of Conservative political thinking" (Hogg, 1947: 32). Because "harmony, not struggle" is the principal political end of the new conservatives, the values of elitism become self-evident to the ruled as well as the rulers. Patriotism, love of God, and mythical heroes become important facets because they promote the stability of the state.

The new conservatism does not restrict its theory of consensus to the political realm alone. In economics, we find that it applies a similar thesis. "Since the industrial revolution," writes Viereck (1949: 12), "conservatism is neither justifiable nor effective unless it has roots in the factories and trade union." Frank Tannenbaum (1951) attempts to provide these roots by presenting the trade union as a far-reaching repudiation of reform and revolution. It is for him "the great conservative force of our time." He resurrects the economics of the corporate state as the inevitable outcome of the natural conservatism of both labor and capital. "The corporation and the union will ultimately merge in common ownership and cease to be a house divided. It is only thus that a common identity may once again come to rule the lives of men and endow each one with rights and duties recognized by all" (Tannenbaum, 1951: 198–199). In consideration of conservatism's commitment to elitist precepts and its utter contempt for labor, it is doubtful whether such a "partnership" can lead to anything other than the Nazi experiment, namely, the absolute and relative deterioration of the workers' conditions. What the new conservative doctrine is actually offering is a joint-stock company of an aristocracy of management and labor. It simply extends the joys of elitism to a select portion of labor.

The metaphysic of present-day conservatism is the idea of consensus. However, nowhere is this metaphysic better refuted than in the pages of its own growing literature. To maintain, on the one hand, that society is a bundle of conflicts between classes, nations, and social systems, and to hold, on the other, that a transcendental spirit is at work blending these conflicts so that the whole pattern emerges as a teleological symphony requires a privileged degree of credulity. The evidence of the social sciences points in the opposite direction. In his constant harking back to the imposing edifice of thirteenth-century feudalism, for example, the new conservative fails to notice that in the very century the City of God had been declared to exist, the seeds of feudal decay had already sprouted roots. The new conservatism desires consensus in a social matrix where men are bitterly divided in their interests. The recognition that different socioeconomic interests prevail explains perhaps why the new conservatism presents a *deus ex machina* called authority to work out what men are unable to resolve in the give and take of the democratic process. In its belief that authority is a prerequisite for the achievement of consensus, the new conservatism is akin to those forms of utopianism that sought to transform society by educating its rulers in the principles of utilitarianism.

William Ralph Inge utilizes the *deus ex machina* based upon authority to demonstrate that the state based on private interests is an eternal verity, "whose type is laid up in heaven." The state becomes the secular expression of Divine Will, "the unifying force which keeps the citizens of a country together" (Inge, 1946: 154–155). The state is an absolute good because it draws its "vitality from the deepest instincts and most firmly rooted habits. Private property, the family, religion, patriotism." And for modern conservative doctrine, any repudiation of such a state must result in a "fiasco" (Inge, 1946: 155). In this form, philosophical conservatism reveals its awareness of social contradictions. For were society a naturally harmonic balance between classes and nations, there would be no need for a state to keep "the citizens of a country together." When conservatism calls upon the divine inspiration of a God-state to maintain an elite in power, it is asking Providence for a restoration of harmony to capitalism, not showing that harmony already is rooted in private-property relations. The appeal to prejudice, myth, and supernatural edict cannot alter basic facts of economic history. To ask Providence to do what people cannot is not to reveal a love of God, but a failure of faith in human powers.

The Conservative Ethic

The moral absolutism of the new conservatism is as much a reaction to the "open society" and "open morality" of pragmatism as it is an attempt to forge a heuristic principle against Marxian ethics. The inherent pluralism of pragmatism makes it impossible to utilize ethics for a predetermined social goal. The steady stream of criticism which the new conservatism has directed at Dewey's instrumentalism is pointedly oriented at his "means-ends continuum." The question John H. Hallowell (1954: 131) poses for pragmatic ethics cannot be evaded: "How is happiness possible without some rational principle in terms of which we can differentiate good pleasures from bad?" A universe without fixed ends, always locating goals in the immediate activities of men, is a universe lacking purpose. It fails to develop criteria for judging both means and ends in terms of a wider setting than individual biological needs. The new conservatism seeks desperately for purpose, for a teleology of morals. What its advocates continually refuse to admit is that purpose can exist without being predetermined.

Modern conservatism is aware that direction is of one of two varieties: the direction of history, what Maritain derisively calls the historical god, or the preordained direction of cosmic will. Since even current conservative doctrine admits that the historical flow forecasts the extinction of absolutist, theologically conditioned morality, there remains but one alternative. To restore purpose into the life of society, it is necessary to give moral law a paramount role, exempting it from the laws of history. Democracy itself is conceived by Hallowell as a series of duties based "upon the reality of a universal obligation to obey moral law." Disobedience to moral authority becomes synonymous with disrespect for democracy (Hallowell, 1954: 124). The moral sanction becomes God's sanction, the moral will becomes God's will, and moral authority becomes the authority of God. Morality becomes a matter of locating the divine pattern and obeying its dictates. Purpose is to be restored to the lives of people by lifting them from the ignoble choice of adopting either a pluralist, directionless ethic sanctioned by a bourgeoisie saturated with utilitarianism or an ethic with a range of applications circumscribed by history and sanctioned by a materialist proletariat. It is a conflict between the idea of history as the interaction and conquest of natural and social obstacles by men and the idea of history as redemption from original sin. History, we are told, "is not as Marx declared it to be, 'the activity of man pursuing his own aims' but rather a dialogue between God and man, with God taking the initiative and man either fleeing or responding to His call. The essential meaning of history is the restoration of personality through redemption from evil" (Hallowell, 1954:100). It is the obvious task of the new conservative to make sure that men respond to rather than flee from this providential call. Here the professor has turned preacher.

The recurrent dilemma of the new conservatism is that in its rejection of a "shallow liberalistic" ethic it moves away from democratic criteria for judging the worth of acts and attitudes. An objective ethic becomes equivalent to a normative and transhistorical ethic. In this form, morality is seen as a matter of discovery rather than a process of development. The determination of who has discovered the True Ethic becomes the focal point of value analysis. The absolutism of this approach does not admit to the existence of alternative ethical programs basic for certain periods and for specific social purposes. Instead, it is compelled to adopt a rigid theological dogma. Those who have accepted such a dogma are said to have discovered the True Ethic; those who have not are said to be lacking an ethic altogether.

The moral authoritarianism of modern conservatism represents a deep mistrust of a scientifically grounded ethic. It is the substitution of an ethic of allegiance for one of empirical procedure. It denies that the framework of human values is human society. The conflict in ideas that exists between social forces is resolved by reference to supernatural dogma. In the footsteps of Saint Augustine, contemporary conservatism bifurcates society into "two cities." The city of man is held to be based upon an egoist morality, while the heavenly city is based on love of God and contempt for self. The possibility of escaping the egocentric dilemma, of acquiring a humane moral code through secular methods, is ruled out. Man, according to the new conservatism and the old theology it mimics, is, in his origins, evil. Redemption comes through renunciation of the worldly and acceptance of the heavenly. The ethical norm in this way comes to be identified with a non-human authority: "The effect of this teaching is not only to distinguish the secular from the spiritual spheres but to place the secular authority under the sanction of a higher authority" (Hallowell, 1954:117). We are presented with gradations of being. The "highest authority" being "secular authority" is the state. The state becomes God in nature. It is the level of being that interprets the normative ethic for the individual. Morality in this fashion becomes a matter of respect for authority, and authority becomes a matter of allegiance. Because the secular state is the disseminator of the providential moral code, any challenge to it becomes heretical.

By lifting the problem of choice from human society, the conservative is able to demand unswerving allegiance to the secular state on the basis of religious sentiment and moral authority. For insofar as the secular authority is the reflection of theological authority, the state must be judged as absolutely good. Criticism of such a Christian state can properly be viewed as an attack on the religious basis of civil society itself. The new conservatism promises a militant defiance of those Jeffersonians who dare to preach the separation of religious and political institutions. It "will seek to expose the reckless vanity of political principles that ignore or deride the quest of God" (Rossiter, 1955:372). This theocratic goal is the natural result of moral absolutism. If the initial premise of human decadence is accepted, if ordinary men are creatures of sin, and if absolution is possible only through a rigorous calculus of duties and allegiances, then indeed to reckon the possibilities of achieving a steadily expanding democratic society is, as the conservative says, a supreme sin.

The entire strength of conservatism's closed ethical system is its ability to sever values from actions. The impact of modern science has convinced the new conservative that in the realm of physical and social events all is flux. The *raison d'être* of conservatism, however, is to emphasize that social life has a special normative feature compelling a value standpoint based on permanence. Faced with a changing world, it must lift the spiritual side of things from their base in material relations. If the conservative philosopher can show that ethics is not subject to change, he can go on to establish a realm of immutable values. If, in the spirit of neo-Platonism, he can further demonstrate that that which is subject to causality (materiality) is unfree, whereas the spiritual alone is connected to free will, then he can show that spirit alone gives man freedom. Man as "flesh" is a "creature of habit, impulse, of passion, driven here and there by the forces of nature which are beyond his control" (Vivas, 1950:341). All efforts at material improvement are therefore wasted, according to Vivas. "But, insofar as man is spirit, he is free. And the law of causality cannot be said to apply to him" (Vivas, 1950:342). The moral law, not subject to causal determination, is thus "above" the laws of nature altogether. In this form the path is clearer, for the supreme edict of the new conservatism, the bedrock of its moral absolutism, is that "the ethical is otherworldly." It turns us away from our social loyalties and conflicts and "toward the source of our freedom and the goal of our salvation" (Vivas, 1950:346).

While Eliseo Vivas is elusive about the exact "source of our freedom," other naturalists doing penance are not as squeamish. The source of freedom is held to be God. The goal of our salvation is regarded as the establishment of the heavenly city on earth. Although this city will establish "moral equality," it cannot change the lordly "conviction that civilized society requires order and classes" (Kirk, 1953:8). But having learned that only the moral realm provides freedom from enslaving causal relations, we can only bear the iniquities latent in civilized society.

The elaborate moral canons of the new conservatism have a quite secular goal of securing a harmonious society based on private property—a hardly novel outcome of a hardly novel philosophy.

Despite its insistence upon the normative foundations of human behavior, the new conservatism does present mankind with a choice that is inescapable. Either the realm of values is subject to causality and scientific analysis or else science and values are mutually exclusive. If the former is true, then the possibilities of developing an organic, naturalistic conception of human nature exist. If the latter viewpoint is true, then any efforts undertaken to change man or his external circumstances are doomed in advance to failure. Morally, the conflict between conservatism and democracy is between the view of human nature as fixed and the view of it as plastic. To deny the malleability of human ethical conduct is to deny the reality of the endless struggle of mankind to utilize an advanced ethic to alter further his social conditions. To assert that man is governed by rigid, predetermined moral dogma is to make social action suspect. It is this sort of resigned belief in the futility of human efforts at improvement that the new conservatism seeks to inculcate. And it seals this resignation with an antiscientific trust in cosmic design.

Pietism

The pietism of contemporary conservatism finds its inspiration, like so many of its other basic tenets, in the doctrines of Burke. Providential guidance is considered the cornerstone of the sociopolitical structure. Prescriptive rights flow from the nature of God in the same way that natural rights are held to flow from the nature of man. The individual is considered to be simply an instrument of Divine Will. The historical evolution of society is regarded as the Divine Will asserting itself in nature: "History is the gradual revelation of supreme design—often shadowy to our blinking eyes, but subtle, resistless and beneficent. God makes history through the agency of man" (Kirk, 1953:36). Not a small amount of attention is focused on humanist and materialist philosophies that have made man his own proper study. The cosmic pietism of the new conservatism is a direct assault on the principle that men, since they are, in fact, independent of supernatural control, have the task of adjusting values so as to enable themselves to alter as well as to comprehend the nature of their lives. To the conservative, this position involves the heresy of self-sufficiency. And the self-reliant individual is not likely to be pious or desirous of supernatural instruction. A naturalistic view of man is a democratic view of man. And as Kirk (1953:119) informs us:

"The pure democrat is the practical atheist: ignoring the divine nature of law and the divine establishment of spiritual hierarchy, he is the unconscious instrument of diabolic powers for the undoing of mankind."

Modern conservatism emphasizes religion as duty rather than religion as social justice. This is indicated by such remarks as: "the first rule of society is obedience—obedience to God and the dispensations of Providence, which work through natural processes" (Kirk, 1953: 59). However, the pietism of the new conservatism must contend with more than the relations of men to Providence. It attempts to show the epistemological basis for such a relation. In the conflict between reason and superstition, conservative doctrine finds its answers. The naive Enlightenment faith in reason as the path to a higher democracy is castigated as a false idol that promotes only the cause of radical incendiaries. Conservativism perceives a great truth, namely, that belief in the nature of man as thoroughly rational excludes the transcendental from social decisions. Action based on reason is judged by Kirk as akin to belief in atheism and materialism. And for the conservative, "the experience of the species is treasured up chiefly in tradition, prejudice, and prescription—generally for all men, and sometimes for all men, surer guides to conduct and conscience than books and speculations." There is a strong current of anti-intellectualism in conservative preachings. It relates reason "to a wasteland of withered hopes and crying loneliness." Irreligious ideas become a sign of "intellectual vanity" (Kirk, 1953:36). At this point, conservatism and pragmatism meet. The anti-intellectualism of both is based on a depreciation of human faculties of reason.

The thoroughness of the conservative attack on reason would shock Thomas Aquinas little less than Denis Diderot. Reason is not even allowed to exist as a theological handmaiden. The new conservative knows "man to be governed more by emotion than by reason" (Kirk, 1953:8). We are warned by the leader of the natural rights school, Leo Strauss (1953:6), that "the more we cultivate reason, the more we cultivate nihilism." To appreciate the extremeness of this view, we should recall the classic defense of Catholicism offered by Aquinas. He bolstered the case for revelation on the power, not the negation, of reason. The great scholastic opposed the idea that myth is a surer guide to Providence than is reason. The orientation of present-day conservatism, however, is more compatible with the mystery cults of antiquity and the irrationalism of Sorel and Pareto than with the sophisticated rationalism of Aquinas.

Our main concern is not the medieval defense of reason, but the present conservative assault on it. Reason is linked with "degradation, the rebellious will of man" (Hallowell, 1954:128). In place of the heady powers of human reason, we are urged to remember that man is bathed in original sin. And if the plunge to a socialist hell is not to be final, we must return to the singular source of goodness, religion. Between Enlightenment and scholasticism the choice must be made. Modern conservativism chooses the latter. The Enlightenment forgot what John Hallowell (1954:128) remembers: that "man is not an autonomous being but the creature of God, his moral weakness is his own, but his moral strength is born of the love of God. What the modern world has almost forgotten is the reality of spirit that ultimately triumphs over material power." Such sentiments rest on the assumption of a human inability to solve the problems of social existence. The full-scale attack launched on Enlightenment principles is on the surface a logical extension of Burkeism. They are that certainly. But more profoundly, the new conservatism sees in Enlightenment thought the taproots of American democracy. The resurrection of pietism requires a negation of the democratic tradition. It is, therefore, important for conservatism to focus its sights on the concepts of self-interest, natural goodness, reason, and happiness—concepts that received dynamic expression in documents such as the Declaration of Independence and the Bill of Rights.

The candor of the new conservatism, its recognizable identification with anti-intellectual and fascist currents, is somewhat jarring to the American saturated in traditions of Enlightenment and utility. American democracy has taken the tenets of eternal progress and happiness, not as abstractions, but as a guide to daily living. A reaction to this tradition on American soil, while clearly not novel, has also quite definitely been a subdued tendency. Even the older forms of conservatism made their opposition to reaction and irrationalism clear. John Adams could still play a vital part in the progress of the American Revolution. What modern conservatism confronts us with is a definite choice between a materialist tradition of freedom through the rational uses of technology, science, and social institutions and a philosophy of myth and prejudice artificially grafted onto the American scene from the backwaters of European idealist currents.

"Absolute democracy" is said to have failed because it leads toward "social disintegration," which in turn raises the specter of "oppressive collectivism." The new conservatism wants to be saved from the consequences of the proposition that society is itself the root source of human happiness and misery. V. A. Demant offers as his salvation from political realities "an organic relation between man's secular and spiritual life." The idea of religion propagated by the new conservatism sheds its monastic garb long enough to tell us that "the 'primacy of the spiritual' must be upheld, not as a retreat from the secular tasks of life, but as a condition of handling them aright" (Demant, 1947:65–66). In plainer language, religion is to be the foundation of society itself.

Conservative pietism is a ladder to the theocratic state. Only a "Christian society" can save mankind from the twin horrors of reason and revolution, from the "old spurious God of the lawless Empire bending everything to his adoration" (Maritain, 1951:187). The perplexing qualities of this position are clear even to some conservatives. If broad social conflict and change result from the iniquities of the material conditions of life, how is it possible for spiritual forces to do more than help us bear iniquities? If genuine change is providential, man is necessarily passive in the face of his everyday socioeconomic relations. It is precisely the fact that men are not simply passive, refusing to await the call of Providence before acting, that makes the conservative dish unappetizing to all but those comfortably situated. It is this overwhelming fact of an age of social and scientific revolution that the new conservatism has refused to acknowledge.

Cosmic pietism, with its emphasis on myth and superstition, is translated into practical affairs as a reawakening of the Crusading Spirit. We are presented with a thorough identification of God with nation, race, and class—particularly the American nation, the Anglo-Saxon race, and the business class. The new conservatism is basically different from its ancestors in that it no longer makes paramount the critique of the bourgeoisie. Instead it places a theological imprimatur on the activities of American financial interests, while damning forever rational and egalitarian societies based on "collectivism." Allan Nevins musters all the tendentious zeal of the new conservatism in practically conceding the inevitability of war with "communist tyranny." Instead, he would have us believe that such an unthinkable holocaust would entitle the American civilization to take its place beside Athenian civilization (Nevins, 1954).

Contemporary conservative pietism employs idealism as a screen to promote a New Holy Alliance. The Atlantic Community is to become a twentieth-century version of Metternich's European Union (Viereck, 1949:132–136). Far from being a humane or judicious conception of the spiritual, the new conservatism uses religion cynically, for adventurist ends. Theoretically, it holds that religion is the basis of society. Practically, it holds that religion is a pragmatic device for maintaining intact a society based on private property, order, and duty. It attempts to provide a cosmic scope for imperial pretentions. A more ironic use of theology is hardly imaginable.

1956

10

The Pluralistic Bases
of
Modern American Liberalism

Classical liberalism is connected in history to the general emancipation of western Europe from the fetters of class structures. The liberal position stemmed from a concern for economic equity no less than from an interest in liberty. In this sense, nineteenth-century liberalism is closer in appearance and in substance to the socialist claims of fraternal brotherhood than to the emphasis of conservative thought upon the right to rule of those with custom and wisdom. Liberalism defined its claims in universalistic terms; it spoke of freeing mankind as a whole. The bourgeoisie, which came to embrace liberalism, was not, however, in complete accord with the doctrine. The bourgeoisie's relationship to liberalism was closer to a kiss of death than an embrace of eternal love— since at precisely the point that the bourgeoisie discovered liberalism, the doctrine ceased to have total critical value and meaning to wide numbers of people. This was the case, at least in the context of western Europe during the nineteenth century.

Liberalism does not precede socialism as an ideology. Historically, it is parallel in time to the maturation of socialist doctrine in Europe. The rivalry between liberalism and socialism is especially bitter and acrimonious precisely because socialists could not place liberalism in the same historical ashcan as they did the capitalist system. Their attempts to engage in the subterfuge of equating liberalism and capitalism failed to convince anyone.

Liberalism does not precede socialism in political life as capitalism is assumed to have preceded communism in economic life. If one examines the history of early capitalism—in sixteenth-century Italy, or seventeenth-century Holland, or even eighteenth-century England—it is evident that the early ideologies of the bourgeoisie had little to do with liberalism as a national policy or a public ideology. In fact, the bourgeoisie often bitterly fought those early reform legislations that in history became connected with their class mission. Even the ideology of latter-day capitalists can only by a considerable stretch of the imagination be connected to liberalism.

Liberals are often persuaded by their adversaries that they simply reflect and represent the capitalist ethos of *laissez-faire et laissez-passer*. But on close examination, one may discover that liberalism and capitalism represent parallel growth patterns. It may be that the liberal tradition has come to stand for capitalist styles and capitalist economies; but if so, this is a very late development in the history of capitalism. There is little historical correspondence between the liberal ideology and its presumed capitalist economic base. At the same time, it is important to recognize that the roots of many forms of socialist ideology, as Marx himself pointed out, lie deep in the feudalistic tradition and in the guild tradition. Thus, socialist ideology also does not necessarily stand as the ideological surrogate for the modern socialist economy. There is an autonomous realm to political ideology that is too often made short shrift of. Not to recognize the autonomous development and special properties of ideologies is to falsify political sociology, to make of it a dialectical monstrosity where every doctrine has its place and every person knows his place.

Let us therefore proceed on the assumption that the time of pure capitalism was in a state of relative decline corresponding to an incline of liberal ideology. As a matter of fact, if we take England as our prime illustration of this hypothesis, the rise of liberalism corresponds with the rise of the political enfranchisement of the masses. And the major victories of the liberal parties in England from the midnineteenth-century Factory Legislation Acts to the midtwentieth-century Nationalization Acts came at the expense of the bourgeoisie. It may be said that liberalism functioned throughout the century as the advanced ideology of the most enlightened sections of the class that despised it. This is as true of twentieth-century United States as of nineteenth-century England. The liberal forces — the New Deal, for example — were despised by the bourgeoisie and by the establishment sectors even though these groups benefited most in the long run from the liberal reforms. If we understand liberalism in this way, we can better appreciate the tensions, ambiguities, and uncertainties that have pervaded the liberal tradition in politics and society.

After making a somewhat ambiguous rejection of the extreme individualist view of libertarianism and opting for a more societal view of liberty within the framework of human obligation, the liberals turned their energies toward a theory of measurement. Societal development through liberalism became the measurement of progress. It was a way of defining where men were, where men are, and where men ought to be. Thus, the degree of liberalism become the measure of growth. Liberalism was the developmental ideology of the nineteenth century, and because of this, it became more than a bourgeois system; it also tried to account for the fact that there were other social classes in ascendancy such as the factory working class. The appeal of the liberal ideology to broad sectors of society, especially in the urban sectors, was made on behalf of the progress, not simply the spiritual achievements, of the human race. It relied upon measurable commodities: the number of literate people, the number of educated people, the rate of gross national production, the growth and spread of urbanism, the growth and spread of secularism. These quantifications were characteristic hallmarks of the liberal measurement of progress; and they were the bedrock benchmarks of industrial Europe and America.

If we turn to the question of the essence of liberalism itself, we come upon what Isaiah Berlin (1954) properly calls two types of liberty: positive liberty and negative liberty. He means by a theory of negative liberty, the desire not to be impinged upon, to be left to oneself. Negative liberty recognizes the self as sacred and inviolable, with special rights as a private being. It acknowledges a private soul with private longings and with certain inalienable rights that do not stem from any contractual arrangement with state authority. The theory of negative liberty is the measurement of how much autonomy a man has in a society. The measure of that autonomy can be very practical: What are the conditions under which a person is penalized and what are the conditions under which a person is praised? Liberalism is an advanced form of calculus, not of hedonism, but of an exchange system based on the assumption that everyone has the ability to assist and to be assisted. Given the fact that society makes certain demands upon a man, how many demands and on what bases? What is a man penalized for? Ethnicity? Nationality? Lack of patriotism? Race? Not voting? Within the framework of ideology, there can be violations of liberty in the name of libertarianism. If one is penalized for not voting, in what way is this an abbreviation of personal liberty? Those nations that boast that 99 percent of the citizenry participate in the vote are perhaps the most suspicious examples of antilibertarian attitudes. Perhaps a nation with 48 percent of its people voting is a better example of respect for the right of the private citizen not to participate. In other words, a theory of negative liberty is concerned with the degree to which personal autonomy is preserved in society. Generally speaking, this cult of the individual has characterized both western European and American varieties of liberalism.

The central European tradition has been different. Its concerns are linked with a theory of positive liberty — that is, the liberty to perform tasks with efficiency and effectiveness. This view can be traced in a direct line from Spinoza through Hegel; and it can be found in Marx and many of the European socialist figures of the nineteenth century. This theory of positive liberty has to do with the notion of mastery, of control, rather than autonomy. The liberty to play an instrument, for example, can only be derived by mastery of that instrument. This notion of liberty carries over into a concept of the state. One cannot be at liberty in a state unless one knows the effective rules of that state, so that liberty depends in part on an appreciation of that system that enables men to survive. Political liberty thus becomes identified with political participation. These are sharply divergent notions of what liberty means. Liberty from (liberty in the sense of autonomy) and liberty to (liberty in the sense of control) provide the poles of the libertarian framework.

These traditions are not easily resolved. To be sure, Isaiah Berlin does his best, but he fails; in the end he is content to stand with a theory of negative liberty derived from the utilitarianism of John Stuart Mill. However, the ambiguities within the liberal tradition are imposed not simply by other forms of political ideologies, but by the metaphysics of the concept of liberty itself. The liberal literature, insofar as there is a conscious liberal literature of the nineteenth or twentieth century, shows that the contradiction between theories of negative and positive liberty becomes increasingly pronounced as liberals become engaged in the political arena. For once the issues are joined at the level of instrumentalities and the gloss of common agreement on goals is pierced, liberalism is subject to the same stresses and strains as is any other political doctrine.

Liberalism as a nineteenth-century doctrine is essentially linked to the belief that each person should count as one irrespective of his property holdings or monetary worth, that in the political arena one citizen is as important as any other citizen. In this way, elitism was challenged, in effect, by maintaining the equality of men in the political arena, irrespective of differences in the economic arena.

But there was a curious anomaly that arose: the fathers of liberalism wanted more than a minimum of liberty. Their real goal was maximum noninterference. But they also understood that prior to their time it was unlikely that such a demand for liberty had ever been made by other than a small minority of highly civilized human beings. If only a small, articulate group of human beings could recognize their right to liberty, in what way could it be said that liberalism is any less an elite doctrine than the conservative doctrine it sought to replace? In short, if the liberal intent is to convince people capable of the exercise of free conscience and if it is true that the exercise of free conscience in all situations is perhaps the most difficult task for all but the smallest minority, then how was liberalism other than another variant of elitism? To be sure, the elite is dedicated to values commanding mass support and even mass sympathy. Nonetheless, while the purposes of liberalism insofar as they are not undermined by the elite formulations themselves remain dedicated to the democratic ethos, there is a recognition that only a small minority of highly civilized men can be liberals in any profound sense.

By the end of the century, the classical liberal position was as much a minority point of view as was any other ideology. It was not only that liberalism resolved itself into a bourgeois position; but rather that even the bourgeoisie was unable to maintain itself in a liberal framework. The class anomaly concerning liberalism continued well into the twentieth century; even at present this dilemma continues to exercise decisive intellectual constraint within the political framework and the state.

What liberalism represents in an American context is, in a theoretical sense, not that much different from what it represented in the last century. But the challenges and the threats are different. The nineteenth-century threat to liberalism was aristocratic. The twentieth-century threat is from the masses. It is not so much that the class strata represented by liberalism has changed as that the opposition to liberalism has changed and broadened. In comparing an enlightened twentieth-century liberal like David Riesman with the best of the nineteenth-century liberals, one finds less difference and more intellectual continuity than in most other political traditions. The shifts in conservative thought between the nineteenth and twentieth centuries were numerous primarily because early conservatism was marginal. There is less discontinuity within the liberal tradition.

Take the question of optimism, or the optative mood, as C. Wright Mills liked to call it. The liberal point of view conveys a long-standing infectious optimism, for liberalism has always been connected with the doctrines of progress and evolution. When liberals speak of change, they usually assume that the organism is susceptible to alteration, and they rarely think of the organism as requiring an exorcism or elimination. Therefore, when liberals speak of men of power, the tendency is to speak of how this power can be acted on.

This strong optimistic mood historically has pervaded liberalism as an assumption, even among the most sophisticated of its adherents—things can be changed by direct action, and the sources of power are divided enough and open enough so that it is possible to act on these sources of power and make the appropriate changes in the system. This is precisely the point in the twentieth century that has so sharply divided the socialists from the liberals. Socialism represents a form of historical pessimism. It represents a statement about the impossibility of effecting change or political action from within. Liberalism makes precisely the reverse assumptions about the openness of the system. Indeed, one might say that optimism enables liberalism to function as a dominant force within current American life, because liberalism provides reinforcement for the theory that the American system is an open system, viable, and subject to change.

This optimism within the liberal framework has to do with effective interaction between selective groups. It is more elite than mass oriented—dominated by the belief in the impact of a letter to a congressman or the effectiveness of a private session between a man of knowledge and one of power. It is faith in legal procedures, in the rule of law. Liberalism in its own way celebrates the ideals of the system. Liberals always act as if the definitions of the social system are circumscribed by constitutional limitations and restraints; as if the formal rule of law is always and everywhere upheld. As a result, no one is more thwarted by the realities of the situation than those who accept the ideals of the system as the norm. Thus, the liberal, acting as if the Bill of Rights exists fully, and as if all constitutional safeguards are upheld, often mistakes normative behavior for juridical ideals.

Liberalism makes the assumption that the rule of mind or of reason will uniformly win out over raw power. Perhaps this is its great virtue; unless men act as if the ideal were at least possible to implement, the ideal can never be realized. It is, therefore, no accident that the victories of liberalism have been legalistic. Organizations such as the American Civil Liberties Union are its ultimate achievements in the practical realm of politics because they take law as sacred and demand that powerful people and the agencies they direct live up to the laws of the society. It is liberalism's strength that it makes this demand, because this provides an idealistic fervor within it that is sometimes thought to have vanished in the dust of English constitutional history.

Lippmann (1922:414–415) summed up with particular clarity the relationship between social stability and faith in reason.

> It is only on the premise of a certain stability over a long run of time that men can hope to follow the method of reason. This is not because mankind is inept, or because the appeal to reason is visionary, but because the evolution of reason on political subjects is only in its beginnings. Our rational ideas in politics are still large, thin generalities, much too abstract and unrefined for practical guidance, except where the aggregates are large enough to cancel our individual peculiarities and exhibit large uniformities. Reason in politics is especially immature in predicting the behavior of individual men, because in human conduct the smallest initial variation often works out into the most elaborate differences. That, perhaps, is why when we try to insist solely upon an appeal to reason in dealing with sudden situations, we are broken and drowned in laughter.

Lippmann never tells his readers whether this derision of reason and stability is to be endured in silence or somehow met full force. It is clear that Lippmann sensed that liberalism functions best in consensus situations, when conflict is low and outbursts at a minimum. But, of course, the evolution of the twentieth century has denied ideal conditions for the perseverance of liberalism.

Within the legal framework of a democratic society, the liberals have no problems; they simply assume that the law must be obeyed at all times. But suppose the demand of the moment is for an illegal act of conscience, not necessarily political but yet clearly illegal—such as the activities surrounding absolute laws of sex, marriage, and divorce. Here the liberals have a genuine dilemma. Namely, do they support free conscience or established precedence? The right of the free conscience stems from roots that are often extralegal in character. Then how does the liberal behave? Does he behave in terms of extralegality or within the framework of law?

If one conceives of liberalism as both a morality and a polity, when the morality is identified with the polity, there is little dilemma in action; but when the demands of the morality contradict the demands of legality, the liberal position either vanishes into a form of acquiescence in law or rejection of law, and therefore a form of radicalism the liberal presumably seeks to move beyond. The rule of law or the rule of men is the liberal's dilemma. He celebrates the former, but is often compelled to act in terms of the latter.

The student movement deserves to be examined from the point of view of liberalism. In many cases, the administration wants civics and the students want politics. The peculiarity of civics is that the norms of legality are always upheld. The administration in such a situation does not always want a rejection of activity as such. They are, rather, interested in civic action. But they fail to appreciate that the student movement is often a demand for politics and that politics in contrast to legislation is often extralegal. Every demand for a change in law is a demand for something other than what presently governs men. The extralegal wing has become the radical wing. Such specialized interest-group movements presume a kind of moral conservatism, even though they exhibit an ideological radicalism. Interest groups reveal a demand for reduced organizational constraints. It is a demand to be irrational, if for no other reason than to deny the rationality that the society wishes to impose. In this way, social protest often is compelled to move beyond liberalism, not so much on ideological grounds, but simply as a means of organizational survival. Often the leading figures in political protest are not the most judicious figures. For many, liberalism becomes a fetter to action, and hence a poor ideology for generating social protest.

For its critics, liberalism offers partiality, fragmentation, and inde-cisiveness. It offers a middle range between whatever is at one extreme end and whatever is said to be necessary at the other. It accepts the partiality of the world in a way that no other doctrine of the twentieth century does. Here again, what appears to critics as weakness is perhaps the ultimate strength of liberalism, for underneath the shibboleths and rhetoric of liberalism is something important. It is the assumption that one can live a life without knowing all the answers. The strength of liberalism is that it does not offer fanaticism, that it makes the assumption that the world is not always going to be fully known, and that men can yet act within a partial frame of reference. The more one emphasizes the fragmentation of the world, the more one must insist on the pragmatic values of men, the less can an argument be made for action as good in itself.

Every action depends in some measure on the belief that the act will bring about the desired change. If there are no warrants that an act will result in the anticipated goals, then how can one assume the necessity for the act as such? The liberal position is dangerous above all for the liberal himself, because at the same time that he must acknowledge the frag-mentary quality of the world, he must act at least as vigorously as those who have a dogma, who have firm solutions. This is where the liberal tradition has had its gravest trials and tribulations. To the degree that it emphasizes the act, to that degree it moves toward fanaticism. To the degree that it emphasized framentation it leads to resignation. So that, at the end as at the beginning, whether from the point of view of action or quietism, theories of positive versus negative liberty, liberalism is a gigantic ambiguity, and perhaps for that reason both a success and a failure—depending on what criteria are used for measuring success and failure.

Charles Frankel (1956), who himself must be ranked a firm advocate of the American liberal system of organization and action, appreciated the degree to which the belief that science represented the consolidation of empirical methods became the great spur to the liberal outlook. He also appreciated the extent to which this identification of liberalism to science was in fact the Achilles heel of that ideology.

> The disasters already accomplished by technology, and the greater disasters that are threatened, have undermined the genial assumption that there is a simple connection between engineering and happiness. The belief that there is a necessary connection between progress in knowledge and progress in morality has been shattered by the spectacle which the Fascists and Communists have placed before us of bestiality joined with technical efficiency. We see that disinterested science means the gradual elimination of mythological codes of thought has been challenged by the emergence, in this most "scientific" of ages, of mythologies whose intellectual quotients are in inverse proportions to the primitive character of the passions they evoke (Frankel, 1956:39–40).

And while Frankel, like Lippman before him, appreciates that the special divination that provides a scientific rationalization for liberalism is simply beyond redemption, lacking any alternatives, he still insists on the need for a nonsanctioned liberalism, something that at least deserves a "fighting chance." In a sense, Frankel, like many other articulate liberals, is himself engaged in the task of unmasking the limits of the liberal doctrine. Upon examination, however, the alternative options appear to be so gruesome to the cultivated mind lurking behind the commodity fetish, that the liberal group remains intact.

The traditional liberal theory of government rests not so much on a theory of checks and balances but, more purposely, on the weighting given to each of the factors comprising governance. For the essence of liberalism is not simply a division of powers among executive, legislative, and judicial branches; nor is it simply the mechanisms for adjudicating the relationships between the three. More profoundly, the nature of liberalism is that it implies the representative will of the people, as expressed in the legislative branch and in the judicial check. This is so over and against potential presidential abuses of power. It is no accident that the traditional liberal formulations always involve the assumption that government governs best when it governs least. Nor is it an accident that from an empirical point of view the liberal credo has found itself, more often than not, opposed to executive power and supportive of judiciary power.

The chief difference between traditional European and contemporary American variants of liberalism is the shift from legislative to executive emphasis. As liberalism has become increasingly linked to the amelioration of social problems, and not just the defense of individual rights, this shift from a suspicion of government to a celebration of government has become pronounced. In a sense, the traditional liberalist formulation was far closer to the modern conservative formulation than either is to a modern liberalism from the New Deal period onwards. The stimulus for such a reformulation of liberalism was the manifest weaknesses of a business civilization no longer able to sustain a *laissez-faire* posture and survive. Under the circumstances, it is quite understandable why liberalism, the cardinal ideology of such a business civilization, also changed its orientation toward federal government.

Louis Hartz (1955), writing at a time when it was still fashionable to declare "that the Bolshevik Revolution represents the most serious threat in modern history to the future of free institutions" (1955:302), nonetheless understood best the reasons why liberalism thrived on American soil. "America represents the liberal mechanism of Europe functioning without the European social antagonisms." In elaborating this point, Hartz indicates that the main danger to the liberal society is not the principle of majority rule, "but the danger of unanimity, which has slumbered unconsciously behind it." That is to say, Hartz has ably argued that liberalism is not simply a credo of the wide-open Jamesian universe, but a fixed dogmatic position that comes close to identifying itself with Americanism and the course of Empire.

> Surely, then, it is a remarkable force: this fixed, dogmatic liberalism of a liberal way of life. It is the secret root from which have sprung many of the most puzzling of American phenomena. Take the unusual power of the Supreme Court and the cult of constitution worship on which it rests. Federal factors apart, judicial review as it has worked in America would be inconceivable without the national acceptance of the Lockian creed, ultimately enshrined in the Constitution, since the removal of high policy to the realm of adjudication implies a prior recognition of the principles to be legally interpreted (Hartz, 1955:9).

This special brand of liberalism takes root in the United States because the democratic system is not one to be fought for, but simply part of the birthright of the American. It is for this reason that liberalism is both so ingrained and yet so dogmatic within the American context.

Conservatism has largely based its claims on elites, and therefore on the will of the executive. Radicalism, too, has based its claims on vanguards who are uniquely qualified and endowed to feel the pulse of the masses. These pulse takers are, in effect, totalitarian equivalents of executive power. But within this framework, liberalism uniquely has seen the legislative and executive branches as those agencies of power that insure legitimate authority and also the rights of the people. This emphasis on the will of the people as individuals, with every man counting as one, better explains the staying power of liberalism as a practice than does the simple division of powers incorporated in the theory of checks and balances. Liberalism has come upon hard times, in part as a consequence of the emergence of executive power as supreme.

Liberalism stands, too, for a sharp demarcation between state power and government power. That is to say, in marked contrast to either extreme conservative or extreme radical regimes, the expression of powers implies a separation of those who have decision-making power— namely, the political branch—from those who carry out the everyday affairs of ordinary men, or what can be called governmental power. That is why the liberal society has come to be clearly demarcated by its separation of the political and the bureaucratic. For separation of the political man and the policy-making man was, in its own subtle way, the extension of the doctrine of separation and the balance of powers. What has taken place over time to erode this situation is the emergence of bigness itself and the veritable collapse of representativism. For one person to represent a constituency of 1,000 is quite different from one person representing a constituency of 500,000. As a result, society's political apparatus has grown distant from the people, and more and more sociopolitical functions are lodged in the hands of policy personnel or bureaucratic officials. Thus a gap emerges between the elected official and the appointed official, a gap that once again adds to the strain on the liberal ethic of every man counting as one. Such an ethic rests heavily on a town hall doctrine of visible elites performing visible tasks. The emergence of antiliberalism—at least as a systematic arrangement— coincides with the enormous growth of technology, large-scale factories, assembly-line production, and the like. When the individual, in fact, counts for less than does the running of a society, the very emphasis on bureaucratic efficiency sets in motion all sorts of potentialities for anomie and alienation, thus also opening the way for the demise of classical liberalism.

In this same vein, liberalism as a classic doctrine rested not only on individualism but also on proprietary rights in a world of small-scale home-owners with small-scale plots of land. The individual's value to the social system was determined, in part, by the value of his property. The erosion of property as a source of wealth—at least as the main source of wealth—and the emergence of commodity goods as the key to the creation of new wealth, removed a major underpinning of the older liberal ethic. The shift from small-scale property to industrial capitalism was itself a main factor in the change in the nature of liberalism (cf. McClosky, 1969).

But if liberalism suffered as a result of the displacement of property relations by industrial relations, it gained at another end—at the sociological end. It opened up vast new channels of mobilization and participation in the social system for the nonpropertied person. The extension of the educational apparatus became the key to upward mobility. It raised a question not of birth, but of performance—and beyond that, introduced the notion that competence rather than excellence was the essential criterion in an achievement society.

Robert Paul Wolff (1968:149) shrewdly points out that contemporary liberalism is more than merely a ritual preference for the middle of the road: "It is a coherent social philosophy which combines the ideals of classical liberalism with the psychological and political realities of modern pluralistic society." Wolff goes on to state the social purposes served by a pluralistic liberalism in America.

> It eased the conflict among antagonistic groups of immigrants, achieves a working harmony among the several great religions, diminishes the intensity of regional oppositions, and integrates the whole into the hierarchical federal political structures inherited from the founding fathers, while at the same time encouraging and preserving the psychologically desirable forces of social integration which traditional liberalism tended to weaken (Wolff, 1968:149–150).

A number of commentators have seen the partial character of liberalism, or better, its failure to acknowledge the possibility of the wholesale reorganization of society. Wolff makes this point with telling effectiveness.

> Pluralism is humane, benevolent, accommodating, and far more responsive to the evils of social injustice than either the egoistic liberalism or the traditional conservatism from which it grew. But pluralism is fatally blind to the evils which afflict the entire body politic, and as a theory of society it obstructs consideration of precisely the sorts of thoroughgoing social

revisions which may be needed to remedy those evils. Like all great social theories, pluralism answered a genuine social need during a significant period of history. Now, however, new problems confront America, problems not of distributive injustice but of the common good. We must give up the image of society as a battleground of competing groups and formulate an ideal of society more exalted than the mere acceptance of opposed interests and diverse customs (Wolff, 1968:161)

It is interesting to note the degree to which discussion of twentieth-century liberalism seems inevitably centered on the United States. The locus of political experimentation has shifted from England, the model of classical liberalism, to the United States, the locus of pluralistic liberalism. And in the shift is also the transformation of liberalism from a political doctrine of ruling through consensus, to a sociological doctrine of accommodating through interest-group determinations. And while it is proper to note that the core problem of liberalism has shifted from law (distributive justice) to economy (the common good), none of the critics has thus far indicated what a better society would look like. For nearly all the critics of liberalism are themselves liberals, or at least antitotalitarians, and this very fact indicates that if liberalism is in deep trouble, its critics are in no less of a bind in coming up with a social system that "works" better.

In an American social order in which everyone counted as one, competence was sufficient; excellence was viewed as an elite importation. Liberalism underwrote the idea of upward mobility with a corollary idea: that all men can do just about all jobs, given half an opportunity; they may not be able to do the job brilliantly or perfectly, but they can do it competently. And in this way, education became a touchstone of the new liberalism—the nonproprietary type.

What has shaken the roots of American liberalism is that the very fact of mass education in the achieving society has created once again a search for distinctness and difference, or an attempt to get beyond competence and once again into something unique. What this has meant is a return to concepts of property—this time, in the form of suburbia and the anti-urban patterns of living. Beyond that, it has also meant the return of ethnicity, race, and all the other demarcations of a special sort that set people apart from each other and that are not subject to egalitarian definitions or educational mobility. Thus, the challenge to the new liberalism is not so much the massification of society as its mythification. The desperate search for individuation in a mass society has taken a distinctively nonliberal turn, and the new ways of racialism and ethnicity certainly demonstrate this fact.

The emergence of a system of checks and balances and the extent of activity caused by educational mobility introduced a further refinement in the liberal credo, namely the notion of institutional autonomies—or what has since come to be known as pluralism, in which religion, education, legislation, and the like, all coexist in harmonious balance, and in which every person can participate—whether he is a member of the Parent Teachers Association or a member of a professional society. The very plethora of voluntary associations in America seems to under-write an era of good will—an era in which pluralism and liberalism became fused into a single uniform doctrine.

In point of fact, examples of this do abound for a society of a plurality of organizational forms and differential memberships. But what has taken place simultaneously to deprive liberalism of its glorious victory is a fusion of economic, political, and military institutions. Whether or not one adheres to a doctrine of power elites, the concentration of power and the disproportionate role played by economic and military institutions has prejudiced the liberal faith in educational, religious, and social institutions. This is to say that pluralism exists but that it exists within a larger context of the concentration of vast powers, directed to areas totally apart from and outside the liberalist notions of mobility and success.

The liberal position shares one fundamental tenet with conservative views of terms of law and order: faith in the concept of authority, in the internalized, individualized expression of wants and needs in behalf of the legitimacy of those who hold power.

Liberalism exists within a pluralistic mosaic where power exists—but only because it is fair in its execution. And in a world where every man does count as one, and where every man does hold property, and where every man does vote—such a system of authority can indeed be said to have prevailed.

What took place is the rise of the delegitimation process along with the mass society itself; the reliance on force and violence rather than rational decision-making—both by those who are the holders of power and those who contest such power—immediately changed the name of this social game from authority to power. The question of law was subsumed under a question of force, and the question of legislation became subsumed under the question of voting blocs and special-interest groups. In such a world, liberalism lost much of its clout, for the whole concept of liberalism as a juridical event rests upon a concept of benign participation and benevolence rooted in education and legislation and moderated by the consensus that prevails between those who rule and those who are ruled. In fact, liberalism never really admitted the existence of a gap between those who rule and those who are ruled, but rather presumed that all men ruled and all men are somehow ruled by others. The very breakdown of a system of balance, the very disequilibrium between the powerful and the powerless, rendered liberalism very weak—if not simply a rationale for the powerful. The hatred exhibited for liberals, from both the conservative and the radical sectors, in no small part stems from the unwillingness of liberalism itself to confront a system not based on harmonies and equalities, but rather on elites and masses, and ruled and rulers, and so forth.

Liberalism survives basically in a situation where long-range goals are feasible and where these goals can be actualized by a consensus apparatus. But to have long-range goals, one must presuppose a social system that can afford time, with fundamental agreements and only some disagreements restricted to tactical questions. To the contrary, radical and conservative doctrines tend to deny the existence of this long range and instead function in terms of a series of crises or the assumption of crises. They tend, therefore, to set up the ideal of immediate gratification and immediate reform, and in this sense, it is simply an empirical issue—whether, in fact, the society has a long time to survive and grow. For if it does, the capacity of liberalism is increased, but if it does not, its capacity is seriously reduced. To a considerable extent, the rise and fall of liberalism in America has to do with assumptions about the long-range viability of the American society itself. The heyday of liberalism coincides with assumptions of that long-range viability, specifically the whole of the nineteenth century, up until World War I. But in a century of total war and in a shrinking imperial system, this same liberalism yielded and buckled before conservative and radical thrusts.

The very items that made liberalism great in the past now cause it great anguish in the present. For liberalism was identified with open-ended theorizing, with evolution, and above all, with the goals of science and its products. All the shibboleths of science were linked into one network of fact and theory: evolution, industry, growth, progress, technology, and science itself. And all these had a ring of goodness that provided easy-to-demarcate signposts of growth, and each piece of evidence of new growth testified to the worth of liberalism itself.

Liberalism was cursed at the moment of its highest successes because the very artifacts produced by technology, and the very theories produced by science, were seen to be at least as destructive of human impulse and human goodness as they were creative. That is to say, the ability to creat mass annihilation, based upon the systematic use of science and technology, was a shocking illustration of the gulf between science and society, between the goods that men produced and the uses to which they were put.

Mills (1963:187–195) outlined five assumptions of liberalism that made this ideology a force in the past, but that as a result of the changed social structure of American society make it no longer viable. First, liberalism assumed a coalescence of freedom and security that tears apart when security no longer is assumed to rest on small holdings, but rather on big absentee ownership—the very sort of ownership that has as its asking price personal freedom. Second, it assumed the preeminence of rural areas and rural values, and this has simply been outstripped by the growth of centralized cities. Third, it assumed the autonomous development of political, social, and economic factors, factors that in the present have been melted and blended. Fourth, it assumed that individualism is the seat of rationality, but the growth of a bureaucratic organization of knowledge had led to the buying and selling of knowledge as a collective community. Fifth, liberalism assumed a ready identification of the holders of power and authority; and it is precisely this that has become difficult to locate and explicate.

But Mills' most telling point is that liberalism, long opposed to Marxism for its severance of means and ends, has simply reversed matters and divested ends from means.

> Liberalism, as a set of ideals, is still viable, and even compelling to Western men. That is one reason why it has become a common denominator of American political rhetoric; but there is another reason. The ideals of liberalism have been divorced from any realities of modern social structure that might serve as the means of their realization. Everybody can easily agree on general ends; it is more difficult to agree on means and the relevance of various means to the ends articulated. The detachment of liberalism from the facts of a going society make it an excellent mask for those who do not, cannot, or will not do what would have to be done to realize its ideals (Mills, 1963:189).

The most telling weakness in liberalism is a consequence of the gap between science and society. Many of its theorists, from James to Dewey to today's liberal voices, assume automatically that the spirit of science is good and that the spirit of liberalism is scientific. But the clear and obvious demonstration that all social systems, fascist or communist, can make use of basic science and can maintain a network of scientific programming and planning sent shock waves into the liberal world. It made evident that the canons of science do not automatically translate themselves into canons of liberalism. And the recognition of this fact, whether it be through the camp at Auschwitz or the bombs of Hiroshima and Nagasaki, ended once and for all the liberal monopoly on science and instead created the possibility of a scientific monopoly of liberalism.

Lowi's (1969:288–314) four counts against the liberal ideology, followed by three counts against its pluralistic rationalization, constitute perhaps the most succinct and damaging indictment delivered thus far. As such, they deserve extensive statement:

> (1) Interest-group liberalism as public philosophy corrupts democratic government because it deranges and confuses expectations about democratic institutions. Liberalism promotes popular decision-making but derogates from the decisions so made by misapplying the notion to the implementation as well as the formulation of policy.
>
> (2) Interest-group liberalism renders government impotent. Liberal governments cannot plan. Liberals are copious in plans, but irresolute in planning. Nineteenth-century liberalism was standards without plans. This was an anachronism in the modern state. But twentieth-century liberalism turned out to be plans without standards.
>
> (3) Interest-group liberalism demoralized government because liberal governments cannot achieve justice. . . . They cannot achieve justice because their policies lack the sine qua non of justice—that quality without which a consideration of justice cannot even be initiated.
>
> (4) Finally, interest-group liberalism corrupts democratic government in the degree to which it weakens the capacity of government to live by democratic formalisms. Liberalism weakens democratic institutions by opposing formal procedure with informal bargaining. Liberalism derogated from democracy by derogating from all formality in favor of informality.

By far the most interesting criticism of liberalism is contained in the third and fourth points. Liberalism has long held that the trouble with most theories of power is that they denigrate or simply ignore the forms of judicial review upon which power is checked by the will of the majority. Here, however, we find Lowi saying that liberalism, by reducing laws to a series of informal norms and interest-group balancing acts, is little else than a veiled form of power concentration theory. The difficulty with this argument is that Lowi is forced into the position that conservatism alone is the defender of the legal framework and the formal polity. But precisely this position serves to blunt partially, if not entirely to compromise, Lowi's radicalism; since at the very least, radicalism is no more concerned with the preservation of the legal edifice than is liberalism.

The criticisms that Lowi offers of the pluralist component in liberalism seem more telling. They reduce to three interrelated propositions (Lowi, 1969:249–296):

(1) The pluralist component has badly served interest-group liberalism by propagating and perpetuating the faith that a system built primarily upon groups and bargaining is perfectly self-corrective.
(2) Pluralism has failed to grapple with the problem of oligopoly or imperfect competition as it expresses itself in the political system.
(3) Finally, the pluralist paradigm depends upon an idealized and almost totally miscast conception of the group. Laissez-faire economics may have idealized the firm and the economic man but never to the degree to which the pluralist thinkers today sentimentalize the group, the group member, and the interests.

It is intriguing to note the extent to which all discussions of liberalism in America are linked to pluralism. And it is clear that it is precisely the difference between the old-fashioned analysis of whole systems and the new-fashioned analysis of situated actions within the system that demarcates European from American liberalism.

1972

11

American Radicalism and the Revolt Against Reason

The American sixties established a new radical element in society. And this has had a perplexing effect. In part, this is so because current radicalism resembles the *fin de siècle* nineties rather than the proletarian thirties. Most people concern themselves more with analogy than with history; hence the radical stance engenders profound doubt as its chief national byproduct. This is the first generation in American society, at least in this century, to combine political radicalism with philosophic irrationalism. As in the age of Sorel, reason has been displaced by passion. Without exaggerating the similarities between Western Europe in 1890-99 and the United States in 1960-69, it might be instructive to pay some attention to these comparisons. The social-science response to technology is to provide an awareness of demands for economic change without disregarding the classical sources of resistance to such change. The gap between the social sources of discontent and the political mechanisms to overcome such discontent has always been a uniquely important problem for radicals. To locate misery and special privilege is one thing; to establish a machinery for tranquility and equity is quite another. For this reason there are special periods marked by a high awareness of discontent and a low ability to remove the objective sources of conflict. The two periods under consideration share such characteristics.

There are roughly nine areas of marked similarity between French social thought in the nineties and the present period in American social life. Perhaps the most obvious, and for that reason elusive, is the stylistic similarity between the last decade of the French nineteenth century and the present decade of our American century. The current style of radicalism is abrasive, physical, impatient, and eclectic. It reflects a concern with the exercise of will over those objective forces that may exist in the world. But what is involved in the radicalism of the present generation as in that of the past is not simply a reemergence of humanism.

The assertion of the primary of the individual will over group interests assumes a strongly moralistic tone. The wills of individuals become objects to be mobilized into one total will. This moralistic style is a ready handmaiden to the "totalitarian democracy" that the historian Jacob Talmon spoke of. It is a fanatic attempt to impose a new social order upon the world, rather than to await the verdict of consensus-building formulae among disparate individuals as well as the historical Muses. Neither history nor humanism, allowing as they do for fragmenting diversity in decision-making and implementation, and for the egotistical needs of political elites, brings all men forward in a unified approximation of total and ideal good. But since without history there is no memory, the Good Myth is transformed into the Myth of the Good.

The emphasis on will is not simply an abstract stylistic response to determinism. Political life does not work in such mysterious ways. Quite the contrary: the answer to why the nineties of the past century and the sixties of the present century reveal striking similarities is the success of industrial capitalism—its ability, then as now, to provide a measure of affluence for a large portion of the citizenry, to integrate the overwhelming portions of the population into the going political system, and to provide multiple channels for expressing resentment, hostility, and special interests. Working-class mobilization into trade unions made nationalism a viable factor in the conduct of World War One; when the chips were down, being German or French counted for more than being a member of the working class. The continued ability of trade unionism to satisfy working-class demands has set up a condition in which class politics, at least in world affairs, hardly exists in the United States. In short, the resurrection of Revolutionary Will, as an expression of the Social Myth, closely followed periods of solid economic achievement, rather than economic crisis, as was the case after the Depression of 1929. The asserted need for Myth shows an inverse correlation with the success of Reality.

In its more specific ideological form, the New Left and the *fin de siècle* Left are both revolts against Marxism as a scientific historiography, and its replacement with Socialism as a vision of the good society. As Sorel clearly perceived, Marxism combines the double strains of humanism and moralism along a horizontal axis, and history and action along a vertical line. He also perceived that the emergence of a victory of radicalism in the twentieth century would necessarily have to tread over the dry bones of the Marxist legacy. And if the decomposition of Marxism seemed to be a premature announcement in the form stated by Sorel, it must certainly seem so no longer. Within radical circles at present, there are continued discussions, not simply between "revisionism" and "orthodoxy," but between alternative options to Marxism no less than within Marxism. In this very fact, "orthodoxy" has been liquidated—not by a frontal assault on shaky tenets, but as Sorel said it would be—through the outflanking maneuvers of empirical science.

The victories that Marxism chalked up in the twentieth century were those that displayed the advantages of will over history. The pure Marxist celebration of determinism slowly ebbed—in the Russian Revolution of Vladimir Lenin in 1917, the Chinese Revolution of Mao Tsetung in 1949, the Cuban Revolution of Fidel Castro a decade later in 1959. These shared the thin silver thread of high leadership quality characteristic of an uncorrupted elite. The overall charisma both of movement and of men took charge. These three revolutions were not predetermined, nor even largely determined by the economic failures of capitalism. Rather, they came as grand spontaneous outbursts to execute the will of the revolution in the present, rather than to await the somber and spurious judgment of objective forces.

In this sense, the very victories attributed to the Marxist legacy were perhaps the most devastatingly undermining aspects of that legacy. Castro did more to destroy Marxian orthodoxy than had a century of anti-Marxist critics. The Sorelian vision that it was not necessarily Marxism as a whole, but Marxism as a deterministic system of science that was "decomposing" was to prove accurate. What remained in Marxism was the hard kernel of moral purpose. Precisely this same kind of attitude seems to underwrite the writings of present-day French revolutionists such as Régis Debray, one of the genuine cultural heroes of the contemporary American Left. A certain amount of naivete, indeed a skepticism about theory as such, seems almost charming in comparison to the rigors Marxists and would-be "students of Marxism" had to endure in the proletarian thirties, in the era of Communist ideological power in the West. The triumph of Marxism as a myth, as a guiding sense of political purpose, rather than Marxism as a blanket science of society, has come to characterize the present generation of the American Left. In this transformation from science to myth—as pretense if not as fact—nothing seems more clearly linked to the New Left as an ideology than the *fin de siècle* irrationalist doctrines of Bergson, Peguy, Le Bon, and this earlier liberation from the rigors of systematic theory.

What flows from this is a concept of will opposed to organization, as purity of conviction is opposed to stifling rationalism. Whether it be the Bourse du Travail or its modern counterpart, the Alinsky Street Corner Club, what seems especially and acutely characteristic is a suspicion of any firm organizational lines of authority as enhancing predetermined and unreal ends distinct from what it is that poor people care about.

There is a strong impulse toward anarchism in this feeling that any tightly knit organization will lead to severe negative repercussions. At present, as in the *fin de siècle* (particularly the work of Roberto Michels on the oligarchical tendencies of all organizational life), there is a strong negative assessment of the value of close organization for ultimate victory. Even in successful revolutions, such as those of China and Cuba, one notes the high degree of totalitarian control; and this socialist practice stands in marked contrast to radical theory. This may simply be a function of the continued survival of the men who made these revolutions. But even so, there is a growing recognition that the problem with revolutions is that they terminate. And the problem becomes: Now what?

The word "organization" is used more in connection with bureaucracy than to express the role of organization in the mobilization of men. But if organization is doomed, what then is the guide of the revolutionary cause? Here we come to the emphasis on will and on the person. The ambiguity left by Marx in this connection, namely, that men make history but that they do so only in ways prescribed by objective circumstances, is resolved by emphasizing the former proposition, that men make history, rather than the latter proposition, that they do so under certain objective circumstances. Phrases in the Cuban Revolution such as "to be a revolutionary, one must make a revolution" indicate the strong impulse toward the role of will. Activism of the self-fulfilling prophecy type is characteristic of the present Left generation. It is precisely what one finds as the main line of development in the work of Sorel and his colleagues.

The assertion of the primacy of will over organization has beneath it an assumption of the prime importance of the person over politics per se. The question for radicals is not simply one of organization or bureaucracy, conditions that are often times discussed simply as negative consequences of the revolution. The main question is the value of political organization in the life of society. Political organization and legitimizing formulas break down, requiring restructure by reform or revolution.

Breakdowns devalue politics because they subject people to one pessimistic outcome after another, to one political scheme and ad hoc supportive apparatus after another.

Political pessimism tended to isolate Sorel from the euphoria of Socialist Party activities of the late nineteenth century, just as it does the contemporary New Left from the dreary vertigo of political party life of the Communist Party in this decade. This discouraging cycle could be broken by maintaining the people's spontaneity, allowing them to function as individuals, united by social feelings and common interest and not obstructed by "pulse-feeling" political mechanisms. Persons associate collectively more stably and satisfactorily through cultural commonalities than by adhering to the political requirements of an organized party. The guerilla movement offers a magnetic model of the transformation of radicalism from a rational to a romantic doctrine precisely because military insurgency offers a style of life free from organized political machinations. Unity is achieved through a common youth culture: savage passion, idealism, thinking in terms of goals rather than interests—these define the "new politics" of the New Left.

To the various charges and criticisms that this emphasis on personal will and opposition to the objectivity of history leads to an irrational society relying ultimately on terror to maintain itself and on a bureaucracy to perform its tasks, the response is remarkably similar in both Sorelian literature and the writings of the contemporary New Left. Basically, the answer given is that therapy is more important than victory. Orientation overrides achievement. Passion and meaning in struggle are more valuable than material accomplishment. Since bureaucracies favor the latter over the former, it is necessary to destroy them periodically in order for the more important commitments to reign supreme. This is more vital than any specific victory of the revolution, since: a) the ultimate contours of a future society cannot be predicted, and b) the victory of the revolutionary factions oftens turns sour precisely because of the failure of its advocates to define a psychology or therapy adequate to the task of restoring purpose to human endeavors.

This therapeutic concern linked men like Sorel with their latter-day "revisionist" counterparts, such as Adam Schaff and Herbert Marcuse. The main idea is simple enough. The purpose of revolution is to create a society better than the existing society. On the other hand, given the fact that few warranties can be made that what is desired will, in effect, come about, the more proximate goal of revolution-making is the therapeutic values that can be instilled in its participants, the revolutionists themselves. Therefore the true change or the essential condition for dramatic change comes not with the triumph of one class over another, or the victory of one nation over another, but rather with the victory that each individual gains in the act of revolutionary performance. This feature of Sorelianism is perhaps the most deeply felt, if not necessarily understood, by the present era of the New Left.

The individualism and intense personalism both of the Sorelian nineties and the present radical sixties prevented the notion of political bureaucracy from becoming too entrenched in each society. But these two movements did even more than that. They helped both societies to confront the radical notion of the mass over and against the socialist idea of class. Such a radicalism seeks a way to describe the nongoverning elements in society in terms conveying their potential unity rather than their fragmented group identity. By focusing on the common features rather than the disruptive details, one is better able, in the absence of the organization normally required to coordinate disparate groups, to promote social unification.

The language of "mass" confronting "elite" is elemental and conducive to moral passion over analysis of various modes of group domination or interaction. The idea of the mass, fuzzy as it would have seemed to the orthodox Marxist, appeared to have many advantages. Above all, it allowed the spiritualization of politics, a salvationary Great Leader able to communicate directly with all people, without the obstructions of class identities to militate against such communication. The faith in the idea of the mass provided a radical glow to what otherwise may have appeared to be intensely individualistic and excessively conservative zeal for the Great Man. The mass is most purely itself without an urban overlay. Sorel emphasizes the pastoral values, the industrial or the high potential of the peasantry for drastic revolution and social change. This is so because they retain an untarnished popular character and represent the real essence of Oppressed Man. Oppressed man is no mere proletariat. He may be a French peasant, a Roman Catholic leftist, a member of an ethnic minority, or a radical cluster. This commonality is a social principle, the herd instinct in social life, a factor making for contact between groups. Leaders are actually intensified cases of what is true for all men, bringing out this elemental collective character. To lead the mass no "vanguard" organization would do. The intelligent, courageous apaches alone symbolize the mass personality. Only they can concentrate their energies and liberate the herd.

Those who endow historic responsibilites upon a "class" and charge men with enough analytic understanding and rational power to read historical law are declared the new utopians—even more contemptible than the original utopians— since they lack even the earlier vision of a good society. The Marxist hero is a teacher-organizer on behalf of the historical law which he is required to unfold. He is a leading strategist of class war and imposes organization to win that war, to fulfill a class responsibility and destiny for social reorganization. But to irrationalist leftism, he is merely preparing another class elite for rule, failing to touch the real wellsprings of unity among men; he is in the Sorelian vision, which has become a New Left shibboleth, a victim of the revolution he serves.

Along with the idea of mass and the ambiguities of stratification as a mandate for revolution and behavior, there is the notion of conspiracy and the direct involvement of the person in the revolutionary process. The notion of conspiracy is raised by Sorel as it is in the sixties not so much as an explanatory device for evaluating political problems, nor as a cynical response to the world. Rather, working with the idea of conspiracy meant that politics would be a consciously shaped process. When shaped by men acting against mass interests, deceit is a valuable political instrument. But then too, by deft moves the holders of power can have their policies quickly undone and can be brought to understand the errors of the conspiratorial theory in an effort to explain corruption but also to provide rapid solutions to it.

Fire can be met with fire. A conspiracy at the top can, under certain conditions, be toppled by a conspiracy from below. Popular insurrection can counter elite conspiracy. If elite conspiracy is supported by technology, particularly by computer devices for the control and maintenance of information about all actors in a political system, it can be overthrown by a popular conspiratorial resort to technology, that of weaponry, firearms. If rulers conspire to deceive and solidify power by technological means, the unruly apaches, acting for the people, can conspire to undo them and can make themselves effective by means of violence.

This generation has seen the removal of moral restraint from political action in the same proportion as the political legitimation of the established system has lost its effectiveness. The novel element in the political equation is not so much violence then, as the emphatic sense of finally being liberated from inherited "bourgeois" restraints on both thoughts and actions.

This neo-Marxist use of conspiratorial theory ascribes to rulerships a characteristic manageable by popular means, even better than that, by a few actors representing a mass interest. Conspiracy can explain politics as a volitional network not subject to "inherent laws," a structure upon which will can act, and, at times, act rapidly and decisively, and may produce extraordinary results. Any young person can enter into a conspiracy rapidly enough; whereas electropolitics requires long-term visibility and mobilization. Conspiratorial politics is oftentimes extralegal politics, whereas electropolitics tends to be politics made, as well as defined, by lawyers. In this special sense, the politics of the 1960s like those of the 1890s were anti-intellectual in that the focus was not on the forms of victory and not on the quality of candidate, but rather on the substance of revolutionary conflict no matter how ugly or brutish the participating individuals or groups may have been in terms of their social ethic or personal style. The fact that electropolitics always seems to lead to something less than a full-scale resolution of the problems of industrial society, and in fact, often stimulates a heightened degree of cooptation of newly mobilized social sectors, leads one to suspect that advocates of conspiracy theories are more concerned with providing a sophisticated antiseptic to those who participate in electropolitics than they are necessarily concerned with the goals of conspiracy.

It is not necessarily the manifest display of raw courage that characterizes the nineties and the sixties—because there are kinds of violence such as imperialist wars that are looked upon with great disdain by radicals of both epochs—rather it is the personal absolution that one finds in the art of politics and the act of conspiracy that becomes important. This links up directly with the therapeutic values of politics rather than any objective goals that might be said to derive from political participation. In this sense, conspiracy theory like political therapy functions as a hedge against personal immorality. This deep fear of the political process as a corrupting element runs deep in the Left from Sorel to Marcuse and Goodman; and it also serves to distinguish liberal political goals from radical social goals.

Even before Trotsky, Sorel formulated the idea of the permanent revolution. He did so, however, not for the purpose of opposing an oppressive bureaucratic structure resulting from a totalistic revolution, but rather to allow for the fact that the quest for change inheres in men and society. Even the best revolution consecrated to any single cause creates a basis for reaction and counterrevolution. It was necessary to conceptualize a means that would allow for change yet not undo the revolutionary victory won at the start. Pioneer socialists, "Utopian" and "Scientific," and even the Russian Bolsheviks who followed them, have tried to deal with revolution as an objective phenomenon, and as such subject to process and change.

In early Marxism and in Bolshevism alike, there is a shared assumption that material changes give rise to spiritual alterations in personality. The latter needs to keep up with the facts of the former. In this way it is claimed that socialism remains scientific and that the basis of socialist man becomes a perpetually revolutionary one. But in the *fin de siècle* interlude, certainly in the time of Sorel's criticisms of "scientific" Marxism, the mood was one of disenchantment with socialist promise, a search for its renewal. It was, in effect, a time when the demand was made that socialist man make an appearance irrespective of a socialist productive base; and a willingness to speculate that maybe only some protosocialist man could create a socialist base. *Fin de siècle* radicalism called for a reversal of causal estimates. A victory in the realm of psychology could take place despite what was occurring in the old, corrupt social order. Nor should this be thought of as simple impatience with history or the vagaries of social change. It became a matter of principle that a special kind of person was required to initiate revolutionary changes.

On this particular point the Sorelian idea links up dramatically with the neo-Marxism of the sixties, a phenomenon that has also weathered disenchantment with old Marxist modes and apologetics, and with its organizational rationalism of the thirties. It too makes assumptions that the purity of personality, the change of life styles, or the redemption of humanity could each arise irrespective of the nature of the political order. The transforming effect of sheer conviction was the new key. The very corruption of the old social order, whether or not it can be adjudicated, whether or not it can be reformed, should not limit the possibilities for personality development. Thus a renewed theoretical emphasis on will derives largely from this desire to bring about a revolution in the psychology of men as a precondition for a revolution in society. And this meant in practice the liberation of radicalism from its own past taboos—sexual as well as political.

Like the *fin de siècle,* the radicalism of the sixties is a reassertion of the priorities of egotism over socialism. For both, the body has a large vote. The main constituency of any social movement is the self. In this special sense, that portion of the New Left most attuned to the Sorelian moral vision are the so-called "hippies" or "street people," who, like Sorel, claim a powerful antipolitical standpoint as a necessary basis for any psychological redemption or moral purification. Antipolitics becomes the essential demonstration effect through which the psychological condition of individuals can be cleansed. Politics as candidacy and advocacy is, like Puritanism, a "hang-up" to be overcome and not a system to be worked.

The final point is also directly linked to the concept of the worth of individual personality. It took the form of a direct assault on the bureaucratic ethos, the administrative style as a feature of all organizations. It is almost as if the individual, by his nature, contained a built-in resistance to organizational life, fearing its capacity to limit and circumscribe human behavior. The assault on bureaucracy, then, was not simply a reflection of antipolitics, either in the *fin de siècle* or in the swinging sixties, but the result of a belief that acquiescence brings about impotence. The stultifying aspects of bureaucracy are widely known by liberals and populists of every sort. The point of difference for revolutionary leftists is that since bureaucracy is an inevitable outcome of maintaining all social revolutions that abolish caretaker classes, it can itself become a conservative and even backward agency unless men work to prevent this from occurring. The permanent revolution, therefore, has as its goal not only the salvation of personality, but primarily its preservation from the effects of the organizational necessities of modern industrial society.

The similarities between the 1890s and the 1960s include the common belief that the revolutionary struggle is not between liberalism and conservatism but between radicalism and liberalism. The assumption is that under reformist pressures some variant of liberalism characterizes official politics. To revolutionize society it is necessary to combat the limitations of liberalism, now associated with official rules. Liberalism reigns in government. It has thus become a force against revolutionary change. It must be reconsidered in view of its new role as an impediment to further social development. Liberalism does not then stand for a way of behaving politically, a mode of creative pragmatism. It is, rather, a ruling and now corrupt conviction.

The ferocity of the assault Sorel launched against the liberalism of his own age is thus theoretically as well as practically induced. For it was liberalism that became identified with the stultifying effects of reason and rationalized organization in society. It was therefore a challenge to liberalism rather than a challenge to knowledge per se that moved men like Sorel to an antirationalist posture.

This is also largely true of the modern Left movement, which came about not so much as an attack on the world of ideas as an attack on the idea that reason is the only mode of knowing. The suspicion is that reason is an ideology that teaches us to stand in the middle of two extremes, unable to act. This identification of liberalism with a spirit of judiciousness and prudence is what continues to make liberalism, at least at the psychological level, the main target for radical jibes. It was the spirit of legitimation and juridical order itself that came under severe attack and reprimand. To attack the legitimation system of the modern Western world was to attack the ideology of that system—which had become and which remains the liberal ideology—an ideology no less elitist because of its tenets than was the conservatism it replaced.

In noting major similarities linking the European 1890s to the American 1960s, at least from the point of view of what was going on in the world of radical behavior and radical thought, we must not forget that there are powerful and significant dissimilarities between these two periods as well. These ought not to go unnoticed if only for the light they may shed on the relationships between the two eras.

First, the Sorelian *fin de siècle* vision was one in which the peasant and proletarian masses were to become the spearhead of any revolutionary change. Sorel's class feeling firmly underlay his mass concept and remained committed to a Marxism, or at least a Bakuninism, which allowed the notion of revolution to take place outside a proletarian vanguard of "organizers." Sorel's vanguard retained psychological propensities to violence and irrationality, which did not necessarily correlate with the stratification system. Nonetheless, the lower classes were to serve as the necessary agency of revolutionary change.

This is obviously not the case for much of the New Left. The new vanguard group, far from being the factory proletariat, is probably the educated sector of society most removed from the processes of production. In point of fact, current radicals are partially composed of groups Sorel and his colleagues considered corrupt, namely, the educated classes. This is largely because American politics is structured to assimilate generational surge as a source of change, its class structure being flexible enough to absorb such pressures. Generational discontinuity and discontent displaces class discontent because classes in American society are plugged into some scheme for sharing in the national wealth and supporting national symbols.

In an individualistic, competitive environment demanding specialized skills as a precondition for participation and advantage, the young are disadvantaged by the system to the extent of challenging it. The challenge may become simply another formula for including new groups or a revolutionary alternative to the system. It thus becomes the young who are most difficult to assimilate and who are most readily alienated. The young become a chief source of challenge and innovation.

The second characteristic stamp of the present generation shows a breakdown in these distinctions between political marginality, revolutionary, and deviant behavior. Hero types are no longer proletarian or productive. They are virile, savage, angry, akin to a popular image of the black, the isolated youth. The educated have lost the tradition of lionizing the productive labors of worker and peasant. It is more important that hero types show authentic inner turmoil, political convictions unmitigated by the complexities of a relativistic and thus immobilizing education. As liberal, middle-class Left elements have moved away from achievement orientations (simply because their parents left precious little to "achieve"), they have lost a radical idealization of earthy labors and have instead idealized poverty as a "way of life." The poor were said to create superior conditions for cooperative community, for ethnic communication, and for personal identity. Class models for reorganization have yielded to racial-ethnic models. The radical young feel charged to revive these values and have, in effect, connected the "culture of poverty" with generational rebellion. Moreover, the "swinging style" of poverty "cultures," such as the black and Puerto Rican, has a natural appeal to those youth searching out an uncluttered life style.

A third difference between *fin de siècle* radicalism and present-day varieties is that *fin de siècle* radicals had a strong military commitment—a commitment to the use of violence as a purifying act while also a necessary compensatory device for the disadvantaged who reveal a lack of political organization. Elements among the Left of the sixties are diffused in pacifist and activist directions. Attitudes toward class wars are as negative as those toward international conflict. Still, this is only partially characteristic of the New Left, which increasingly has taken a guerilla "line" on black violence. Whether the martial spirit will be sustained in the future and become completely characteristic is difficult to predict.

For the *fin de siècle* it was still possible to have a martial ethic linked to a socialist destiny. In an age of superweapons the display of armed heroes is menacing in proportion to the technological destructive power at their command. The same capacity to exercise a radical ideology over a large group of people now demands a commitment to the idea of pacifism or, at the least, to the notion of international peace.

The main differences, then, are not so much ideological as they are functional. Successful revolutions in Russia, China, and Cuba indicate that the dialogue of the nineties was concerned with what would yet come to be. The dialogue of the present radical generation must always start from the fact that socialist revolutions have in fact succeeded. They are capable of pointing to pragmatic successes much in the same ways and in the same areas of production as capitalism. Radicalism is thus subject to the kind of withering criticism Sorelians were spared, considering that the latter were concerned with the future and not with the defects of the accomplished socialist fact.

Our own decade may show a radicalism more in tune with the

irrational style than even that of the *fin de siècle.* The attack by the Left on society has become totalistic. It has joined political marginality to social deviance in ways thoroughly alien to Sorel and his age. It has become an attack on socialism as well as capitalism. It has become an attack on industrialism as well as agrarianism. It has become an attack on technological achievement no less than on those who would engineer the soul. This kind of assault is atypical and uncommon even for the most violent proponent of the Marxist vision—orthodox or revisionist.

Within an American context, it has indeed become simpler to argue a case for social radicalism as something apart from political revolution. In the *fin de siècle,* the case for radicalism and for revolutionary politics was still inextricably linked. This very linkage is now threatened by withdrawal of huge portions of the underclass population from legitimizing the behavior of public officials. The problem of compromise plagues the radicals more in the Swinging Sixties than in the Gay Nineties because accommodation has become the dominant motif of politics between nations no less than within a nation. This cannot easily be acknowledged, much less countenanced, by radical irrationalists.

What is to be found in the historical context is a coexistence over a long period of time between different social systems, their adaptations to each other and to unique circumstances. In other words, there has not been a historical displacement of one system by another, or one pure form of statecraft by another; rather there has occurred the crystallization of new mixtures. Many similar ideological starting points take different forms in different nations, inducing similarities and differences unforeseen by political leaders—such as the fact that bureaucratic socialism in an East European country may have as much in common with bureaucratic capitalism in a West European country such as France than either may have with the underdeveloped areas of the world.

The alienated sense of being extrinsic to power remains just as true for the New Left as it was for the Sorelian Left. Socialism and capitalism continue to coexist in peaceful disharmony. So too do radical and reactionary demands for violence coexist in a form not too far removed from its *fin de siècle* formulation. Fascism returns in the United States not as a right-wing ideology, but almost as a quasileftist ideology, an ironic outcome that Sorel anticipated in his own writings when he celebrated Mussolini and Lenin as if they were really two peas in one pod. A curious and bitter irony is that after two world wars and two additional undeclared world wars against underdeveloped nations, we have now come full cycle: the ideology of Left and Right have partially coalesced into a general assault on the present moment in history. Activism itself has become a style that is ironically neutral and employable by Left and Right. In the larger sense, all political behavior has become "extremist"—that the Left has partaken of this bitter feast is only a reflection of the larger failure of the American political culture to make a convincing case in the cynical world we inhabit.

1968

12

Capitalism, Communism, and Multinationalism

An advertisement in *The New York Times* (October 1, 1972), placed by the World Development Corporation, read as follows:

A well-known party is looking for revolutionary ideas. It may come as a surprise, but the communists are no longer claiming they've invented every good idea under the sun. On the contrary, they're eagerly hoping that Westerners may have invented a few before them. The fact is that the communists—in particular the East Europeans— are building a broad consumer society. They're in a hurry. And they're in the market for advanced technology in a staggering number of fields. The point is this: if you own the patented or proprietary technology that East European countries need, you could work out some highly profitable arrangements. Sell technology to the communists? Can it even be done? The answer is that today it finally can be done. And is being done. In fact, over the past couple of years, major American corporations have been doing it with increasing frequency. Naturally, the technology must be non-strategic. Exactly how do you go about it? You go about it with infinite patience. As you can imagine, selling American technology in Eastern Europe is a highly complex economic, political and technical problem. Obviously, it's absolutely crucial to develop the right contacts and the right communication. That's where we, World Patent Development Corp. come in. For years now, we've maintained close technological contacts with the proper governmental agencies in all East European countries. Because of our unique position, we've been able to locate markets and negotiate licensing agreements for the sale of almost every kind of technology.

Conversely, we're also presiding over the transfer of East European technology to the West. In fields ranging from synthetic copolymers to pollution control equipment. From advanced textile equipment to natural cosmetics.

This is a far cry from Cold War rhetoric; and helps place in perspective the obvious thaw *cum* rapprochement reached between Nixon and Kissinger for the American side and Brezhnev and Kosygin for the Soviet side. The emergence of the multinational corporation is the paramount economic fact of the present epoch and helps to explain current trends in the political sociology of world relations.

Research on multinational corporations is extensive and still mushrooming. At this point, the literature on multinationals constitutes something of a multinational enterprise unto itself, with a major annotated bibliography (Burtis, et. al., 1971), and a special issue of the American Academy of Political and Social Science (Blake, 1972) attesting to the popularity of this subject. Yet one aspect of multinationalism seems to me to be of considerable importance but has thus far been significantly underestimated. Orthodox economists have been busy focusing on the impact of multinationals on sovereignty, while radical theorists have been busy focusing on the impact of multinationals on underdeveloped areas. As a result, the extraordinary impact of the multinational corporation on relations between capitalist and socialist states has been largely ignored.

The overriding ideological posture of the twentieth century has been the Manichean struggle for supremacy between capitalism and communism. From this posture flows the utopian fantasy of the chief protagonists: that the struggle will be resolved by the conquest of communism and equality over capitalism and inequality. A further consequence has been the derivation of a counterutopian literature reversing good and evil, excoriating communism for creating a totalitarian nightmare that can only be halted by a total allegiance to democratic life as expressed at the present moment in Western history by the "West," a term serving as a banal euphemism for the capitalist nations.

Two real-life events of macroscopic proportions broke this ideological-utopian barrier: first, the rise of a Third World in Africa, Asia, and Latin America with the attendant pluralization of economic forms, political systems, and social doctrines; and second, the rise of multinational corporations primarily loyal to their own industrial growth and financial profitability, rather than to the nation of their origin. Multinationalism involves commitments that, whatever their intentions, have taken us beyond a model premised on a showdown struggle between old capitalism and new communism; or to use the oracular vernacular, classical democracy and modern totalitarianism.

The historical fact is that the phase of Third World nation-building that extended from 1945 to 1970 has now brought about a fully crystallized world system (Horowitz, 1972). More speculative and contentious, because it is of more recent vintage, is the function and role of the multinational corporaticns in this world system, and their impact on capitalist-communist dichotomous relations. It is curious, but a fact nonetheless, that despite the amount of information available on particular multinationals, little attention has been given to how this industrial phenomenon as a power unto itself affects the United States' relations with the Soviet Union, and by extension, the structure of capitalism and communism as competing world empires.

The Nature of Multinationalism

Definitions of the term "multinational corporation" vary. Recently, several works (Kindleberger, 1969; Bock and Fuccillo, 1972) have sought to distinguish between international, transnational, and supernational firms. But for our purposes, such taxonomies can be subsumed under the operational definition stated here. Nonetheless, for the most part, there is agreement on the following operational guidelines:

(1) Multinationals are corporations that operate is at least six foreign nations.

(2) Multinationals are corporations whose foreign subsidiaries account for at least 10 to 20 percent of its total assets, sales, or labor force.

(3) Multinationals have annual sales or incomes of more than 100 million dollars (which effectively reduces the number of firms we are dealing with to approximately 200, of which 75 percent are primarily affiliated with the United States).

(4) Multinationals have an above average rate of growth and profit margins when measured against exclusively national firms.

(5) Multinationals are found most often in high technology industries, specifically those that devote a high proportion of their resources to research, advertising, and marketing.

On the assumption that the term multinational may still be strange to some, let us try a simple definition: a multinational corporation is one that does a sizable portion of its business outside the borders of the nation in which it has its primary headquarters. One important argument against this definition is that multinationals are simply and historically an extension of the national corporation, doing business abroad. By that definition, nothing qualitative has changed, rather the volume of commodities sold abroad has increased. Here, multinationalism is viewed simply as imperialism by another name. The difficulty with this argument is that everything novel about the present situation is omitted for the sake of maintaining the myth of economic determinism.

It is true that the multinational is an old phenomenon that has achieved new dimensions in recent years. Many firms, like Singer Sewing Machines, National Cash Register, Unilever, General Motors, etc. have been conducting overseas business for many years; it is, however, the fusion of these older firms with more basic (in the sense of having the capacity to produce high-level technology) industrial firms, such as Xerox Corporation, International Business Machines, British Petroleum, Phillips of the Netherlands, International Nickel, etc., that has tipped the balance within them from national to international corporate participation. Since each of these giants of industry reveals annual sales that exceed the individual gross national product of all except several dozen nations, the political and economic power they wield is obviously potent, although highly diffuse.

What we witness now is more than old wine in a new bottle. That which is new about multinationals can be summarized as follows: firms that in the past maintained classical imperial relations, i.e., importing raw materials and exporting finished commodity goods at superprofits, have new arrangements. Now they share research and development findings and also patent rights distribution; manufacture in the economic periphery at lower costs rather than produce the same goods in the cosmopolitan center (which has the additional payoff of quieting nationalist opposition); develop profit-sharing arrangements between local firms and foreign firms, which involve training and tooling. Beyond that, one finds a reverse multinationalism, one based on raw materials rather than on finished goods. Thus, the oil-rich countries of the Arab Middle East form a bargaining collective to do business directly with major oil companies of the West. Thus there takes place bartering and bargaining between national governments, such as the Arab oil states joined by Venezuela, Iran, Nigeria, Indonesia, and other members of OPEC, with private sector multinationals like the powerful oil corporations of America and Western Europe (Tanzer, 1969; Adelman, 1970).

That which is new about the multinational is not simply the transcendence of the nation-state boundaries to do business, an old ploy of corporations in wealthy nations, but more profoundly, a reduction in profits through increased payment of high prices for raw materials (like petroleum) and the acceptance of lower prices and hence less profit for finished manufactured goods (such as automobiles). This is the aspect of multinationals that most sharply points to the need for a modification of classical and new forms of Marxism-Leninism alike, since the very essence of politics as a reflexive form of national and economic exploitation is exactly what is reversed. What we have now is economics as a reflexive form of political exploitation and domination. The connections and conflicts between the international economy and the national polity is of considerable intrinsic interest to the study of multinationalism; however, it is tangential for the purposes of this study. It also has the advantage of being perhaps the best research area in the field of multinational corporate analysis, thanks in no small part to the work of Raymond Vernon (1971) in calling attention to the impact of multinational corporations and national sovereignties. Other works which have taken up this issue that deserve attention are those of Eisenhower and Frundt (1972), and Bruyn (1972), both of which adopt a more radical stance than that of Vernon, but nonetheless raise the same fundamental set of considerations. For the specific impact of multinationals on United States foreign relations, see Ray, 1972:80–92.

The Buying of Western Capitalism by Eastern Socialism

The post-World War Two thrust of nationalism prevented any undue optimism about the ability of socialism to triumph as a world system and as an international ideology. Indeed, so intense did nationalist sentiments become in Third World areas of Asia, Africa, and Latin America that the Soviets, after much hesitation, had to readjust their policy and ideology and finally recognize a third way, something more than capitalism and less than socialism (Thornton, 1964); or in my own terms, a cross between a Keynesian economic mechanism and a Leninist political machinery. But in that act of recognition, the dream of an international proletarian revolution, with or without a Soviet vanguard, gave way to more parochial dreams of peoples' democracy and socialist republics that would no more dare try to transcend nationalist sentiments than would the older capitalist regimes in Western Europe. Between 1945 and 1970, the nationalist thrust profoundly diminished belief in a socialist utopia.

When internationalism finally did make its move, it did so in corporate rather than proletarian guise. The multinational corporation, pointing to an international brotherhood of the bourgeoisie and the bureaucracy, to a transcendent class loyalty considerably beyond the national aspirations of even the United States or any other principal capitalist social system, discredited the socialist utopia no less than had the earlier nationalist phase. For the multinational is a giant step toward an international economy no less remote from the socialist brotherhood than national socialisms. The multinationals offer a basket of commodity goods that the socialist states, no less than the Third World states, desire. The relative ease with which such multinationals of the capitalist sector penetrated the societies and economies of the socialist sector stands in marked contrast to the difficulties involved in concluding the most elemental treaty arrangements between East and West at the policy and political level. Doing things in a businesslike way has become as much a touchstone for rational efficiency in the Soviet Union as it is in the United States. The culture of multinationalism had reached Eastern Europe and the Soviet Union long before the actual economic penetration, with the mass consumer demands of the Soviet public following the Stalin period. It is plain to see, therefore, that multinationalism, like nationalism in an earlier era, has stymied the socialist utopia, at the very same time that it has improved the commodity conditions of the socialist nations.

One need only consider the extensive trade agreements reached between the United States and the Soviet Union in September 1972 to gauge the velocity and the extent of multinational penetration.

White House adviser Henry Kissinger, negotiating in Moscow between September 11 and 14, achieved substantial progress in trade talks with the Soviet Union. The White House got a report from Mr. Kissinger of a "great breakthrough" that could result in completing a broad multi-billion-dollar agreement with the Russians ahead of the original target date, the end of 1972. On September 14, the U.S. Department of Agriculture confirmed a private sale of 15 million bushels of American wheat to Communist China, the first to that nation in many years. A few days earlier, the Boeing Company announced sale of 10 of its 707 jetliners to the Red Chinese for 125 million dollars in cash. The chairman of Occidental Petroleum Corporation, Armand Hammer, said in Moscow on September 14 that details of the trade pact his firm had signed in June with the Soviet Union were being arranged. Among other things under consideration, said Mr. Hammer, were sales of chemical fertilizers and construction of a 70-million-dollar U.S. trade center in the Russian capital, complete with a 400-room hotel . . . reports from Moscow indicate that the overall trade agreement now being negotiated could increase business between the two countries to as much as 5 billion dollars a year by 1977. At present, U.S.-Russian trade amounts to about 220 million dollars annually. That figure, however, does not include around a billion dollars in purchases by the Russians of American grain in recent weeks. Still remaining to be resolved before final agreement on the overall trade pact was the issue of Lend-Lease debt owed the U.S. by Russia since World War II. The sticking point is said to be over the amount of interest due. Agreement also was reported near on a maritime pact that would guarantee to U.S. and Russian ships at least a one-third share each of the cargoes involved in the billion-dollar grain sale to Russia (*U. S. News and World Report,* October 1972).

The question then becomes: Can the Soviet Union maintain its basic commitment to *production development* rather than to *consumption modernization* in the face of foreign business penetration? Obviously the Russians and to a lesser degree the Chinese think the answer is yes. However, the inexorable logic of consumer orientations brings forth the argument that satisfying immediate needs of a social sector able to pay is more important than delaying such gratifications in favor of long-range goals of economic equality at home and certainly more important than fulfilling ambitious goals of national liberation abroad.

The political potential of multinationals, even those dominated by the United States, are revealed by their use in East European nations like Rumania and Hungary. One finds Pepsi Cola Corporation, Hertz Rent-a-Car Agencies, Pan American, and ITT-supported hotels in the center of Bucharest, and, of course, the most conspicuous multinationals in such a country are Western-dominated commercial airlines.

Joint marketing ventures are becoming increasingly popular. Production may take place at an Eastern plant, a Western plant or both concurrently. As a rule, the communist partner is alloted sales exclusivity in its own and in other Eastern markets, while the Western partner concentrates on the remaining territories. An example is an agreement under which the Simmons Machine Tools Company of Albany, New York, sells in the United States equipment manufactured by Czechoslovakia's Skoda.

A new class of contracts calls for one side to assist the other in markets (usually those of less developed countries) which happen to be more easily accessible to it for geographic, economic or political reasons. Hungary has helped to pioneer this particular method. Nikex, a foreign trade organization acting on behalf of a domestic enterprise, has contracted with the West German Rheinstahl group to co-produce semi-hydraulic mining equipment of a type which it has hitherto been importing. Manufacturing responsibility and local sales were assigned for five years to the Hungarian industrial enterprise. Nikex was given international distribution in Turkey and India (where bilateral treaties facilitate its access) and eventually in other foreign markets, when production outstrips demand. The West German firm has undertaken to supply all necessary technical aid as well as special parts, castings and equipment.

Joint efforts in the service industries offer exceptional latitude for foreign management and profit participation. A significant straw in the wind is the willingness of Russia's Intourist travel agency to rent automobiles under a royalty remunerated Hertz franchise. Avis is not too far behind in other East European regions.

In 1967, Intercontinental Hotels Corporation, a fully-owned subsidiary of Pan American Airways, in conjunction with Tower International, a company controlled by the Cyrus Eaton group of Cleveland, entered into agreements for the construction and operation of luxury hotels in Hungary, Rumania and Czechoslovakia. The Western firms are assisting with design, construction, personnel training, supervision, bookings and, above all, finance (interestingly enough obtained in part from the Soviet-owned Moscow Narodny Bank in London). An important aspect of the agreements is a license to use the Intercontinental name as a magnet for foreign tourists. Compensation is akin to, and in many respects better than a profit participation, namely, a percentage of the hotels' gross, hard currency receipts over a term of years, payable in convertible funds free of withholding taxes (Pisar, 1970:352–353).

Such firms, doing business on a licensing basis in East Europe, open up channels of communication to the West. And if the socialist republic's dependence on the Soviet Union is lessened symbolically more than in reality, it nonetheless has the effect of displaying the physical presence of the West in Eastern Europe. Beyond that, it permits higher numbers of international conferences at which Westerners participate and interact with participants from China and the Soviet Union. In short, the multinational firm encourages a country like Rumania to strive to become a Switzerland of the East Socialist bloc; a place where Israelis, Albanians, Russians, and Chinese meet freely and to the greater benefit of the open-ended socialist regime. In such a context, for one to speak of the corrupting influence of multinationals is to rave like a Puritan Divine against autonomy. In the East European setting, national sovereignty is strengthened not weakened by the existence of the multinational corporations. This is, of course, at considerable variance with the impact of multinationals in a Western European context. For example, the combined power of Dutch multinationals (Royal Dutch Shell, Unilever, KLM Airlines, Phillips) is much stronger in the Netherlands than the government and its various agencies. Indeed, Holland shows how national sovereignty can be weakened rather than strengthened by multinationalism.

Vernon (1971:259) has indicated his own belief that labels of socialism will do as much to promote as to dissuade multinationals from penetrating the socialist and Third World sphere.

The fact that many less-developed countries associate themselves with some form of socialism needs no detailed documenting. The number may even have increased somewhat in the course of time. It is not clear, however, just what that espousal means for the role of the multinational enterprise. During recent years, several genuinely socialist countries have been exercising enormous ingenuity to find a way of assigning a role to foreign-owned enterprises in their economies. The Yugoslavs, of course, have moved furthest in this direction; by 1970, foreign-owned enterprises were in a position to negotiate for rights that were the de facto equivalent of those available in such nonsocialist states as Mexico or Brazil.

Many other less-developed countries—for example, Pakistan, Tunisia, and Iraq—though committed to socialism of some sort, have nevertheless cultivated a certain deliberate ambiguity over the future position of multinational enterprises in their economies. As India edges her way toward national identification with socialism, it is not at all clear that the country's policies toward foreign investors will grow any more restrictive. Besides, the actual shift of less-developed countries toward state ownership of the means of production has not been irrevocable—witness the cases of Indonesia and Ghana. Neither is it clear that the countries that do not yet see the future in these terms will eventually make the shift. Mexico, with her abiding coalition of local big business, bureaucracy, and a single party of ambiguous ideology, seems as likely a model as Guinea; Yugoslavia, with her bent for improvisation and pragmatism, seems no less likely a model of the future than Cuba.

The idea of a single world market has so deeply permeated Soviet socialism that the USSR is now in the position of accepting as part of its own economic codebook the rules on any given day of the much reviled free market economy. The recent "wheat deal" between the superpowers indicates an increasing sophistication by Soviet "business" in precisely these areas of market management and manipulation. The Soviets sent forth twenty buying teams to negotiate independent of one another and also without any apparent overall coordination. But of course, it was the existentially a high level of commercial orchestration that enabled the USSR in one fell swoop to fulfill an agrarian internal need for wheat, and buy a surplus amount at a low cost for resale on the world market at a high profit. The Soviets in this way have become part of the "paper economy"—for the wheat deal involves the movement of money no less than the transfer of a basic crop.

The Soviets have done as well in the area of natural gas as in wheat negotiations. In 1966, they negotiated with Iran to purchase gas that had previously been flared off in the fields because there was no market for it at that time. In turn, the Iranians received Soviet financing and assistance to construct the necessary pipelines and associated equipment as well as a steel mill. While the Iranians gained a valuable steel plant, the Soviets began negotiating its sale of the Iranian gas to both East and West European nations. These deals culminated in sales equal to the total Iranian gas supply. The Soviet purchase price from Iran for the natural gas was 19 cents per thousand cubic feet, while its sale price was nearly double that price, or 37 cents. This deal, profitable as it was to the Soviets, was equally advantageous for the United States, who, without this gas arrangement, would have had to pay 87 cents per thousand cubic feet to Algeria for such gas purchases, or similarly high prices to Middle East nations in the proximate future. (Vinnedge, 1972:558–559). The rise of sophisticated multinational dealings across East-West boundaries clearly services the major powers at the expense of Third World nations.

The following observation in a new text on business internationalism makes clear this new source of Soviet commercial management.

> As computer communications technology continues to advance it seems quite likely that a single world market for shares of corporations will emerge. Ultronics, a subsidiary of General Telephone and Electric, recently teamed up with Reuters to organize a world-wide system providing price quotes on corporate shares and commodities. At present the system is operational in Europe and covers some 10,000 stocks and commodities. Stock exchanges included are Dusseldorf, Frankfurt, Hamburg, Munich, London, Amsterdam, Milan and Zurich. Outside Europe, there are *Stockmaster* subscribers in Hong Kong, Beirut and Latin America. Japan and Australia are also subscribers. Even the Soviet government has toyed with the idea of subscribing to *Stockmaster* in Moscow. The result of this information becoming available globally is the gradual emergence of a single world market for securities (Brown, 1972:228–229).

Borrowings by the Soviet Union and the Comecon Nations (Council for Mutual Economic Assistance) are done almost exclusively in the Eurodollar market of Europe. American lenders account for a considerable portion of this amount. Hard currency indebtedness of Comecon nations to Western banking interests has soared in the era of détente. By 1974 the totals owed were 22.5 billion dollars. The size of the Soviet economy and its gold reserves make the Communist nations a "safe" investment. Soviet and Comecon interest payments buoy Western banking capitalism; while such loans in hard currency buy technology for Eastern communism.

What we have then is the emergence of huge trading blocs that regulate relationships between East and West. The increasing concentration of capital in the West permits a movement from multinational corporation to an interrelated fiscal network that readily connects up to the Soviet interrelated fiscal network.

The Selling of Eastern Socialism to Western Capitalism

The fundamental antagonism within the socialist bloc has been the development of an industrial society without a corresponding modernized society. The Soviet Union can mount trips to outer space, but cannot satisfy consumer demands for automobiles; it can launch supersonic jet aircraft, but cannot supply the accoutrements of personal comfort to make such travel enjoyable. It can mass-produce military hardware, but cannot individualize stylistic consumer components. In every aspect of socialist society, the duality between industrialism and modernism has emerged as a central factor. In this, the socialist sector is the opposite of the Third World, where modernization is purchased at the cost of development; where production is increased with relatively low technology inputs, and produce is exchanged for commodity goods produced in the advanced capitalist sector. Both the Second World and Third World need and want consumer goods from the First World. The Third World pays for such consumer goods with agrarian goods, while the Second World wants to pay for such consumer goods with industrial products.

Lessening tensions since the end of the Stalin era in 1952 have led to the opening of consumer valves in the Soviet Union and hence the maintaining of tight political, statist controls, the assumption being that the stability of the socialist bureaucratic regimes will become correspondingly greater as the demands for consumer gratification are increasingly satisfied. Thus far, this theory has in fact proved correct. Protest in the socialist bloc has been limited to a narrow strata of intellectuals who have subsequently been declared malcontents or madmen in the face of the general satisfaction with the level of available consumer goods. Whatever the long-term secular trends may be, and whatever the consequences to socialist legitimacy and class interests, the fact remains that consumer orientations have worked. Multinational penetration must therefore be seen as part of a general commitment of the Soviet leadership to obtain political quietude through economic gratification.

The most obvious commodity that the Soviets have to sell is not agrarian products, and certainly not consumer goods—both of which are in profoundly short supply within the socialist orbit—it is technology. The Soviet Union has a high technological sophistication, built up over more than fifty years of emphasis on industrialization at the expense of nearly every other economic goal. To an increasing degree, American companies looking for ways to reduce costs in their own research and development are buying the latest Soviet technology. The trend is most apparent in the metallurgy field, as is made clear in the following report, filed jointly by Boris E. Kurakin, spokesman for the official Soviet buyer, Licensintorg, and by Henry Shur, president of Patent Management (*The New York Times,* August 25, 1972).

> The Soviet Union constitutes the world's largest single concentrated source of high technology with proven industrial results which eliminate the risk of costly R. & D. efforts for United States industry. The U.S.S.R. demonstrably excels in many areas of metallurgy, production and fabrication of metals and welding.

Another *New York Times* (April 17, 1972) report indicates that as the Soviet Union moves closer to a consumer-oriented society its attitudes toward banking and saving have tended to show a corresponding transformation.

> . . . as economic priorities slowly shift in these countries to meet consumer demands, so are the pressures rising for more trade with the West and some kind of accommodation to the West's monetary system. Official Japanese sources said last week in Tokyo the United States was planning to propose creation of a new group of 12 nations—Japan, the United States, France, Britain, West Germany, Spain, Canada, the United Arab Republic, India, Australia, Brazil and Mexico. There is a major difference with the West centers on the distribution of new man-made, internationally managed reserve assets such as the Special Drawing Rights (SDR's) now in circulation. SDR's are now distributed on the basis of relative economic strength, as measured by the quotas Western countries have with the International Monetary Fund.

Since consumer goods are purchased largely through Western-dominated multinationals, the character of international banking communism has drawn closer to that of international banking capitalism, in short, to the essence of banking principles, profits from interests on loans secured by equity arrangements.

> In their desire to facilitate trade with capitalist countries, the Communist countries of Eastern Europe are operating one of the fastest growing banking systems in the West. "No longer can you say a bank is Russian, Hungarian, German or even American," observes Mr. Steindling. "Banking is international in the East as well as the West, and the standard by which all banks are judged is not nationality but whether

or not they are making a profit." One criticism of Communist bankers is that they are not so attuned as Westerners to assessing credit risks because of their background in a state economy where enterprises do not run the risk of failing. The Communists use a foreign banking network because in trade with the outside world, they have to avail themselves of the monetary system of the West. The Communist bankers' main job is to arrange credits for financing East-West trade at attractive rates of interest for the Communist borrower. If a German exporter sells $1-million worth of machine tools to Russia, the Russian bank—in this case the Ost-West Handelsbank in Frankfurt—will probably purchase the promissory note of the Russian importer.

Last year the Soviet Union, Czechoslovakia, Poland, Hungary, East Germany, Bulgaria and Mongolia, members of the Communist economic bloc known as COMECON (Council of Mutual Economic Assistance) subscribed $350-million, of which $100-million was in hard currency, to form a Communist Investment Bank in Moscow. This $100-million is just one example of assets pumped through the Communists' Western banking apparatus in the international capital market, earning good rates of interest for the Communist lenders, and symbolizing at least in financial terms a coming together of East and West (*The New York Times*, October 2, 1972).

Coming into existence is a banking network that has the capacity to rationalize multinational exchanges. Banking capitalism links up with banking socialism precisely because banks are involved in similar international activities and similar investments in profitable enterprises. In the absence of direct industry-to-industry contracts, given East-West structural constraints at the manufacturing level, the banking system is the fluid that pumps life into an East-West economic détente. And it is this détente that permits arms reduction negotiations to take place in an atmosphere of political *entente cordiale*.

The Fusion of Capitalism and Socialism as Social-Science Ideology

The multinationalist framework has made a cultural impact on an East-West accommodation more significant than that made in the past by any other influence. Led by the United States and the Soviet Union, scientific academies of a dozen nations have set up a "think-tank" to seek solutions to problems created by' industrialization and urbanization of societies. Such problems as pollution control, public health, and overpopulation are to be studied by an International Institute of Applied Systems Analysis with overseas headquarters in Vienna, Austria. Even the broad composition of this new knowledge industry reflects multinational thinking. Its director will be a professor of managerial economics at Harvard, and its council chairman will be a member of the Soviet Academy of Sciences, Jerman M. Gvishiani, and, incidentally, the son-in-law of Premier Aleksei N. Kosygin (*Science,* October 13, 1972). In this remarkable display of East-West fusion, representatives from Czechoslovakia, Bulgaria, Poland, and East Germany will be joined by representatives from Japan, Canada, Great Britain, West Germany, and Italy. The director of the program, Dr. Howard Raiffa, indicated that the accumulated findings of management techniques, particularly as these have evolved in the aerospace industry, would be applied to a wide variety of health and welfare problems in Eastern Europe. He noted that a "likely first task would be concerned with energy: an analytical study of short and long range projections of the world supply of energy sources, future technologies and hazards of each source" (*The New York Times,* October 5, 1972).

It is evident from the tone and substance of these preliminary guidelines for this international think-tank that it will be technocratic and nonideological in nature; in short, the perfect cultural and educational coefficient of a multinational expression for international cooperation. The same report points out that:

> The United States was "giving more than it's getting" in connection with the institute, but the investment was worthwhile because of its potential impact upon both the Soviet managerial class and East-West ties. Dr. Raiffa said in a position paper that the institute would have "a selective approach which will concentrate on a few problems at a time with the understanding that these problems will vary through time."

The rise of a multinational cultural apparatus has been made possible by the widening exchange of scientists, scholars, and performers from East to West and West to East. But underneath such widening contacts, indeed, presupposing these contacts, has been the declining fervor of ideology. Both Marxism and Americanism have yielded to considerations of efficiency and effectiveness, and with this yielding has come a vigorous effort to provide methodological guidelines for the development of accurate and universally applicable data. The new technology, with its potential for simultaneous translation and rapid publication, has also served to bring East and West together. This coalescence occurs precisely in areas of intellectual activities relatively uncontaminated by inherited ideological sore points. Hence it is that such diverse subjects as futurism, computer technology, machine learning, etc., by virtue of their newness, foster greater joint efforts. But of course, it is just these areas that also happen to be most significant from the viewpoint of multi-nationalist exchanges of goods and services.

Multinationalism and the End of Classical Imperialism

The rise of multinationalism corresponds to a concomitant transformation of imperialist relations. What commenced as the classical military occupation of foreign territories in the preimperial, colonial period, shifted to the export of banking and industrial wealth owned by the advanced powers and exchanged for the mineral wealth and natural resources of the peripheral colonized area. Whatever the merits of economic arguments concerning the relative value of agricultural and industrial products, the historical fact is that underdeveloped areas were, and still are, characterized by an agrarian base dependent on export of raw materials and the import of finished goods and commodities. Over time this pattern has begun to break down, the first piece of evidence of this breakdown being the failure of the masses to participate in the selective distribution of commodities, creating huge riots and revolutions in overseas developing areas. Thus, the contradictions between the national middle classes and the rest of these underdeveloped societies subjected classical imperialism to intense pressures by indirection. National liberation and socialist movements of various types and structures simply invalidated the classical model of colonialism.

To stop the erosion of their international position, the imperial powers altered their strategies, and beyond that, altered their profit picture. Marx pointed out in *Das Kapital* that within a domestic context the percentage of profitability is less decisive than the maintenance of profits. The increase in product utilization is a means of stabilizing and increasing profits in absolute terms, in monetary amounts rather than in percentile units. Hence, capital-intensive industries permit less overt exploitation without a systemic collapse. This same phenomenon has occurred in an international context: a shift occurs lowering the percent of profits but not the actual flow of funds. The multinational corporations establish local participation in factory and industrial management, train local talent to assume tasks requiring special technical competence, move toward joint ownerships with local middle classes or local bureaucratic classes (if dealings are with the socialist bloc), transfer factories and technicians when necessary; and in short do everything other than surrender their positions as profit-making units operating in an overseas climate. This overseas climate has become increasingly antagonistic to the signs and symbols of imperial enterprises, while desperately demanding more of the goods and uses of these same foreign firms (Boddewyn and Cracco, 1972). Hence, the multinationals become involved in bridging the gap between revolutionary nationalism and establishment internationalism. They do this by acquiescing to the symbolic demands of nationalists and revolutionists, while satisfying the very real economic demands of the conservative middle-sector elements in Third World societies.

The rise of the multinational corporation has given increased weight to Lenin's initial focus on imperialism, albeit in a manner perhaps not entirely foreseeable by the master builder of Russian Bolshevism. At the turn of the twentieth century, the basic imperial powers engaged in banking-industrial capitalism were the United States, England, France, Germany, Japan, and Russia. After the Soviet revolution, the Marxists postulated that Russia would be out of the imperialist orbit for all time. After World War One it was further postulated that the imperialist powers would redivide Europe so as to limit and minimize German participation in the Imperial Club. After World War Two, this same set of theories further deduced that the back of Western European capitalism had been broken, and that certainly both German and Japanese capitalism had been brought to heel. Now, a quarter-century later, we have witnessed a certain Grand Restorationism, of which the multinational corporation is merely the advanced guard. For what we now witness is precisely the same cluster of nations that prevailed at the turn of the century controlling the overwhelming bulk of the international economy. The economic mix has changed; it is now far more favorable to the United States than it was in 1900. But also, curiously, it is now more favorable to Japan and Germany than it was at the turn of the century.

After two immense world wars, both presumably involving, if not entirely defined by, the imperialist inner struggle, and after a presumed social revolution that shook the earth's foundations for ten days at least, we are faced with a curious similitude that takes us back to the century's starting point. This is not to suggest at all that the world has stood still. It is to say that the staying power of powerful nations has remained quite durable, whatever the rotation of political power may have been at any given time span within the twentieth century. One might say that all political revolutions have a very similar concern for the maintenance and eventual extension of economic dominion—a fact of life that was as true for German fascism and Japanese militarism as it is for Soviet communism and American capitalism. Here we have one of those long-run secular trends displaying the remarkable potency of economic factors in social life; whatever the exigencies of political game-playing may necessitate.

The multinationals, by serving to alter the fundamental relationships between the bourgeoisie of advanced countries and the bourgeoisie of the peripheral countries, have also served to change the terms of the international game. The difficulty with much Marxian thinking in the current era is the supposition that dependence and underdevelopment are the handmaidens of backwardness whereas in fact what one observes increasingly throughout the Third World is a correlation of dependence *and* development. And this is as true of Soviet penetration in Cuba as it is of United States' penetration in Brazil. For what is involved is the internationalization of the notion of the senior and junior partner arrangement, which more fittingly and accurately describes present developmental realities than does the conventional model of superordination and subordination. By internationalizing capital relations, multinationals have also internationalized class relationships. Obviously, the situation with Soviet satellites is more complex, since all trade and aid relations are filtered through a grid of political and military tradeoffs; yet the same principle clearly obtains. This means that multinationalism permits development while at the same time maintains a pattern of benign dependence.

This new situation is made perfectly plain by Richard Barnet (1972: 237) in drawing our attention to the elimination of world war as a mixed blessing: one that permits world order within a multinationalist context sanctioned by the major powers.

> The essence of imperialism, regardless of the economic system from which it proceeds, is the unjust bargain. Human beings are used to serve ends that are not their own and in the process they pay more than they receive. The effort by two hundred multinational corporations (or twenty or two thousand) to rationalize the world economy is part of an imperialist pattern of a new dimension. The mineral resources of the earth will soon be under the control of four centers of power: the predominantly American multinational corporations, the predominantly European multinational corporations, the Soviet state enterprise, and the Chinese state enterprise. If the attempt of a few hundred corporate managers in multinational private and state enterprises to determine how and where the resources of the whole earth shall be developed is successful, these members of the new international managerial class will for practical purposes be the first world conquerors in history.
>
> While it is claimed by the apologists for the multinational corporation that the peaceful division of the world is the most "rational" way to

exploit resources, expand productivity, and promote the good life for the greatest number, the interests of the great corporate units conflict with the basic human needs of a majority of the world's population. The supreme value pursued by the new breed of corporate managers is efficiency. This is an improvement, to be sure, over glory, *machismo,* and the excitement of winning, which, it will be recalled, are so important to the national security managers. For those who can make a contribution to the rationalized world economy there will be rewards. But the stark truth is that more than half of the population of the world is literally useless to the managers of the multinational corporation and their counterparts in Soviet and Chinese state enterprises, even as customers.

It need only be added that since these large masses of no importance to the multinational and state enterprises have no apparent mechanism for realizing their own aspirations through official channels, new forms of political and economic competition may emerge in this epoch.

The Reemergence of Proletarian Internationalism as a Function of Multinationalism

The strangest, or certainly the least anticipated, consequence of the multinational corporation is the reappearance of militant unionism. The emergence of worker resistance to the multinationalist attempt to seek out the cheapest supply of labor as well as raw materials wherever that condition might obtain is still in an infant stage, but clearly on the rise. Highly paid West German optical workers must compete against low-paid workers from the same industries in Eastern Europe. Auto workers in Western Europe find themselves competing against workers in Latin America producing essentially the same cars. Chemical plants of wholly owned United States subsidiaries are put up in Belgium and England to capitalize on the cheaper wage scales of European chemical workers and to gain greater proximity to retail markets. Even American advertising agencies are protesting the manufacturing of commercials in Europe. Such stories can be repeated for every major multinational firm and every nation.

One may well appreciate the rationale offered by the multinationals. They can take advantage of the protectionist system of closed markets in the United States while pursuing an antiprotectionist approach for trading abroad. They can thereby derive the payoffs of selling to the American worker at American market prices while employing workers overseas at lower European wage scales. Investment abroad is also a way to get beyond antitrust laws that apply fully within the United States but scarcely at all in other countries. As Gus Tyler (1972:56–57) has observed: "For all these reasons—cheap labor, tax advantages, protected markets, monopoly control—as well as for other reasons of proximity to materials or markets, the giant conglomerates of America are moving their investments massively overseas. The result has been a rising threat to American employment and trade: jobs have not kept up with either our growing population or market; exports have not kept up with an expanding world trade." In a fierce critique, he sees the situation created by multinationalism as destructive of nationalism no less than of unionism.

> The multinationals have turned this old-fashioned world topsy-turvey. The modern "cosmo-corporations" are stateless, reaching across national boundaries, often owned jointly by major corporate investors of several countries. By their integrated international organization, they have made the phrase "comparative advantage" for any nation a meaningless term. Capital, technology, management know-how, merchandizing, machinery, invention—all these "advantages" can be shipped anywhere anytime. Even raw material is hardly an advantage as multinationals of many nations move in on the lands that have natural resources, such as oil. The "advantages" offered by various locations are primarily "political," like low wages, tax benefits, protected markets, government subsidies or market monopolies (Tyler, 1972:59).

This new situation, whatever the merits or demerits of the rationalizing capacity of multinationals, has created a partially revivified working class that shows, unlike its responses to earlier periods, greater class solidarity than cross-class national solidarity. Certainly, in the major wars of the twentieth century, the working classes consistently lined up behind nationalism and patriotism and in so doing have frustrated just about every prediction made on their behalf by left-wing intellectuals. Now, precisely at that moment when so much left-oriented rhetoric has itself become infused with an antiworking-class bias, we bear witness to the emergence of proletarian militance; this time as a function of self-interest rather than lofty ideology.

The organization of working-class life is still along national lines; but when confronted with middle-class internationalism, i.e., as represented by the multinationals, it must either create new trade union mechanisms or revitalize old and existing ones.

> Foreign resentment against U.S. multinationals flares up most dangerously when these corporations do to the workers of other countries what they have been doing to American workers all along: shut down a plant for company reasons. Within two weeks, General Motors closed down a plant

with 685 employees in Paris, because of Italian competition, and Remington Rand closed down a plant with 1,000 employees to relocate in Vienna. The French government—then under Charles de Gaulle—decided to get tough with the U.S. multinationals; so GM opened a plant in Belgium instead of France and proceeded to ship the product into France—duty free (Tyler, 1972:62).

It is intriguing to note how a relatively insular trade-union movement such as the British Trades Union Congress (TUC) has vigorously responded to multinationals as a threat. It has put forth demands for making union recognition a precondition for setting up foreign subsidiaries in the United Kingdom; and likewise to have organizations such as the Organization for Economic Cooperation and Development (OECD) serve as agencies for funneling and channeling working-class demands on wider multinationals.

The British trade unions cannot rely solely on government action; other policies would be necessary to reach their objectives *vis-à-vis* multinationals. One step would be to become much more "professional" in their approach to negotiations with international companies. This will entail spending more money and resources on services to support negotiating teams, particularly to service such teams with information. The British Government's Industrial Relations Act may help since it obliges all firms to provide information to trade unions for collective bargaining purposes. As yet, however, no one is sure what the nature of this information will be (Gennard, 1972:5).

But while British responses have been legalist and proffered through government agencies, European workers on the mainland have become more direct and forthright in their dealings with multinational-led strike actions and corporate lockouts.

The International Federation of Chemical and General Workers' Union has acted as a coordinating body for different unions in various countries in negotiations with St. Gobain, a French-owned glass manufacturing multinational. Some success for international action coordinated through International Trade Secretariats has been achieved; for example: In 1970, strikers at May and Baker, a British subsidiary of Rhone-Poulenc, won a 16 percent pay rise "largely due to large-scale international intervention" at the company's French headquarters and at other May and Baker plants in the Commonwealth. Peugeot workers in Founee threatened a 15 minute stoppage in 1968 to back 1,000 workers suspended in an Argentinian subsidiary. After two days, the company agreed to take back nearly all the suspended workers (Gennard, 1972:7).

This renewed working-class activity has had a stunning effect on East-West trade union relations. It is axiomatic that socialism does not tolerate or permit strikes since, in the doctrine of its founders, socialism is a workers' society, and a strike against the government is a strike against one's own interest. That such reasoning is a palpable hoax has never been denied. Indeed, the leaders of Poland, Hungary, and other East European states have become quite sensitized to such mass pressure from below. Yet the impact of this reasoning is that strike actions have been rare, and met most often with repressive measures. The concept of working-class international action between laborers in "capitalist" and "socialist" countries has been virtually nonexistent. Nevertheless, such is the force of multinationalism that even these deep political inhibitions are breaking down. We may be entering an era of working-class collaboration across systemic lines, not unlike the coalescence between the bourgeois West and bureaucratic East.

> Recent work stoppages and unofficial "wild cat" strikes in Poland, Yugoslavia, Sweden, Germany, Belgium, Switzerland, Holland, United Kingdom, Italy, and elsewhere, emphasize the growing opposition to centralized union authority and policies. By their nature, the national centers, like national governments, are best (perhaps uniquely) suited to deal with problems in the marginal areas of the lowest paid, least trained and poorest organized. For this reason, they tend to emphasize narrowing of the gap between the highest and lowest paid categories and raising of millions of working poor up into the middle-income brackets. This is an aim upon which there is universal agreement in principle and much sanctimonious moralizing. Practice is another thing entirely. In an economy which is disaggregating and in which challenges to central authority are being mounted everywhere, the levelling precept runs counter to the current of social change.
>
> No particular group really believes—usually with justification—that sacrificing wages on its part is really going to help anyone else, least of all the lower categories. Official appeals for solidarity are always vague as to how the sacrifice of the better off is to be given to the less fortunate. As long as the firm, plant or industry remains the basic unit of the economy in which most of the wealth and decision-making power of society is centered, workers must seek to maximize their share of national revenue in terms of such units. This explains why most of the unofficial strikes in Sweden, Germany and Belgium, for instance, the heightened militancy in Italy, and the rejection of contracts in the USA and elsewhere, were provoked by the highest paid workers rather than by the lowest. The revolt in the shipyards of Poland was a revolt of the better-off workers in the economy, and the strongest and most stubborn opposition to the Czech repression is located in the best paid chemical and metal industries (Levinson, 1971:209–210).

Several important features of this special variant of proletarian internationalism must be distinguished: (1) It cuts across national lines for the first time in the twentieth century. (2) It cuts across systemic lines, being less responsive now to Cold War calls for free labor or socialist labor than it ever was at any earlier time in the post-World War Two period. (3) The vanguard role in this effort is being assumed by the workers in the better-paid and better-organized sectors of labor; in the specialized craft sector more than in the assembly-line industrial sector. (4) While new mechanisms are being created to deal with multinational corporations, the more customary approach is to strengthen the bargaining position of available organizations, such as the International Metal Workers' Federation and the International Federation of Chemical and General Workers' Unions.

What we have then is an intensification of class competition, but on a scale and magnitude unlike the conventional national constraints. It is still difficult to demonstrate or to predict whether such class struggles can be as readily resolved short of revolution in the industrial areas as those in the previous epoch were resolved in the national areas. In effect, if Marxism as a triumphal march of socialism throughout the world has been thoroughly discredited, it manages to rise, phoenixlike, out of the bitter ashes of such disrepair. The intensification of class struggles at the international level remains muted by the comparative advantages of multinationalism to countries like Japan and the United States. But if such comparative advantages dissipate themselves over the long pull of time (and this is beginning to happen as less-developed nations begin to catch up), then the quality of class competition might well intensify.

The Theory of Big-Power Convergence and Multinational Realities

Multinationalism has served to refocus attention on the theory of convergence: that particular set of assumptions that holds that over time the industrial and urbanizing tendencies of the United States and the Soviet Union will prevail over systemic and ideological differences and will form a convergence, or at least enough of a similitude, to prevent major grave international confrontations (cf. Brzezinski and Huntington, 1964: 429–430). The convergence theory does not postulate that the two systems will become identical but rather that what will take place is a sort of political twin-track coalition network. Convergence more nearly represents a parallelism than a true merging. In this sense, multinational corporation interpenetration is quite distinct from convergence, since what are involved are the linkages of the two superstates at the functional economic levels but continued disparity at the political organization level. In an interpenetration such as that being brought about by the multinationals, systems of society do indeed meet and cross over. The lines of intersection are clearly evident as the data show; and the implications of such a development extend far beyond a formal proof for any doctrine of political science or economics.

The evidence for the convergence theory has been generally made much stronger by the rise of multinationals. And without entering into an arid debate about whether capitalism and socialism can remain pure and noble if this can take place, the empirics of the situation are clear enough: the United States and the Soviet Union (whatever their economic systems can be called) have shown a remarkable propensity to fuse their interests at the economic level and collapse their differences at a diplomatic level, for the purpose of forming a new big-power coalition that dwarfs the dreams of Metternich for a United Europe in the nineteenth century. Indeed, we now have a situation in which the doctrine of national self-interest has been superseded by one of regional and even hemispheric spheres of domination by the two major world superpowers (Weisband and Franck, 1971).

The issue of systemic convergence is certainly not new. The pros and cons of this debate have been well articulated by intellectuals and politicians alike. The existence of commonalities between the major political and economic powers has long been evident. Geographical size, racial and religious similitudes, even psychological properties of the peoples of the USA and the USSR, all conspire to fuse American and Soviet interests. What has been in dispute is whether such root commonalities are sufficient to overcome long-standing differences in the economic organization of society, ideological commitments, and political systems of domination. This argument remained largely unanswered and unanswerable as long as the mechanism, the lever, for expressing any functional convergence remained absent. The unique contribution of multinationalism to the debate over convergence between the major superpowers is precisely its functional rationality, its place in contemporary history as the Archimedean lever lifting both nations out of the Cold War. Multinational links take precedence over political differences in prosaic but meaningful ways. They serve to rationalize and standardize international economic relationships. They demand perfect interchangeability of parts; a uniform system of weights and measurements; common auditing languages for expression of world trade and commerce; standard codes for aircraft and airports, telephonic and telegraphic communications; and banking rules and regulations that are adhered to by all nations. Convergence takes place not so much by ideological proclamation (although there has even been some of this) but primarily by organizational fiat; that is, by seeming to hold ideological differences constant, while rotating every other factor in international relations.

What lies ahead? Even as we enter the multinational era, questions arise as to the efficacy of this resolution for world society. Some critics see the social structures of modern business as being in contradiction with the larger value complex of society (Brown, 1972:131); while crusaders see the multinational corporation as the beginning of a true internationalism (Turner, 1971:185–187). Most recently, it has been suggested that the multinationals may resolve certain issues in relationship to the underdeveloped regions and the Third World as a whole. It has recently been suggested (Adam, 1971:63) that beyond the multinationals might be the antimultinationals or regional organizations serviced by public institutions.

It is debatable whether world corporations allocate resources in the most efficient way. They do contribute to the (relatively) quick diffusion of many innovations. However, the question of efficiency hinges on the direction of change rather than the rate of change. In an oligopolistically organized market structure the choice of the consumer is manipulated: far from being offered the full range of choices possible, the consumer is provided only with products manufactured (rather more than less) in accordance with the predictions of the corporations on what the consumer wants. It is the corporations who decide which of the new possibilities offered by science should be made use of. If one of the main criteria of efficiency is the optimal satisfaction of consumer wants, this can be attained only when large numbers of independent decision centers exist.

The polar opposite of the world corporation is the antimultinational corporation. The latter is a public institution which organizes many industries across one region, substituting regionalization for internationalization. The boundaries of an enterprise are thus to be contained by the boundaries of the political unit, in order to render possible the control of the enterprise, the elimination of oligopolistic waste and regional imbalances. Owing to the aeronautical and electronic revolutions which greatly reduce costs of communication, regional groupings can obtain new knowledge easily and cheaply; this increases their chances to preserve their economic independence.

The difficulty with this small-power formula is that regionalism already exists, in the form of the European Common Market, the Latin American Free Trade Federation, Comecon, etc. These agencies, while serving the nation-states who are member-states reveal precisely the indebtedness to political pressures of power blocs that the multinationals

serve to move beyond. The ideology of antimultinationalism as super-
statism thus becomes a special variant of world political readjustments.
And if it may serve to keep in check the multinationals, it does so at the
expense of any real movement beyond the current political immobilism.
If multinationalism is not exactly the fulfillment of an egalitarian dream,
the return to more parochial forms of socioeconomic organizations is also
clearly no real improvement.

Multinationalism has played a major role in establishing détente as the
central thrust in big-power settlements. Its doing so has profoundly
lessened the bargaining power of smaller nations vis-à-vis the superpowers. But whatever problems this leaves in its wake, this myth-
breaking development at least makes possible a more realistic international political climate.

Pax Americana Plus Pax Sovietica: The Politics of Multinationalism

The politics of multinationalism is not so much an illustration of convergence as it is an example of pragmatic parallelism. One has only to
compare and contrast the position of Michael Harrington (1972:570) on
Nixon's program with Weisband and Franck's (1971:37–38) approach to
Brezhnev's program to see how this parallelism operates—with or without a broad solution to theoretical disputations on convergence.

Harrington points out that underlying the Nixon-Kissinger position is
a shared metaphysical belief that the division of the world is both
necessary and desirable.

> Internationally, then, Nixonism has a profoundly conservative, shrewd
> yet utterly flawed approach. It seeks a Metternichian arrangement among
> the superpowers, capitalist and Communist, according to which change
> would be relegated to controllable channels. In pursuit of this goal it is,
> unlike the moralistic policy of Dulles, willing to strengthen the power of
> its enemies if only they will accept the model of a global equilibrium.
> Nixonism is rhetorically dedicated to the virtues of the global division of
> labor but actually committed to utilizing America's state power to social-
> ize the enormous advantage of our corporations on the world market. . . .
> Capitalist collectivism, in other words, wants to make a deal with bureau-
> cratic collectivism to preserve the status quo.

Weisband and Franck, aside from assigning causal priority for this
doctrine to the West, assert nonetheless that the Brezhnev approach to
peaceful coexistence represents a similar attitude toward big-power
sovereignty over smaller areas.

The Brezhnev doctrine, which continues to govern the policies of the Warsaw Pact governments, to some degree represents a trade-off or division of the world by the Soviet Union and the United States into spheres of influence or "regional ghettos." Not that our policy-makers in Washington planned it that way: little or no evidence has been adduced to show that the U.S. government ever willfully intended to trade control over Latin America for recognition of absolute Soviet dominance over Eastern Europe. Nor can it be said that any actions we have taken in relation to Latin America are the same as Russia's brutal suppression of Czechoslovakia. . . . What we do wish to assert is that virtually every concept of the Brezhnev doctrine can be traced to an earlier arrogation of identical rights by the United States vis-à-vis Latin America. . . . it is important to realize that the search for new norms in the world must begin with a clear understanding that we, as much as the Russians, bear responsibility for conceptualizing the Brezhnev norms. . . . In the Soviet view, regional determination and prerogatives take precedence over those of the international community including the United Nations.

Curiously enough, the conncection between international politics and the rise of multinationalism was clearly articulated, even by the above prescient commentators on international affairs. Lesser analysts seem to prefer to think of the new Nixonism as some sort of magical mystery tour: a transformation of high spiritual beliefs into policy matters. My contention is that the current foreign-policy initiatives of Henry Kissinger derive directly from a new awareness of the consequences—political and economic—of the changes in corporate relationships brought about by the power of the multinationals. American policy-makers have finally recognized that this industrial change has necessitated an end to the Cold War and the substitution of a new detente based on economic realities. President Nixon, throughout the 1972 year, clearly articulated such a geopolitical realignment based on economic realities.

As early as January 1971, Nixon articulated the point of view that he sustained on his diplomatic initiatives in Moscow and Peking:

We must remember that the only time in the history of the world that we had any extended periods of peace is when there has been a balance of power. It is when one nation becomes infinitely more powerful in relation to its potential competitor that the danger of war arises. So I believe in a world in which the United States is powerful. I think it would be a safer world and a better world if we have a strong, healthy United States, Europe, Soviet Union, China, and Japan, each balancing the other, not playing one against the other, an even balance.

The peculiar linkage is China, since it alone has yet to participate fully in the multinational system. Further, it can be said to be by far the poorest of the countries with which power balance has to be sought. But with that admittedly crucial exception, and this can be argued to be a requirement of political trade-off preventing undue Soviet impact on the Western world and undue Japanese presence in the Eastern world, what Nixon has outlined is quite clearly the politics of multinationalism, and not of capitalism triumphant or socialism defeated. The trade and aid agreements between East and West during this period serve to confirm the accuracy of this appraisal. Even China is entering the multinational race with its increased sale of specialized consumer goods to the United States and its purchase from Boeing Aircraft of an international fleet of advanced jets.

This new Metternichian arrangement among the superpowers is precisely a repudiation of the earlier moral absolutism of anticommunism and anticapitalism. In a sense, and one step beyond an acknowledged end of the Cold War, this geopolitical redistribution may also solve a major problem of the multinational corporation, its transcendence of the limits and encumbrances placed by national sovereignty. By an international linkage of the superpowers, the problems of multinational regulation, which loom so large in the established literature, can be rationalized, if not entirely resolved, by appeals to commercial rationality rather than political sovereignty.

The thesis presented by George Kennan (1972:13) that the end of the Cold War came about as a result of a series of victories of the United States over the Soviet empire is simply untenable. The plain fact is that Stalinism was remarkably legalistic in its foreign policy, whatever its extralegalities were internally. Beyond that, the Soviet empire has neither shrunk nor disappeared. Current Soviet policy, especially as it affects Eastern Europe, can only be described as extremely aggressive. It is precisely the absence of victory, the existence of a thoroughly stalemated situation, that led the major powers to reconsider their collision course—a course that could threaten both empires at the expense of outsider factions in the Third World, China, and even nonaligned nations like India, waiting in the wings to pick up the pieces.

What has happened is that advances in both the political and social realms have come about in rapid succession as a result of the multinational economics; namely, arms control agreements, direct executive rapprochement, new trade and purchasing agreements, and exchanges of research and development technology in basic fields. These have signaled the real termination of the Cold War. Multinationalism, in its very extranational capacities, has served to rationalize this new foreign-policy posture on both sides. Terms like "have" versus "have-not" states have come to replace and displace an older rhetoric of capitalism versus socialism, not simply as an expression of the uneven international distribution of wealth, but as an indication of the current sponginess of any concept of capitalism or socialism. Precisely the inability of the Cold War to be resolved through victory has led to a feeling on the part of elite leadership in powerful states that the coalition of the big against the small, of wealthy against impoverished, and even of white-led nations against colored-led nations can alone guarantee the peace of the world and the tranquility of potential sources of rival power like China in the East or Germany and France in the West. With one fell swoop the mutual winding down of the Cold War settles the hash of rival powers and determines the subordinate position of the Third World for the duration of the century. The cement for this new shift in fundamental policy is the multinational corporation. An end to ideology? No. An end to capitalist and communist rhetoric? Perhaps. An end to the Cold War epoch? Probably.

1974

IV

SOCIOLOGICAL POLITICS

13

The Rise and Fall of Project Camelot

Introduction to an Essay

American lives have become intertwined with the fate of government contracts. The granting of an award to an aircraft company in California is an occasion for loud newspaper headlines and can create in-migration patterns overnight. By the same token, the cancellation of a contract to a shipbuilder in New York is also an occasion for front-page newspaper stories. In short order, the boomtown can be made into a ghost town. Management and labor, ministers and bankers, Republicans and Democrats, all seem to have a common desire to get hold of government funds irrespective of their private philosophies of government. Academic establishments are no exception, as any investigation of federal aid-to-education programs will reveal.

With this as background, the cancellation of a social-science contract by an agency of the government can hardly be expected to create a furor among the American people. However, while it might seem that the rise and fall of Project Camelot fits a general government pattern, it has now become evident that its cancellation by the Defense Department is an event of special meaning and particular consequences for the social-science industry. The sound and fury generated by Project Camelot—from Washington to Moscow, involving scholars from Norway to Chile—signify much more than the rise and fall of a single project. Camelot's fate may prove to be the harbinger of vast changes in the structure and function of the social sciences.

The value problems for social scientists are the same whether scholars work for a ten dollar per diem or a one million dollar per annum. What are the vital connections between science and policy, between public findings and secret data, between the myths of society and the facts of sociology, between objectivity and commitment? Yet if the "stakes" of a project do not qualitatively alter the value questions, they do drastically affect a considerable number of scholars and in so doing alter the practical stakes. A multimillion-dollar government "sponsor" has expectations and demands that differ significantly from that of a university bestowing honor or status. The scope of a project therefore decisively influences expectations and outcomes.

These comments introduce a project, the meteoric rise of which is exceeded only by its equally decisive demise. Project Camelot came into being in 1964 as an offspring of the Army's Special Operations Research Office (SORO), with a fanfare befitting the largest single grant ever provided for a social-science project. Its termination less than a year later was registered with an official military dispatch that was as lame as it was tame. *What* is the "story" behind Project Camelot? *Who* was in back of it? *How* was it funded? *When* did it start? Above all, *why* did it fail?

Perhaps the best way to begin is with the description of Project Camelot offered in the rather decisive document, dated December 4, 1964, mailed to a select list of scholars around the world:

> Project Camelot is a study whose objective is to determine the feasibility of developing a general social systems model which would make it possible to predict and influence politically significant aspects of social change in the developing nations of the world. Somewhat more specifically, its objectives are:
>
> First, to devise procedures for assessing the potential for internal war within national societies; second, to identify with increased degrees of confidence, those actions which a government might take to relieve conditions which are assessed as giving rise to a potential for internal war; and *finally,* to assess the feasibility of prescribing the characteristics of a system for obtaining and using the essential information needed for doing the above two things. The project is conceived as a three- to four-year effort to be funded at around one and one-half million dollars annually. It is supported by the Army and the Department of Defense, and will be conducted with the cooperation of other agencies of the government. A large amount of primary data collection in the field is planned as well as the extensive utilization of already available data on social, economic and political functions. At this writing, it seems probable that the geographic orientation of the research will be toward Latin American countries. Present plans call for a field office in that region.

An examination shows that the statement of purpose raises as many questions as it resolves. I should add that these questions are not resolved in the more extensive and elaborate documents subsequently published. For to devise procedures for assessing the potential for internal war within national societies—even if the results were to help determine the "feasibility" questions as to whether such internal war is plausible and under what conditions—is not to settle "policy" issues: Would the findings be the same if the "incumbents" are Communists and the "insurgents" are Restorationists? To what extent is the data-gathering process determined by social-science needs or by American foreign-policy needs? The draft proposals make the assumption that governments are somehow always in the position to take actions to relieve conditions that give rise to a potential for internal war. This philosophical voluntarism goes untested. Thus the *scientific limits* of Project Camelot are never stated.

Obviously, if governments were in a voluntaristic position, there would never be any revolutions, planned or spontaneous. An essential dilemma in Project Camelot is that it never settled the issue of primary concern: How does one assess the characteristics of a social system or evolve instruments for obtaining and using essential information? The problem of the relationship between "pure" and "applied" social science is involved from the outset. The question is how far and with what legitimacy can the social scientist pursue this inquiry. Much more important than responding to every wild allegation about Camelot in the overall picture is to determine the precise character of social-science values in a context of extreme political and professional tensions.

Project Camelot: A Collective Self-Portrait

I would like to offer a collective portrait of how the personnel working on Project Camelot viewed their own participation and what they felt to be the shortcomings of the project. As a result of data gathered in direct interviews, there appeared to be general consensus on the following six points.

First, those who went to work for Project Camelot felt the need for a more appropriate big-range social science. They wanted to create a social science of contemporary relevance that would not suffer from a parochial narrowness of vision to which their own professional backgrounds (largely in sociology and psychology) had conditioned them. Most of the men viewed Camelot as a bona fide opportunity to do unrestricted fundamental research with relatively unlimited funds at their disposal. Under such optimal conditions, these scholars tended not to look a gift horse in the mouth. As one affiliate indicated: there was no desire to inquire too deeply as to the military source of the funds or the ultimate purpose of the project.

Second, a number of those affiliated with Camelot felt that there was actually more freedom under selective sponsored conditions to do fundamental research in a nonacademic environment than could be found at a university or college. One project member noted that during the fifties there was far more freedom to do fundamental research in the RAND Corporation than in any college or university in America. Indeed, once the protective covering of RAND was adopted, it was almost viewed as a society of Platonists permitted to search for truth on behalf of the powerful. A neo-Platonist definition of the situation by the men on Camelot was itself a constant in each of the interviews conducted.

Third, a good many of the Camelot affiliates felt distinctly uncomfortable with military sponsorship, especially considering the present U.S. military posture. But their reaction to this discomfort was that "the Army had to be educated." This view was sometimes cast in neo-Freudian terms; namely, that the Army's bent toward violence ought to be sublimated. Underlying this theme was the notion of the armed forces as an agency for potential social good; an enlargement on the idea that the discipline and the order embodied by an army could be channeled into the process of economic and social development in the United States as well as in many parts of the Third World.

Fourth, there was among the Camelot social scientists a profound belief in the perfectibility of mankind, particularly in the possibility of the military establishment performing a major role in this general process of growth. This perspective was the Enlightenment syndrome. Like the eighteenth-century *philosophes,* many members of the Camelot staff shared a belief in the worth of rational persuasion. Just as Voltaire and Diderot thought they could change the course of universal history by bringing the message of social utility to the monarchs of Europe—to Catherine of Russia, to Emperor Joseph of the Austro-Hungarian Empire, and to King Louis of France—the men of Camelot believed that they too, in some like manner, could affect the course of events. They sought to correct the intellectual paternalism and parochialism under which Pentagon generals, State Department diplomats, and Defense Department planners seemed to operate.

Fifth, one might say that a major long-range purpose of Camelot, at least for some of its policy-makers, was to prevent another revolutionary holocaust. At the very least, there was a shared belief that Pax Americana was severely threatened and deserved to know its own future. The policy-makers of Project Camelot may be criticized for a certain *jeune naïveté* on this point; but surely, once Americanism as an ideology is accepted as a basic positive value it is difficult to condemn the policy-makers for corruption. The Camelot personnel were upset by those social scientists willing to try nothing and criticize everything, who considered themselves to be in the forefront of applied social science, and saw little difference between scholars engaged in the war against poverty and those directly concerned with the war against violence.

Sixth, what became particularly apparent from speaking with Camelot personnel is that none of them viewed his role on the project as a form of spying for the United States government or for anyone else. The only person who even touched on this discordant note was an assistant professor of anthropology whose connection with the project was, from the outset, remote and tenuous. So far were Camelot people from thinking of their work in cloak-and-dagger terms that none of them interviewed was even convinced that the armed forces would take his preliminary recommendations seriously (even though that remained the hope of each). There was perhaps a keener commitment on the part of the directing members of Camelot neither to "sell out" nor to "cop out" than there generally is among scholars with regular academic appointments. This concern with the ethics of social-science research seems to result from their having confronted, in a daily situation, the problems of betrayal, treason, secrecy, and abuse of data. Even though a university position may ultimately derive from federally sponsored research, the connection is often too remote to cause any steady *crise de conscience.* Another factor seemingly involved is that government work, while well paid, remains professionally marginal. And the sense of marginality undoubtedly causes many federally linked scholars to ponder steadily their policy "roles."

From the outset of their involvement, a number of men had serious doubts about the character of the work they would be doing and about the conditions under which it would be done. But these doubts were more sophisticated than the common garden variety of criticisms one might have anticipated.

It was pointed out, for example, that the U.S. Army tends to exercise a far more stringent intellectual control of research findings than does the U.S. Air Force. As evidence for this, it was stated that SORO had fewer "free-wheeling" aspects to its research designs than did RAND. One "inside" critic went so far as to say that he knew of no SORO-sponsored research that had a "playful" or unsponsored quality, such as one finds to be a steady diet of RAND. "It was all grim stuff," I was told by one staff man; and by another, that "the self-conscious seriousness gets to you after a while."

Another line of criticism was that the pressures on the "reformers" (the men engaged in Camelot research often referred to themselves in this way) to effect recommended changes were much stronger than those on the military. The federal bureaucracy expected social scientists to be social reformers, while the military was expected to behave in a conservative manner. What gave an aura of role confusion, no less than role displacement, to several Camelot officials was a vaguely perceived organizational disequilibrium between researchers and sponsors. It was felt that a relationship of equality between sponsors and researchers did not exist, but rather one of superordinate military needs and subordinate academic roles. On the other hand, some Camelot officials were impressed by the disinterestedness of the military and thought that, far from exercising undue influence, the army personnel were loath to offer opinions even when requested.

Yet another objection made from within was that if one had to work in the policy sciences, if research that would have international ramifications was to be conducted, it might better be performed under the auspices of conventional State Department sponsorship. "After all," I was told, "they are at least nominally committed to civilian political norms." There was a considerable reluctance to believe that the Defense Department, despite its superior organization, greater financial affluence, and executive influence, would actually improve upon State Department styles of work or accept recommendations at variance with Pentagon policies.

There seemed to be few expressions of disrespect for the work being contemplated by Camelot or a disdain for policy-oriented work in general. This consensus obtained despite the fact that the scholars engaged in the Camelot effort incorporated in their outlook and orientation two rather distinct sets of vocabulary. Their role disorientation led to a scientific eclecticism. The various documents reveal a military vocabulary provided with an array of military justifications, often followed (within the same document) by a social-science vocabulary offering social-science justifications and rationalizations. The dilemma in the literature emanating from Project Camelot, from the preliminary report issued in August 1964 until the more advanced document issued in April 1965, was the same: an incomplete incorporation of the military and sociological vocabularies.

It might be doubted that a synthesis between military and sociological "styles of work" was possible, given the exclusively heuristic concerns of the Army's interest in the dynamics of insurgency and counterinsurgency and the more general theoretical concerns of the cadre of Camelot in the process of revolution-making. If an anology may be permitted, and perhaps forgiven, in light of the yet-to-be-discussed points, there is a sense in which a criminologist is dedicated to the liquidation of crime and not just to the incarceration of criminals. What was it that the men of Camelot were dedicated to liquidating? Was it conflict in general? Was it counterinsurgent movements? Was it Communist-led revolutions? Was it the social source of discontent? Would any recommendation criticizing the military as a fomenter of discontent (especially in Latin America) be made? In short, the preeminence of a "systems" approach rather than a "problems" approach led to exaggerated model-building techniques that obfuscated rather than clarified major issues. Many Camelot scholars came to this same conclusion. But unfortunately, it was understood too late—only when the project was declared null and void.

The Web of Tangled Events

As is often the case, the explosion of a big event begins in unpredictable circumstances and in unlikely surroundings. The actual crisis over Camelot came to a boiling point as a result of a congruence of several events. It involves a network spreading from a professor of anthropology at the University of Pittsburgh, to a professor of sociology at the University of Oslo, to another professor of sociology at the University of Chile in Santiago, and finally, to events that took blace behind U.S. embassy walls in Chile. From there on, the Camelot story moved to Washington: demands for a hearing, outcries from congressional figures, pained expressions of grief by State Department officials, revanchist sentiments of anger by Defense Department officials, confusion by military intellectuals, and finally, the official announcement and resolution of the problem by presidential epistle.

In May 1965, Chile was the scene of wild newspaper tales of spying and academic outrage at being recruited for spying missions. This was high irony, since in the working papers of Project Camelot, it is stated that the criteria for study "should show promise of high payoffs in terms of the kinds of data required," and apparently Chile did not meet these requirements. The "model nations" for the study of Latin American revolutions and coups were to be Argentina, Guatemala, Venezuela, Bolivia, Colombia, Cuba, El Salvador, Dominican Republic, Peru,

Brazil, and "special cases," Mexico and Paraguay. In the preliminary design, Chile was not included among those nations to be given even a casual treatment.

How it was that Chile became involved in Project Camelot's affairs brings us directly to a consideration of Hugo G. Nuttini, Assistant Professor of Anthropology at the University of Pittsburgh, citizen of the United States, and former citizen of the Rupublic of Chile. From his opening inquiry to the directors of SORO it is clear that Nuttini desired to participate in Project Camelot in whatever capacity was deemed most useful.

The reaction to his desire for participation was extremely cautious and quite restrained. Whatever Mr. Nuttini was or was not, he certainly was not an employee or staff member of Project Camelot. He was finally asked to report on the possibilities of gaining the cooperation of professional personnel with Project Camelot and in general to do the kind of ethnographic survey that has mild results and a modest honorarium of $750. But Mr. Nuttini had an obviously different (and more ambitious) definition of his role; and despite the warnings and precautions that Rex Hopper, then newly appointed head of Project Camelot, placed on his trip (especially Hopper's insistence on its informal nonaligned quality), Nuttini somehow managed to convey the impression of being a direct official of Project Camelot and of having the authority to make proposals to prospective Chilean participants. Here was an opportunity to link the country of his birth with the country of his choice.

At approximately the same time, Johan Galtung was invited to participate in a June conference that would present a preliminary research design for the study of internal war potentials and the effects of government action on such potentials. The proposed plan for the conference had as its basis the December 4th memorandum. The fee for participation of the social scientists attending would be $2,000 for four weeks. Galtung, who was in Chile at the time and was associated with the Latin American Faculty of Social Science (FLACSO), replied in his letter of April 22, saying that he could not accept participation in Project Camelot for several reasons. He could not accept the role of the Army as a sponsoring agent interested in a study of counterinsurgency. He could not accept the notion of the Army as an agency of development rather than an agency for managing conflict or perhaps even promoting conflict. He could not accept the "imperialist features," as he called them, of the research design. Finally, he could not accept the asymmetry of the project. He found it difficult to understand why it was that just as there were studies of counterinsurgency there should not also be studies of the social effect of counterintervention, studies of the conditions under which Latin American nations might intervene in the affairs of the United States. Obviously and openly, Dr. Galtung had spoken to others in Oslo, Santiago, and throughout Latin America about the project. He clearly had shown the memorandum of December 4th to many of his colleagues, and presumably it was from his copy of the memorandum that a Spanish-language version was fashioned and circulated.

On the same date as Galtung's letter to Hopper, April 22, Nuttini had a conference with the Vice-Chancellor of the University of Chile for the purpose of discussing at greater length the character of Project Camelot. After half an hour's exposition, Professor Fuenzalida, invited to attend this "briefing session" by the Vice-Chancellor, asked Nuttini point-blank to specify the ultimate aims of the project, its sponsors, and its political implications. Before an answer was forthcoming, Professor Fuenzalida, apparently with considerable drama, pulled a copy of the December 4th circular letter form his briefcase and read a prepared Spanish translation.

At the same time, the authorities at FLACSO turned the matter over to their associates in the Chilean Senate and in the left-wing Chilean press. They blazed forth with banner headlines and with such terms as "intervention," "imperialism," and the "scandal of Project Camelot." This rhetoric was undoubtedly reinforced by the May 1965 events that saw United States troops once more occupy Santo Domingo in the Dominican Republic. After several days of extremely heated University denunciations and a rather complete stand within the Chilean mass communications network against Project Camelot, United States Ambassador to Chile Ralph A. Dungan sent forth his own protest to Washington, which asked for an unconditional cancellation of Project Camelot's Chilean activities.

The public disclosures of the Chilean "situation" heightened the uneasiness felt even by those sectors in Chile who were pro-American over the expansion of Defense Department activities. Foreign Minister of Chile Miguel Ortíz warned in an interview against allowing the economic and social development plans embodied in the Alliance for Progress to become overshadowed by strategic considerations of fighting nonexistent insurgency movements. By the last week of June, both progovernment Christian Democratic and opposition Left Socialist newspapers throughout Chile condemned the "brazen intervention" by the U.S. Defense Department engaged in the realization of a vast continental spy plan known as "Operation Camelot." The papers, employing strong nationalist language, went on to say, "that the worthy and virile reaction of our country to the United States plan to carry out an apparently inoffensive sociological study in our midst is acquiring justified resentment." All newspapers agreed that Project Camelot was "intended to investigate the military and political situation prevailing in Chile and to determine the possiblity of an antidemocratic coup." After this rather universal Chilean reaction it was clear that Project Camelot could not survive, in Chile at least.

Events from that point on switched to Washington, where State Department officials and congressional reaction created sufficient pressure to halt Project Camelot in midstream, or more precisely, before it ever really got underway.

There was considerable fortuitousness on the Washington side, no less than on the Santiago side. At the time United States Ambassador to Chile Ralph A. Dungan sent through his telegrams requesting clarification of Project Camelot, what it was, and who was sponsoring such operations in Chile. The State Department member of Camelot Core Planning Group, Pio Uliassi, was casting considerable doubt on the Defense Department's sponsorship of efforts, which, he held, more properly belonged to the State Department. As a result of Uliassi's attitude, or rather the negative reaction to his recommendations, there was a steady deterioration of relations between Camelot sponsors and State Department consultants. Indeed, informal charges that the State Department representative on the Core Planning Group amounted to a courier role rather than a creative role only served to increase mutual suspicion and hostility.

As Camelot became increasingly autonomous, communications between its sponsors and the State Department sharply dwindled. Even before the Chile flare-up, it was clear that State Department officials wished to restore their former control over research projects on foreign areas. The Chile explosion, and the letters from Ambassador Dungan, only permitted what was smoldering behind the scenes to come into the open. The analysis of Project Camelot, issued from what *The Washington Star* mistakenly termed a "low-ranking State aide," formed the basis of a report to State Department officials that underlay later requests to kill Camelot at the earliest possible time. The report mentioned the following points:

The Camelot officials considered the State Department official on the Core Planning Group to be an observer rather than a recognized authority able to give counsel. Coordination of Camelot plans for Chile were so lacking that not only was there a breakdown in communications between the State Department and Camelot but also between Army personnel and

Camelot officials. Camelot officials, through their participation in a future publication entitled Conflict, would in effect attempt to make political judgments that up to the present were exclusively in the hands of the State Department.

When Ambassador Dungan's communications reached Washington, there was thus already a considerable amount of ferment about Project Camelot. The demands for a congressional hearing were quick to follow. Senators Fulbright and McCarthy asked for early hearings. And in a private hearing on Camelot held in early July before the House Foreign Affairs Committee, the text of which was not released until December, Representatives Fraser, Rosenthal, Fascell, and Royball questioned Theodore Vallance on the worth and sponsorship of Camelot. The remarks were cast in terms of military intrusion into foreign-policy areas, such as, the lack of coordination between government agencies that leads to dangerous duplication of effort and embarrassing results. Finally, the question of the general allocation of responsibilities was raised. It soon became evident to all interested parties that if SORO as a whole were to be saved, Project Camelot as a part of that whole would have to be sacrificed.

In quick succession, Dean Rusk and Robert S. McNamara, respective heads of the State Department and Defense Department, announced their agreement in principle on future lines of responsibility and communication concerning foreign-area reasearch projects. Next, Ambassador Dungan let it be known that Chile would be spared any embarrassment by Project Camelot, regardless of the ultimate outcome of the project. A week later, announcement was made by the Defense Department that Project Camelot was cancelled on the grounds that its original doubt about the practicality of officially sponsored research on other nations had been verified by the reaction in Chile to news of the project. Shortly after this remarkable case of political clairvoyance, questions were raised, both at the official and journalistic levels, about similar projects sponsored by the Defense Department concerning French Canada (Project Revolt) and rural politics in Colombia (Project Simpatico) and Project Michelson, sponsored by the Navy Department, which sought to analyze "goals and goal structures" of the United States, the Soviet Union, and the Chinese People's Republic. In each case, the damage that could be done by "sociological snoopers" was raised. The damage done by journalistic gibing was, however, not mentioned.

While the fate of the various projects ostensibly similar to Project Camelot remains to be decided, it is evident that future sponsorship of foreign-area research by agencies other than those sanctioned by the

State Department is quite unlikely. This is the essence of President Johnson's memorandum to Dean Rusk. The key paragraph in his communication stated that "no Government sponsorship of foreign area research should be undertaken which in the judgment of the Secretary of State would adversely affect United States foreign relations." The request for "procedures" to assure that this ruling will be carried out has already been put into effect. The Special Operations Research Office of American University, while financed by the Defense Department, will, in all likelihood, become increasingly responsive to State Department needs and wants in the area of foreign-nation research or, failing that, return to formalistic information services for the Army. The exact lines of authority are yet to be worked out. But Army officials have already considered this yet one more instance of State Department control of military affairs and Defense Department unresponsiveness to military needs. Thus, in its own way, the termination of Project Camelot contributed in no small measure to the smoldering debate between military and civilian personnel in the Defense Department, no less than to the more generic competition for authority in foreign affairs between State and Defense Departments.

On the Advisability of Project Camelot

The end of Project Camelot does not entail the end of the Special Operations Research Office nor does it imply an end to research designs that are similar in character to Project Camelot. In fact, the termination of the contract does not even imply an intellectual change of heart on the part of the originating sponsors or key figures of the project.

One of the characteristics of Project Camelot was the number of antagonistic forces it set in motion on grounds quite apart from what may be called considerations of scientific principle. The project was criticized and attacked far more in terms of extrinsic issues of strategies and timing than on intrinsic issues of research design. The mystique of social science seemed to have been taken for granted by friends and foes of the project alike.

The State Department grounded its oppostion to Camelot on the basis of the ultimate authority it has in the area of foreign affairs. There is no published criticism of the design itself. Congressional opposition seemed to be generated by a concern not to rock any foreign alliances, especially with Latin America. Again there was no statement about the ineffectiveness of the project on scientific or intellectual grounds. A third group of skeptics, the academic social scientists, thought that Project Camelot and studies of the processes of revolution and war in general were better left in the control of major university centers and in this way kept free of direct military supervision. However, with the subsequent revelations of university participation in far more covert military and paramilitary activities, such criticisms were not militantly pursued. The Army, for its part, while it offered a considerable amount of support at the informal level, did nothing to contradict Secretary McNamara's order cancelling Project Camelot. Not simply did military influentials feel that they had to execute the Defense Department's orders, but they themselves were probably dubious of the value of "software" definitions of "hardware" systems.

A number of issues which were peripheral to Project Camelot became important in debates concerning its continued funding. In particular, the "jurisdictional" dispute between Defense and State loomed largest. Essentially, the debate between the Defense Department and the State Department is not unlike that which obtains between unions of electricians and bricklayers in the construction of a new apartment house. What union exactly is responsible for which processes? Less generously, the issue is who controls what. The umbrella of responsibility, expertise, and clear lines of authority is, at the root, a question of power and domination. At the policy level, Camelot was a program tossed about in a larger power struggle that has been going on in government circles since the end of World War II, or it may have reflected that particular historical juncture when the Defense Department emerged as authentic competition for honors as the most powerful bureau of the administrative branch of government.

In some sense, too, the divisions between Defense and State are outcomes of the rise of ambiguous politico-military conflicts such as Korea and Vietnam, in contrast to the more precise and diplomatically controlled "classical" world wars. What are the lines dividing political policy from military posture? Who is the most important representative of the United States abroad, the ambassador or the military attaché in charge of the military mission? When soldiers from foreign lands are sent to the United States for political orientation, should such orientation be within the province of the State Department or the Defense Department? When undercover activities are conducted, should the direction of such activities belong to military or political authorities? Each of these is a strategic question with little heuristic or historic precedent. Each of these was profoundly entwined in the Project Camelot explosion. It should be plain that the State Department was not simply responding to the recommendations of Chilean left-wingers in urging the cancellation of Camelot. They used the Chilean hostility to "interventionist" projects as an opportunity to redefine the ratio of forces and to express the lines of power existing at present between the two leading government executive agencies.

The folklore of Washington admits that the primacy of the American ambassador in foreign countries is a polite fiction. The competition he has—from military missions, special roving emissaries sent directly from the presidential office, and from undercover men, sent from the Central Intelligence Agency or the Federal Bureau of Investigation, who often work independently of and even at cross purposes with the ambassador— is not to be dismissed lightly. Perhaps, as a retaliation for these abuses and indignities of his office, the ambassador has sought to reaffirm his own role. And one way has been to control the types of research and investigatory projects planned by itinerant Americans for the nation where he is in residence.

Just why an ambassador should have the right to control scientific research is difficult to explain. Such responsibility assumes an intellectual sophistication that is precisely most noticeable by its absence in our Latin American ambassadorial staff. Yet, within a fortnight after Ambassador Ralph Dungan voiced his strong opposition to Project Camelot, the Ambassador to Brazil, Lincoln Gordon, did likewise over a project supposedly similar in character but in an earlier stage than Camelot. What seems evident from this resistance to social-science projects is not so much a defense of the sovereignty of nations where ambassadors are stationed as it is a defense of the position that conventional political channels are sufficient to yield the information desired or deemed necessary on policy grounds. It further reflects a latent State Department preference for politics as an art rather than politics as an object of science. At the theoretical level, this represents the Machiavellian notion that manipulation rather than clarification is the key concept. In any event, this is what Americans stationed abroad often appear to be concerned with. Whatever the proper stance, whether politics is an art rather than a science or whether conventional diplomatic corps members are more likely to garner meaningful information than newly arrived social-science researchers, it is evident that a combination of conventional and novel intraservice rivalries played a larger part in the termination of Camelot than objective conditions may have warranted.

Congressional reaction to Project Camelot followed the particular representative's or senator's feelings toward military sponsorship of research. Their feelings toward social-science involvement in problems of military science and technology were also clearly at stake. From the remarks reported, Congressmen were either positive toward the military and negative toward social science or negative toward the military and positive toward social science. In such instances, what emerged was a cognitive bind. Thus, most members of Congress, when they were informed of the Camelot situation, were pleased at any resolution that would not add stress to their own perceptions. At other times, those negative toward the military used the occasion to criticize the Defense Department's sponsorship of types of research based on intervention in the affairs of other nations, while those negative toward social science used the occasion to note the ineffectual and impotent character of social science vis-à-vis the smooth operations of good diplomats. Project Camelot was thus caught in a pincer maneuver, and it could neither extricate itself nor rely on its associates to "save" it.

Congressional reaction seems to have been that Project Camelot was bad because it rocked the diplomatic boat in a sensitive geopolitical area. And the first rule of a bureaucratic apparatus is to avoid organizational turmoil, exorcize it befor it spreads. Underlying congressional criticism is the plain fact that most Congressmen are more sympathetic to State Department control of foreign affairs than they are to Defense Department control. In other words, despite military-sponsored world junkets, National and State Guard pressures from the home state, and military training in the career profiles of many congressmen, the sentiment for political rather than military control is more agreeable to them. Hence, their negative response to Camelot is perhaps a function of their general sentiments regarding the State and Defense Departments.

One reason for the violent response to Project Camelot is the singular sponsorship of it by the Department of Defense. The fact is that Latin Americans, in particular, have become quite accustomed to and conditioned by State Department approaches and involvements in the internal affairs of various nations. The Defense Department is a newcomer, a dangerous one, inside the Latin American orbit. The train of thought connected to its activities is in terms of international warfare, spying missions, military manipulations, etc. The State Department, for its part, is often a consultative party to shifts in government and has played an enormous part in either fending off or bringing about *coups d'état*. This State Department role has by now been accepted and even internalized by many smaller nations (and some large ones as well) in the Third World. Not so the Defense Department's image role. The State Department has legitimate claims to have an embassy and legation in Chile; the Defense Department is viewed as an alien force in a country such as Chile—especially since it has such direct ties to the military solution to all political problems—a long-standing anathema to Chilean Christian democracy.

Were Project Camelot to have had State Department sponsorship, it is interesting to conjecture on how matter of fact the reaction to it might have been. The hysteria over Project Camelot was in part due to the popular and diplomatic view that the Defense Department is an alien force in Chile, and hence, its sponsored activities are inherently worse than those initiated by the State Department. But whether this is actually a fault that can properly be placed at the doorstep of Project Camelot is highly conjectural. In point of fact, academic and intellectual criticism of Project Camelot from American colleges and universities, at least, has been sensitive to the complexity of the issues involved. It is true that social scientists of Latin American universities and research centers, notably those of Santiago and Buenos Aires, raised serious ideological objections to the project. But even these remarks are notable for their reserve. It was noted that the "ideological orientation" of Project Camelot was integrated into the research programs in a way that would permit "the generation of hypotheses." It was also noted that the political goals and the military sponsorship of Project Camelot are professionally inadmissible. The questioning of the utility of further collaboration between North American and Latin American social scientists seems to be more rhetorical than threatening. Yet, such doubts rest on criteria that are themselves quite ideological and political. In the main, then, Latin American social scientists, while uniformly negative toward Project Camelot, have not made the kinds of distinctions that would point to a sociologically worthy alternative approach to applied research.

Social scientists in the United States have, for the most part, been reluctant to express themselves publicly on the matter of Camelot. The reasons for this are not hard to find. First, many "giants of the field" are involved in government contract work in one capacity or another. And few souls are in a position to tamper with the gods. Second, information on Project Camelot, even at this late date, has been of a newspaper variety, and professional men are not in a habit of criticizing colleagues on the basis of such information. Third, many social scientists doubtless see nothing wrong or immoral in the Project Camelot designs. And they are therefore more likely to be either confused by or angered with the critical Latin American response to the project directors.

There are nonetheless many "informal" and "private" remarks made about Project Camelot that indicate wide discontent with its approach and with the general turn to federally sponsored research involving social scientists. Area specialists in particular have been vociferous in criticizing the "amateurishness" of Camelot's design. Several scholars complained bitterly that it made their task of collecting data on the main social sectors of vital South American nations much more difficult. One advanced student working on the effects of the Roman Catholic Church on the developmental process of Mexico was told that he could no longer count on Church support since the data would obviously show a left-wing tendency in the Church and thus anger and perhaps alienate powerful forces in the United States. Perhaps most tragically, there is the case of an advanced doctorate candidate at a West Coast university who had completed his data collection on social stratification in Chile, only to find his materials confiscated by customs authorities. And I am told by another young scholar who just returned from two years in Chile that Camelot "jokes" are now in evidence among the younger Latin American intelligentsia. However, what has to be noted is that serious critical analysis of Project Camelot remains at the private level or at the denunciatory stage. These comments usually concern the way in which the sponsors of Camelot went about their work rather than the contents of their outlook.

One of the cloudiest aspects of Project Camelot is the role of American University. Its actual supervisory role over the contract appears to have begun and ended with the 20 percent commission a university receives as expense funds on most federal grants. Thus, while there can be no question as to the "concern and disappointment" of President Hurst R. Anderson of American University over the termination of Project Camelot, the reasons for this regret do not seem to extend beyond the formal and the financial. No official at American University appeared to have been willing or capable of making any statement of responsibility, support, chagrin, opposition, or anything else related to the project. The issues are indeed momentous and must be faced by all universities at which government-sponsored research is conducted: the amount of control a university administration has over contract work; the role of university officials in the distribution of funds from grants; the sort of relationships that ought to be or are expected to be established once a grant is issued; whether project heads should be members of the faculty, and if so, whether they have the necessary teaching functions and opportunities for tenure as do other faculty members.

The difficulty with American University is that it seems to be remarkably unlike most other universities in its permissiveness. The autonomous character of this university is questionable. The Special Operations Research Office received neither guidance nor support from university officials. From the outset, there seems to have been a "gentleman's agreement" not to inquire or interfere in Project Camelot on the part of the university but simply to serve as some sort of camouflage. Such a form of economic opportunism on the part of an institute of higher education can only be considered reprehensible, a symbol of maximum university weakness and disarray. Were the American University genuinely autonomous, it might have been able to lend highly supportive aid to Project Camelot during the crisis months. The fact that American University maintained an official silence preserved it from any congressional or presidential criticism but at the same time pointed up some serious flaws in its administrative and financial policies.

The relationship between Project Camelot, Special Operations Research Office, and American University reflected shortcomings in lines of organizational authority. When the tail wags the dog, the dog must obviously become an appendage. And this is approximately what happened. American University seems to have been little more than window dressing, a fund repository raking off several hundred thousand dollars for administrative services and having no control over the project and little contact with its directors. The stationery itself would indicate what the lines of power were, since *Special Operations Research Office* was originally set in larger type than *American University*. The relationship of Camelot to SORO as a whole presented a similarly muddled organizational picture. The Director of Project Camelot was nominally autonomous and in charge of an organization rivaling in size and importance the overall SORO operation. Yet, at the critical point, the decision taken on the part of SORO was ultimately to protect itself by sacrificing what nominally was its limb. That this part happened to be a vital organ may have hurt, but the loss of the organ was considered scarcely fatal. In fact, the issue of SORO's strategy of yielding up Camelot as a sacrifice to the pagan gods remains a continually debated issue.

Under such circumstances, many social-science institutes throughout the major university centers in the United States wondered out loud why the work of Project Camelot was not allocated to them on the basis of competitive bidding or simply awarded to the capable institutes outright. While social scientists in American academic life are increasingly well funded in their research projects, it is nonetheless the case that they badly lag behind their colleagues in the natural sciences both in the amount of monies received from the government for research purposes and in the conditions under which these funds can be manipulated. The huge amounts, relatively speaking, put at the disposal of Project Camelot were considered another effort to prevent social scientists at major universities from partaking of these funds. It was said, and not denied by the relevant officials, that the Defense Department felt more comfortable in a controlled research situation than they might have in a free research situation. The retort of university-oriented social scientists has been that it is precisely the mistakes made by Project Camelot directors that are best avoided by the kind of atmosphere present in universities rather than in "think-tanks" provided by the armed forces.

The directors of Project Camelot tried to meet such objections by not "classifying" any of its research materials, so that there would be no stigma of secrecy. They also tried to hire, and even hire away from academic positions, people well known and respected for their independence of mind. The difficulty was that even though the stigma of secrecy was formally erased, it remained in the attitudes of many of the employees of Project Camelot. Many of the middle-echelon, less-sophisticated personnel unfortunately thought in terms of secrecy, clearance, missions, and the rest of the bureaucratic ethos that powerfully afflicts the Washington scientific as well as political environment.

It is apparent then that Project Camelot had much greater difficulty hiring a full-time staff of high professional competence than in getting part-time, summertime, weekend, and sundry assistance. Few established figures in academic life were willing to surrender the advantages of their tenured positions for the risks of a project.

Military opposition to Project Camelot was either nonexistent or confined to the general worth of social-science projects. Those men in the armed forces who have a positive orientation toward social science— having worked with social scientists and social materials in the preparation of foreign-area handbooks or having utilized the valuable armed forces organizational and communication studies made by social scientists—were of course dismayed by the cancellation of Project Camelot. In addition, there was a group of military officers who were themselves trained in various social sciences and, hence, saw in the attack on Camelot a double attack—upon their role as officers and their professional competence. But the Army was so clearly treading in new territory that it could scarcely jeopardize the entire structure of military research to preserve one project.

It can be argued that this very inability to preserve Camelot, threatening other governmental contracts with social scientists, no doubt impressed a number of armed forces officers. But this consideration had to be weighed against the overall dangers to military policy. And there is an old military adage that where possible the fight should be conducted on grounds and in terms chosen by the attacking force.

The claim is made by the Camelot staff and various aides that the civilian critics of the project played into the hands of those sections of the military predisposed to vetoing any social-science recommendations. The claim that "software" can never assist "hardware" has indeed been made more than once. But it will be asked, if this is the case, why the military offered such a huge support to the social-science project initially. The answer to this is easier to find than might first be imagined. Four million or seven million dollars is actually a trifling sum for the military in an age of a multibillion-dollar military establishment. The amount is significantly more important for the social sciences where such contract awards remain relatively scarce. Thus, a set of differing perceptions arose as to the importance of Camelot: an Army view that considers a four-to-seven-million-dollar grant as one of many forms of "software" investment and, in contrast, a social-science perception of Project Camelot as the equivalent of the Manhattan Project, which led to the manufacture of the atomic bomb.

The Feasibility of Project Camelot

While most public opposition to Project Camelot centered on its advisability, a considerable amount of scientific opposition centered on its feasibility. This contrasted with the stated attitudes expressed by most of the men I contacted who were involved with Project Camelot. For them, the issues generated were not so much technical as ideological. A curious linguistic dimension frequently cropped up: Camelot personnel would speak of the "Chilean mess" rather than the "Camelot mess" as the outsiders held. Nor should this perspectival distinction be lightly dismissed. In fact, no public document issued by the Camelot directors contested the possibility that, considering the successful completion of the data-gathering stage of the project, Camelot personnel could indeed establish basic criteria for measuring the level and potential for internal war in a given nation. Thus by never challenging the feasibility of the work, the political critics of Project Camelot were providing backhanded compliments to the efficacy of the project design.

From a social-scientific viewpoint, however, more than political considerations are involved. It is clear that for social scientists, particularly those not directly connected with Project Camelot but having a shared interest in problems of the military, revolutions, the developing regions, and their potencies, the critical problems presented by Project Camelot are scientific. In what follows, I shall attempt to summarize what were the most frequently expressed objections to the research design and those that I, in particular, consider to be most relevant.

The research design of Camelot was from the outset plagued by ambiguities. The documents never quite stated whether the purpose of the contract was to study counterinsurgency possibilities or the revolutionary process as a natural event. It was also difficult to determine whether this was to be a study of comparative social structures, a study of a single nation "in depth," or a study of overall social structures with a particular emphasis on military possibilities. While many factors were included for future study, no assignment of relative weight was given. In this way, the methodological relativism of the design contributed to heightening the ambiguity. The organizational support for such ambiguity stemmed from the different perspectives expressed by senior Camelot scientists.

In the four parts of the "master publication" there seem to be at least four different methodologies employed: a social-systems design; a design based on analytic case study materials; a study of internal conflict by means of manual and machine simulation; and an ethnographic report on internal war potentials, which in turn incorporates an appendix attempting to link the report to mathematical functions of authority and competition. Clearly, in a project of this size there was room for different methodological approaches. However, it is not clear just what the relationships were between the individual parts of the project and between each part and the whole. While no one was able to explain these discrepancies, there was a candid admission that they did indeed exist but would have been "worked out" during the life of the project. In other words, though it was the case that most criticisms leading to the termination of Project Camelot were not directed to its intellectual potential, it was especially at the latter level that Camelot personnel thought there was a great deal to be desired. Indeed, a considerable internal opposition (especially on the part of Camelot's advisory committees) to the program was grounded in just these questions of methodology.

An aspect of the research design that unquestionably gave rise to serious criticism and skepticism about Project Camelot was the platitudinous and programmatic content of the original research proposals. An "orientation" that is "scientific," offering a "balanced course between theoretical and empirical work," bringing to bear "all the relevant disciplines and talents required," will obviously raise doubts as to the viability of the methodology. Further, the "over-all outline," while spoken of, failed to materialize in the documents. They are highly eclectic, drawing upon theoretical design effort, analytic case studies, survey research, and "comparative analysis." The only criticism in the documents is reserved for the efforts of an "individual scholar with limited resources." While this may have been useful in stimulating federal financial support, the fact is that the encouragement of "lone wolf" attitudes, of separate research by individuals on their own, may have considerably reduced the suspicion held that Project Camelot was, in Johan Galtung's words, an example of "managerial sociology" or some sort of medieval Jesuitical collectivity.

Eclecticism damaged the scientific aims of the Camelot research. What took place, as illustrated in the main summary, is that the four different research associates of the working group presented an outline in four parts, in a manner that by no means made evident that unified results were either anticipated or even plausibly to be expected. Had the four sets of working papers been presented as just that—four sets of papers—instead of a "unified front" of ideas and attitudes, the scientific character would have been enhanced, and the policy-oriented aspects could have been placed in a larger perspective of social-science scholarship. This said, it must also be noted that the many people who had the opportunity to criticize were quite reticent. The Project Camelot working groups, when they did make criticisms, found a ready response from the project directors. Also, the first year on any project of such scale cannot be expected to yield sophisticated conclusions.

There was a noticeable tendency toward the use of hygienic and sanitized language in the descriptions of the project. We are told about a "precipitant" of internal war as being an "event which actually starts the war." Whereas "preconditions" are "circumstances which make it possible for the precipitants to bring about political violence." Obviously, "events" do not start wars, only *people* do. "Precipitants" do not bring about political violence, only *participants* do.

This is followed by a general critique of social science for failing to deal with social conflict and social control. And while this in itself represents an admirable recognition, the tenor and context of the design make it plain that a "stable society" is the considered norm no less than the desired outcome. The "breakdown of social order" is spoken of accusatively. Stabilizing agencies in developing areas are not so much criticized as presumed to be absent. A critique of U.S. Army policy is absent because the Army is presumed to be a stabilizing agency. Rather than reflecting love for the Army, the formulations simply assume the legitimacy of the Army tasks. "If the U.S. Army is to perform effectively its part in the U.S. mission of counterinsurgency it must recognize that insurgency represents a breakdown of social order. . . ." But such a proposition has never been doubted—by Army officials or by anyone else. The issue is whether such breakdowns are in the nature of the existing system or a product of conspiratorial movements. Here the hygienic language disguises the antirevolutionary assumptions under a cloud of powder-puff declarations.

Sanitary terminology is also evident in describing political regimes and in determining nations to be studied. Studies of Paraguay are recommended "because trends in this situation [the Stroessner regime] may also render it 'unique' when analyzed in terms of the transition from 'dictatorship' to political stability." What "transition"? Since when have social scientists perceived dictatorship and political stability as occupying the same level of meaning? No dictatorship has ever been more "stable" than Hitlerism. One might speak of the transition from dictatorship to democracy or from totalitarianism to authoritarianism. But to speak about changes from dictatorship to stability is an obvious rubric. In this case, it is a tactic to disguise the fact that Paraguay is one of the most vicious, undemocratic *(and stable)* societies in the Western Hemisphere.

These typify the sorts of hygienic sociological premises that have extrascientific purposes. They illustrate the confusion of commitments among Project Camelot spokesmen. The very absence of ideological terms such as "revolutionary masses," communism, socialism, capitalism, etc., intensifies the discomfort one must feel on examination, since the abstract vocabulary disguises rather than resolves the problems of international revolution. It does not proceed beyond U.S. Army vocabulary, not because this vocabulary is superior to revolutionary vocabulary, but simply because it is the language of the donor. To have used clearly political rather than military language would not "justify" governmental support. Furthermore, shabby assumptions of academic respectability replaced innovative orientations. In fact, by adopting a systems approach, the problematic, open-ended, and practical aspects of the study of revolutions were largely omitted; and the design of the system became an oppressive curb on the contents of the problems inspected.

This points up a critical implication of the Camelot affair. The importance of the subject being researched does not uniquely determine the importance of the project per se. A sociology of large-scale relevance and reference is all to the good. It is important that scholars be willing to risk something of their reputations in helping to resolve major world social problems. But it is no less important that in the process of addressing their attention to major international problems the autonomous character of the social science disciplines, their own criteria of worthwhile scholarship, not be abandoned. It is my opinion that the ambiguity, asymmetry, and eclecticism of the fragmented and programmatic nature of even the most advanced documents circulated by Project Camelot lost sight of this "autonomous" social-science character in the pursuit of the larger demands of society.

It never seemed to occur to the Camelot directorship to inquire into the chances and desirability for successful revolution. This is just as solid a line of inquiry as that which was emphasized: namely, Under what conditions will revolutionary movements be able to overthrow a government? Furthermore, they seem not to have thought about inquiring into the role of the United States in these countries. This points up the lack of symmetry. The project need not have focused exclusively on the North American presence. However, the problem should have been phrased to include the study of "us" as well as "them." It is not possible to make a decent analysis of a situation unless one takes into account the role of the different people and major groups involved. In its initial stage at least, there was no room in the design of Camelot for such contingency analysis.

This one-sidedness is not unusual in sociology. As a result, shortcomings in this approach did not glare up at any of the key participants to the project. Camelot did not seem sufficiently different from ordinary sociological practices to warrant any special precautionary measures. And the precedents relied upon were indeed of a reassuring variety.

An early example was industrial sociology, where many people worked for many years on essentially managerial problems. But there were some sociologists with an affinity for labor who saw through the business bias and began to complain about a sociology that simply performs the dirty work of industrial management. An even stronger case is medical sociology. In that field, almost everyone took (and still takes) for granted the proposition that what the doctors want and think is good for everyone. Until *Boys in White,* it never occurred to anyone to ask how things might be from the patient's point of view. Later, there were other exceptions, research that insisted on treating doctors just like anyone else. The nature of the asymmetry in Project Camelot is two-fold. First, it failed to ask *all* the questions that need to be asked. Second, it did not open to investigation the motives and biases of the sponsoring agencies.

In short, many sociologists are used to asking their questions improperly simply because to do so may serve heuristic ends in a marketable way. When they are presented with the opportunity to influence policymakers as in the case of Project Camelot, they can do little better than puff up stale methodological forms for new use. They are also the primitive substantive guidelines used. The Enlightenment assumption that people in power need only to be shown the truth in order to do the right thing is unacceptable. Nevertheless, it is clear that some well-intentioned people have accepted elitism as an exclusive framework. They need to be reminded that this is by no means the only possible position.

In discussing the policy impact on a social-science research project, we should not overlook the difference between "contract" work and "grants." Project Camelot began with the U.S. Army, that is to say, it was initiated for a practical purpose determined by the client. This differs markedly from the typical academic grant in that military sponsorship is distinctive for its "built-in" ends. The scholar seeks the grant, whereas this donor stipulated projected aims. In some measure, the hostility for Project Camelot may be an unconscious reflection of this distinction between grants and contracts, a dim feeling that there was something "nonacademic," and certainly not disinterested, about Project Camelot irrespective of the quality of the scholars associated with it.

This raises the yet deeper issue: Are social scientists to approach contract work in the same spirit as they approach grant work? Does contract work, once accepted, signify broad acceptance of the terms of the contract, or is it simply a formalism, a cover-all enabling the scholar to proceed at his will to do as he wishes? The originating statements about the nature of Project Camelot are ambiguous on this point. They promote contractual obligations of working within the Army's project design and yet indicate the free-funding characteristics of the grant. In all likelihood, contributing scholars viewed Camelot funds much as they would any other funds received from a private donor.

Project Camelot documents suffered greatly from the sin of pride. They made a fine show of incorporating many social scientists and diverse points of view. There was no effort to impose ironclad a priori theoretical outcomes. However, the assumption that Project Camelot was somehow essential and vital to the national interests went undisputed. All available scientific thought was to be fed into Project Camelot, while the utilization of all this input was left unexplained. This assumption of critical importance was undoubtedly a primary factor in why the men of Camelot were shaken when the Chilean story became public knowledge. It brought home the fact that what is essential for some may be insignificant for others.

Characteristic of all research projects is an inflated sense of self-importance. This is necessary if for no other reason than that it would be hard to generate enthusiasm and self-sacrificing work without the myth that what one does is potentially earth-shattering. This very impulse toward self-importance on the part of Camelot returns us to the basic verities of the relationship between things that are scientifically valid and things that are socially important.

The Ethics of Policy Research

Just what are the limits and obligations, no less than the rights, of the scientific researcher to investigate the viscera of another society on behalf of a government foreign to that society? This question, which in effect is nothing short of the nature and limits of sovereignty and legitimacy, can perhaps be more readily understood by reference to an example from "middle-range" research. By placing secret recording devices in a juryroom in order to study its decision-making process, have sociologists not also violated the basis of jury procedures by tampering with their sovereignty as such? Is the information yielded worth the costs involved? The same question must be raised in connection with Camelot and the study of a foreign nation in depth.

The issue of "scientific rights" versus "social myths" is perennial. Some maintain that the scientist ought not penetrate beyond legally or morally sanctioned limits and others argue that such limits cannot exist for science—at least not for an applied science. In treading on the sensitive issue of national sovereignty, Project Camelot reflected and became subject to the generalized dilemma. For this matter of the legitimate rights of the army, of scientists, of the sovereignty of the national entities chosen for scrutiny, was bound to be felt as well as stated with some indignation. In sheer deference to the scientific researcher, in recognition of him as a scholar, he should have been invited to air his misgivings and qualms about government and especially army-sponsored research, to declare his moral conscience. Social scientists were mistakenly approached as skillful, useful potential employees of a "higher" body, subject to an authority greater than their scientific calling.

What is central is not the political motives of the sponsor. For social scientists were not being enlisted by Camelot in an intelligence system for "spying" purposes. But given the social scientist's professional standing, his great sense of intellectual honor and pride in his subtle and far-reaching capacities, he could not be "employed" without damaging his self-image and stature. His professional authority should have prevailed from beginning to end with complete command of the right to thrash out the moral and political dilemmas as he viewed them. The Army, however respectful and protective of free expression at the formal level, was "hiring help" and not openly submitting military problems to the *higher* professional and scientific authority of social science.

To be a servant of power is distinct from being a wielder of power. The relationship of a professional savant to a policy-maker is different from that of the psychoanalyst to a patient. Not only does the psychoanalyst exercise a legitimate form of superordination; but such a role of dominance derives from a public acceptance of his intellectual skills. In the case of the social and political scientists on Project Camelot, the limitations of social research were never made clear. Had the Army approached the problem the way a patient going to an analyst might, namely, that something was chronically wrong and it ought to be repaired, some balance might have been maintained. But the right of the armed forces to cancel its contract with Camelot was never placed in question. This relationship of inequality at the informal level at least corrupted the lines of authority and profoundly limited the autonomy of the social scientists involved.

The social scientists of Camelot contributed to this imbalance by an ingenuous eagerness to adopt or incorporate an alien vocabulary no less than an alien set of sociological assumptions. It became clear that the social scientist as servant to power was not so much functioning as an applied social scientist as he was performing the role of supplying information and making evaluations. What happened in Project Camelot is that values and heuristics were linked in an illicit alliance. The uniform assumption made by Camelot personnel was that the scientific worth of the project was uniquely determined by the scope and social significance of the project, thus ignoring the important function of independent criteria in measuring scientific research.

What is at stake in a practical way is the extent to which the social importance of a work can justify its scientific character. Project Camelot failed to respond to this problem of linking importance to quality. The question of who sponsors research is not nearly as decisive as the question of ultimate use of such information. The sponsorship of a project, whether by the U.S. Army or by the Boy Scouts of America, is in itself neither good nor bad. Sponsorship is a factor for consideration only insofar as the intended outcomes can be predetermined and the parameters of those intended outcomes tailored to the sponsor's expectations. The defenders of Camelot failed to penetrate to the nature of objections because the formulations made by its spokesmen were in terms of the independence and freedom of the project, whereas the critics of the project never really denied this freedom and independence but questioned instead the purpose and character of these intended results.

The sensitivities of the project to political issues are an independent dimension. It is not simply a question of the character of the project but of the political atmosphere in which a project is placed on the marketplace.

At the time of Camelot, the American intervention in the Dominican Republic took place. The occupation by United States troops had a catalyzing effect on the rest of Latin America, particularly on a country such as Chile, which did not go along with various rulings of the Organization of American States. Chile thus became acutely sensitized to the possibilities of the overthrow of its own regime. One accusation went so far as to say that the purpose of Camelot was the overthrow of the constituted Chilean government, much as the government of Brazil had been overthrown a year earlier for its intransigence to earlier OAS efforts with respect to Cuba. However groundless such accusations against Camelot may have been, the failure of the project directors to take the political situation into account led them to make assumptions about foreign receptivity to the project's design that simply were unreal and insensitive. It may be that the very multitude of purposes leads to a gigantic problem. Be that as it may, men continue to seek out the purpose of life; and research projects which fail to address themselves to the fact that nations, like persons, are jealous of their rights—real or presumed—cannot help but lead to disastrous consequences.

It would be a gross oversimplification to assume that the theoretical problems of Project Camelot derived from the reactionary character of the project's designers. The director went far and wide to select men for the advisory board, the core planning group, the summer study group, and the various conference groupings who were in fact more liberal in their orientations than any random sampling of the sociological profession would be likely to turn up. But in a sense this search for broad representation was itself a problem rather than a solution. To choose a panel of experts with the deliberate aim of assembling representatives of particular approaches—from believers in maximum usage of counterinsurgency techniques to believers in the utter inefficacy of counterrevolutionary tactics, and from advocates of massive deterrence to adherents in civil disobedience—is not as fallacious in itself as it is in its expectations. It is fanciful to expect such people to adjudicate their differences by analogy with the committed procedure of a bureaucratic organization. It should surprise no one that the result is more often a common denominator than a well-rounded position or design. The premium on accommodation is great enough so that the April 1, 1965 Report suffers at once from four weakened formulations without arriving at the much-vaunted well-rounded position.

The representation of this confusion between science and policy is made often and in a way which is often self-contradictory. For instance, in his reply to the Argentine sociologists' declaration, Professor Hopper says that "there is no ideological orientation of the project beyond the conviction that the scientific method is useful and therefore ought to be applied to the research objectives of the project." However, in nearly every page of the various working papers, there are assertions that clearly derive from the American military policy objectives rather than the scientific method. The steady assumption that internal warfare is damaging and is a state in which "a government might take [steps] to relieve conditions which are assessed as giving rise to a potential for internal war" itself disregards the possibility that a government may not be in a position to take actions either to relieve or to improve mass conditions, or that such actions as are contemplated may be more concerned with reducing conflict than with improving conditions. The added statements about the U.S. Army and its "important mission in the positive and constructive aspects of nation building" assume the reality of such a function in an utterly unquestioning and unconvincing form. The idea of applied science, of a selective program of assistance to some social forces at the expense of others, should not be taken as a mandate for disregarding the rules of the scientific game. And the first rule is not to make assumptions about friends and enemies in such a way as to promote the use of different criteria for the former and the latter.

The many diverse studies being conducted of foreign nations will continue. The military will press on for more exact information, particularly in areas close to the military buffering point, and finally the social scientists will press on in their search for a policy-oriented El Dorado. They are no more likely to give up the search for policy relatedness than the military is willing to give up the search for scientific information. The questions raised by the birth and death of Camelot only introduce in modern guise the problems long raised by Kant in philosophy and Weber in sociology, and which continue to plague the social science world.

The story of Project Camelot was not a confrontation of good versus evil: not that all men behaved with equal fidelity or equal civility—that obviously was not the case. Some men were weaker than others; some more callous and some more stupid. But all this is extrinsic to the problem of Camelot. The heart of the question must always be: What are and are not the legitimate functions of a scientist?

One interesting sidelight is how little the question of communism came into focus, and yet it is clear that one's attitude toward Left and Right, toward social reform and social change, toward Americanism or anti-Americanism, form the warp and woof of the attitudes expressed on the project. In some sense, this is an ultimate vindication of social science as a human science, since the ideological goals sought are clearly fused to the organizational instruments used.

Project Camelot was intellectually and ideologically unsound. More significantly, Camelot was not cancelled because of its faulty intellectual approaches. Instead, its cancellation came as an act of government censorship and an expression of the contempt for social science so prevalent among those who need it most. Thus it was political expedience, rather than Camelot's lack of scientific merit, that led to its termination: it threatened to upset State Department relations with Latin America. Giving the State Department the right to screen and approve government-funded social-science research projects on other countries, as the President has ordered, is a supreme act of censorship. Among the agencies that grant funds for such research are the National Institutes of Health, the National Science Foundation, the National Aeronautics and Space Agency, and the Office of Education. Why should the State Department have veto power over the scientific pursuits of men and projects funded by these and other agencies in order to satisfy the policy needs—or policy failures—of the moment? President Johnson's directive was thus a gross violation of the autonomous nature of science, even though the project itself may well have been a gross violation of sound canons of morality and methodology.

We must be careful not to allow social-science projects with which we may vociferously disagree on political and ideological grounds to be decimated or dismantled by government fiat. Across the ideological divide is a common social-science understanding that the contemporary expression of reason in politics is applied social science, and that the cancellation of Camelot, however pleasing it may be on political grounds to advocates of a civilian solution to Latin American affairs, represents a decisive setback for social-science research.

Project Camelot: A Retrospective Evaluation

As in all major events, the passage of time does not so much diminish interests as it alters persepctives. Issues have arisen that will occupy and preoccupy the attention of social scientists and policy-makers for years to come. Here, we can only allude to some of the new perspectives that have emerged in the wake of Project Camelot. We shall concentrate on three points—each of which has come up quite frequently in correspondence and conversations on Project Camelot. These may not be the central issues for the public at large, but they certainly appear to be central for the social-science community.

A big issue is whether or not the social scientist should work for the government (or at least for certain agencies within the government). In our terms, this is the conflict between "selling out" on one side and "copping out" on the other. This conflict can only be resolved by a firm concept of *autonomy*—both organizational and ideological. In a world of power, it seems to be more sober to develop countervailing modalities of power than to huff and puff at the walls of the national sovereignty. At this level, the trouble has been that social-science organizations make far too few demands upon federal agencies. At times, it appears as if the leadership of social-scientific organizations still does not believe that the successes of the social sciences are real. Having been reared in a period of relative deprivation for the social sciences, the social scientists view all funds as big and all projects as wonderful. Perhaps if we were to realize that the social sciences are no longer at the stage of primitive accumulation, we might be able to resolve this dilemma of selling out versus copping out.

Some critics of Camelot are vigorous in affirming the right of the State Department to censor projects of a social-science nature. They say that the problem is not one of substance but of subjects: that is, Who is in charge of these programs? I believe this to be an irrelevant consideration. The need of the moment is not for more liberal-minded censors (although it may be for more liberal attitudes in general) but for an end to censorship as such—benign or malignant. To borrow a thought from the late Bernard Shaw: censorship, mild or severe, is severe. The problems presented in the design of Project Camelot cannot be resolved by presidential fiat or administrative edict but only by the constant checking and crosschecking that define the methods of social-science research.

Other critics of Camelot wish to place a moratorium on social-science work for or under federal sponsorship. It is my view that a less drastic, but perhaps far more effective, way of gaining respect for the social sciences would be an across-the-board change in the format of the higher arts of grantsmanship: the need for more grants (scientifically initiated research) and fewer contracts (agency-initiated research); the need for a financial pool arrangement, that is, on every grant received there should be a portion set aside (preferably under the supervision of either the university or the social-science institute processing grants) without regard to either the disburser or recipient of the grant; the need for more emphasis on individuals and less on collectivities. The big whopping grants given to teams may have so many dysfunctional byproducts (the creation of new bureaucratic substructures, the mediocrity of the finished product, etc.) that it may be time for the social-science agencies themselves to begin researching the shortcomings of team efforts (as in the past they did of individual efforts) and request, even demand, of federal and private agencies more concern for and attention to the needs of the individual scholar.

Equation of policy research with applied social science in general is perhaps summed up by the word "instrumental." The assumption of those who argue on heuristic grounds appears to be as follows: *if all reasearch conducted by scholars for the government is operational and if such operational research is subject to some form of control then any research done for the government is subject to control.* We should deny the premise and therefore the logic of bureaucratic reasoning which raises doubts as to the credibility of social-science research in area studies. Precisely this recourse to operational definitions of government-sponsored work may stimulate, rather than curb, subterfuge in assignment of funds and create a broad-scale suspicion (among Latin Americans at least) that even university-based research is not necessarily liberated from government-determined operational needs.

It is perfectly fair to expect that the division of federal agencies responsible for sensitive work be made as clear as possible and with a minimum of embarrassment to our own personnel—researchers and diplomats alike. It is also the responsibility of the State Department to conduct foreign affairs in a way that will neither discredit our own people nor outrage the people of the host countries. It is also fair to expect the State Department to prevent the kind of executive agency rivalries that would lead to chaos and competition rather than useful information. But the terms of the presidential mandate under which the review board has been set up are frighteningly extensive. They are likely to inhibit not only the operational research represented by Camelot but also the kind of independent research—let us say on the consequences of United States intervention in the Dominican Republic—that may be either noninstrumental or downright counterinstrumental in character.

The problem with Project Camelot is not exclusively political but also methodological. The identification of revolution and radical social change with a social pathology is the final proof, if such were necessary, that the functionalist credo of order, stability, pattern maintenance, stress management, and so forth, does indeed reveal strong conservative drives. However, a cautionary note should be added: the fact that certain functionalists and systems designers employ their method for conservative goals does not mean that all functional or structural social scientists are conservative—or, for that matter, that the goals of Project Camelot created a need for such a strict methodology. Examination of the documents shows that there is scant evidence of a direct linkage between functional analysis and ideological faith. Some men connected to the project even revealed a somewhat Marxist methodological preference.

If Project Camelot has served to focus the attention of social science on the acute problems of the interconnections between organization and research, ideology and science, then its "unanticipated consequences" will have by far outweighed the discomforts and even the agonies of the present moment. Project Camelot, by raising in the sharpest way the question of the *credibility* of American social science precisely at that point in time when the problems of data reliability seem to have been resolved, is an issue of paramount significance. The coming of age of American social science has been a painful experience. But could it have been otherwise?

1965

14

Social Scientists
and
Military Commissars

"The bonds between the government and the universities are . . . an arrangement of convenience, providing the government with politically usable knowledge and the university with badly needed funds." The speaker of these words, Senator J. William Fulbright, went on to warn that such alliances may endanger the universities, may bring about "the surrender of independence, the neglect of teaching, and the distortion of scholarship." Many other distinguished Americans are disturbed by the growing number of alliances between the military and the university. The Department of Defense (DoD) is the most sought after and frequently found sponsor of social-science research. And the DoD is sought and found by the social scientists, not, as is often imagined, the other way around. Customarily, military men provide only grudging admission of the need for behavioral research.

There are four distinct reasons why the DoD is sponsoring more and more social-science research. *First:* money. In fiscal 1968, congressional appropriations for research and development amounted to the monumental sum of $14,971.4 million. Of this, an incredible $13,243.0 million, or about 85 percent, was distributed among three agencies whose primary concern is the military system: the Atomic Energy Commission, the National Aeronautics and Space Administration, and the DoD. The figure for the DoD alone is $6,680.0 million. This means that a single federal agency commands nearly two-fifths of the government research dollar. So it is easy to see why so much effort and energy is expended by social scientists trying to capture some of the monies the DoD has to experiment with. As bees flock to honey, men flock to money—particularly in an era when costly data processing and data gathering strain the conventional sources of financing.

Second: the protection from political scrutiny given research undertaken for the DoD. I am referring to the blanket and indiscriminate way in which congressional appropriations are made for both basic and applied research. Policy-linked social scientists operate under an umbrella of secrecy established by the DoD's research agencies. So-called security demands eliminate the threat of harassment by congressional committees. Attacks over supposed misallocations of funds and resources—such as those directed against the National Institutes of Health by congressional appropriations committees and the General Accounting Office—are not made against academics with DoD funding.

This dispensation allows DoD to remain free from attacks despite the fact that its allocations for research and development are not itemized the way allocations are for Health, Education, and Welfare. This auditing cover allows DoD even greater flexibility than its already swollen funds would indicate to do experimentation. Such a *carte blanche* situation probably places far less strain on social scientists than would be the case if they worked for other agencies. In the world of research, power provides the illusion of freedom.

Third: the relatively blank-check congressional approach to DoD funds and the security umbrella of the auditing system provide social scientists with unlimited resources. DoD allocations are not broken down into subagencies, nor are any of their specialized activities or services checked —unlike the usual scrutiny directed at other agencies.

That this condition has not gone entirely unnoticed is shown by the congressional demand that as of 1968 the DoD be called to account on an appropriation budget.

Fourth, the DoD's connection with "national security"—which protects the DoD and those who work for it—offers great temptation to social researchers interested in the "big news." For it enables the DoD not only to outspend such agencies as the National Science Foundation in university-based activities, but also to penetrate areas of non-Defense research that are central only to the social-science researcher. Programs to support juvenile-delinquency research (Project 100,000) and others to upgrade academic institutions (Project Themis) are sponsored by the DoD rather than by the Office of Economic Opportunity and not simply because of their disproportionate fundings. Just as important is the legitimation the DoD can provide for policy-oriented researchers in sensitive areas.

These are the main reasons why many social-science researchers are now enlisting the support of the DoD in their activities—despite the negative publicity surrounding Project Camelot and other such fallen angels.

The Setting

Instead of the expected disclaimers and denials from university officials, these men—from both administrative and academic sides—have rushed in recent months to take up any slack in secret research study on campus, asking that the number of projects they are already handling be increased. Arwin A. Dougal, assistant director of the Pentagon's Office for Research and Engineering, has indicated that while some major universities are gravely concerned about academic research for military ends, most universities realize how important "classified research" is to the national security. Indeed, Dougal has said that many professors involved in secret research actually try to retain their security clearances when their projects are completed. Rather than disengaging themselves, they, like many other university leaders, are eager to participate to an even greater extent.

Symptomatic of the ever-tightening bond between the military and the social scientist is a "confidential," 53-page document entitled *Report of the Panel on Defense Social and Behavioral Sciences.* It was the offspring of a summer 1967 meeting, in Williamstown, Mass., of members of the Defense Science Board of the National Academy of Sciences. This board is the highest-ranking science advisory group of the Defense Department. The meeting's purpose: to discuss which areas of social-science research would be of most use to the Department of Defense (DoD).

The Report of the Panel on Defense Social and Behavioral Sciences throws a good deal of light on current relations between the national government and the social sciences. Unlike Project Camelot, the abortive academic-military project to investigate counterinsurgency potentials in the Third World, this report was not inspired by government contractual requests. It is the work of leading social scientists who have been closely connected with federal research. Unlike *Report from Iron Mountain,* this report can hardly be described as a humanistic hoax. The authors are known, the purpose of the report explicit, and the consequences clearly appreciated by all concerned. What we have in this report is a collective statement by eminent social scientists, a statement that can easily be read as the ominous conversion of social science into a service industry of the Pentagon.

Most of the scholars who prepared this report have one striking similarity—they have powerful and concurrent academic and government linkages. They move casually and easily from university to federal affiliation—and back again to the university.

The panel's chairman, S. Rains Wallace, the exception, is president of the American Institutes of Research, a nonprofit organization that does research under contract for government agencies, including the DoD. Gene M. Lyons, who is executive secretary of the Advisory Committee on Government Programs in the Behavioral Sciences of the National Research Council (affiliated with the National Academy of Sciences), is also a professor at Dartmouth College. (He maintains, however, that he attended only one day of the meeting, and as an observer only.) Peter Dorner, functioning through the Executive Office of the President on the Council of Economic Advisers, is also a professor of economics at the Land Tenure Center of the University of Wisconsin. Eugene Webb, listed as a professor at Stanford University, is now serving a term as a member of the Institute for Defense Analysis, specifically, its science and technology division. Other panel members—Harold Guetzkow of Northwestern University; Michael Pearce of the RAND Corporation; anthropologist A. Kimball Romney of Harvard University; and Roger Russell, formerly of Indiana University and now Vice-Chancellor for Academic Affairs at the University of California (Irvine)—also shift back and forth between the polity and the academy. It is plain, then, that these men have penetrated the political world more deeply than did members of past project-dominated research activities.

In addition to this similarity, nearly all these social scientists have had overseas experience and are intimately connected with federal use of the social sciences for foreign-area research. Yet, as in the case of Camelot, this common experience does not seem to produce any strong ideological unanimity. The men range from relatively conservative political theorists to avowed pacifists. This underscores the fact that patriotism and professional purpose tend to supersede the political viewpoints or credos these men may adhere to.

The Report

The Report closely follows the memorandum that John S. Foster, Jr., director of Defense Research and Engineering of the Department of Defense, issued to the chairman of the panel. Foster's marching orders to the panel members requested that they consider four topics: "high-payoff" areas in research in which it would be reasonable to expect large profits over the next three to ten years; research to solve manpower problems; Project Themis, a DoD project for upgrading the scientific and engineering capabilities of various academic institutions so that they can do better research for the Defense Department; and, finally, broad-ranging government-university relationships.

Before commenting on the report, let me provide a summary of its findings and recommendations. To begin with, the report urges increased effort and funding for research on manpower, in all its aspects; for research on organization studies; for research on decision-making; for increasing the understanding of problems in foreign areas; and for research on man and his physical environment.

Under "Manpower," we read, among other things: "In order to make full use of the opportunities provided by Project 100,000 [to make soldiers out of rehabilitated juvenile delinquents] both for the military and for the national economy, we recommend that fully adequate funds be invested to cover all aspects of the military and subsequent civilian experience of the individuals involved."

Under "Organization Studies": "Research on style of leadership and improved methods of training for leadership should be revitalized."

Under "Decision-Making": "Techniques for the improvement of items which might assist in forecasting alliances, neutralities, hostile activities, etc., and for use in tactical decision-making need to be expanded, applied, and tested in the real world."

Under "Understanding of Operational Problems in Foreign Areas": "Despite the difficulties attendant upon research in foreign areas, it must be explicitly recognized that the missions of the DoD cannot be successfully performed in the absence of information on (a) sociocultural patterns in various areas including beliefs, values, motivations, etc.; (b) the social organization of troops, including political, religious, and economic; (c) study and evaluation of action programs initiated by U.S. or foreign agencies in underdeveloped countries.

"Solid, precise, comparative, and current empirical data developed in a programmatic rather than diffuse and opportunistic fashion are urgently needed for many areas of the world. This goal should be pursued by: (a) multidisciplinary research teams; (b) series of field studies in relevant countries; (c) strong representation of quantitative and analytic skills; (d) a broad empirical data base."

Under "Man and His Physical Environment": "Continuing and additional research are needed on the effect of special physical and psychological environments upon performance and on possibilities for the enhancement of performance through a better understanding of man's sensory and motor output mechanisms, the development of artificial systems which will aid performance, and the search for drugs or goods which may enhance it."

Under "Methodology": "We recommend increased emphasis upon research in behavioral-science methodology. While this is basic to all of the areas listed above, it needs to be recognized as worthy of investment in its own right. The systematic observations of the many quasi-experimental situations which occur in everyday military activities must be made possible if we are to learn from experience. We recommend that a capability be established in one or more suitable in-house laboratories to address the question of how the logistical problems of such observation can be solved."

On "Government-University" relations: "There is disagreement concerning the involvement of first-rate academic groups in behavioral science research relevant to long-term DoD needs. The task statement implies that DoD has not been successful in enlisting the interest and service of an eminent group of behavioral scientists in most of the areas relevant to it. This panel does not concur. We therefore recommend that the [National Academy of Sciences] Panel on Behavioral and Social Sciences be asked to address this problem and to determine whether, in fact, an acceptable proportion of first-rate academic workers are involved in DoD behavioral-science research.

"More high-quality scientists could probably be interested in DoD problems if DoD would more frequently state its research needs in terms which are meaningful to the investigator rather than to the military. . . . Publicity concerning the distinguished behavioral scientists who have long-term commitments to the DoD should be disseminated as a way of reassuring younger scientists and improving our research image."

The Panelists

Why did these distinguished social scientists accept the assignment from the DoD? Most of them seemed particularly intrigued by the chance to address important issues. They viewed the work done by the DoD in such areas as racially segregated housing, or the rehabilitation of juvenile delinquents through military participation, as fascinating illustrations of how social science can settle social issues. It is curious how this thirst for the application of social science led the panelists to ignore the *prima facie* fact that the DoD is in the defense business and that therefore it inevitably tends to assign high priority to military potential and effectiveness. Further, the question of what is important is continually linked to matters of relevance to the DoD. In this way, the question of professional autonomy is transformed into one of patriotic responsibility.

In general, the idealism of social scientists participating in DoD-sponsored research stems from their profound belief in the rectifiability of federal shortcomings, as well as in the perfectibility of society through the use of social science. Despite the obviousness of the point, what these social scientists forget is that the federal government as well as its agencies is limited by historical and geopolitical circumstances. The federal bureaucracy is committed to managing cumbersome, overgrown committees and data-gathering agencies. It is further committed to a status quo merely for the sake of rational functioning. It can only tinker with innovative ideas. Thus federal agencies often limit investigations to perfecting the instruments of government. Social scientists and their designing mentality, their strain toward perfection, appear unrealistic to those charged with government operations.

The social scientist often imagines he is a policy formulator, an innovating designer. Because of the cumbersome operations of government, he will be frustrated in realizing this self-image and be reduced to one more instrumental in light of what he can do. He gets caught up in theoryless applications to immediacy, surrenders the value of confronting men with an image of what *can be,* and simply accepts what others declare *must be.* Thus, what the social scientist knows comes down to what the Defense Department under present circumstances can use.

Although the initiative for this report came from the social scientists, the DoD provided the structure and direction of its content. To a remarkable degree, the study accepted DoD premises. For example, the two major assumptions that influenced its thinking are stated baldly. First, since the DoD's job now embraces new responsiblities, its proper role becomes as much to wage "peacefare" as warfare. Peacefare is spelled out as pacification of total populations, as well as a role in the ideological battle between East and West. Toward such ends, it is maintained, social science can play a vital part.

Nowhere in the document is the possibility considered that the DoD ought not to be involved in many of these activities—that perhaps the division of labor has placed too great an emphasis upon this one agency of government at the expense of all others. Nor is it anywhere made clear that educational and antipoverty programs similar to those the DoD is engaged in are already underway in other branches of government—that

DoD activities might be duplicating and needlessly multiplying the efforts of the Department of Health, Education, and Welfare or the National Science Foundation.

The second explicit assumption that the group makes is that hardware alone will not win modern wars; manpower is needed, too. Here the panelists see social science as providing data on the dynamics of cultural change and a framework for the needs and attitudes of other people. Here, too, there is a remarkable absence of any consideration of the sort of "manpower" deployed in foreign environments; or of the differing responses of overseas peoples to such manpower. The foreign role of the U.S. Defense Department is simply taken as a given, a datum to be exploited for the display of social-science information. In this sense, U.S. difficulties with foreign military activities can be interpreted as a mere misunderstanding of the nature of a problem. Expertise and objectivity can then be called upon where a policy design is lacking or failing. Thus even the DoD can mask policy shortcomings behind the fact of a previously inadequate supply of data. In this way, the credibility gap is converted into a mechanical information gap—which is exactly what is done in the report. All efforts, in other words, are bent to maximizing social-science participation rather than to minimizing international conflict.

Still a third assumption of the panel participants—one that is not acknowledged—is that their professional autonomy will not be seriously jeopardized by the very fact of their dependence upon the DoD. Indeed, many scholars seem to have abandoned their primary research interests for the secondary ones that can be funded. And the main responsbility for this shift lies not with the DoD but with the social-science professions and the scholarly community at large. As one panel member ironically noted, in response to my questionnaire, the position of the DoD is an unhappy reflection of university demands that individual scholars and university presidents pay for expanding university overhead and enlarged graduate programs—rather than any insistence by federal agencies that the nature of social science be transformed. Another panel member indicated that, whatever dishonor may exist in the present relationships between social science and the DoD, the main charge would have to be leveled at the professoriat rather than the funding agencies. And while this assignment of priorities in terms of who is responsible for the present era of ill will and mistrust can be easily overdone and may lead to a form of higher apologetics in which there is mutual accusation by the social scientists and government policy-makers, it does seem clear that the simplistic idea that the evil government corrupts the good social scientist is not only an exaggeration but, more often, a deliberate misrepresentation.

The Findings

Reexamining the specific findings of the first section of the report, "High Payoff Research in Development Areas," leaves no doubt that the panelists mean by "high payoff" those potential rewards to be netted by the DoD, rather than advantages to be gained by social scientists. This is made explicit in the section on "Manpower," in which the main issues concern problems of improving the performance of soldiers equipped with high-level technology. It is in this connection that the panelists heartily approve of Project 100,000. Although (with the exception of two panelists) there is a special cloudiness as to the nature of Project 100,000, the panelists have no doubt that the employment of delinquents in this fashion makes the best use of marginal manpower for a "tremendous payoff" in the future efficiency of the defense establishment.

A number of the report's recommendations amount to little more than the repetition of basic organizational shibboleths. But even at this level, special problems seem to arise. There is confusion in the minds of the panelists, or at least throughout the report that they prepared, about what constitutes internal DoD functions as opposed to those belonging to general military functions. The phrase "military establishment" functions as an umbrella disguising this ambiguity. Not only is the relationship between a civilian-led DoD and a "military establishment" unresolved, but beyond that the panelists appear willing to discount the organizational intermingling of the DoD with other governmental agencies—such as the Census Bureau, the Department of Labor, and the Department of Health, Education, and Welfare.

This leads to a tacit acceptance of DoD organizational colonialism. Not only is the DoD urged to be on the lookout for other agencies' collecting similar data and doing similar sorts of analyses, but also, to exert a special effort to use the work of outside agencies. On behalf of "cooperation," may I say that without it there exists the possibility of invasion of privacy and other violations of individual rights: in fact, this is a common problem when any single department functions as a total system incorporating the findings of other subunits.

The report contends that those parts of the armed services responsible for developing basic information about decision-making have done their work well. It is interesting that no examples are given. Moreover, the military and civilian personnel who provide support for decision-making within the military establishment are said to have a rare opportunity to contribute to this steadily improving use of sound decision-making models for areas like material procurement for frontline battle medical services. Nothing is said about the nature of the conflict to be resolved or the values employed in such decisions.

While several members of the panel, in response to my questionnaire, indicated that they held this report to be an indirect resolution of problems raised by Project Camelot, the formulations used in the report are similar to those used in the Camelot study concerning overseas research.

The report states: "Comparative organizational work should not be done only within civilian groups such as large-scale building and construction consortia and worldwide airlines systems, but also within foreign military establishments." In Project Camelot, the same desire for military information was paramount. Curiously, no attention is given to whether, in fact, this is a high-payoff research area; or if it is, how this work is to be done without threatening the sovereignty of other nations. In other words, although the report superficially is dedicated to the principle of maximum use of social science, this principle is not brought into play at the critical point. The ambiguities and doubts raised by previous DoD incursions into the area of foreign social research remain intact and are in no way even partially resolved.

The panelists are dedicated to the principle of high-payoff research, but appear to be disquietingly convinced that this is equivalent to whatever the members of the panel themselves are doing, or whatever their professional specialties are. Thus a high-payoff research area becomes a study of the effect of isolation upon individual and group behavior; or the area of simulation of field experiences that the military may encounter; or the study of behavior under conditions of ionizing radiation. It is not accidental that in each instance the panelists themselves have been largely engaged in such kinds of work. One is left with the distinct impression that a larger number of panelists would have yielded only a larger number of "high-payoff" areas, rather than an integrated framework of needs. This leads to a general suspicion that the report is much more self-serving than a simple review of its propositions indicates.

The references to methodology again raise the specter of Camelot, since it is evident that no general methodology is demonstrated in the report itself and no genuine innovations are formulated for future methodological directions. There is no discussion of the kind of methodology likely to yield meaningful predictions. Instead, the DoD is simply notified of the correctness of its own biases. We are told that "predictive indicators of a conflict or revolutionary overthrow are examples of the type of data which can gain from control applications." No illustrations of the success of such predictors is given. The purpose turns out to be not so much prediction as control of revolutionary outbreaks. This, then, constitutes the core methodological message of the report.

Project Themis

As for Project Themis, designed to upgrade scientific and engineering performances at colleges and universities for the benefit of the Defense Department, the project titles at the institutions already selected do not furnish enough information to assess the actual nature of the research. A proposal of more than $1.1 million for research into "chemical compounds containing highly electro-negative elements" was turned down by the dean of faculties at Portland State College. Said he: "I know what the proposal was talking about. It could very easily be interpreted as a proposal involving biological warfare. The proposal could be construed as committing the university to biological warfare."

Among the universities now contracted for Project Themis work is the University of Utah, with the project title "Chemistry of Combustion." Newspaper accounts during the summer of 1967 indicated clearly that this project was aimed at improving missile fuels. Additional illustrations could be given, but the point is clear: Project Themis is what it claims to be, a program to involve universities in research useful to the Defense Department.

The panelists assure us that "DoD has been singularly successful at enlisting the interest and services of an eminent group of behavioral scientists in most of the areas relevant to it." They go on to say that, indeed, "the management of behavioral science research in the military department should be complimented for long-term success in building the image of DoD as a good and challenging environment in which to do both basic and applied research." No names are cited to indicate that there are eminent clusters of behavioral scientists working in the DoD. Nor is there an indication whether "the eminent men" connected with DoD are in fact remotely connected as part-time consultants (like the panelists themselves) or intimately connected with basic work for the government. And even though Foster's letter indicates that there is a problem of recruitment and government-university relations, the panel simply dismisses this as insignificant. Yet members go on to note that the DoD image is perhaps more tarnished than they would like to think; that, for example, the Civil Service Commission discriminates against the behavioral scientist with respect to appointments, and that it is hard to persuade behavioral scientists that the DoD provides a supportive environment for them. Despite the censure of the Civil Service Commission, it is claimed that the DoD has not been as attractive and as successful in social-science recruitment as we were earlier led to believe.

More damaging is the allegation of the panelists that quality control of research at universities is not in any way superior to that exercised within other research sources, such as the DoD. They tend to see "quality control" as something unrelated to university autonomy and the objectivity of their research. Lest there be any ambiguity on this point, they go on to indicate in an extraordinary series of unsupported allegations that the difficulty is not one of social-science autonomy versus the political requirements of any agency of government, but rather one of bad public relations—which is in turn blamed mostly on "Representatives of Civilian Professional Organizations" who lack a clear picture of DoD requirements yet testify before congressional committees, which, in turn, are backed up by social and behavioral scientists who regard these DoD activities as a threat to academic freedom and scientific integrity, and who "are usually ignorant of the work actually being performed under DoD's aegis."

The specific committee hearings referred to are nowhere indicated. Certainly the various hearings on such proposed measures as a national social-science foundation or on social accounting do bring out in those testifying the highest amount of professional integrity and concern. Perhaps the conflict stems from the fact that DoD intellectuals are concerned precisely over the nonpolicy research features of such proposed legislation.

Finally, the panelists offer a gentle slap on the wrist to defense research managers who allegedly lack the time to address themselves to these kinds of problems. In short and in sum, the report ignores questions having to do with social-science autonomy as if these were products of misconceptions to be resolved by good will and better public relations between the DoD and the academy. That such conclusions should be reached by a set of panelists, half of whom are highly placed in academic life, indicates the degree to which closing the gap between the academy and the polity has paradoxically broken down the political capabilities of social science by weakening its autonomous basis.

The panelists have enough firmness of mind to make two unsolicited comments. But the nature of the comments reveals the flabbiness that results from the tendency of social scientists to conceive of their sciences as service activities rather than scientific activities. They urge, first, that more work be done in the area of potential high-payoff fields of investigation that might have been overlooked in their own report, given the short time they had available in preparing it. They further urge the establishment of a continuous group with time to examine other areas in greater depth and to discuss them more deliberately, so that high-payoff areas can be teased out and presented for cost considerations. In other words, the unsolicited comments suggest mechanisms for improving these kinds of recommendations and making them permanent. They do not consider whether the nature of social science requirements might be unfit for the bureaucratic specifications of Foster's originating letter.

Advise and Dissent

In some ways, the tension between social scientists and policy-makers has provided each group with a reality test against which basic ideas could be formulated about policy issues. But the very demand for a coalescence of the two—whether in the name of "significant" research or as a straight patriotic obligation—must, inherently, corrupt social science and impoverish policy options.

The question that the report raises with great forcefulness is not so much about the relationship between pure and applied research, as it is about what the character of application is to be. Applied research is clearly here to stay and is probably the most forceful, singular novel element in American social science in contrast to its European background. What is at stake, however, is a highly refined concept of application that removes theoretical considerations of the character and balance of social forces and private interests from the purview of application. The design of the future replaces the analysis of the present in our "new utopian" world.

The panelists simply do not entertain the possibility that the social world is a behavioral "field" in which decisions have to be made between political goals no less than political means. Reports cannot "depoliticalize" social action to such an extent that consequences do not follow and implicit choices are not favored. Innovation without a political goal simply assumes that operations leading to a change from one state to another are of value. The report does not suggest, much less favor, significant political changes in the operations of the DoD; and its innovative efforts are circumscribed to the area of improvements rather than opened wider to include the possibility of complete changes. However, efficiency is a limited use of applicability because it assumes rather than tests the adequacy of the social system.

The era of good feelings between the federal government and social science, which characterized the time of the outbreak of World War II and extended through the assassination of President John F. Kennedy, no longer exists. In its place there is now the era of tight money. The future of "nonprofit" research corporations tied to the DoD is being severely impeded from both sides. Universities such as Pennsylvania, California, and Princeton have taken a hard look at academic involvement in classified research for the Pentagon. Princeton, with its huge stake in its international-relations programming, is even considering canceling its sponsorship of a key research arm, the Institute for Defense Analysis. On the other side, many of the "hard" engineering types have continued to press their doubts as to the usefulness of software research. And this barrage of criticism finds welcome support among high-level military officers who would just as soon cancel social-science projects as carry out their implications.

With respect to the panelists, it must be said that a number of them have indicated their own doubts about the report. One of the participants has correctly pointed out that the report has not yet been accepted by the DoD, nor have the findings or the recommendations been endorsed by the National Academy of Sciences. Another member claimed that his main reason for accepting the invitation to serve on the panel was to argue against the Defense Department's decision to bring the universities into operations such as Project Camelot. He went on to point out that his mission was unsuccessful, since he obviously did not influence the other panelists.

A third panelist points out that the Camelot type of issue was not, to his recollection at least, a criterion in any discussion of the topics. Yet he strongly disclaims his own participation as well as membership in the National Academy of Sciences Advisory Committee on Government Programs in the Behavioral Sciences. He also indicates that his panel had nothing but an administrative connection with the National Academy of Sciences, and he, too, seems to indicate that he had an ancillary advisory role rather than an integrated preparatory role.

Trying to gauge the accuracy with which the final report represented a true consensus of the panelists proved to be most difficult. While most panelists, with hedging qualifications, agreed that the report reflected an accurate appraisal of their own views, the question of the actual writeup of the document brought forth a far from consistent response. One panelist claims that "all members contributed to the basic draft of the Report. Each assumed responsbility for composing a section, all of which were then reviewed by the panel as a whole." Another panelist declared his participation only "as an observer," and denied his involvement in any final writeup. Yet a third panelist denied that he had had any role in preparing the report.

A final, and still different, version was stated as follows: "The report was written by members of the committee and the overall editing and bringing-together responsibility was undertaken by Rains Wallace. One or two members of the committee were assigned to specific topics and drafts were prepared at Williamstown. These went to Wallace, who organized them, did some editing, and sent them back to us. Each person responded and the final version was then prepared by Wallace." In other words, the actual authorship of a document that was released "in confidence" over the names of some of America's most distinguished social scientists is either the work of all and the responsibility of none, or perhaps—as is more likely the case—the work of one or two people and the responsiblity of all.

FAR vs. DoD

The issuance of this report, even in semiprivate form, reveals the extent to which a gap exists between the thinking of the two chief departments most directly involved in sensitive research and in research in foreign areas—namely, the Department of Defense and the Department of State. Indeed, the issuance of this report is likely to exacerbate the feelings of high officials in the State Department that the Defense Department position represents an encroachment.

The memorandum issued in December 1967 by the Department of State's Foreign Area Research Coordination group (FAR), in which is set forth foreign-area research guidelines, represents a direct rebuke or, at the very least, a serious challenge to the orientation that the report of the Defense Science Board represents. It is a high point in federal recognition that real problems do exist.

The FAR Report is broken into two different sections with seven propositions in each section. First under "Guidelines for Research Contract Relations Between Government and Universities" are the following:

(1) The government has the responsibility to avoid those actions that will call into question the integrity of American academic institutions as centers of independent teaching and research.

(2) Government research support should always be acknowledged by sponsor, university, and researcher.

(3) Government-supported contract research should, in process and results, ideally be unclassified, but given the practical needs of the nation

in the modern world, some portion may be subject to classification. In questionable areas, the sponsor should lean toward making public whenever possible the results and findings of government-supported research.

(4) Agencies should encourage open publication of contract research results.

(5) Government agencies that contract with university researchers should consider designing their projects so as to advance knowledge as well as to meet the immediate policy or action needs.

(6) Government agencies have the obligation of informing the potential researcher of the goals to be met, of any special conditions associated with the research contract, and generally of the agency's expectations concerning the research and the researcher.

(7) The government should continue to seek research of the highest possible quality in its contract program.

A second set of seven recommendations is listed under "Guidelines for the Conduct of Foreign Area Research Under Government Contract" and these too bear very directly on the panel report and do so most critically and tellingly.

(1) The government should take special steps to ensure that the parties with which it contracts have the highest qualifications for carrying out research overseas.

(2) The government should work to avert or minimize adverse foreign reactions to its contract research programs conducted overseas.

(3) When a project involves research abroad, it is particularly important that both the supporting agency and the researcher openly acknowledge the auspices and financing of research projects.

(4) The government should under certain circumstances ascertain that the research is acceptable to the host government before proceeding on the research.

(5) The government should encourage cooperation with foreign scholars in its contract research program.

(6) Government agencies should continue to coordinate their foreign-area research programs to eliminate duplication and overloading of any one geographical area.

(7) Government agencies should cooperate with academic associations on problems of foreign-area research.

These recommendations (with allowances made for the circumstances of their issuance) unquestionably represent the most enlightened position yet taken by a federal agency on the question of the relationship between social science and practical politics. These sets of recommendations not only stand as ethical criteria for the federal government's relationship to social scientists, but—even more decisively—represent a rebuke to precisely the sort of militarization of social science that must ultimately issue into covert international operations. The reassertion by a major federal policy-making agency of the worth to the government of social-science autonomy represented the first significant recognition by a federal agency that Project Camelot was only a consequence, not the cause, of the present strains in social science-federal bureaucracy relationships.

1968

15

The Pentagon Papers
and the
Tragedy of American Research

Few major political events, particularly those directly linked to the forging of American foreign policy such as the publication of the Pentagon Papers by *The New York Times* and the *Washington Post,* can be fully described without accounting for the role of the social scientist. In this case, the economists clearly performed a major role. From the straightforward hawkish prescriptions offered in 1961 by Walt W. Rostow to the dovishly motivated release of secret documents on the conduct of the war in 1971 by Daniel Ellsberg, the contributions of social scientists were central. As a consequence, it is fitting, nay imperative, that the import of these monumental events be made plain for those of us involved in the production and dissemination of social-science information and insight.

The publication of the Pentagon Papers is of central importance to the social-science community in at least two respects: social scientists participated in the development of a posture and position toward the Vietnam involvement; and at a more abstract level, the publication of these papers provides lessons about political participation and policy-making for the social sciences.

We live in an age in which the social sciences perform a special and unique role in the lives of men and in the fates of government, whatever the status of social-science theory. And because laymen no longer ask "Is social science scientific?" but rather "What kinds of recommendations are offered in the name of social science?" it is important that social

275

scientists seek out any special meaning of the Pentagon Papers and documents, over and above the general and broad-ranging discussions that take place in the mass media. Thus, my effort here is not to be construed as a general discussion of issues, but rather as a specific discussion of results.

Findings

The Pentagon's project director for a *History of the United States Decision-Making Process on Vietnam Policy* (now simply known as *The Pentagon Papers*), economist Leslie H. Gelb now of the Brookings Institution, remarked: "Writing history, especially where it blends into current events, especially where the current event is Vietnam, is a treacherous exercise." Former Secretary of Defense Robert S. McNamara authorized this treacherous exercise for a treacherous conflict in 1967. In initiation and execution this was to be "encyclopedic and objective." The actual compilation runs to 2.5 million words and 47 volumes of narrative and documents. And from what has thus far been made public, it is evident that this project was prepared with the same bloodless bureaucratic approach that characterizes so much federally inspired social science and history. The Pentagon Papers attempt no original hypothesis, provide no insights into the behavior of the "other side," make scant effort to separate important from trivial factors in the escalation process; they present no real continuity with past American foreign policy and in general eschew any sort of systematic survey research or interviewing of the participants and proponents. Yet, with all these shortcomings, these materials offer a fascinating and unique account of how peace-keeping agencies became transformed into policy-making agencies. That this record was prepared by 36 individuals, including among them political scientists, economists, systems analysts, inside dopesters, and outside social-science researchers—tells us something else in addition to who its authors were: more interesting, it tells us how easily the government has learned to entrust its official records to mandarin types, who in exchange for the cloak of anonymity are willing to prepare an official record of events. An alarming oddity is that, in part at least, the chronicle was prepared by analysts who were formerly participants.

For those who have neither the time nor the patience to examine every document thus far released, it might be worthwhile simply to summarize what these documents contain. In so doing, it becomes clear that the Vietnam War was neither a Democratic nor a Republican war, but a war conducted by the political elite, often without regard to basic technical advice and considerations, and for reasons that had far less to do with curbing communism than with the failure of the other arms of government to curb executive egotism. With the publication of these papers this country's overseas involvements have been chronicled with a precision never before available to the American public. Indeed, we now know more about decision-making in Vietnam than about the processes by which we became in the Korean War. For instance, we have learned that:

1. The United States ignored eight direct appeals for aid from Ho Chi Minh in the first half-year following World War II. Underlying the American refusal to deal with the Vietnamese leader was the growth of the cold war and American opposition to assisting a communist leadership.

2. The Truman administration by 1949 had already accepted the "domino principle" after the National Security Council was told early that year that the neighboring countries of Thailand and Burma could be expected to fall under communist control if Vietnam were controlled by a communist-dominated regime.

3. The Eisenhower administration, particularly under the leadership of Secretary of State John Foster Dulles, refused to accept the Geneva accords ending the French-Indochina war on the grounds that they permitted this country "only a limited influence" in the affairs of the fledgling South Vietnam. Indeed, the Joint Chiefs of Staff opted in favor of displacing France as the key influence rather than assisting the termination of hostilities.

4. The final years of the Eisenhower administration were characterized by a decision to commit a relatively small number of United States military personnel to maintain the Diem regime in Saigon and to prevent a detente between Hanoi and Saigon.

5. The Kennedy administration transformed the limited risk gamble into an unlimited commitment. Although the troop levels were indeed still quite limited, the Kennedy administration moved special forces units into Vietnam, Laos, and Cambodia—thus broadening the conflict to the area as a whole.

6. The Kennedy administration knew about and approved of plans for the military *coup d'état* that overthrew President Diem. The United States gave its support to an army group committed to military dictatorship and a no-compromise policy with the Hanoi regime.

7. The Johnson administration extended the unlimited commitment to the military regime of Saigon. Between 1965 and 1968, under this administration troop levels surpassed 500,000 and the United States partici-

pation included the management of the conflict and the training of the ARVN.

8. After the Tet offensive began in January 1968, Johnson, under strong prodding from the military Chiefs of Staff and his field commanders, moved toward full-scale mobilization, including the call-up of reserves. By the termination of the Johnson administration, the United States had been placed on a full-scale war footing.

Among the most important facts revealed by the Papers is that the United States first opposed a settlement based on the Geneva accords, signed by all belligerents; that the United States had escalated the conflict far in advance of the Gulf of Tonkin incident and had used congressional approval to legitimate commitments already undertaken rather than to answer new communist provocations; and finally, that in the face of internal opposition from the same Department of Defense that at first had sanctioned the war, the executive decided to disregard its own policy advisers and plunge ahead in a war already lost.

Decisions

Impressive in this enumeration of policy decisions is the clinical way decisions were made: the substitution of war-game thinking for any real political thinking; the total submission of the Department of State to the Department of Defense in the making of foreign policy; the utter collapse of any faith in compromise, consensus, or cooperation between nations; and the ludicrous pursuit of victory (or at least nondefeat) in Vietnam are all so forcefully illustrated in these Pentagon Papers that the vigor with which their release was opposed by the Attorney General's office and the executive branch of government generally can well be appreciated.

A major difficulty with the thinking of civilian supporters of the military is that they study war while ignoring politics. The recent disclosure of the Pentagon Papers bears out this contention with a vengeance; a hothouse scientology emerges in which the ends of foreign policy are neatly separated from the instruments of immediate destruction. That a certain shock and cynicism have emerged as a result of the revelations in these papers is attributable more to the loss of a war than to the novelty of the revelations. The cast of characters that has dragged us through the mire of a bloody conflict in Southeast Asia, from Walt W. Rostow to Henry A. Kissinger, remain to haunt and taunt us. They move in and out of administrations with an ease that belies political party differences and underscores the existence of not merely a set of "experts" but also a well-defined ruling class dedicated to manufacturing and manipulating political formulas.

The great volume of materials thus far revealed is characterized by few obvious themes: but one of the more evident is the utter separation of the purposes of devastation from a comprehension of the effects of such devastation. A kind of Howard Johnson sanitized vision of conflict emerges that reveals a gulf between the policy makers and battlefield soldiers that is even wider and longer than the distance between Saigon and Washington. If the concept of war gaming is shocking in retrospect, this is probably due more to its utter and contemptible failure to provide battlefield victories than to any real development in social and behavioral science beyond the shibboleths of decision theory and game theory.

"Scientists"

A number of researchers as well as analysts of the Pentagon Papers were themselves social scientists. There were political scientists of considerable distinction, such as Morton H. Halperin and Melvin Gurtov; economists of great renown, such as Walt Rostow and Daniel Ellsberg; and systems analysts, such as Alain C. Enthoven. And then there was an assorted group of people, often trained in law, such as Roger Fisher and Carl Kaysen, weaving in and out of the papers, providing both point and counterpoint. There are the thoroughly hawkish views of Walt Rostow; and the cautionary perspective of Alain Enthoven; and the more liberal recommendations of people like Roger Fisher. But it is clear that social scientists descend in importance as they move from hawk to dove. Walt Rostow is a central figure, and people like Carl Kaysen and Roger Fisher are at most peripheral consultants—who, in fact, seem to have been more often conservatized and impressed by the pressurized Washington atmosphere than influential in the liberalization or softening of the official Vietnam posture.

The social-scientific contingency in the Pentagon, whom I christened the "new civilian militarists" a decade ago, were by no means uniform in their reactions to the quagmire in Vietnam. Political scientists like Morton Halperin and economists like Alain Enthoven did provide cautionary responses, if not outright criticisms, of the incessant requests for troop build-ups. The Tet offensive, which made incontrovertible the vulnerability of the American posture, called forth demands for higher troop levels on the part of General William C. Westmoreland and Maxwell Taylor. Enthoven, in particular, opposed this emphatically and courageously:

Our strategy of attrition has not worked. Adding 206,000 more U.S. men to a force of 525,000, gaining only 27 additional maneuver battalions and 270 tactical fighters at an added cost to the U.S. of $10 billion per year raises the question of who is making it costly for whom. . . . We know that despite a massive influx of 500,000 U.S. troops, 1.2 million tons of bombs a year, 200,000 enemy killed in action in three years, 20,000 U.S. killed in action in three years, 200,000 U.S. wounded in action, etc., our control of the countryside and the defense of the urban areas is now essentially at pre-August 1965 levels. We have achieved stalemate at a high commitment. A new strategy must be sought.

In the same month, March 1968, that Enthoven prepared this critical and obviously sane report, he wrote a curious paper on "Thomism and the Concept of Just and Unjust Warfare," which, in retrospect, seemed to be Enthoven's way of letting people like myself know that he was a dissenting voice despite his earlier commitment to war-game ideology and whiz-kid strategy.

As a result of these memoranda, Assistant Defense Secretary Paul Warnke argued against increased bombing and for a bombing pause. He and Assistant Secretary of Defense for Public Affairs, Phil G. Goulding, were then simply directed to write a draft that "would deal only with the troop issue," hence forcing them to abandon the internal fight against an "expansion of the air war." And as it finally went to the White House, the report was bleached of any criticism. The mandarin role of the social scientists was reaffirmed; President Johnson's commitments went unchallenged. The final memo advocated deployment of 22,000 more troops, and approved a 262,000 troop reserve build-up; it urged no new peace initiatives and simply declared that a division of opinion existed on the bombing policy, making it appear that the division in opinion was only tactical in nature. As the Pentagon Papers declared:

Faced with a fork in the road of our Vietnam policy, the working group failed to seize the opportunity to change directions. Indeed, they seemed to recommend that we continue rather haltingly down the same road, meanwhile, consulting the map more frequently and in greater detail to insure that we were still on the right road.

One strange aspect of this war-game strategy is how seldom the moves and motives of the so-called "other side" were taken into account. There is no real appreciation of the distinction between North Vietnam and the National Liberation Front of South Vietnam. There is not the slightest account taken of the actual decisions made by General Giap or Chairman Ho. The Tet offensive seems to have surprised our grant strategists as much as it did the political elites for whom they were planning. While they were beginning to recognize the actual balance of military force, Wilfred Burchett had already declared, in 1967 to be exact, that the consequences of the war were no longer in doubt—United States involvement could not forestall a victory of the communist factions North and South. Thus, not only do the Pentagon Papers reveal the usual pattern of ignorance of the customs, languages, and habits of the people being so brutally treated, but also the unanticipated arrogance of assuming throughout that logistics would conquer all. Even the doves like George W. Ball never doubted for a moment that an influx of a certain number of United States troops would in fact swing the tide of battle the way that General Westmoreland said it would. The argument was rather over tactics: Is such a heavy investment worth the end results? In fact, not one inner-circle "wise man" raised the issue that the size of the troop commitment might be basically irrelevant to the negative (from an American viewpoint) outcome of the Southeast Asian operations. One no longer expects good history or decent ethnography from those who advise the rulers, but when this is compounded with a heavy dose of impoverished war gaming and strategic thinking in the void, then the question of "science for whom" might well be converted into the question of "what science and by whom."

All this points up a tragic flaw in policy-making by social-science experts. Their failure to generate or to reflect a constituency outside themselves made them continually vulnerable to assaults from the military and from the more conservative sectors of the Pentagon. This vulnerability was so great that throughout the Pentagon Papers one senses that the hawk position was always and uniformly outspoken and direct, while the dove position was always and uniformly ubiquitous and indirect. The basis of democratic politics has always been the mass participation of an informed electorate. Yet it was precisely this informed public, where a consensus against the war had been building, that was cut off from the policy planners and recommenders. Consequently they were left in pristine isolation to pit their logic against the crackpot realism of their military adversaries within the bowels of government.

Disclosures

Certain serious problems arose precisely because of the secrecy tag; for example, former Vice-President Hubert Humphrey and Secretary of State Dean Rusk have both denied having any knowledge whatsoever of these papers. Dean Rusk went so far as to say that the research methodology was handled poorly: "I'm rather curious about why the analysts who put this study together did not interview us, particularly when they were attributing attitudes and motives to us" (*The New York Times,* July 3, 1971). Perhaps more telling is Dean Rusk's suggestion that the Pentagon Papers have the characteristics of an anonymous letter. Along with Dean Rusk, I too believe that the names of the approximately forty scholars connected with the production of these papers should be published. To do otherwise would not only prevent the people involved from checking the veracity of the stories attributed to them but, more important, would keep the social-science community from gaining a clearer insight into the multiple roles of scholars, researchers, professors, government analysts, and policy-makers. The nature of science requires that the human authorities behind these multivolumes be identified, as in the precedent established by the identification of the authors of the various bombing surveys done after World War II and the Korean War.

One serendipitous consequence of the Pentagon Papers has been the development of a more meaningful perspective toward the proposed "Code of Ethics" being advanced by so many social-science professional associations. They all deal with the sanctity of the "subject's rights." All sorts of words guarding privacy are used: "rights of privacy and dignity," "protection of subjects from personal harm," "preservation of confidentiality of research data." The American Sociological Association proposals, for example, are typical:

> Confidential information provided by a research subject must be treated as such by the sociologist. Even though research information is not a privileged communication under the law, the sociologist must, as far as possible, protect subjects and informants. Any promises made to such persons must be honored. . . . If an informant or other subject should wish, however, he can formally release the promise of confidentiality.

While the purpose of this code of ethics is sincerely geared to protect individuals under study, if it were taken literally, a man like Daniel Ellsberg would be subject to penalty, if not outright expulsion, on the grounds that he was never granted permission by the individuals concerned to make his information public. Many professional societies, in their zeal to forge an ethical code, forget that the right of the private subject to confidentiality does not automatically signify the needs of government to become more overt and less covert. The truly difficult ethical question comes not with the idea of maintaining confidentiality, but with determining what would be confidential, and when confidentiality should be violated in terms of a higher principle. All social-science codes of ethics presume an ethical standpoint limiting scientific endeavor. but when it is expedient to ignore or to forget this ethical code, as in the case of the Pentagon Papers, the profession embarrassingly chooses to exhibit such a memory lapse. The publication of the Pentagon Papers should once again point the way to the highest obligation of social-science organizations: to the truth, plain and simple, rather than the codes of ethics presume an ethical standpoint limiting scientific endeavor, but when it is expedient to ignore or to forget this ethical code, as in the case of the Pentagon Papers, the profession embarrassingly chooses to exhibit such a memory lapse. The publication of the Pentagon Papers should once again point the way to the highest obligation of social-science organizations: to the truth, plain and simple, rather than the preservation of confidentiality, high and mighty. And unless this lesson is fully drawn, a dichotomous arrangement will be made—making public the documents of public servants whose policies they disapprove of and keeping private the documentation on deviants whom supposedly the social scientists are concerned with protecting. This is not an ethical approach but rather an opportunistic approach. It rests on political and professional expediency. The need therefore is to reassert the requisites of science for full disclosure and the ethics of full disclosure as the only possible ethics for any group of professional scientists. If the release of the Pentagon Papers has done nothing else, it has reaffirmed the highest principle of all science: full disclosure, full review of the data, full responsibility for what is done by those who do the research.

Secrets

Another area that deeply concerns the social scientist and that is highlighted in the Pentagon Papers is the government's established norms of secrecy. While most officials in government have a series of work norms with which to guide their behavior, few forms of anticipatory socialization have applied to social scientists who advise government agencies. The professionalization of social scientists has normally been directed toward publicity rather than secrecy. This fosters sharp differences in opinion and attitudes between the polity and the academy, since the reward system for career advancement is so clearly polarized.

The question of secrecy is intimately connected with matters of policy between the standing practice of policy-makers (particularly in the field of foreign affairs) is not to reveal themselves entirely. No government in the game of international politics feels that its policies can be candidly revealed for full public review; therefore, operational research done in connection with policy considerations is customarily bound by the canons of government privacy. But while scientists have a fetish for publicizing their information as a mechanism for professional advancement no less than a definition of their essential role in the society, the political branches of society have as their fetish the protection of private documents and privileged information. Therefore, the polity places a premium not only on acquiring vital information, but also on keeping silent about such information precisely to the degree that the data might be of high decisional value. This leads to differing premiums between analysts and policy-makers and to tensions between them.

Social scientists complain that the norm of secrecy oftentimes involves yielding their own essential work premises. A critical factor reinforcing an unwilling acceptance of the norm of secrecy by social scientists is the allocation of most government research funds for military or semimilitary purposes. Senate testimony has shown that 70 percent of federal funds targeted for the social sciences involve such restrictions.

The real wonder turns out to be not the existence of the secrecy norm but the relative availability of large chunks of information. Indeed, the classification of materials is so inept that documents (such as the Pax America research) designated as confidential or secret by one agency may often be made available as a public service by another agency. There are also occasions when documents placed in a classified category by sponsoring government agencies can be obtained without charge from the private research institute doing the work.

The norm of secrecy makes it extremely difficult to separate science from patriotism and hence makes it that much more difficult to question the research design itself. Social scientists often express the nagging doubt that accepting the first stage—the right of the government to maintain secrecy—often carries with it acquiescence in a later stage— the necessity for silence on the part of social researchers who may disagree with the political uses of their efforts.

The demand for government secrecy has a telling impact on the methodology of the social sciences. Presumably social scientists are employed because they as a group represent objectivity and honesty. Social scientists like to envision themselves as a wall of truth off which policy-makers may bounce their premises. They also like to think that they provide information that cannot be derived from sheer public opinion. Thus, to some degree social scientists consider that they are hired or utilized by government agencies because they will say things that may be unpopular but nonetheless are significant. However, since secrecy exists, the premises upon which most social scientists seek to work are strained by the very agencies that hire their services.

The terms of research and conditions of work tend to demand an initial compromise with social-science methodology. The social scientist is placed in a cognitive bind. He becomes conditioned not to reveal maximum information lest he be victimized by the federal agencies that employ his services. Yet he is employed precisely because of his presumed thoroughness, impartiality, and candor. The social scientist who survives in government service becomes circumspect and learns to play the game. Consequently his value to social science becomes seriously jeopardized. On the other hand, once he raises these considerations, his usefulness to the policy-making sector is likewise jeopardized.

Social scientists believe that openness is more than meeting formal requirements of scientific canons: it is also a matter of making information universally available. The norm of secrecy leads to selective presentation of data. The social scientist is impeded by the policy-maker because of contrasting notions about the significance of data and the general need for replication elsewhere and by others. The policy-maker who demands differential access to findings considers this a normal return for the initial expenditure of risk capital. Since this utilitarian concept of data is alien to the scientific standpoint, the schism between the social scientist and the policy-maker becomes pronounced precisely at the level of informational accesibility. The social scientist's general attitude is that sponsorship of research does not entitle any one sector to benefit unduly from the findings—that sponsorship by federal agencies ought not to place greater limitations on the use of work done than does sponsorship by either private agencies or universities.

Loyalties

A major area that deeply concerns social scientists is that of dual allegiance. The Pentagon Papers have such specific requirements and goal-oriented tasks that they intrude upon the autonomy of the social scientist by forcing upon him choices between dual allegiances. The researcher is compelled to choose between participating fully in the world of the federal bureaucracy and remaining in more familiar academic confines. He does not want the former to create isolation in the latter. Thus, he often criticizes the federal bureaucracy's unwillingness his basic needs: the need to teach and retain full academic identity; the need to publicize information; and above all the need to place scientific responsibility above the call of patriotic obligation—when they may happen to clash. In short, he does not want to be plagued by dual or competing allegiances.

The norm of secrecy exacerbates this problem. Although many of the social scientists who become involved with federal research are intrigued by the opportunity to address important issues, they are confronted by some bureaucracies that oftentimes do not share their passion for resolving social problems. For example, federal obligations commit the bureaucracy to assign high priority to items having military potential and effectiveness and low priorities to many supposedly idealistic and farfetched themes in which social scientists are interested.

Those social scientists connected with the government, either as employees or as consultants, are hamstrung by federal agencies that are in turn limited by political circumstances beyond their control. A federal bureaucracy must manage cumbersome overgrown committees and data-gathering agencies. Federal agencies often protect a status quo merely for the sake of rational functioning. They must conceive of academicians in their midst as standard bureaucratic types entitled to rise to certain federal ranks. Federal agencies limit innovating concepts to what is immediately useful, not out of choice and certainly not out of resentment of the social sciences but from what is deemed impersonal necessity. This has the effect of reducing the social scientist's role in the government to that of ally or advocate rather than innovator or designer. Social scientists begin to feel that their enthusiasm for rapid change is unrealistic, considering how little can be done by the government bureaucracy. And they come to resent involvement in a theoryless application to immediacy foisted on them by the "new utopians," surrendering in the process the value of confronting men with the wide range of choices of what must be done. The schism, then, between autonomy and involvement is as thorough as that between secrecy and publicity, for it cuts to the quick well-meant pretensions about human engineering.

The problem of competing allegiances is not made simpler by the fact that many high-ranking federal bureaucrats have strong nationalistic and conservative political ideologies. This contrasts markedly with the social scientist, who comes to Washington not only with a belief in the primacy of science over patriotism but also with a definition of patriotism that is more open-ended and consciously liberal than that of most appointed officials. Hence, he often perceives the conflict to extend beyond research design and social applicability into one of the incompatible ideologies held respectively by the social scientists versus the entrenched Washington bureaucrats. He comes to resent the proprietary attitude of the bureaucrat toward "his" government processes. The social scientist is likely to consider his social-science biases to be a necessary buffer against the federal bureaucracy.

Elitists

The publication of the Pentagon Papers sheds new light on political pluralist and power concentrationist hypotheses. When push finally did turn to shove, President Nixon and the government officials behaved as members of a ruling class and not as leaders of their political party. President Nixon might easily have chosen to let the Democratic Party take the blame and bear the brunt of the assaults for the betrayal of a public trust. Indeed the Nixon administration might have chosen to join the chorus of those arguing that the Democratic Party is indeed the war party, as revealed in these documents; whereas the Republican Party emerges as the party of restraint—if not exactly principle. Here was a stunning opportunity for Mr. Nixon to make political capital on a no-risk basis: by simply drawing attention to the fact that the war was constantly escalated by President Truman, who refused to bargain in good faith with Ho Chi Minh despite repeated requests; by President Kennedy, who moved far beyond anything President Eisenhower had in mind for the area by making the fatal commitment not just to land troops but to adopt a domino theory of winning the war; by President Johnson, whose role can well be considered as nefarious: coming before the American people as a peace candidate when he had already made the fatal series of commitments to continue escalation and warfare. That President Nixon chose not to do so illustrates the sense of class solidarity that the political elites in this country manifest; a sense of collective betrayal of the priesthood rather than a sense of obligation to score political points and gain political trophies. And that too should be a lesson in terms of the actual power within the political structure of a small ruling elite. Surely this must be considered a fascinating episode in its own right: the reasons are complex, but surely among them must rank the belief that Mr. Nixon behaved as a member of the ruling elite, an elite that had transcendent obligations far beyond the call of party, and that was the call of class.

One fact made clear by the Pentagon Papers is the extent to which presidentialism has become the ideology and the style in American political life. The infrequency of any reference to the judicial situation with respect to the war in Southeast Asia and the virtual absence of any reference to congressional sentiments are startling confirmations of an utter change in the American political style. If any proof was required of the emerging imbalance between the executive and other branches of government, these papers supply more than is needed. The theory of checks and balances works only when there are, in fact, groups such as senators or stubborn judges who believe in the responsibility of the judiciary and legislative branches to establish such check and balance. In the absence of such vigor, the war in Southeast Asia became very much a series of executive actions. And this itself should give pause to the advocates of consensus theory in political science.

The failure of the Vietnam episode has resulted in a reconsideration of presidentialism as the specific contemporary variant of power elite theory. The renewed vigor of Congress, the willingness, albeit cautionary willingness, of the Supreme Court to rule on fundamental points of constitutional law, are indicative of the resurgence of pluralism. In this sense, the darkest hour of liberalism as a political style has witnessed a liberal regrouping around the theme of mass politics. Even the domestic notions of community organization and states' rights are indicative of the limits of presidentialism—so that Mr. Nixon, at one and the same time, is reluctantly presiding over the swan song of presidentialism in foreign affairs and celebrating its demise in domestic affairs. The collapse of the Vietnam War and the trends toward neoisolationism are in fact simply the reappearance of political pluralism in a context where to go further in the concentration of political power in the presidency would, in all likelihood, mean the upsurge of fascism, American style. If the concept of a power elite was reconfirmed in the Pentagon Papers, so too, strangely, was the concept of political pluralism in the public response to them. The countervailing influence of the Supreme Court was clearly manifested in the ringing affirmation of the First Amendment, in the denial of the concept of prior restraint and prior punitive actions, and in the very rapidity of the decision itself. This action by the judiciary, coupled with a show of muscle on the part of the Senate and House concerning the conduct of the war, military appropriations, boondoggles, and special privileges for a handful of aircraft industries, in its own way served to underscore the continued importance of the open society and the pluralistic basis of power. Even executives, such as Hubert H. Humphrey, have declared themselves in favor of full disclosure and reiterated the principles guiding the publication of the Pentagon Papers. Power elites operate behind a cloak of anonymity. When that cloak is lifted, an obvious impairment in the operational efficiency of elites occurs. What has happened with the release of the Pentagon Papers is precisely this collapse of anonymity, no less than of secrecy. As a result, the formal apparatus of government now asserts its prerogatives. This does not mean that the executive branch of government will be unable to ever recover from this blow at its prestige or that it will no longer attempt to play its trump card: decision-making by executive fiat. It does mean, however, that the optimal conditions under which power elites operate have been seriously hampered. The degree of this impairment and the length of time it will obtain depend exclusively on the politics of awareness and participation, no less than the continuing pressures, of those sections of the public interested in lowering the secrecy levels in high-level international decision-making.

Probably the most compelling reasons given for President Nixon's bitter opposition to the release of the Pentagon Papers are those provided by Melvin Gurtov, one of the authors of the secret Pentagon study and an outstanding political scientist specializing in Asian affairs. He speaks of three deceits in current American Vietnamese policy: "The first and most basic deceit is the Administration's contention that we're winding down and getting out of the war." In fact, Vietnamization is a "domestic political ploy that really involves the substitution of air power for ground power." The second deceit is that "we're truly interested in seeing the prisoners of war released." Gurtov notes that "as far as this administration is concerned the prisoners of war are a political device, a device for rationalizing escalation, by saying these are acts that are necessary to show our concern for the prisoners." The third deceit "is that under the Nixon Doctrine the United States is not interested in making new commitments in Asia." In fact, the administration used the Cambodia coup "as an opportunity for creating for itself a new commitment in Southeast Asia, namely the survival of a non-Communist regime in Phnompenh." This outspoken position indicates that the defense of the power elite of the past by President Nixon might just as well be construed as a self-defense of the power elite in the present.

Conspiracies

The Pentagon Papers provide much new light on theories of power elite and diffusion and also provide an equal measure of information on conspiracy theory. And while it is still true that conspiracy *theory* is bad theory, it is false to assert that conspiracies do not exist or are not perpetrated by the government. It might indeed be the case that all governments, insofar as they are formal organizations, have secrets, and we call these secrets conspiracies. From this point of view, the interesting question is how so few leaks resulted from an effort involving so many people and of such great magnitude as setting policy in the Vietnam War. Rather than be surprised that these papers reached the public domain four to six years after the fact, one should wonder how the government was able to maintain silence on matters of such far-ranging and far-reaching consequence.

Cyrus Eaton, American industrialist and confidant of many communist leaders, indicates that the Vietnamese almost instantaneously were made aware of United States policy decisions. But I seriously doubt that they actually had copies of these materials. Rather, like the American public itself, they were informed about the decisions but not the cogitations and agitations that went into the final decisions. Perhaps this is the way all governments operate; nonetheless, it is fascinating—at least this once—to be privy to the process and not simply the outcome and to see the foibles of powerful men and not just the fables manufactured for these men after the fact.

These papers underwrite the commonsense view that governments are not to be trusted and to undermine the more sophisticated interpretation that governments are dedicated to the task of maintaining democracy at home and peace abroad. As bitter as it may seem, commonsense cynicism has more to recommend it than the sophisticated, well-elaborated viewpoints that take literally the formal structure of government and so readily tend to dismiss the informal response to power and pressure from men at the top. The constant wavering of Lyndon B. Johnson, his bellicose defiance of all evidence and information that the bombings were not having the intended effect, followed by the shocking news that lieutenants like Robert McNamara had decided to change their positions in midstream (which almost constituted a betrayal in the eyes of the President) were in turn followed by a more relaxed posture and a final decision not to seek the presidency. All this forms a human drama that makes the political process at once fascinating and frightful; fascinating because we can see the psychology of politics in action, and frightful because the presumed rationality is by no means uniformly present.

The publication of the Pentagon Papers, while a considerable victory for the rights of a free press and of special significance to all scientists who still uphold the principle of full disclosure as the norm of all political as well as scientific endeavor, is not yet a total victory for a democratic society—that can only happen when the concept of secrecy is itself probed and penetrated, and when the concept of undeclared warfare is finally and fully repudiated by the public and its representatives. The behavior of the government in its effort to suppress publication of the Pentagon Papers cannot simply be viewed as idiosyncratic, but rather as part of the structure of the American political processes in which the expert displaces the politician, and the politicians themselves become so beholden to the class of experts for information that they dare not turn for guidance to the people they serve. For years, critics of the Vietnam War have been silenced and intimidated by the policy-makers' insistence that when all the facts were known the hawk position would be vindicated and the dove position would be violated. Many of the facts are now revealed—and the bankruptcy of the advocates of continued escalation is plain for all to see. It is to be hoped that this will strengthen the prospects for peace and firm up those who, as an automatic reflex, assume the correctness of the government's position on all things military. It is also to be hoped that the principle on all things military. It is also to be hoped that the principle of democracy, of every person counting as one, once more will become the source of fundamental decision-making and political discourse.

1971

16

The American Way
of
Spying

I

The thin line between intelligence and surveillance, between the public's right to know and the citizen's right to privacy, is the foundation of much current American soul searching. Both positions—the right to knowledge and the right to privacy—are firmly entrenched in the constitutional tradition. Thus, the existence of investigatory agencies is troublesome to the extent that they involve us in a legal double-bind—a veritable contradiction between competing needs in a modern society. The limits of privacy come full force up against the limits of knowledge. And choices are made in terms of shifts in the moral sentiment more than by new legal foundations of the social order.

In American social history issues of ideology are fought out and masked by contrasting administrative claims. This was made virtually certain given the fact that the American polity derives from the legal premises of a checks and balances system that shared power prevents its undue exercise. Thus, the legislative branch stands in the forefront of those demanding the right to know about the entire gamut of CIA activities; arguing, in effect, that the agency is ultimately responsive to Congress since it alone is the repository of the popular will. The executive branch is obviously reluctant to pursue such a line of reasoning; its growth in power since the end of the Second World War clearly derives from the secrecy implicit in a policy-making (in contrast to a polity-making) approach. The steady stream of publications issuing forth from hearings and testimonies held by both branches of Congress is a firm indicator that the right of the public to information on all agency activities is about the only mechanism available to prevent yet a further erosion of legislative powers and their transfer to executive branches. Thus, politically, no less than ideologically, the current revaluation of CIA activities involves principles of a fundamental sort—the sort that ultimately may redefine who governs and, beyond that, the limits of governance.

The Federal Bureau of Investigation and the Central Intelligence Agency have been with us for quite some time. Their activities are hardly esoteric or mysterious. So the question becomes: Why has the role of intelligence-gathering agencies and federal police bureaus come under widespread critical examination at this point in our national history.?

The answers are obviously complex and multiple: the dismay and disgust of the public with the Watergate break-in and its aftermath, and the obvious collusion of party officials with federal agencies in first creating a police-state climate, and second in supressing the full story. Then there is the general mistrust of federal bureaucracy, a realization that the need to know has spilled over into a desire to dominate—a far less noble purpose; and the sense that the only way to restore confidence in government is to expose illegitimate behavior by those who transgress the legitimate boundaries of government. Finally, there is international pressure, from Latin America to Asia, to curb the overseas operations of intelligence-gathering units that, in fact, act as counterguerilla units beyond the boundaries of national sovereignty.

For the most part, discussions about the CIA and other information-gathering agencies that spin off into action roles confuse the moral purposes of such activities and their empirical efficacy. It is one thing to express a sense of rage about CIA spying activities on American citizens or foreign governments and quite another to demonstrate the degree of success such activities have achieved. In these murkier waters, one does find countervailing forces at work—not only civil libertarians versus civil disrupters, but competition between agencies such as the FBI and the CIA, which itself muffles, if not quite mitigates, spying activities.

In my opinion, we must combine the best of critical social science and investigative reporting to express a sense of the system as well as a sense of outrage. The restoration of international law, the new resolve toward congressional inquiry and control, the distinction between democratic restraint and antidemocratic opposition, the further distinction between the national interest and narrow commercial or military interests, all indicate ways in which the government can better serve its citizenry.

Spying is not, strictly speaking, an American preserve, nor is the illegal use of surveillance personnel to harass a native citizenry an American monopoly. However, it is of little worth to cite instances of terror and police spying abroad, or for that matter, historical illustrations of this phenomenon. The purpose of democratic government is normative and not simply comparative. The recitation of transgressions elsewhere, on the fatuous assumption that the role of government is more gracious and generous now than in the past eras, simply misses the point. Democracy is an ideal of equity we are collectively dedicated to achieving; it is not an equivalent of Pax Americana that must be bullishly supported wherever and whenever opposition movements, parties, or systems arise.

As a result, the following seven-point minimal policy program that can and should emanate from this current round of congressional hearings and presidential commissions is indicated:

A national civil liberties commission paralleling the existing national civil rights commission should be created. This group should be appointed by Congress, should perform its duties with maximum autonomy and noninterference from other government agencies, and ought to function as a special ad hoc group of the Government Operations Committee of the United States Senate. The various commissions recently appointed to study CIA violations have in common a dangerous politicization; hence it is likely that nothing of consequence will result. On the side of softsoaping CIA covert operations is the Presidential Commission headed by Vice-President Nelson Rockefeller and on the side of what has been called the Senate "cabal" to get the CIA is the Senate Select Investigating Committee headed by Frank Church. Most past commissions have had the benefit of social and behavioral science personnel who filed reports with meat and meaning. The present concurrent investigating commissions seem destined to generate more heat than light and, more pointedly, result in a zero effect, with the recommendations of the different commissions and subcommissions canceling out one another. What is needed is a single autonomous commission with political inputs for the Congress, the executive, and the judiciary branches, but with leadership and direction provided by constitutional lawyers and political scientists.

The jurisdictional disputes between agencies such as the CIA and the FBI should be brought out into the open to determine if either agency has assumed greater police roles than is constitutionally warranted. Beyond that, specialized subagencies, like the passport division of the State Department, should be explicitly prohibited from making special arrangements and deals with the CIA that could lead to the creation of special files for surveillance purposes and blacklists that might inhibit citizens engaged in private activities of tourism or commerce.

The CIA should limit its intelligence-gathering operations generally. At the optimal level, they do little more than repeat data and information found in social and political science, often naively, and without the balance manifested in scholarly research. CIA sponsorship of research, often having little or nothing to do with threats to American interests, only conservatizes scholarship and inhibits the open exchange of information.

A definition of the intelligence-gathering functions of the CIA must be established that is not so broad and diffuse as to permit the funding of conduits in areas ranging from broadcasting to publishing to student associations. It is always possible to justify and rationalize sub-rosa activities in the name of intelligence, when in point of fact the underwriting of otherwise legitimate expressions of communication for propaganda purposes serves only to discredit honest operations and to cast grave doubts on the CIA's integrity by its uniform alignment with right-wing and conservative enterprises and causes that might otherwise be unable to survive. The CIA is entitled to support research and to publish results. But it should be made by statute to declare such support openly and, wherever possible, to publish its results in official government documentation centers rather than privately endowed firms.

Diplomacy, not counterinsurgency, should dominate in policy-making abroad. The ambassadorial functions should be greatly strengthened, so that spying and surveillance activities do not take place independent of state department control, to the embarrassment of United States foreign policy. From India to Chile, normal relations with the United States have been strained as a result of CIA secrecy. A recommendation to move cautiously in setting up new intelligence-gathering units and to rely instead upon existing agencies was made as early as February 1947, by General George P. Marshall in a memorandum to the President. "The Foreign Service of the Department of State is the only collection agency of the Government which covers the whole world, and we should be very slow to subject the collection and evaluation of this foreign intelligence to other establishments, especially during times of peace. The powers of the proposed agency seem almost unlimited and need clarification."

The fiscal cover under which the CIA has been permitted to operate should finally be lifted. The General Accounting Office and the citizenry have a right to demand the same public disclosure of the amount, distribution, and allocation of funding as is expected of any other federal agency. Indeed, the FBI is subject to a far greater auditing responsibility than the CIA and yet manages to carry out its assignments without jeopardy. The risks to specific assignments are virtually nonexistent. But the risks of continuing constitutional violations are great in the present atmosphere of fiscal secrecy.

The major question is not simply the illegal "domestic" spying activities of the CIA, but whether its overseas activities should be restricted to information-gathering rather than manifest support of conservative regimes and the fomenting of opposition to radical regimes. A simple rule in this connection is to have the CIA do unto other governments as they do to us. That is to say, since the Soviet Union engages in large-scale and illegal spying activities, the activities of the CIA inside the Soviet Union should be commensurate with that nation's acts inside the United States. But for nations such as Uruguay or Pakistan, who have neither the ability nor interest to conduct spying missions in the United States, the same rules should apply to United States' behavior inside those Third World nations. Real opposton to CIA activities inside other major world powers is clearly not in dispute; but rather CIA activities against small and relatively defenseless countries whose rights to select and implement policies are seriously undermined by CIA interference and involvement.

These seven items are not intended to provide a definitive list of suggested policy changes in the conduct of American surveillance activities, but the are aimed at moving us beyond the moral torpor that has seemingly gripped our political leadership since the Vietnam War began in earnest a decade ago and also beyond the political infantilism of dismantling the intelligence effort unilaterally and without regard to real world conditions.

What the various executive and legislative hearings on the CIA are likely to demonstrate is only a cluster of confirmations about atrocities already reported: assassination attempts against Left and Right leaders hostile to presumed Americn overseas interests, stimulating political crisis by supporting oppositionist groupings, and cloak and dagger code-breaking and gun-slinging operations having more technological than political meaning. Some exact details might prove titillating or intriguing, but none are likely to cause any fundamental reestimations of the CIA's potential for damage.

What then does the current animus toward the CIA signify? The most obvious explanation is also the most likely. From 1964 to 1974, the American people underwent a gradual but authentic change in their sense of national priorities. Economy, ecology, and environment, the three national "E's" displaced militarization, modernization, and mobilization, the three international "M's." And as the stalemated situation of the fifties led to the military defeats of the late sixties, attitudes toward redirecting our priorities hardened. Defeat has had a sobering effect on the American public; and if it would be a mistake to judge the mood of America as isolationist, it would be folly to believe that internationalist sentiments have remained firm. Even a minimal, nonmilitary task force stationed in the Middle East has come upon severe critical public reaction. The line between internationalism and imperialism has become thin—made more so by the incessant rhetoric of nationalism pouring forth from Third World nations that have been the recipients of unwanted CIA "favors."

Thus it is that the demise of the CIA is far less a function of its own bunglings and failures than of a shifting mood in America. A vanguard police force is less urgently needed in a period of national retrenchment than in a period of world war and cold war involvement. Thus it is that the CIA is a victim of international pacification. It is not that we have decided that now is the time to gloss over or launder the atrocities and bigotries it has committed in the name of American foreign policy, but simply that now is the time to recognize that all organizations—secret as well as public—are subject to the iron law of public purpose even more than to an iron law of private survival.

II

Just as there is a peculiar imbalance in spy activities—a sort of asymmetry between those who do the spying in contrast to the innocents spied upon, or even worse, between assassins and the assassinated, so too there is an asymmetrical relationship at the other end of the spectrum. Those standing four-square for overtness and probity show too little understanding or appreciation of the existence of an international espionage system, and of linkages between such federally sponsored agencies as Interpol. One is constantly informed of dirty tricks and covert operations as if they were an American monopoly. The spy system is an integrated effort, part of a superstructure of mutual antagonisms inherited from World War Two and later the cold war. Because there is no Soviet group equivalent to the Senate Investigating Committee, a sense of the "other side" is completely absent in the volumes prepared by the Congressional investigators. The workings and operations of Soviet intelligence, the OGPU and NKUD, are left to the imagination, or for those who are really curious, to a review of the archival research performed by American scholars of an earlier era.

It is strange to read about the evils of covert operations and how they are in violation of international law. One is reminded that the conflicts between the titanic philosophies of Kant and Hegel still persist, with the Kantians acting the role of good guys in search of world order through world peace. On the other side stand the young Hegelians of power politics, like Henry Kissinger and Andrei Gromyko, who are fully aware that the nation is still the basic organizing unit of law, and as such it is uniquely the source of organized terror, systematic espionage, and of distinctions made on a daily basis between public propaganda and privileged information. This Hegelian component in the structure of the world helps account for a universe without trust; spying becomes the only mechanism available to make public, or at least inform the other side of, the doings and wrongdoings of the protagonists. In an odd way, the madness of nationalism helps explain the rationality of the espionage system. It also helps determine why investigations, hearings, and conferences, both of a formal and informal sort, while helping us understand the nature of a spying universe, tend to do little to move us beyond such a universe. As long as the nation has an organized existence, indeed organizes our basic economic political activities, to that degree spying will be with us. Allen Dulles, Richard Helms, William Colby, all knew this lesson well. The magnitude, the awfulness of the spy system is not simply a function of its current range of activities, but of the fact that the bigger the nation, the more it wants to know and needs to know about other potential claimants to power.

Throughout the many pages of testimony and scholarship concerning CIA activities one is repeatedly struck by a central problem shared by all spy networks. Each of them operates in such a veil of secrecy that their own national leadership is unaware of their doings. Moreover, such agencies conduct their affairs in a world where their mandates are clear at the individual level, but incredibly cloudy at the general level. They know who to kill, who to spy upon, and what crucial information is needed to make a bigger and dirtier (or smaller and cleaner) bomb. But they do not seem to have the foggiest notion of the consequences of their activities. CIA leadership presumes that the agency serves not just as an intelligence-gathering unit abroad, but as a stabilizing factor promoting a world in which democratic policies can be more readily implemented. In point of fact, the actual activities described before the Church Committee hearings, particularly the assasination attempts, are as ludicrous as they are (often) unsuccessful. The CIA officials are prisoners of their own broadly interpreted mandate. The assassination of General René Schneider in Chile did not lead to an overthrow of Salvador Allende but to the strengthening of his regime. The attempted assassination against Fidel Castro likewise mobilized the Cuban population against the foreign aggressor and deflected any internal criticism as divisive. One develops the astonishing feeling from reading Colby's various statements to congressional and paracongressional bodies that beyond the drying up of information, little can be said in defense of the CIA. If that is the situation, given the misinformation gathered, the double-crosses and political misconceptions, from the Bay of Pigs invasion to the Vietnam War, the CIA is already a fossil.

The difficulty in the CIA position is that it sees its activities as entirely legitimate. But it does not identify the political mandate underlying that legitimation. While it wishes to make clear that the CIA mandate is in the field of foreign intelligence, and that past activities within the United States have been illegal and excessive, that really is not the point. The main issue is whether foreign intelligence is feasible when there is no overall sense of the milieu in which actions are performed. The contradiction in its position is manifest. If the Cold War has genuinely been wound down, and an era of détente exists, how can a mandate issued in one era be satisfactorily negotiated in another? On the other hand, if the mandate of the CIA has changed, does that mean that the policy of détente is merely chimeric, a legal fiction which itself disguises the continuing battle between the superpowers? In these kinds of questions one senses an acute lack of awareness by the protagonists, by those who attack the spy networks, and by those who are seeking to expose these networks.

If the problem of those in charge of the espionage system is a painful lack of awareness of the consequences and meaning of their activities, one must be candid and say that their mindlessness, in some portion at least, is matched by the pillars of community conscience by those who seek the immediate end of all spying activities, and by those who think of spying as an American preserve. There is a tragic ahistorical quality in many of these papers. Nearly all read as if Pearl Harbor had never happened, as if it would be an embarrassment to raise such consideratons, as if in the atomic age no one would dare to start a war that would be *prima facie* suicide.

But if the nation-state does exist, and aggression is a genuine characteristic of nations no less than individuals, then the lessons of history cannot be overlooked. This embarrassment with the past is intriguing. A kind of holier-than-thou attitude prevails among critics of the CIA, and is so much the rage of the moment that one can hardly get beyond the dissident member of the audience who questioned Colby: "How many did you kill in Vietnam?"; only to be indignantly ansered: "I didn't kill any"; followed by deriseive laughter from the audience. This sense of moral outrage in my estimation is a function of naiveté—based on an assumption that American purity has been soiled—as if this nation has been uniquely touched by Providence and people like William Colby ate from the apple. of desire and destroyed our political innocence. I do not believe opponents of the CIA have a right to such naiveté. We are obligated to remember Pearl Harbor, no less than agencies involved in spying are obligated to remember American democracy. CIA actions may have negative consequences, but so may the destruction of agencies.

The consequence of this Mexican stand-off between those defending the agency's right to gather information and those who are outraged by the excesses of spying is a tragic absence of serious policy recommendations. All we are offered in this regard is a promise that the Central Intelligence Agency will use the word "foreign" prefacing "intelligence," while opponents will probably settle for nothing less than the dismantling of the agency as a whole, to be replaced by some indeterminate, more nobly organized agency. What is odd, what is missing, are policy recommendations that make sense and are sensible, that can overcome the polarization brought on by congressional revelations of agency excesses, wrongdoings, and malfeasance. Policy recommendations might have been some of the following: a continuing Senate Surveillance Committee, or a special ad hoc group appointed by the government operations committee of the United States Senate; a much sharper definition of the areas of responsibility of the CIA and the FBI; a constant comparison of CIA-sponsored intelligence-gathering versus the information publicly available through responsible scholars and networks involved in international relations and information-gathering generally; a clear definition of what constitutes intelligence-gathering, in order to limit spying activities in the world of publishing, broadcasting, student organizations, and the like; and an end to a special fiscal covering and a greater accountability, especially to the General Accounting Office and the citizenry generally. One might also suggest that instead of gathering scholarly information for intelligence in counterinsurgency, radical channels of information might be used; perhaps these channels would be more efficacious in bringing about a more balanced foreign policy and a greater sense of the American situation to the rest of the world.

Despite the hoopla surrounding the Staff Report of the Select Committee to Study Governmental Operations with respect to Intelligence Activities in Chile (1975) the contents of the report on covert action between 1963 and 1973 are hardly earth-shattering. The report itself concludes: "In Latin America particularly, even the suspicion of

CIA support materially hampered Allende's rise to power, or for that matter, stimulated his tragic demise." The data provided by the report show no significant correlations between increased military assistance and sales and the Allende period. Well might this be the case since the Chilean military almost uniquely in Latin America had, up to the Pinochet period, an almost fanatical devotion to legality and civilian administrative rule. So CIA involvement in Chile did not mean total support of the military. Indeed, the rightist plot to kidnap and abduct the Chief of Staff of the Chilean Army, René Schneider, was undertaken precisely to overcome the military's stiff commitment to democratic norms. But even at this level, CIA involvement is moot, for as the report makes clear: "The CIA had been in touch with that group of plotters, but a week earlier had withdrawn its support for the group's specific plans." Even the nefarious half-million-dollar effort by ITT to prevent the election of Allende brought no CIA involvement: "The CIA learned of this funding but did not assist in it." Little wonder that the Senate Report remains inconclusive: a slap at the CIA for defining its intelligence-gathering functions in "far too broad" a manner, but hardly the exposé we were led to believe was in the offing.

The Select Committee's report on Alleged Assassination Plots (1975) is more meaty, for in this area the CIA clearly crossed the line, in several instances, from knowledge of plots to direct engagement of paid minions to perform assassinations. Officials of the United States government initiated plots to assassinate Fidel Castro (unsuccessful) and Patrice Lumumba (successful); they encourged or were privy to plots to kill Rafael Trujillo, President Diem, and General Schneider. But here we find the anomaly that our officials were acting against right-wing dictators, and as a result stimulated movements for social and political change. The report clearly indicates that the CIA and others exaggerated perceived threats to American national security as a result of the cold war. What the authors of the report do not ask is whether they have underestimated foreign dangers as a consequence of détente. The most telling point is that cloak and dagger activities took place in a cloak and dagger atmosphere; that is to say, even high government officials knew little or nothing of covert CIA operations. It is for this reason that such wide use could be made of underworld criminal elements—often from the same groupings that were engaged in the Watergate break-in. The recommendations are again exceedingly fragmentary, of the thou-shalt-not-hire-criminals-to-do-dirty-works variety. But the conclusion is revealing: we are reassured that "the events described do not represent the real American character," whatever that may be, but some sort of aberration. The essence of the recommendation is that "The United States must not adopt the tactics of the enemy." Ah! So there is an "enemy" after all, if only in the last page of the report, marked "epilogue." But one may ask what sort of report might have been drawn if Epilogue had turned into Prologue: if the description of the strategy and tactics of the OGPU (the Soviet United State Political Administration) had formed the essential backdrop against which the dialectic of covert operations was played out.

The CIA File edited by Borosage and Marks (1976) is based on a series of papers initially delivered in September 1974 under the sponsorship of the Center for National Security Studies, and cohosted by Senators Philip A. Hart and Edward W. Brooke. The appearance of past director William E. Colby in a question-and-answer guise gave the conference considerable public exposure long before the present round of investigations on clandestine CIA activities. Indeed, one would have to say that the people included—outstanding journalists like David Wise and Thomas B. Ross, political scientists such as Richard A. Falk, Morton H. Halperin, and Richard J. Barnet, lawyers like Robert Borosage and Herbert Scoville, Jr.—provide the ideological and intellectual vanguard that makes possible a critical public reaction to the news that the CIA mandate to investigate had spilled over to clandestine operations, from intervention into the political structure of other nations to assassination of undesirables as defined by the agency.

One wonders whether the repugnance for the CIA is based on its specific political activities or upon animosity for the political posture of the United States in the past decade. As Victor Marchetti in his own overview makes clear, the CIA's predecessor, the World War II Services (OSS), performed exactly the same sort of extralegal role, and provided a guideline for the postwar CIA activities. But what becomes clear as one goes through these essays is the private agenda of these critics of American foreign policy. They exhibit such a uniform dissent from such policies that they lash out at instrumentalities of foreign policy, and the CIA as the weakest legal chink in that armor, rather than examine the nature of that policy commitment directly. As a result, one is left with the uncomfortable feeling that agency practices are repugnant less in themselves than for the specific policies their government has mandated.

In a real sense, the choice at this point in time is not simply the status quo versus changes in that status quo, but whether in fact the intelligence system is to be dismantled or be limited. If the former, what insurances and guarantees of the behavior of the great powers in the world are to be provided? If the latter, what forms of supervision could prevail that would maintain civilian authority and democratic goals over these agency processes?

Given all the investigation committees, there is still little information on who these covert operators are. I do not simply mean their names and addressses, which are now being provided by newspapers in Paris, Madrid and Lisbon—and even Washington—but what are their backgrounds? What makes them tick, psychologically and sociologically? Are they frustrated novelists, or are they terminal Masters' candidates denied jobs at Brookings? Are they would-be engineers who want to create systematic unity in the world and found their way to the CIA as the means to impose such unity? Are they failures, miscreants, and misfits? Or are they the stuff of heroes? None of these volumes on the CIA tells us anything about its people. They remain as cloudly and hidden at the end of the books as at the beginning. From my own point of view, unless they become at least as clearly etched as their critics, the spying world has nothing to worry about. For all of the moral criticism, all of the collective outrage or guilt does not touch the soft center of personal biography. "They" still know considerably more about "us" than vice versa. So the agencies of spying come up with the last laugh. They remain as covert as ever—not about what they do but about who they are. That is the most glaring omission in the present discourse concerning spying in America.

1976

V

MILITARY
POLITICS

17

Arms, Policies,
and
War Games

Who are the civilian militarists? First, they are men who make military policy without being officially connected to any branch of the army, navy, or air force services. Second, they are men trained in the strategy and tactics of military terrorism who, under the protection of university and government agencies, claim and proclaim their "neutrality" with respect to social and political issues.

In these pages the names of many of these men appear: Herman Kahn, Thomas C. Schelling, Henry A. Kissinger, and Albert Wohlstetter. While it is clear that they exhibit many policy differences in their thinking, a collective portrait does nonetheless emerge. They have a shared philosophy, a narrowly conceived utilitarianism in which each person or each side always acts in terms of national self-defense. They replace problems of principles with matters of strategy. They prefer thinking about the unthinkable at the cost of any examination of what is possible or preferable. They inhabit a world of nightmarish intellectual "play," while ridiculing the "ossification" of American military posture. They seem to prefer "advisory" positions and leave to politicians the actual tasks of acting out their recommendations. (How else can they claim to be value neutral with respect to scientific canons?) In brief, they are "military" minds with "civilian" status. Hence I have designated them "the new civilian militarists"—the real-life counterparts of the devotees to "fail-safe" technological politics.

It has been suggested by the more Panglossian elements in American intellectual circles that the new civilian militarists are not really taken seriously by the United States government; hence, Why should they be taken so seriously by those concerned with survival in a thermonuclear age? The mass-circulation weeklies have punctured this naive academic myth more forcefully than the professional journals (see Enthoven, et al., 1962; *Business Week,* 1963). The description of the Pentagon's "Whiz Kids" makes crystal clear the policy-making and policy-planning roles of the new civilian militarists. What emerges from a collective portrait are the following facts and figures:

(a) They are the principal advisors to the Department of Defense.

(b) They have the direct "ear" of the American President and other members of the Executive's "official family."

(c) They belong primarily to the technological sector of the American professional elite—with a preponderance of engineers, physicists, and economists.

(d) They have so outflanked military "tacticians" that, in the words of the article, the military "themselves are now bringing in younger, university-trained soldier-scientists to act as the military equivalent of the Whiz Kids."

(e) For the most part, the new civilian militarists received their nurturing in the training grounds of the RAND corporation—making studies of conventional and nuclear war and studying the worth of such bulwarks of peace-making as the Strategic Air Command (SAC), Tactical Air Command (TAC), and the Air Defense Command (ADC).

The position of the civilian militarists was aptly summed up by Peck, when he said: "Defense is really the dominant problem of our times." It is the burden of this work to show this to be incorrect; to show in contrast that *disarmament* is really the dominant problem of our times. In the crucible of this debate inheres the furies that will either consume us or preserve us.

Contrary to the propaganda barrage, even the word "war" has become obsolete as a description of the present potential for total annihilation in a universe of "overkill." The assumption made in the following pages is simple, but, I believe, sober: the alternative to annihilation is not deterrence or truce; it is disarmament. The cornerstone of classical warfare is victory and defeat. The basis of thermonuclear annihilation is the destruction of both self and other.

In opposition to my assumption stands an emerging body of statistics developed by experts whom I have termed the New Civilian Militarists, henceforth called NCM. Before offering my analysis, I think it only fair to present the rationale and conclusions of these experts who operate out of RAND, ITEK, the Hudson Institute, and the various Centers of International Relations, and something of the framework within which their calculations are made.

During the last several years a great deal has happened both in the strategy and tactics of war-making and in the technology of human destruction. Unfortunately, advances registered by the strategists of peace during this same period have not kept pace. Indeed, the gap between military preparation for conflict and civilian strategy for cooperation continues to widen. While the former becomes more precise, the latter becomes more strident. In addition, men of learning are being pressed into military activities, while, as yet, pitifully few military men are adopting civilian attitudes.

This is understandable. Thermonuclear weapons one thousand times as devastating as those that laid ruin to Hiroshima and Nagasaki have been developed and made operational. Even cautious statisticians indicate that from one-third to one-half the populations of the United States and the Soviet Union would be annihilated in any multistrike hydrogen bomb exchange. Scientists have surmised the terrors of somatic and genetic dislocations that would follow in the wake of thermonuclear exchange. The only question is the extent of the damages to human organisms. These are but a few of the consequences predicated for a post-World War III epoch. And in a world lacking transcendent goals, or even common survival attitudes, extreme pessimism finds its bizarre counterpart in an optimism bred by impregnable weapons systems.

Such information tends to blunt rather than stimulate interest in the problem of disarmament. The typical psychic reaction of a cancer patient doomed to die within a stipulated period of time is known as privatization; it takes the form of retreat from worldly concerns or of accelerated ego gratification. The same is true of widespread social *anomie* in general. Retreatism is the sociological counterpart of cynicism.

But so far no military analysis has demonstrated that society is in the position of a cancer patient. We have every right to assume the possibility of a durable and valid peace between men and nations. Yet what we are witnessing is a form of privatization in which society knows the facts, but feels impotent in the face of them. Why? And what can be done to release our thinking so that we face reality and seek a resolution of the arms race? Why should "thinking about the unthinkable" not be enlarged to include thinking of alternatives to the arms race as such?

The problems of deterrence and disarmament are unfortunately meshed. To discuss them in general terms would, at best, lead to soothing abstractions and sentimental aphorisms. Neither will get us out of this period of privatization. I shall therefore concentrate on a discussion of recent trends in arms control and argue the thesis that arms control is not a substitute for a general disarmament policy, but its very opposite. Further, the very substitution of the one for the other in the name of *Realpolitik* is another aspect of the privatization process (at the national level), subverting rather than supporting the search for peaceful alternatives to thermonuclear depopulation.

Familiar to those conversant with the dialogue between the advocates of deterrence and arms control on the one hand and those of disarmament on the other are the men who project concepts of strategy and tactics strongly influential in military and political thinking about United States arms policy. Responsible to no political group and only indirectly involved in the actions they propose or foresee, these advisers have developed what may be called "game policy" as a means of evaluating contingencies in international politics; that is, they have used the principles of good and bad moves in the artificial world of game-playing to calculate risks and anticipate the moves of "imaginary" enemies in the world of international political strategy.

The development of this line of thought had, in part at least, origins in the correct assumption that the new role of the Soviet Union as a thermonuclear power of at least equal strength to the U.S. required a revaluation of the strategy and tactics of war-making no less than a revaluation of the goals and consequences of foreign policy. It was in the despairing aftermath of the Sputnik launchings that most of this new thinking about our arms control was undertaken. Academic strategists in the United States who, until the Soviet thrusts into outer space, were tolerated as purveyors of mathematical paradoxes, came to be respected as necessary adjutants in policy decisions. The forms of deterrence developed by these strategists have influenced military and political thinking on United States arms policy to an extent and in a manner we shall now attempt to explore.

The NCM have the following thoughts, paraphrased for quick study, on U.S. arms policy:

A policy of disarmament should be made contingent upon the aims of national policy and national security. All stages in arms control therefore should be tactical representations of national self-interests. The escalation or deescalation of the arms race or the feasibility of disarmament is not to be decided on central principles of foreign policy, but rather in terms of deterrence strategy.

The United States and the Soviet Union are in a delicate balance of terror, which reduces itself to a bipolar arms race. This can be thought of as a kind of two-player game. Other "players" tend to form partnerships or alliances with one of the sides. As of now, these "Nth" players contribute to the symmetry of the terror balance because two nations hold the overwhelming majority of the blue chips—in this case, thermonuclear warheads. But this terror balance is in an unstable equilibrium, threatening to become more delicate and less balanced with the passage of time since initial strikes and retaliations are programmed to occur within minutes and even seconds of each other, opening the possibility for mistakes in calculation. An additional unstable element is the "Nth" player (such as China or France) who has independent geopolitical interests.

In the thermonuclear age the aggressor has the advantage because of the destructive power of modern weapons. According to the game-theory principles of von Neumann and Morgenstern, a player can score a gain of predictable dimensions irrespective of what the other player does or is planning to do. This increases the rate and tempo of thermonuclear arms build-up and places an enormous premium on cheating, bluffing, blitzkrieg tactics, and the "game of chicken."

In view of this situation, disarmament cannot lead to a final resolution of outstanding world problems since maintenance of the delicate balance of terror rests on the assumption of relatively equal strengths by the conflicting powers, an equilibrium that cannot be shown to obtain at any given moment. Thus arms control, defined as the maintenance of symmetry between conflicting players, is the only fruitful line of political discourse.

Popular thinking, including that of most military strategists, rests on the false premise that present-day weapons would destroy mankind if used. What Herman Kahn calls "Doomsday" weapons can be programmed in the near future, although the likelihood is slim since it is a tactical absurdity to program self-annihilation as a means of victory. According to this line of thought, anywhere from ten to one hundred million people might perish in a hydrogen exchange, but it would not be a total disaster, it would not be an "overkill" situation, since man and his cultural institutions would still survive, however mutilated.

Given this set of conditons, discussions between the United States and the Soviet Union ought to be used to provide us with the answers to the following questions: How rapid a thermonuclear retaliation should be programmed? Under what conditions ought we to make the first strike?

How rapid would be the recovery rate from such a war? What are the prospects for a reestablishment of social and political hegemony after a nuclear conflict? All of these questions are based on the assumption that a thermonuclear war, while it would represent an *unprecedented* catastrophe, would by no means be an *unlimited* one.

We ought to prepare now for the eventuality of a thermonuclear war, rather than assume its impossibility. In addition to clearcut psychological advantages in terms of mobilizing the population, this allows for the development of radiation meters for evaluating the extent of somatic damage, area evacuation programs, and experiments to create chemical and biological counteragents to nuclear damage. An advantage in terms of military policy is also involved, since victory might well be determined by which population is able to recover quickest.

Finally, the problems for the period following a thermonuclear conflict are those of the forms of survival and reconstruction, problems that do not exist in a pacifist stance that assumes that all forms of human life would perish. Plans to meet postwar problems should be made and would include exploration of the kinds of checks needed to prevent violation of agreements arising from negotiated settlement.

These policy assumptions and observations of the NCM have created a stir in political circles, military agencies, civilian defense organizations, and academic institutions. Contrast the views of historian H. Stuart Hughes and mathematician James R. Newman, both committed to disarmament rather than arms control. Hughes describes Kahn, an extreme advocate of game theory among the NCM, as "the master strategist of the midtwentieth century," and says "what Kahn tries to do is to look thermonuclear war in the eye and to treat it as a reality rather than a bad dream" (see Hughes, 1961). Newman, for his part, doubts the very reality of Kahn's work, *On Thermonuclear War,* and asks, "Is there really a Herman Kahn? It is hard to believe. Doubts cross one's mind almost from the first page of this deplorable book: no one could write like this; no one could think like this. Perhaps the whole thing is a staff hoax in bad taste... this evil and tenebrous book with its loose-lipped pieties and its hayfoot-strawfoot logic, is permeated with a bloodthirsty irrationality" (see Newman, 1962).

Hughes may make too generous an estimate of the scientific worth of the war-game theoreticians, while Newman undervalues the work of the NCM in setting forth the actual climate of policy in which discussions on the arms question are taking place. We can afford neither the luxury of uncritical praise nor cries of outrage at those who define the military realities of the present world. The fact that so expert an authority on nuclear weapons as Jerome Weisner can act as sponsor to the NCM and persuasively argue their case for world peace would make it plain that it is not the morality of Kahn, Wohlstetter, Kissinger, Schelling, and Brodie that needs scrutinizing, but rather the scientific adequacy of their claims. In fact the NCM have changed the content of the traditional relationship between governemtn and academy. In former years, the problem was why there was such a complete bifurcation of the two. Now, the problem is locating the legitimate limits of the interpenetration of one into the other.

In order to explore these views on deterrence and the rival solutions to the problems posed, I shall now remark on a series of logical paradoxes in which the NCM seem inextricably involved.

The NCM insist that their conditions for a successful arms control program are both realistic and practical. But their claim of "thinking about the unthinkable" does not justify their lack of consideration for basic "thinkable" factors that exist: psychological factors such as different attitudes toward war, different ways of deciding what is rational, different ideas of right and wrong, different approaches to reality and truth. These must be taken into account. But these considerations upset the symmetry of a game-theory approach. The actual social and political problems of the moment belong to a historical period designated "post-World War II." the striking characteristic of the NCM is that they carry on analysis in an "as if" gambler's universe of "post-World War III." This is an *Alice in Wonderland* methodology that fails to tabulate all the social, political, and economic factors that must be considered for an accurate set of forecasts.

The purpose of scientific inquiry is to arrive at accurate forecasts. To assume a universe of two players displaying symmetry in everything from morals to weapons is to start out divorced from reality. Such essential factors and variables as the function of the United Nations as a mediating force in military and jurisdictional disputes, the role of "third force" nations such as England and France (which do have atomic weapons), and the role of "third world" nations such as India and China (which are likely to have a nuclear striking force in the near future) are discussed, notably by RAND experts, as if the nations necessarily must be partners in one or the other of two coalitions engaged in a simple two-player game, and not independent variables possessing unique interests and ambitions.

Even if we consider the social universe as militarily symmetrical, there is the matter of rifts within each side. These may take the form of a schism within each side over policy questions as such. For example, should the United States intervene directly in Laos, the Congo, or Cuba? If so, what are the ground rules of such intervention? What are to be the relations between legal sovereignty and political objectives? The rules of a game are, after all, enshrined in custom and tradition. In addition, such games are programmed for a conditional victory permitting the further playing of games. The same cannot be said of intentional political relations where the final answer is annihilation. Here rules, when present at all, are vague and subject to sudden (and arbitrary) reinterpretation. The NCM are too ready to disguise an elitist manipulation of human beings behind a theory of games, without seriously coming to grips with political behavior.

The NCM use language loosely. They employ the rhetoric of disarmament problems when they mean arms control problems. Often, they talk of arms control when they mean deterrence through arms escalation. If this were purely semantic, one could assume it would be corrected in the course of further explorations. But the difficulty seems to inhere in war-game theory proposals as such. The concept of deterrence, for example, is sometimes employed as the strategy of the first strike and other times as the strategy of retaliation to a first strike. In the work of Kahn and Schelling the notion of deterrence enters the analysis only in terms of a response to a strike, whereas in the work of Kissinger and Wohlstetter, deterrence means the maximization of balance factors over terror factors. The NCM critique of the "Maginot mindedness" of Pentagon officials, who note that "if these buttons are ever passed they have failed in their purpose," is in fact a criticism of the deterrence policy in the ordinary meaning (as used by Hedley Bull and the British strategists)— the prevention of military attack and/or unilateral build-up.

The NCM have redefined deterrence to mean willingness to fight thermonuclear war. Thus the issue game theory raises is not deterrence as such. If the retaliatory capacity of both players is the measure of deterrence then it is the key in the game of war. The theory of the first strike rests on the belief that large-scale advantages accrue to that nation-player who first uses thermonuclear weapons. The NCM thus do not rule out the possibility that our side may be the first to strike, since such a decision would upset the delicate balance of terror. They also suggest programming our thermonuclear effort in terms of split-second retaliation to any strike, the size of the retaliation to be determined by the extent of the original strike as well as the military and political objectives sought. At the same time they advocate invulnerable (Polaris-type) launching sites that would permit a delayed retaliation and thereby provide flexibility of response.

Here the dilemma hinges on an interpretation of the concept of deterrence. Is it aggression, prevention of aggression, or retaliation to aggression? Until the logical status of this concept is made plain, war-game theory can only contribute to the heightening of tensions by casting serious doubt on the worth of disarmament negotiations or even on any serious effort to limit conflict through staged programming if it should come in limited form.

Classic definitions of warfare imply that there will be a victory and a defeat. The NCM, however, have redefined warfare in terms of equilibrium so that any specific gains from thermonuclear conflict seem to be liquidated. They envision the "phasing in" of a brief war, after which both sides will suspend hostilities, at least temporarily, and arrive at some settlement. War is defined as a minimum-maximum affair; that is, it is defined in terms of the number of people who can be sacrificed in a thermonuclear holocaust without disrupting the possibility of playing out the game at a later stage. Thus they talk of limiting thermonuclear war and at the same time have redefined the concept of deterrence so as to make limitation extremely unlikely.

As in a game of chess between associates, the enjoyment of convivial rivalry takes precedence over who wins any particular contest. Here the best analogy would be a medieval joust in which the contestants say to one another: "That was a fine game. We ought to meet again next year and perhaps the outcome will be different." Only in the case of the NCM calculations the "recovery period" would be "spaced" by decades rather than years. But this can be done only if the rules of the thermonuclear game are strictly enforced. The players must not program "Doomsday machines" (to use Kahn's pithy phrase), and mankind must be willing to consider itself as a pawn or sacrificial lamb, without hope of victory or even the opportunity for a new beginning provided by default.

Ignoring the pathological aspects of this approach, we might mention possibilities that somehow have escaped the notice of most war-game theorists. Measuring economic recovery rates may be quite meaningless when employee or employer suffer radiation injuries or loss of kin. The rate of economic growth is in part contingent upon psychological factors: on the capacity for delayed gratifications, on the desire to expend energies in certain directions with a minimum of returns—in short, on the very factors likely to be absent during and after a nuclear exchange. This brings us to two points of even greater substance. If we assume that men cannot rationally settle affairs except within the spectrum of terror, how can we presume that "Doomsday machines" will never be programmed? Conversely, if we believe that man has sufficient reason to stop short of doing violence to self-interest, why not assume that bilateral disarmament could take place prior to any thermonuclear strike? If, as the NCM claim, man can distinguish between warfare and annihilation, then the need for a terror balance to maintain peace seems nonexistent. If, on the other hand, national interest is the basic motivating force, applicable without assurance of reason, then the only alternative to annihilation is disarmament. In either case arms control seems an unstable halfway house between war and peace.

The NCM take a utilitarian view of human behavior, assuming that self-interest mysteriously and automatically adds up to the general interest—that what one nation defines as good for itself must likewise be good for the "other" nation. Yet game theory permits a definition of common interest only in the context of an explicit contractual agreement, a coalition. It fails to prescribe in those situations in which a coalition is not effected, such as secret and unilateral renewal of tests. It ignores the entire question of bluffing and cheating previously referred to. Thus, from the *strategic* point of view any firm decision not to renew thermonuclear weapons testing is irrational, a violation of self-interest. Yet from a *policy-making* point of view, such a decision is absolutely necessary. To maintain a retaliatory equilibrium in nuclear deterrence requires at times a flat rejection of rationality. An example of this was President Kennedy's statement at the height of the Cuban crisis of October 1962; he said that in a worldwide nuclear war "the fruits of victory would be ashes in our mouth," and added, "but neither will we shrink from that risk at any time it must be faced" (see Kennedy, 1962).

Thus, if we define interest and reason as equivalents, we conclude that any lessening of the arms race injures one or the other "players." But if we define interests apart from reason, that is, if we set up reason as something apart from the modification and adjudication of the claims of interests, we are out of the realm of game theory as such and into social science. The aims of retaliatory equilibrium clearly are not the same as those of rational equilibrium. Retaliatory equilibrium must simplify the terms of the game and establish strategic notions of friend and foe. It must project symmetrical models into an asymmetrical political climate and rules-of-the-game comprehension into a context of social disorganization and political disequilibrium. Useful as it may be to their calculations, the NCM do a dangerous thing when they substitute stereotypes for typifications. Such substitution disguises the divergent, even conflicting, aims of strategic and policy decisions.

The NCM develop a theory of strategies supposedly based on a consideration of mutual strengths and weaknesses of the players. For their theory to be made operational they must assume the morality of the players involved. The problem of cheating heavily clouds the worth of war-game theory. For while calculations of mathematical probablities necessarily assume that all players are fully aware of the rules and scrupulously abide by them, in reality this means that military-game theorists must plan our foreign policy on the known or assumed military capacity of the Soviet Union, while expecting the Soviets to base their policies on the morality of the United States. How can we safely assume that the Soviets have no immediate war aims? How can they assume that the United States might not suddenly decide that it would be to our advantage to start hostilities?

Even if impartially considering the interests of both sides, strategic thinking is limited to consideration of the interests of one side at a time and so may unavoidably come to a conclusion that may be mutually disadvantageous from a strictly military position. Where would such a conclusion take into account a morally valid perspective in policy-making and decision-taking? Even if it made good military sense to base policy considerations on Soviet war-making potentials and to ask the Soviet Union to base its policies on United States' moral fiber, it does not make commonsense. Nor does Schelling's position of establishing mutually agreed upon rules of behavior solve the dilemma. Such a consensus transcends the realm of self-interest for either side. It assumes a superordinate set of values that moves out of the framework of interest thinking as such.

While the NCM maintain an aura of detachment about larger social issues, it is quite plain that the forecasts they make have pessimistic, even fatalistic premises. Their efforts tend to generate the conditions they assume and thus bring about the very results they prophesy. Such prophecy takes on the power of self-fulfillment, as Robert K. Merton and before him W. I. Thomas have pointed out, because when "men define situations as real, they are real in their consequences." The danger of the self-fulfilling prophecy has frightening dimensions when applied to the assumption that nuclear war may take place, on however limited a scale.

The Pentagon warriors inculcate this argument by means of an illicit transference from strategic options to policy proposals. By an exclusive focus upon immediate military targets, the civilian militarists have made it appear that game theory is synonymous with war games. In a recent report on their activities, William Beecher gave the following information: "In the Pentagon, the Joint Chiefs of Staff have a crew of specialists who can test the validity of and anticipate the requirements for contingency war plans. . . . Should they be asked to check on any drawingboard plan for possible invasion of Cuba, the specialists could speedily estimate chances of success and even predict how many gallons of gasoline and how many spare parts for light tanks would be needed" (Beecher, 1963). While the possibilities of such computations are undoubtedly correct, the implication that war with Cuba is necessary is shabbily made part of the calculations. It is never mentioned that the same sort of gaming calculations can be made in terms of anticipating the requirements of wide-scale industrial reconversion to peacetime economy. In other words, the value system of the war gamers is built into the calculations based on the inevitability of mass conflict.

Further problems arise in the transition from personal alarm and fear to expressions of such emotions through public outcry and resentment. Such outcries need institutional channels to be effective. The NCM claim that open consideration of post-World War III conditions can alert the public to the dangers of such a war. But since every effort of the NCM is based on the possibility, if not the inevitability, of such a war, thoughts are focused on post-war survival, not deterrence; indeed, deterrence takes on the meaning of combat readiness, if not actual combat. Without institutionalized efforts at peace-making, the prophecies of the NCM may become real, not because they are based on accurate predictions, but because people have unknowingly accepted as fact the assumptions provided by the NCM.

The works of Edward Teller and Albert L. Latter exemplify another form of this pessimistic prognostication. They minimize the threat to life and limb from atomic fallout and offer the consolation of metaphsics in place of science. "That will happen which will happen and what is to be we know not. God alone knows." Such a thoroughly unscientific theory of determinism surrenders a priori the possibilities of working out alternative models for peaceful relationships. Indeed, the work of Teller indicates that from an NCM viewpoint, the very attempt to reach an international accord itself would put "our" side at a gaming disadvantage—since part of the game of war is not to betray to the "other" side knowledge of the basic orientations of "our" side.

An essential premise of NCM thinking is the assumption of perfect rationality and communication even in times of extreme duress. What if one power should overestimate the signs of belligerence of another power and wrongfully prepare to launch a preventive first strike? By preparing its own strike, this power might cause the rival power to instigate a crucial preemptive attack before the first power pressed the "panic button." Even assuming that the military is "rational" in starting a war (because the intelligence services checked all available data on "victory" possibilities), it is vital to the NCM position that the opponent be equally "rational" and have an equally perfect communication network (also in terms of his "victory" possibilities) in graduating the level of his response. The possibility that, in times of emergency, breakdowns in rationality and communication will occur is not considered. Only on this *irrational* assumption of perfect rationality at all times and at all levels of the decision-making apparatus can the NCM predict the responses of the enemy. If this strangely cooperative enemy will make clear in advance his retaliation at the 50-million-death level while generously desisting from an attack that would take 200 million lives then game-theory strategy works. If, in the midst of war the enemy replies with full available force, he breaks the rules, and the game theory has failed. This belief in absolute strategic rationality assumes that sudden and capricious warfare, though launched in the fury of the moment, would aim simply at immobilizing the enemy's second-strike retaliatory capacity (since victory would otherwise be meaningless).

Equally questionable is the policy assumption that miscalculated decisions to start a war can be eliminated and that a halt can be called before the ultimate gambit of an exchange of cities. Both sides could then apologize and retire for a period into a "postattack recuperation," during which time future plans for warfare could be calculated. But in nuclear war it is useless to regret errors, since it is impossible to retract them before their consequences are realized in massive destruction. There is no ambiguity, slender margin for error, no stand-off time connected with an atomic bomb.

The NCM assume that even under stress conditions militarists can perceive the difference between the long-range and the short-term interests of the enemy accurately enough to calculate the exact type of attack to be expected. It seems almost superfluous to note that nothing in the history of warfare or in the nature of men in times of ultimate challenge permits so optimistic a reading of events. In talking about World War IV, V, and VI, the NCM cater to the false illusions of those who imagine they can survive a thermonuclear blast. This is a dangerous and distorted misuse of the survival instinct of mankind. It is a play on utilitarian sentiments, while it suppresses peaceful options to World War III as the most readily available way for this survival instinct to fulfill itself.

Although the claim is made by and for the NCM that they are neutral with respect to the values of war and peace, they do place a premium on a warrior ethos, if not on destruction as such. A main argument advanced by some of the game theorists is that preparation for war is necessary to justify the human quest for knowledge. An even greater distortion of the history of science is the thesis that society does not accept the desire for knowledge unless it is somehow connected to war. As evidence of this, the educational build-up that followed the launching of the Soviet Sputnik is cited. But in fact, scientific discovery may or my not be used for warfare. It is, and always has been, totally independent, a variable, unpredictable, and beyond predetermined calculation. To attach positive values to world annihilation because it stimulates scientific invention is sheer fantasy. The abstract concept of game theory itself developed as a branch of pure mathematics, long before the current war-game theories were stimulated by military questions. Probability theory does not depend on warfare for its existence. The use of a theory ought not to be confounded with its origins.

A contrast of Soviet military policy, as summarized by Raymond Garthoff (1963) and H. S. Dinerstein, with our own NCM proposals reveals several important differences. For the Soviets, survival is not an issue in war. For the NCM, it is often the only issue. For the Soviets, military action is subordinate to and answerable to overall political aims. In NCM policy-making, the military action creates its own aims. For the Soviets, in the thermonuclear era as before, the primary objective of military operations is the destruction of hostile military forces, not the annihilation of the economic or population resources of the enemy. For the NCM, there is no longer any clearcut distinction between military and civilian objectives. It must be pointed out, however, that recent trends in Soviet military theory have drawn closer to NCM thinking on a number of subsidiary points, such as the mutual advantages of instantaneous communications and the relative upgrading of nuclear strikes at the expense of conventional military delivery systems. Nonetheless, there remain fundamental differences in the respective definitions of the present military-political situation (see Sokolovskii, 1963).

The NCM envision a brief war with several strikes and have little or nothing to say about military operations beyond this thermonuclear phase. This is in flat contradiction to the Soviet theory of protracted war. In Soviet policy, along with conventional methods of destruction would follow nuclear strikes. NCM policy seems geared to either unconditional surrender or a conditional surrender based on a restoration of the *status quo ante*. While the NCM consider arms escalation to be a negotiable matter between the contending parties, Soviet policy flatly rejects escalation. The prospect of a conflict in which low-yield atomic weapons could be employed without either combatant rushing for its most powerful weapons is unrealistic in the extreme to the Soviet militarists. And it can hardly be called cheating when the side that uses full force when attacked has never accepted the rules of those who operate on an assumption of limited retaliation.

In other words, the NCM of the United States and their opposite numbers on the Soviet side are operating with considerably different rule books. In any kind of game this means chaos. Game theory applied to war sows the seeds for the most dangerous sort of miscalculations when either side overlooks the differences in the options, directives, and goals of the other side. It is precisely this absence of agreement on rules, as well as the absence of superordinate goals, that frustrates disarmament negotiations. The NCM cannot disregard this absence of agreement and simply move as if agreement exists when it does not. The reason for such a skip in reasoning may be the probability that once such rules were established, the very *raison d'être* for the NCM, in fact for war itself, would disappear.

That the NCM have gained such a wide hearing is more a consequence of the general breakdown in the disarmament dialogue between the great powers than an indication of any intrinsic merit in game-theory proposals. In different ways, but with convergence at the functional level, the United States and the Soviet Union are witnessing what C. Wright Mills described as "the rise of the cheerful robot and the technological idiot." If war-game theory does nothing else, it can alert us to the dangers of mathematical techniques uninformed by the content of the social sciences and humanities. This separation of rational thinking from human reason and experience, so clearly embodied in the NCM approach, has several and diverse roots, perhaps the most important being the isolation of "is" questions from "ought" problems. What began as science's proud declaration of independence from political or theological edicts has, through the mechanism of *expertise,* spilled over into the totally different assumption that indifference to value issues—indeed, even stupidity in the face of them—is the proper image of the true scientific mind. The NCM claim this attitude without due regard for its nihilistic content. They provide policy-makers with carefully sifted information, comparative analyses of data, and the likely consequences of taking or not taking the line of action indicated. What the policy-makers do with such information is their own business. Division of responsibility is absolute.

Who, then, is responsible? Surely there is a moral undercurrent in the method that sees the game theorist as diagnostician and society as his patient. But the NCM expert does not and cannot stand totally outside society. He is part of it, and he is affected by the total situation, even as he attempts to prescribe medicines to make it healthy once again. Laski's thoughtful criticism of *expertise*, made several years ago, pertains (Laski, 1960; cf. Wilhelm, 1964):

> It is one thing to urge the need for expert consultation at every stage in making policy; it is another thing and a very different thing, to insist that the experts' judgment must be final. For special knowledge and the highly trained mind produce their own limitations which in the realm of statesmanship, are of decisive importance. *Expertise*, it may be argued, sacrifices the insight of common sense to intensity of experience. It breeds an inability to accept new views from the very depth of its preoccupation with its own conclusions. It too often fails to see around its subject. It sees its results out of perspective by making them the center of relevance to which all other results must be related. Too often, also, it lacks humility; and this breeds in its possessors a failure in proportion which makes them fail to see the obvious which is before their very noses. It has, also, a certain caste spirit about it, so that experts tend to neglect all evidence which does not come from those who belong to their own ranks. Above all, perhaps, and this most urgently where human problems are concerned, the expert fails to see that every judgment he makes not purely factual in nature brings with it a scheme of values which has no special validity about it. He tends to confuse the importance of his facts with the importance of what he proposes to do about them.

That the overwhelming majority of men are capable of seeing beyond the immediate gratification of their own and their nation's desires into the wider consequences of a course of action indicates that the use of reason is possible in relation to problems of war. Certainly, the change in scientific and industrial conditions and the creation of powerful weapons of annihilation have served to minimize the self-interest arguments for war at the center of NCM proposals. Before we can accept the approach of the game theorists, we must accept their assumption that life is a game and that players will accept rules set up for them by others. It is the quality of such reasoning that we will not question.

Is there not at least a minimum credo agreed on through such agencies as the United Nations? Have we not come to accept as a set of beliefs about man, the world, and social values certain standards? These are not rules of conduct. They are not assumptions. They are not deterrents or theoretical agreements. They are beliefs with which a large part of mankind agree. Man has a right to, indeed needs to, maintain life. The question of what to do with it is not involved. His material needs must be supplied. How and through which social structure at what given time these needs can best be met are open questions. People need freedom to shift, choose, and alter their conceptions of what constitutes progress or prosperity, even though entrenched political and economic interests may not welcome such shifts and revisions. Men do not need to agree on systems of government in order to secure peace. But they do need to find unity on how to go about pursuing basic goals. The method of science does not exclude the making of decisive choices in moments of crisis. But it cannot be separated from the responsibility of reminding the decision-makers of alternate views, especially if such views are unpopular and apt to be overlooked for reasons having little to do with their scientific cogency. There is a place for a kind of methodological common ground that defines the character of scientific rationalism—but from such ground, dogmatic statements about the ultimate constituency of life cannot be made.

Human reason is a handmaiden to the actual processes taking place in society and nature. When it becomes more, when it tries to spin a web of pure thought, it parts company with life. Games and game analogies cannot deal with actual conflicts of interest between peoples and nations with different aims and goals. Reason cannot delegate to itself responsibilities it cannot fulfill. On the other hand, when reason becomes less than an intelligent, persuasive means of overcoming the paradoxes in society, it abandons men to the power of unreasoned action.

The NCM oscillate between a stand of arrogance in selection of such assumptions as are suited to a game-theory approach and an abrogation of the historic identification of the sciences with the deepest causes of human survival and growth. Even military men have noted the absence of "qualities of humility and tact" in NCM dealings with other public officials (see White, 1963). To stay within the paradoxical findings of the New Civilian Militarists is to surrender to the dangers of pessimism and cynicism, to move in a never-never land of war-game theory. Reality lies beyond games of bluffing, chicken, and all-or-nothing stakes. There remains a world of reason that recognizes the importance of social history and political diplomacy in thinking about policy options.

1962

18

Noneconomic Factors
in the
Institutionalization of War

We want peace, just as we want utopia, just as long as we are pretty sure of
not getting it. When the choice is placed before us, however, as it seems to
be in the modern world, between utopia or, at least, peace, which is
something less, or annihilation, our embarrassment may become so acute
that we choose annihilation. One sees this in the conventional cartoon
image of peace as a wispy and rather bedraggled female in a bedsheet
holding a wan olive branch as a corsage. She is not a girl that any red-
blooded American or Russian would particularly want to go out with,
much less make love to. Still, she haunts us. It is a specter even more
frightening, perhaps, than that which Karl Marx invoked in 1848, because
we have always thought in terms of war as a last resort. Now there may be
no last resort, except doomsday, which is no resort at all. There is no
defense, no isolation, no protection from the awful task of living together
with monstrously strange bedfellows.

—Kenneth E. Boulding

The problem of converting world-war industry to peacetime enterprise
is being seriously posed for the first time since the outbreak of World
War II. Thus far, the center of concern has been the economic feasibility
of the transition process for an industrial complex. There are also
noneconomic factors responsible for a lag in technical know-how that
slows down the reconversion process and the practical implementation of
steps toward industrial reconversion. Five major noneconomic deterrents are: absence of awareness of the necessity of conversion; rise of new

industrial activities heavily dependent upon the continuation of arms spending; belief in armaments as a bulwark of social solidarity; acculturation to patterns of secrecy and coercion; fear that industrial reconverson will lead to deterioration of the Western alliance. Under critical examination, these factors prove to be insubstantial. However, disarmament and conversion to peacetime industrial policies are two programs that would have to be phased in sociologically as well as economically. A policy of heavy arms expenditures has generated profound social and political disorientation. No major shifts in the production orientation of American industry will occur until doubts about the future of the American economy are either assuaged or overcome in the face of the greater problem of the future of the human community as such.

Whenever the question of the costs or benefits of the arms race arises, there is a common propensity to deal with the matter in economic terms. Perhaps this is as it should be, since monetary and fiscal considerations do seem to determine what can be done to alter an industrial apparatus of incredible complexity tooled up for a quarter-century to handle military assignments. But even more knowledgeable economists have clearly indicated that the 10 percent of the national budget directly allocated to arms production is not a "necessity" from an economic viewpoint (Benoit, 1960, 1963; Royce, 1962). Even though exact knowledge on the phasing time, economic costs, and manpower shifts of any transition to peacetime production is available, the prospects for such a momentous industrial and commercial retooling remain dim because of social and political considerations. Why should it be the case that, in the midst of this intellectual know-how, there is such a paucity of activity oriented toward the realization of that long-postponed and ephemeral phenomenon—a peacetime economy?

This is obviously an extremely difficult problem, one that can only be tentatively answered. In order to confront this major issue directly, I shall outline each issue separately and then indicate recommendations to reduce the amount of expenditures for military and paramilitary purposes at a minimal *social* cost. What follows is predicated on two premises, one ethical and the other political. My first premise is that the chief task confronting Americans is disarmament and not deterrence— that is, a peace based on the institutionalization of world law and juridical limits to sovereignty as well as weaponry and not a peace grounded on a presumed "delicate balance of terror" (Horowitz, 1963a, 1963b). The second premise is that bilateral settlement between East and West, specifically between the United States and the Soviet Union, is now eminently possible and even imminent (Horowitz, 1963c, 1963d).

Such bilateral negotiations cut through the fog of rhetoric introduced into the situation by unilateralists on one side and by the still more menacing new civilian militarists on the other. Neither moralism nor gamesmanship is relevant in the present context.

The first point that must be considered, and one so obvious as to be often overlooked, is the simple unawareness that an economy on a permanent war footing carries with it menacing possibilities. The plain fact is that many Americans imbibe the economic benefits of the arms race in the form of steady work, good living and working conditions, high wages, and often professional standing. Indeed, the study of international conflicts has itself been professionalized and institutionalized to an amazing degree. It does not require an economic determinist to realize that such benefits drown out the overall need for a reduction of tension through a reduction in arms production. Taken in its broadest sense, arms production covers military personnel, operations, and maintenance of the war industries, as well as military hardware as such. The arms industries present a pattern of high growth combined with minimum sales risk—which makes resistance to change quite understandable. The following reveals the pattern of this growth:

> Expenditures of the Department of Defense have risen from $19.8 billion in fiscal year 1951 to $43 billion in 1961, or by over 100 per cent, a growth rate far in excess of that of any other major areas of the American economy. At the present time, Defense Department purchases of goods and services are equal to almost one-tenth of the gross national product. The proportion reached peaks of 48 per cent during World War II and 12 per cent during the Korean War, but was, of course, lower during the interwar period of the cold war. An abrupt change in the nature of the external threat would probably cause another major shift in the proportion of the country's resources devoted to armaments (Widenbaum, 1963).

The problem with most business enterprises presently engaged in direct or subsidiary forms of arms production is not that they are fearful of an economic retooling, or even that they fear their survival possibilities in a peacetime economy, but simply that no thought has been given to remobilization of the economy in a nonmilitary direction. Peaceful production is not a felt need because the syndrome of high wages and solid profits has essentially remained unbroken in the American economy ever since 1939, when the nation first went on a partial defense mobilization. And when "recessions" did take place, such as the one of 1949, the Korean War—and the rise in some spending—mitigated its economic effects.

In a major survey of defense industry planning for the future, Philip Shabecoff and Joseph Lelyveld were compelled by the evidence to conclude that most defense contractors "have no idea at present of how to plan for a sharp reduction in defense spending. A few companies are confident they would be able to make a smooth transition to civilian business. Fewer still report that they have actually done some long range planning in this area." (Shabecoff and Lelyveld, 1963). The general consensus among military producers and contractors is that no arms reduction will take place and that, if it does, the problem could be most pragamatically meaningful through yet further government help. There is, in short, a profound inability of defense contractors such as Lockheed Aircraft, General Dynamics, Boeing Company, North American Aviation, to mention only a few, to take seriously their own faith in the private-enterprise system. What they have become used to is government subsidization of private profits—something radically different from the confrontation of buyers and sellers in a symbolic market place. Thus, the lack of awareness of the need to disarm is reinforced by the absence of competitive capitalism!

The basic correctives for this institutional unconsciousness require, at the outset, a clear separation of issues. National interests must be distinguished from commercial interests. In this way, it might be made plain that the policy of the United States is dictated by considerations larger than those motivating defense contractors. This would spark an interest in conversion, if for no other reason than that entrepreneurial survival would once again become a real factor. Where this has been done, where federal cutbacks on military hardware have been effected, the business establishment has proven most resourceful in maintaining high productive levels and full employment after a relatively brief crisis period.

Senator George McGovern has proposed a five-billion-dollar cutback in arms spending. But, more important, he indicated ways in which the effects of this cutback could be mitigated and overcome. First, he proposed that all industries having more than 25 percent of their production in defense contracts be required to establish an "operating conversion committee to prepare for possible alternatives in the event of a loss in military contracts." Second, he proposed a government board whose main task would be to assist businesses in the process of considering conversion. What makes such conversion relatively simple is the concentration of defense contracts in the very large corporations and in engineering firms that perform specialized services. This would make it possible to have conversion to a peacetime economy without any overall disruption to the social fabric. One economist has seen the problem as a short-run effort to shift $22 billion now allocated for defense purposes to the larger civilian economy (Vickrey, 1963).

One contribution of the New Civilian Militarists to the present unconscious state of industrialists has been the oft-repeated statement that "arms control will not cut defense cost" (Schelling and Halperin, 1962) but what is neglected is the possibility that a policy of *disarmament* would indeed cut such costs. This reinforces the decision-makers in the war industries who view any policy other than arms control as dangerous to their continued welfare. This, coupled with a fear that marketing commercial products would be unprofitable, has made defense contractors perhaps the most conservative force in American society. What is needed to unfreeze these attitudes is first a clear-cut federal policy indicating that arms control is only the first phase of arms reduction. This done, the federal administration must assist in the opening up of certain highly monopolized peacetime enterprises, such as the automobile and electronics industries. There is a need for new capital investment in old industries no less than for the creation of new types of commercial production.

Federal initiative in planning would enable defense contractors to consider the larger implications of converting their plants to peacetime uses. A temporary downward adjustment need not lead to industrial calamities or financial bankruptcies. And even the extent of such a downward turn in the short run is problematic, since economists are now in a position carefully to "phase in" peacetime production with a minimum amount of disruption. One thing is not possible: for defense contractors to lobby against federal spending for civilian purposes while at the same time urging increased federal contracts for defense purposes. To call one kind of spending socialistic and the other patriotic is simply to confuse the ineluctable fact of federal direction of the economy with the tentative forms of such direction through monetary allocation (Galbraith, 1958).

A second problem in defense spending is that many new industries have emerged as a result of the cold war, so that the problem for General Electric might be reconversion but for General Dynamics it is a simple conversion *for the first time* to peaceful production. The war industries have no built-in agencies for unguided conversion. And since this is true for many firms doing military work on contract, the traditional arguments against federal planning are largely obsolete and meaningless.

A subsidiary argument employed in defense of high military budgets is that such spending stimulates discovery and the application of discovery. The one strong point in this line of reasoning is that the process of application of scientific invention is often an unprofitable venture, one that cannot be maintained without heavy federal subsidization. But the conclusion drawn—that peacetime production would involve a cutback not only in military production but in scientific technology as well—simply does not follow. For what would be involved is not a withdrawal or retrenchment in federal spending per se but simply the reallocation of funds for nonmilitary purposes.

What must be made clear is that the argument for peacetime uses of industry does not imply a nineteenth-century neomercantilist view of balancing the budget. Indeed, it might conceivably be the case that a real adjustment of the economy may entail higher rather than lower, more and more rather than fewer, federal outlays. Highway construction, foreign assistance, space exploration, and civilian uses of energy sources may be applied for war or peace. But the application in one direction or another is something quite apart from the quantity of federal expenditures or even taxation.

The problem is ideological in character. Americans are accustomed to government spending being paired with military requisitions, because they view the military establishment as intrinsically national in character. But if any conversion is to be successful, an entirely novel concept—in American ideology at least—must be institutionalized; namely, the infusion and intrusion of government planning of commercial and industrial enterprises. Without becoming tendentious, it is plain that the Tennessee Valley Authority (TVA) and the Missouri Valley Authority (MVA) are just as legitimate allocations of federal funds as are those to aircraft or rocket production. The argument that "to try any large part of a conversion process centrally would raise severe problems" (Raymond, 1962) mistakes the nature of democratic polity. This is not a plea for increased management of individuals but a recognition that there remains a need to increase the management of things. This, at any rate, is a likely consequence of any serious reconversion of scientific and industrial initiative.

A third major obstacle to conversion and reconversion is the directly ideological notion of having a "national purpose." The manifest function of such a program is to define the goals for Americans at midpassage: to determine the American posture toward the Communist bloc nations, toward newly emerging nation-states, and, above all, toward our own future aims and ambitions. The latent function of such a frenetic search, doomed to failure by the very nature of a pluralistic society exhibiting contrasting goals and instrumentalities, is to provide what Durkheim called the "collective conscience" with a sense of cohesion. It has become clear even to the rhetoricians of the cold war that anticommunism is itself a negative response with built-in boomerang effects. Without a positive program, Americans entered the present decade immunized to a considerable degree against cold-war policies, and this led to a fractionalized public opinion. A feeling that everything was done from the top and that the "little man" counted for naught translated itself into negative attitudes toward armed service, civil defense, and other citizen-participation activities. But, instead of making adjustments, policy-making tended to become increasingly strident, making for a reinforcement of the rhetoric of oversimplification.

Both as participants and as leaders, members of the corporate structure adhered to policies calculated to retain a cold-war consensus, rather than to alter the character of this consensus. The cold war, which had functioned as an exclusive mode of expression of American political leadership in the postwar period, had succeeded in institutionalizing itself. To dislodge the cold war from its gray eminence required the sort of broad-scale political reorientation that defense contractors were least suited to carry forth and those best suited, such as labor organizations and voluntary associations, were least able to carry forth. The concept of anticommunism, negative and frustrating though it may be, is at least a political cement. The Communist menace served to justify resistance to all kinds of social innovation. As one anthropologist has recently observed, "The view of the Soviet Union as a deadly adversary that at any moment may destroy us also makes real disarmament unlikely; and suggests that instead of getting rid of our arms we will merely rest on them" (Henry, 1963). That this carries within itself a paralyzing and narcotizing effect on significant action was held to be less important than that the society should have no rallying ideology. That in the process of combating erosion, through a self-conscious definition of national purpose, Americans have subjected themselves to a still deeper erosion, a fear of the consequences of unsanctioned change, is only now being recognized and, even now, in private pronouncements rather than in public policies.

The comment by David Riesman on this quest for a singular purpose deserves serious attention:

> There is something oddly regressive in the spectacle of the United States reducing itself to the size of a new nation that needs a manifest destiny. . . .
> Affluence ought to mean abundance of purposes, and intense exploration and discovery of new ones, both individual and collective. It might mean a stronger concern for the purposes of others who have not yet reached the dilemmas of abundance (Riesman, 1963).

But this narrowing-down process, this search for ideological uniformity disguised as a commonly inspected and arrived at social consensus, is indicative of widespread fear that only a monolith can overcome a monolith, that only a bureaucratized state can defeat another bureaucratized state. The strength of our conservatism stems from the same psychological sources as the strength of communism in the developing regions: a fear that democratic-process consensus structures are indeed weaker than totalitarian command structures. The war industries, the military establishment, the defense-department engineers turned strategists underwrite this fear—since they have moved policy-making out of the public political arena and mimetically reproduced elitist modes of operating on the body politic. The problem is that this produces a boomerang effect.

By thoroughly dulling the sense of mass participation in political life, these groups have moved the society to a form of "privatization" that seeks gratifications in personal and egotistic fashions—not only without regard to the consequences of such behavior for an anticipated "enemy" but, more profoundly, without due regard to the human consequences for one's own family, community, or nation. The reconversion of industry to peacetime uses should have as its essential byproduct a corresponding rise in public participation in public affairs—and only those who are profoundly hostile to democratic norms will find such an outcome objectionable.

The fourth point to be noted is the internal system of secrecy and coercion that has become legitimated. If we assume—and I daresay this is more than an assumption—that any society tooled up for "spontaneous" outbreak of thermonuclear warfare requires a significant quantum of coercion and the institutionalization of this coercion in the form of police, federal investigators, congressional investigators, and the like, then it can be seen that the maintenance of a high military budget directly affects the lives of many people who are described as dissidents in relation to the cold war. It can only be considered Pollyannish to hold that an invisible consensual blanket alone guarantees active participation in the cold war. The element of coercion, while more sharply limited in the United States by countervailing and juridical limitations than in the Soviet Union, is nonetheless present (Horowitz, 1962).

The armaments industry, with its emphasis on clearance, surveillance, and security, legitimates coercive intervention in the lives of private citizens. Since the "next war" will be between arms and arms, rather than men and men, this stress on secrecy generates a growth in the command mechanism. This is still more apparent in the Soviet Union, where munitions production is the responsibility not of the military establishment but of economic agencies. Since the midthirties, planning agencies have specialized to this end (Bergson, 1961). Thus, such policing agencies, whether from the East or West, have a vested interest in the maintenance of a huge armaments industry.

This is a matter that cuts both ways. It is a relatively stable law of organizational behavior that a bureaucracy attempts to maximize its power and to retain this power beyond the point of external necessity. Organizations do not vanish because their need has been obviated—they simply search out new rationalizations for their perpetuation. A number of press reports have indicated a frantic interaction between corporation lobbies and the military establishment to sway senatorial sentiment away from the test-ban treaty (Childs, 1963). It may be gathered, in view of the minimal basis of the test-ban treaty, that far more powerful forces would be mobilized in the event of any bilateral treaty entailing actual arms reduction in its provisions.

What is urgently required is the widest sort of public education on the problems of transition to peace. The current tendencies to maximize the coercive apparatus pose a genuine threat to American democracy. A wide exercise of political rights is far less of a risk than an uncritical commitment to a society of secret agents. The increased demand of nuclear scientists for freedom of movement and less secrecy is an indication that one major veto group is cognizant of the relationship between secrecy and coercion.

Substantive arguments against an excess of coercion in a cold-war atmosphere are: first, it is difficult to differentiate or to limit coercion so that it does not become terroristic; second, the secret society is inhibiting to traditional American rights of communication and transportation; third, it inhibits the growth of science—which requires the widest access to information and verification of data. On this point, it is now clear that the institutionalization of the cold war, far from stimulating scientific progress, actually serves to inhibit it, by creating an atmosphere of closure about information and the exchange of ideas. Thus, the overall consequence of the reduction in arms spending would be a general liberation from the world of secrecy. As long as the arms race continues, the most that can be hoped for is an enlightened leadership that is willing and ready to smother its critics with a consensual blanket.

This is not a simplistic matter of America's "will" to fight for freedom, or the Soviet Union's "will" to fight for communism. It is a question of a higher will to survive despite differences. Once the threads of the cold war start coming apart, the entire garment is subject to abandonment

(Osgood, 1963; see also Sorokin, 1960). The struggle now is thus between those desiring to patch up the traditional alliances and those seeking a detente with the Soviets. Political decisions will ultimately determine the rate at which the cold war will be converted into a peaceful competition of social systems. One significant feature of the Kennedy administration was the belief within its higher echelons that such a peaceful struggle can be won; the assumption is that "time" is on the "side" of capitalist America, rather than on the side of communist Russia. Whether this optimism is warranted or not, its very permeation of administrative policy-making bodies serves to increase the possibilities that conversion and reconversion of the industrial base are in the offing.

The fifth point that requires attention is the relationship between what Kenneth Boulding has aptly termed "the world war industry" and foreign affairs. In some measure, although to what extent it is difficult to say, the world-war industry is an inhibiting factor on social change. Armaments reinforce regimes with which the United States and the Soviet Union respectively have working relations and thus draw the nations of the world into the bipolarization that has obtained since the close of the Second World War. This monopolization of military hardware serves to make the world dependent on the leading powers to a degree that cannot be described as healthy. The argument adduced by some to the effect that we have "allies" while the Soviets have "captives" (Kissinger, 1962, 1963) simply ignores the social function of military establishments in Latin America no less than in Eastern Europe—a function of maintaining a status quo that can hardly be said to constitute a popular will.

The political argument is that to reduce investment in armaments is to invite chaos around the world, particularly in developing areas—but this argument is strictly political in character. From an economic standpoint, the General Agreement on Trade and Tariffs (GATT) report on *Measures for the Economic Development of Under-Developed Countries* demonstrates that the developing regions have needs of such enormous proportions that they alone could absorb the 10 percent of the gross national product siphoned off for military spending (Schelling, 1957). Import requirements of these areas will double—from $27 billion in 1960 to $43 billion by 1970—even if it is assumed that the growth rate in these areas remains constant. The need in these areas for American consumer goods, the need for American technical manpower in all sorts of projects, from land clearing to dam-building, would likewise grow. But the purely economic standpoint is inoperative while such political considerations as the character of the social structure and political agencies in these countries are subject to constant scrutiny and veto by Washington or Moscow. Thus, the external aspects of the heavy armaments industry operate to keep change at a minimum. If every social change in Latin America, Asia, or Africa is to be greeted by the war cry of treason then the actual economic redistribution of production will be seriously handicapped.

The world-war industry prevents real dramatic shifts in the social structure, and then the "backwardness" of foreign areas is used as an argument to prove that a political crisis would flow from the conversion of industry, from the production of armaments to the production of non-military goods. The statement by Roger Hagan on the reasons for the polarizing simplicity of the cold war helps to explain why such an undue faith in military hardware continues to blunt the implementation of broad-scale reform programs that would be based on principles of relative equality.

> So much has the political career of much of Congress come to depend on anti-Communist hoopla that one can almost infer that the fight against subtlety has become a matter of survival for vast elements of our society. For behind the Congressmen are millions of Americans whose style of life, whose sense of meaning, and whose manner of economic endeavor and personal encounter have come to depend upon being publicly patriotic and firm. In a society outdistancing its roots and values and trying to fill the gap with the public virtues of boosterism, the Cold War has become Babbittry gone mad, and it is impossible to be optimistic about the chances for altering the image of Soviet aggressiveness sufficiently to erode the bed-rock argument against nuclear parity (Hagan, 1963).

In such a context, the economic arguments for conversion and reconversion away from the "milorg" (military organization) to the "firm" (nonwar industry) come upon this bedrock of an oversimplified image of *Realpolitik.* What may disrupt the present equilibrium is the bifurcation going on in the Socialist bloc, which may compel a reappraisal of present alignments and alliances and which may open the possibilities for at least a pragmatic settlement of East-West differences. This will take place if by no other device than a redefinition of just who and what is East and who and what is West. But, without such an overall *political* settlement, the chances that the economics of armament production will be reduced in its capabilities and capacities are severely limited.

One final problem that remains knotty is that the bulk of Americans remain "economic determinists." They more readily see the results of large arms budgets in advantageous terms than in disadvantageous terms. The need is to gain a public awareness of the broad psychosocial consequences of the large output for armaments. A modest beginning has been made by the United Nations—which has emphasized a number of basic sociological advantages to a conversion of the international economy to peacetime production. First, the general level of living would rise since federal agencies would begin to devote far more attention to matters of social welfare, health, and education. Second, a reduction in the armaments industry would accelerate the tendency toward the shorter work week, experimentation in types of work habitats, and also in new forms of planning automation without creating undue social disruption. Third, a conversion to peacetime production would decrease the sort of tensions that lead to privatization and a general fear that there are no tomorrows. Personal planning would have meaning, and the frenetic behavior characteristic of the younger generation could be expected to diminish. Fourth, distinctions between have and have-not nations would be alleviated at least in terms of invidious comparisons in the military sphere. A byproduct of this would be a lower expenditure on nonprofitable and rapidly obsolete military hardware and a higher expenditure on commodity production. Fifth, the value system itself would undergo transformation. The faith in raw power could be expected to give way to negotiation and tension management through rational and juridical means. Sixth, cultural contacts would increase with the added possibility that deeper understanding would open yet newer horizons for settlements. Perhaps we will know that a basic change has taken place when the slogans of nations undergo a similar change. When peaceful competition gives way to peaceful cooperation, then the possibility of strengthening a *de facto* settlement by social and personal feelings of kinship will itself become a factor in securing a more perfect machinery of conflict resolution (United Nations, 1962).

Given the trepidations of many Americans about the costs of disarmament, it is necessary to conduct reconversion and conversion within a fixed period of time, This period must be definite and with finite limits on sociological as well as economic grounds. First, the quicker the conversion the less likely will it be that wrong decisions will be made as a result of procrastination. Second, people are more likely to be convinced of the value of a reconversion policy if it is connected with a general policy of arms reduction or disarmament of a specific type. Third, the development of a "crash program" for retraining personnel while retooling factories for peacetime enterprise would serve to reassure the involved publics that conversion does not axiomatically entail unemployment or lower income (see Economist Intelligence Unit, 1963). But of course, such measures are linked to the ability and willingness of governments to engage in a permanent redistribution of investment consumption and expenditure, which, in turn, is based on the biggest assumption of all—the possibility of an extended and durable peace.

Before long, let us hope, resources now allocated to the maintenance of military establishments will be released. This very process will create the basis for beneficent social uses of natural and human resources (U.S. Arms Control and Disarmament Agency, 1962). The breakup of the Communist bloc as a monolithic unit has moved with surprising speed— especially when it is considered that the hegemony of the capitalist democracies was maintained for a far longer time, for centuries not just decades. New forms of social behavior and political organization are being considered. Once they are available as alternatives, the fear of totalitarian *coups d'état* will be considerably less. It is highly questionable if any size military build-up can successfully cope with world communism in a frontal assault. The experiences of Korea, South Vietnam, and Germany indicate that direct military confrontations are now, at best, ambiguous, indecisive, and incapable of victory, but it is quite possible that the new *Realpolitik* will involve arms reduction and arms elimination and, in this form, institutionalize free choice and democratic norms.

From a pragmatic point of view, police actions, counterinsurgency guerilla actions, and volunteer Hessians have failed, each in its turn. The first failed in Korea, the second failed in South Vietnam, and the third failed in Cuba. The age of "winning" a global conflict, after the spread of nuclear weaponry to more than one country, has decisively ended. Logically, the age of defeat has also ended. Hence, if all future military actions must result in settlement, it seems eminently reasonable to suggest that agencies for settlement can be institutionalized without recourse to the symbolic, and now largely vacuous, threat of extermination.

There is no day of peace. A secure peace comes closer to realization as our sensitivity to the needs of social development increases. There is no perfect planning for World War Three because the contingencies cannot be accounted for. Likewise, there is no perfect plan for phasing in industrial conversion to nonmilitary production. On the other hand, the *prima facie* priority that planning for peace ought to have over planning for war is the result of our new realization that war in our age, like peace, would be largely a matter of impetus and impulse. The trajectory to be ridden—reconversion of industrial production on one side or continued military production on the other—may well prove decisive in pushing us toward the stars, cooperatively, or toward the abyss, collectively. The element of risk cannot be eliminated—no more by exponents of disarmament than by those urging continued arms spending. The question really is not *how much* but *just what* are the Americans and Soviets willing to risk?

1964

19

Organization and Ideology in the Antiwar Movement

The organizational basis of the current antiwar movement is profoundly nontotalitarian and self-consciously anti-Stalinist. In this special sense, the critics are correct in calling the movement "anarchistic." Party doctrine in which, as Martov facetiously pointed out, "the Party is divided into those who sit and those who are sat upon," no longer exists. Local control is central. And just as individuals are encouraged to "do their thing," organizations are likewise exhorted to "do theirs" as well. This marks a self-conscious return to the American anarchist tradition, particularly its transcendentalist wing from Thoreau to Lysander Spooner.

The antiwar movement is no longer confined to totalitarian models derived from the thirties, when both the extreme Right and Left were tied to the ideological and functional needs of foreign powers such as Nazi Germany and Stalinist Russia; it has been able to extricate itself wholly from both Spenglerian and Marxian forms of historicism. "Laws of History" (which have always implied the serious study of social background) have given way to the "Will of the People" (which always implies the resentment by activists against those who take history too seriously). The availability of successful foreign models of revolutionary change that have been "stage jumping" in character—such as that of the Soviet Union, China, and Cuba—precisely reinforces the trends toward domestic anarchism in the current antiwar movement. Thus, while it is important to recognize the degree to which the antitotalitarian qualities of the current antiwar movement have spilled over into an antirationalistic bias, it is no less important to recognize the intense moral concern the movement represents.

The dilemma with the "movement centers" is that in exchange for maximizing spontaneous activity and automatic political behavior, they also permit, or indeed almost make inevitable, a higher degree of violence than is the case for those movements marked by the older leftist style of control from the top down. Since a great many of the movement centers are comprised of militant groups, their demeanor in crisis situations, such as those that arose in Chicago during the convention, tends to embrace the entire phalanx of resisters, including the pacifist-oriented groupings. The indiscriminate response of the police to threats to their social control of a situation only reinforces the schisms within the peace movement between traditional pacifists and politicized radicals.

The problems are particularly acute for those portions of the antiwar movement dedicated to nonviolent methods and equally acute for those sectors of the police who might prefer the use of more confined and moderate treatment of antiwar demonstrators. It is not that the militant wing of the New Left should be prevented from pursuing its own tactics, but rather that in this very endeavor it tends to overwhelm more pacifist-inclined elements. Ironically, this same situation is reported with respect to police and National Guard behavior. In every demonstration there is a small cadre of officers who appear ready, and a large body of policemen who appear reluctant, to engage in direct confrontation either with fists or with billy-clubs, mace, or other weapons of limited destruction (cf. Kifner, 1968). The agony of the situation is that, while pacifists and policemen deny the existence of such tactical and even principled cleavages, neither side is remotely willing to isolate the precise source of violence. To do so would yield an impression of internal dissensions and "fink"-like behavior. Thus, the problem of personality and social structure remains without hope of easy solution.

Not only were the antiwar protesters violent in their tactics. As a corollary, the counterdemonstrators, who were largely passive in earlier years, have also become more violent. Most counterdemonstrators earlier had heckled the antiwar protesters, taunting them with "Communist" or "pinko" as well as earthier derogatory terms. Some had thrown eggs or tomatoes at the demonstrators. In April, the counterdemonstrators, seemingly less organized than any of the antiwar groups, started tearing down signs set up by the war protestors, breaking through lines, and trying to start fist fights.

The significant point is that the escalation of the Vietnam War has been matched by the escalation in antiwar protest actions. A certain Europeanization of populist politics has set in. This involves a sharp condemnation of orthodox parliamentarian politics as such and moves, inexorably, into a framework in which direct confrontation becomes the supreme test of worth. This might be considered the middle-class adaptation of the *foco* in guerilla struggles, in which the will of the people is asserted through the participants at specific points of struggle. A *fin de siècle* phenomenon reappears: the goals of the struggle become fluid, indefinite, and even suspect, while the forms of struggle become sharper and more consuming. In the America of today as in the France of 1898 the struggle is the message.

Antiwar organization is an amorphous, almost amoebalike phenomenon. But insofar as there is any clear pattern of development in the organizational structure of the antiwar movement in the United States, it may be said to have emerged in three stages—each within the marginal context of radical politics. First, covering a period roughly between 1952 and 1956, there was a discernible ideological thawing out of the communist-oriented Left. Out of the ashes of the McCarthy assault on the feeble American communist organization, and out of a corresponding period of "thaw" in the Soviet Union and its loosening effects upon communists everywhere, there emerged left-wing efforts at ideological independence and more democratic organizational procedures. The second period, between 1957 and 1965, involved the rebirth of issue-oriented leftism. In this period new radical groups were formed that were primarily involved in the struggle for the rights of blacks: on the educational, economic, and political levels.

For the pacifist wing, the second stage was characterized by a touching faith in the rationality of all men and in individual, dramaturgical acts: individuals sailing into the Pacific Ocean atom bomb test areas (sponsored by the Committee of Nonviolent Action—CNVA—founded in 1957); Quaker demonstrations against land-launched missiles in Omaha, Nebraska; and various lengthy cross-national "walks for peace" (cf. Lynd, 1966:310–376).

But by 1965 several major events took place. On the one hand, there was the growing nationalization of black radicalism, which took on separatist overtones and sought exclusively black leadership. On the other hand, United States' involvement in Vietnam led to her becoming a party to war, a fact that became dramatically real for the American population in 1965. Now the white radical movement had its ready-made ideological issue. This third period was first discerned late in 1964 after the student revolt at Berkeley, which injected into the radical main-stream a student militancy for university and, finally, social reform on a broad scale. Thus an initial left-wing thaw issued into the radical plural-ism of blacks, students, and sympathetic liberal professionals.

The first major antiwar strategy following the escalation of the Vietnam War early in 1965 was that of the teach-in (Menashe and Radosh, 1967). It reflected not only an urge to "dialogue," but also the implicit threat that the American university system would be converted into a politically relevant complex as an answer to the war. The intel-ligentsia in the United States, which in all past wars of the century was solidly behind the prowar consensus, this time made a decisive break with its own tradition. Yet the genteel nature of the resistance to war fol-lowed closely the general pacifist response still dominant. The uses of reason were sure to triumph over the forces of might (cf. Menashe and Radosh, 1967). It is not that the teach-in concept has been totally abandoned, but rather, as in the March on the Pentagon, that it was fused to active resistance and massive disruption (cf. Dellinger, 1967:4–5).

If the black nationalist movement was cutting its ties from the ortho-dox white liberal antiwar supports, the same was not true in reverse. For the number of blacks involved in antiwar protest movements has most often come from the upper leadership level of the black protest move-ment, while whites, sensing the vitality the black movement holds for radicalism as such, have consistently sought to attach themselves to civil rights struggles. It is this white attachment to black protest that has been responsible for the tactical resemblances of the antiwar movement to the black liberation movement and that stimulated overlapping memberships and actions. In fact, the present antiwar movement grew out of the stimulus provided by the civil rights movement. From 1954 through 1964—that is, from the Supreme Court desegregation decision to the Mississippi voter registration drive—blacks and whites acted together primarily through SDS, SNCC, and CORE. And many civil rights organizations, like SNCC, participated in the antiwar movement, at least at the leadership level. In the 1967 spring mobilization, Stokely Carmichael's contingent of black people marching to the United Nations from Harlem was the rallying point and the highlight of the antiwar protest movement of the day.

The reasons for this sequence of development are complex. Generally, the claims of blacks to full citizenship rights are understandable to Americans on pragmatic and moral grounds, even if these remain unful-filled. Furthermore, their "cause" traditionally has been espoused by every leftist radical group. Strategies and tactics vis-à-vis this cause have sometimes united and sometimes splintered the Left. Nevertheless, it has remained the least controversial issue the Left has put forth insofar as the general public response is concerned. Thus, black protest can generate a momentum to which other issues may become attached—filling out the chorus of radical voices.

By contrast, antiwar movements may appear tainted by unrealistic idealism or even unpatriotic treachery. American masses are not likely to sympathize with such movements standing independently of morally acceptable ones. The aspirations of blacks follow the traditional struggle for equality by minority and ethnic groupings: there were the struggles of the labor movement for recognition by the larger society, and there were working-class struggles for more popular educational and cultural opportunity. Moreover, each of these were legitimized by some formula familiar and drawn from American liberalism. However bitter working-class conservatives may be toward extending voting franchise and property rights to include yet another outsider group, their own definition of Americanism leaves them hard-pressed to deny equal treatment (even if separate) to the black people.

The antiwar movement has been predominantly middle class in background and remains so to this day. This may help to explain working-class and lower-class opposition to the movement. Stevedores, shopkeepers, sales clerks, mechanics, factory laborers have always been ambivalent and suspicious of causes espoused by the middle class. Education is viewed paradoxically, as effete and yet as a model for imitation. Given the educated middle class character of the antiwar movement, it represents to many working-class Americans a defection from within. War always elicits feelings of patriotism. The demand to rally behind the nation, without regard for the actual merits of its position, is precisely how "loyalty" comes to be defined. Loyalty is valued more highly than rationality and discussion. Thus, the facts about any war come to be subsumed to the emotions appropriate to all wars.

By contrast, the American black has traditionally been presented as a dilemma and a challenge. Thus it is easier for most of these same working-class Americans to appreciate aggression provoked by the history of racial discrimination and impoverished economic conditions. Furthermore, the black subculture shares many ideals with "grass roots" American culture. The readiness to live with and face violence and death are central virtues for both. It is no accident that the dominant American culture and black militants thus come to share and express resentment for gun-control legislation or any curb on the right to bear arms (see Marx, 1967:170–177).

The antiwar movement, quite to the contrary, has for the most part been in the forefront of efforts to initiate gun-control legislation and to expand such legislation to institute arms control at police and military levels. We are not here concerned with the purposes to which violent means are employed by one or another social group, but with the fact that the antiwar movement has challenged the basis for resolving problems in American society. Thus, whatever alliance exists between black militants and white antiwar groups is an uneasy one, due not simply to the different composition of each sector of the New Left, but to the different conceptions of strategies and tactics used to achieve their respective ends.

A theme behind most white movements is the idea of self-leadership. They all seek "freedom"; and the freedom sought is the expression and creation of individuality. It is freedom from organization, groups, and ultimately from rules as such. The black movements seek freedom from white control, not from the constraints of black society. The blacks are trying to create, rather than eliminate, organizational constraints. They do not seek freedom to "do your own thing," but to do the black thing, to find their own identities in subjecting themselves to the discipline of their own groups. This is the meaning of dressing, eating, and thinking black— to stand side-by-side with their "soul brothers." In part, the different styles of black and white protest, the tendency to fractionalization among the whites and to solidarity and discipline among the blacks, are due precisely to contrasting views on organizations, no less than to the content and programs of the respective movements. The white movements draw extreme ideological inferences from the liberal ethic, putting the autonomy of the individual above all organizational constraints. It is the extreme secularized form of Luther's "every man his own priest." The black movement tends to be antiliberal, dogmatic, sectarian in its direction, affirming the value and supremacy of the group above the individual. In short, for the white movement, the "struggle is the message," but for the black movement the struggle is the necessary price of success.

The black liberation movement makes explicit demands upon the sociopolitical order. The question of violence and nonviolence is largely tactical—the Southern Christian Leadership Conference notwithstanding. The antiwar movement, or at least a dominant wing, retains the belief that its goal is the limitation and ultimately the liquidation of violence. This schism between violence as a tactic (blacks) and violence as an evil (antiwar advocates) separates the two groups and helps to reveal existing differences between black protest and antiwar protest movements. It is clear that militant blacks are largely disinterested in the course of the war in Vietnam. Indeed, some participants in the black movement seem to think that the war actually may benefit blacks in terms of occupational status. It is not an accident that a basic pitch made by antiwar advocates is that the costs of the war deprive blacks of equality. In fact, little evidence exists that any real correlation of the two phenomena exists. For example, were the war in Vietnam to cease immediately, the overall size of military expenditures for a variety of reasons (rational and irrational) would remain constant over the next five years at least (Weidenbaum, 1967:60–75; Little, 1965:7–9). On the other hand, the structure of the antiwar movement is clearly affected by the comparative lack of black participation. Yet it must continue on its collision course with the military even if this leads to a confrontation with that large portion of the black community that casts its lot with the Establishment. Certainly one of the fascinating aspects of the future of the antiwar movement is precisely the postures adopted toward black protest movements that have an avowedly and explicitly violent character. The emergence of organizations such as the Black Panthers in San Francisco-Oakland, the Blackstone Rangers in Chicago, and the Zulu Twelve Hundreds in St. Louis, to name but a few, places a great strain on the antiwar movement—not only philosophically, in terms of goals sought, but practically, in terms of tactics employed.

At the Columbia University disorders in the spring of 1968, and again at the antiwar demonstrations in Chicago in the summer of 1968, the increasing gap between student movements and black movements became apparent. Black demands were made largely for increased participation, while the antiwar movement increasingly acted in terms of its sense of alienation.

Given the unique role of the student movement in the current antiwar effort, some detailed analysis of this social stratum is in order—not only to show why students become participants but as an indication of the ferocity of police reaction and black indifference. For the most part, the backgrounds of participating and sympathetic students in the antiwar movement are not strikingly unusual. There are three broadly discernible groups in the student wing of the antiwar movement.

One: Students from families with middle-class, social-service-minded backgrounds. Whether manifesting a high degree of "Christian compassion" or being college-educated social workers, these individuals can be characterized as noticeably committed to helping the less fortunate. These students often carry the liberal implications of their home experience to greater lengths than parents would have encouraged—but they are not faced with active parental opposition. Many report early experiences of contact with the poor, or, idealizing even to the point of romantic daydreams, a Jew, a black, or someone considered "outside" community, parental, or general social approval.

Two: Students from small-town or suburban communities and strictly conventional homes. These students are faced with a range of parental behavior from physical punishment for political activities to consistent pressure to end political affiliation. These students do not clearly recall early contact with the poor but always sympathized with the "underdog." They are largely inflamed by parental authority and conventionality. Humanizing contact with poverty usually occurred after joining the movement.

Three: Students with parents who were, or are, Communists, Trotskyists—some variety of traditional radical. These are a small, vocal minority within the movement. The parents of these students encourage participation. They are well-versed in Marxist literature, able to take the lead in discussions and other activity. There was frequent contact with small circles of radical friends of parents throughout childhood. The participation of these students has often led to "focus treatments" on the part of right-wing publications. In addition to exposés from the Right, a god-that-failed disenchantment, which is a byproduct of committed Marxist participants, is now receiving an airing (Luce, 1966).

Research reveals a number of things about students who participate in peace marches and peace activities:

(a) Demonstrators, in contrast to leaders, were quite young—the median age being 18-19.

(b) They had no well-formed, comprehensive political ideology.

(c) Many students (though not usually leaders) morally opposed the cold war and nuclear weapons—in spite of little or no personal religious commitment. Their statements and actions seemed to be idealistic protests for purity.

(d) The age period in which first feelings for social or political "causes" are most likely to develop, data suggest, is 12 to 15.

(e) The majority of students came from politically liberal families, but they were "rebelling" in going far beyond parental experience in the realm of public action. About one-fourth of the students characterized their homes as politically conservative or reactionary. Some demonstrators appeared to display a quality of simultaneous rebellion against identification with parental images.

(f) Older demonstrators, in their middle twenties, seemed to form a separate psychosocial population from the younger students.

(g) Opposing pickets from conservative student groups indicated the existence of strong differences in belief and behavior. Comparing the two groups along the psychosocial dimension of trust and distrust is especially interesting (cf. Solomon and Fishman, 1964:55; Flacks, 1967: 52–75).

The similarity of backgrounds reveals the distinctiveness of the student's *social* movement. Though each student may have had unique experiences leading him to antiwar participation, his involvement is better explained politically. The strong reaction against conditions and policies in the United States, catalyzed by demands for black rights, has made organization possible and optimism plausible. It is a time that calls forth the "political moralist." As Keniston (1968a:247–256) indicated in his study of the Vietnam Summer Project of 1967, "although in behavior most of these young radicals were rather *less* violent than their contemporaries, this was not because they were indifferent to the issue, but because their early experience and family values had taught them how to control, modulate, oppose, and avoid violence."

A better appreciation of what is involved in the antiwar movement as a social whole comes from matching ongoing ideologies with social class support. In the first place, there are two broad classifications of antiwar ideologies. The first universal might be called "pacifist," the other "political." Pacifist types tend to be selective in their opposition to modern war.

The most conspicuous type of pacifist is the absolute pacifist, morally committed to total restraint from bodily harm to others or to himself. This type is usually a religionist or, more specifically, someone who has found little comfort in the organized religions and yet maintains strong theological preferences. As were Tolstoy and Gandhi, these are often men of letters and learning who cluster in marginal religious groups, such as the Fellowship of Reconciliation or the Ethical Culture Society, to support premises of absolute pacifism. Such men are in the established sects, professions, and occupations.

The second major type consists of religious pacifists per se, those who offer a literal interpretation of the commandment against killing. This group, aside from the political substratum itself, receives support from many of the less educated or at least those less linked with intellectual pursuits who nonetheless deplore violence because of their early church training. Here, traditionalism rather than marginality seems to be the key.

The third kind of pacifist might be called the "thermonuclear pacifist." Here tactical considerations outweigh all other factors. Students in particular espouse, not so much the virtue of life, but the terrors of ultimate weapons. In a sense, thermonuclear pacifists juxtapose conventional war with nuclear annihilation. Recent literature of the culture heroes of the New Left indicates that technological features of modern warfare rather than prohibitions on conflict are central to this group. And the thermonuclear pacifists are by far the largest cluster of people who employ the rubric of pacifism.

As for the political types, they too can be divided into logical (and historical) groups.

First, there are the isolationists, people who are strongly nationalist and who employ the ideology if not the rhetoric of keeping Americans from dying in overseas warfare. The halcyon days of the isolationist movement took place prior to World War II. The America First movement linked up nicely the rhetoric of extreme nationalism with the claims of European fascism—that a policy of nonintervention was best suited to American foreign-policy goals.

The ecological settings in which the isolationist wing of the antiwar movement had its greatest strength—Chicago, St. Louis, Dallas—indicate that the agrarian sector, or at least the midwest organized working class, was greatly committed to this framework. This kind of ideology is still prevalent, judging by the information available in the editorial columns of midwest newspapers in such middle-sized cities as Topeka, Omaha, or Joplin. The transformation of the agrarian middle class into a *nouveau riche* urban middle class had tended to wipe out this isolationist wing of the antiwar movement, not to mention the fact that fascism as a world historic force was destroyed as the result of World War II. Yet this type of position remains in evidence not so much in the antiwar movement as currently constituted as it does in the unorthodox sentiments expressed in the major parties and reflected in the national polls on the war.

The second political type might be called the "federalist." He believes in one world, in a "United States of the World." He sees the "war system" as a product of competing nation-states; the solution, therefore, is a unified political world system. But the federalists too are found at the margins of orthodox politics. When the equilibrium between the underdeveloped world and the fully industrialized world was replaced by an open and intense rivalry after World War II and when the major powers retained their strong nationalist sentiments in the structuring of the United Nations, the federalists lost favor. The formation of a United Nations Organization, which recognizes rather than ostracizes national sovereignties, has effectively liquidated federalism as a political force and eroded its base in any social sector of the population.

The third political type to be found in the antiwar movement, and by far the most numerous, is issue oriented. He is specifically concerned with ending the war on poverty, is frustrated by the war overseas—or perceives the Vietnam War as a direct threat to students' careers via the military draft, as well as to his own vision of what the good society should be.

There is an obvious overlap between the thermonuclear pacifists and the issue oriented political types. Both groups draw their greatest sustenance from the 8 million student population, the 20 million black population, and the more than 6 million persons of Mexican and Puerto Rican backgrounds. And this huge "underclass" can command the support of at least a healthy minority of the "intellectual class."

A fourth political type is antiwar only in a limited sense: he is opposed to the Vietnam War *because* America intervened against the revolutionary side. He advocates revolution as the only way to create needed social, political, and economic changes in the Third World. He supports wars that aid the revolutionary cause and opposes wars that injure such causes. This type defines himself as anti-imperialist and believes that the United States' economic, political, and military presence must be expelled from the Third World, by revolutionary military means if necessary. For this group, the successful Cuban Revolution serves as a model.

The anti-imperialists seek an NLF victory rather than simply an end to the war in Vietnam. They oppose actions that would end the war on terms they consider unacceptable, just as North Vietnam in the Paris Peace Talks indicates an unwillingness to negotiate an end to the war on unfavorable terms. This group is not essentially antiwar since it accepts war as a legitimate and valid military strategy.

This group seeks an end to imperialism rather than an end to war. It is opposed to the negotiated settlement of the war on any terms except the total and unconditional withdrawal of American troops. It is opposed to gun-control legislation in America, on the grounds that such legislation would deprive the revolutionary movement in this country of access to weapons. Finally, it is beginning to talk about revolutionary confrontation with the American military—in the form of police and National Guard. In this respect, it sees the role of police in America as similar to the role of the American military in Vietnam and many other nations. Both are a force that must be defeated for a successful revolution to occur. There exists within the American antiwar movement an element, numerically small but increasingly influential (or at least vocal), that is anti-American rather than antiadministration.

The correlation between all these types and their social bases of support would require extensive empirical analysis. Some studies indicate that key leadership of the student wing of the antiwar movement had parents who were themselves radicals. This supports the thesis of generational revolt (cf. Flacks, 1967). For our purposes it is sufficient to point out that participation of marginal political types and deviant social subcultures indicates the drawing power of the antiwar issue as a vehicle for expressing a fundamental sense of alienation. For one thing is clear: any minimization or elimination of thermonuclear pacifists and issue-oriented "peaceniks" would quickly reduce the size of the antiwar movement to the sectlike proportions it had in more tranquil times.

The continuation of the Vietnam War provides common ground for the diverse organizational and ideological facets of the antiwar movement. And as the war escalates and endures, the claims of the "anti-imperialists" tend to be substantiated in the eyes of the "issue-oriented" participants. It also inhibits major differences between the various factions from surfacing. Though not fatally flawed by the factionalism of the past, the peace movement is fractionated and atomistic. Some 150 organizations are classified as anti-Vietnam protest groups; 75 to 100 are specifically antidraft. Any organizational chart grossly misrepresents the fluidity and disorganization of the groups; however, it does give some sense of the movement's scope.

The National Mobilization Committee to End the War in Vietnam, known in some quarters as MOB or "the Mob," tops the pyramid by reaching down to contact leading national and community coalition groups. In New York, the Fifth Avenue Peace Parade Committee to End the War in Vietnam, once headed by Mobilization director David Dellinger, performs the basic organizational work needed for mass rally. Most large cities have similar coalitions.

Responsible for activating the long list of national and local groups in its area, the Fifth Avenue Peace Parade Committee will contact a number of adult peace, and primarily pacifist, groups: Women Strike for Peace, SANE, War Resisters' League, Committee for Nonviolent Action, the Student Peace Union, and the Student Mobilization Committee are primary. There are three groups for veterans—Veterans for Peace, Vietnam Veterans to End the War in Vietnam, and Veterans and Reservists to End the War in Vietnam, of which the last is the most militant. That is, they are more willing to use direct action, risk arrest, and turn in their military medals and papers. Antidraft organizations include the Resistance (supporters of draft-card burnings, draft refusers, and allied seminary students who refuse religious deferment and insist on conscientious-objector status) and black antidraft groups. Most professionals, from writers to academicians, have numerous ad hoc organizations aimed at war protest just as the clergy and religious organizations do. These include the Episcopal Peace Fellowship, Concerned Clergy, Catholic Peace Fellowship, and American Friends Service Committee. Since the Spring Mobilization in 1967, Reform Democratic Clubs have participated in the New York movement, helping in turn to transform the war issue into a respectable political one. Other political organizations contacted for mass mobilizations are the left-wing, multiissue groups like the Communist Party and the Socialist Workers Party. Some unions, such as the ILGWU, Local 1199 of the Amalgamated Workers Union and District 635, are also counted on for support. Currently the emphasis in New York is on geographical organizing on a block-by-block level. Charles Street and West 84th Street have groups whose major goal is peace in Vietnam.

Including the local, citywide, regional, and national committees, by 1968 there were in all some 150 groups. Some perform distinctive roles. Women Strike for Peace, for example, is as much a fund-raising as it is a direct-action group. Membership lists, of course, overlap as people ally themselves with church, professional, and single-issue organizations.

The characters and relations of these diverse organizations are fluid. Despite its overwhelming publicity and tactical advantage, SDS is not viewed by most people in the coalition organizations as influential in the mobilizations. "They usually come in at the end," as they did at the Pentagon. Once dominant in the early peace movement, the Committee for Nonviolent Action, founded by the late A. J. Muste, is now at best a regional grouping in the northeast. Committed to nonviolent action as a total philosophy of life, it is most similar to the Gandhian spirit of civil disobedience.

Youth Against War and Fascism consider themselves to be radical. In New York they marched without a permit, as did the Committee to Aid the Liberation Front and the Veterans and Reservists. Most noteworthy is the increasing militancy of the clergy, from support for halting the bombing in 1965 to the October 1967 Call to Resist Illegitimate Authority. At that time 320 clergymen pledged to aid and abet draft refusers and to transform synagogues and churches into sanctuaries for conscientious objectors. Also important is the formation in September 1967 of Business Executives Move for Vietnam Peace. Most are managers or owners of middle-sized businesses.

The mobilizing role of the intellectuals can scarcely be underestimated. They challenged the basic assumption of the war and they examined the inconsistencies and inaccuracies in statements made by government officials. Beyond that, they dramatized the generalized destructiveness associated with the strategy of the war of attrition. In other words, they offered the counterlegitimacy of Science over and against the legitimacy of Government. And for that reason their authority far exceeded their numbers.

In a sense, the very unity of the intellectuals depended upon the binding force of the war issue. Through criticism of the Vietnam conflict, journalists could challenge the premises of the day-to-day conduct of the war; logicians and philosophers could challenge the inconsistencies of the war rationale; scientists could decry the growing uses of bacteriological and chemical weaponry; and literati could once more take up the classic claims of humanism and civilization.

The intellectuals were more important in mobilizing sentiment than even past clusters of men of ideas were in respect to revolutionary parties. The reason is precisely that classical political leadership does not exist in the antiwar movement. And in such a context, only the force of ideas, the men of ideas, come to gain universal attention. The heroic dimensions of poets like Robert Lowell, philosophers like Herbert Marcuse, journalists like Bernard Fall, and novelists like Mary McCarthy and Norman Mailer loom larger precisely because standard political types are held in disrepute.

Antipolitics, or better, the politics of moralism, characterizes the antiwar protest movement, as it has traditionally characterized intellectual postures toward political leadership. This frame of mind was well summed up by the freelance photographer at the Pentagon March who observed: "There was no leadership, that was what was so beautiful. The leaders all think they're leaders, but this just happened." And not waiting for the Fifth Avenue Peace Parade Committee to put out a call to picket Hubert Humphrey's opening campaign at the Labor Day Parade, large numbers of individuals turned out to protest his stands on the war and on the Chicago demonstrations.

To say that the movement is "organized" would give exaggerated credit to the leadership and the methods used for mobilizing mass demonstrations. Loose confederations or temporary coalitions today exist as pragmatic necessities in the new world of leftist politics. Students, upon whom the movement is largely based and through whom it has become legitimate, disdain the old-time popular front and its factionalism. Despite the peace movement, the styles of the young—in rhetoric, dress, and language—have changed. For them, existential action plus the rhetoric of contemporary revolution is a style as well as an ideology. Small groups, organized for specific ends, become the ideal.

The ones that carry with them some mystical aura, some communism of the mind as it were, become those that the students take particular pleasure in identifying with.

The newer-style antiwar leader is basically a model and not a chief. He does not function as a classic charismatic, much less bureaucratic, head. Many leaders are heroes of the movement's past crusades, serving as models for the followers who can then pattern their behavior and action in the same way, although they would not be available to "take orders" from the leaders if the latter tried to give them. This is a new political reality. Because of the ease of communication among "mass intellectuals" in American society, it is relatively simple to start a nationwide movement based on emulation. However, "responsible authorities" can only seem to appreciate such phenomena by thinking of organization—secret or manifest. The point is that a high degree of organization is not necessary if the communication of ideas and sentiments is rapid and extensive enough to persuade some segment of the public to become involved in mass activities.

The Youth International Party, or Yippies, particularly demonstrate the theatrical, half-for-real sensibility that appeals to the students' sense of humor and sense of outrage at the war. Despite their reputation (one estimate placed their number at ten), their only outstanding accomplishment is their finely developed sense of public relations. One could say that they attack the mimeograph machine more than the on-duty patrolman. But the Yippie myth prevails and grows stronger as more people—even those who are unsympathetic—believe what they say.

For the young, then, such older, left-wing political groups as the Communist Party and the Trotskyite Socialist Workers Party are "out of it." Ironically, official response to the demonstrators is directed toward these outsiders. During the early days of the movement, it was common to hear political leaders call the demonstrators Communists or victims of Communist exploitation.

Students have become increasingly militant and intransigent as the war has progressed. The peace movement has filtered down into the high schools. In some measure, the peace issue seems to highlight fears of the military draft and also discontent with school programs and administrations. The campuses are now the pacesetters for the peace movement. The formation in 1968 of the Student Mobilization Committee to End the War in Vietnam formally indicated the passing of power to the young. What was once disregarded by the adult peace movement has now become its central strategy. The SDS policy of grass roots, community organization over mass mobilization was recently adopted by the National Mobilization Committee.

Propaganda of the word, characteristic of the genteel tradition from which the antiwar movement emerges, has been replaced by propaganda of the deed, a characteristic of the younger and more recent entries into protest and confrontational politics. In this sense there has been a startling change from alienation to commitment and now to revolution-making.

The peace movement of the past deeply linked most *traditional* organizations involved to various American elites. Peace groups, from the Carnegie Endowment for International Peace to the United Nations support agencies, have maintained long and strong ties to Congress. Organizations such as SANE are committed to maintaining ties with the Establishment and with the various elements within the governmental structure of power. The newer organizations often ignore tie-ins with established power. In fact, they repudiate precisely these connections as futile and even faulty in conception. Thus, the gulf is not simply between newer violent types of response and older nonviolent types of organizations. Often the correlation can be made between the *newer violent* organizations and appeals to mass action and the *older nonviolent* organizations and appeals to elite decision-making.

The antiwar movement has evolved into a frontal assault on traditional American notions of patriotism. The symbolic defiance of common American values has reached a point where the burning of the American flag or the raising of the Viet Cong flag is now something of a ritual. The New York demonstrations in April 1967 used the California demonstrations as a model. Nearly all these confrontations between demonstrators and counterdemonstrators took place over control of the Viet Cong flag. In point of fact, however, the peace movement itself was torn over the question of symbolic assault on American patriotism versus discussion with the power system over the "real issues." Organizations such as SANE and the American Friends Service Committee were particularly divided over the new tactics. Only with great difficulty did the movement as a whole reconcile itself to wholesale assaults on the American value system. The switch is hard for the traditionalists of protest, who are sentimental about traditional American symbols. The new protesters, however, burn the flags but still consider themselves the true embodiment of these symbols.

Symbolism has always been a consistent element of the antiwar protest, from the place of action—the Pentagon and Independence Hall—to its timing—Thanksgiving Day, July 4th, the anniversaries of

Hiroshima and Nagasaki. The most symbolic acts—burning draft cards and carrying the Viet Cong flag—have generated the most violence. They assault the romantic, irrational, and powerful identification of man with country.

This, too, illustrates that violence is often a consequence of behavior. It is not the purpose of antiwar rallies to become military battlefields. The natural history of the crowd situation itself breeds violence. Conflict occurs mostly in unstructured situations where mass congregations of people with different points of view coalesce into opposing (but reinforced) factions. They become enmeshed in a zero-sum situation where one side or the other is compelled to retreat or surrender.

The definite shift from the politics of symbolic opposition to the actual prevention of war activities that support and sustain the war is another mark of the movement today. The direct action, of course, tends to raise the ante and to increase the level of violence. Confrontations may be prolonged and involve such fundamental questions as the control of property, the authority of university officials, and even the ownership of buildings, streets, and empty lots. The amount of violence seems to be directly related to the intimacy of the participants with the institution under attack. Confrontation sought and made with such sensitive federal military functions as ROTC training programs yields the most violence. Though this may mark a turn to guerilla insurgency, it more obviously reflects an escalation in the symbolic struggle.

The terms of dialogue in American life have been directly affected by the antiwar movement. The increasing frustration over the conduct of the Vietnam War has polarized a population reared on a diet of victory and defeat and unable to accept a permanent state of war. As the Vietnam War has continued, it has also become the subject of popular debate. The question of American overseas commitment has been picked up by orthodox political actors and not just theatrical leftists.

When the government mobilizes support and force, opposition groups work extra hard to weaken the government stand. Thus, as the government and the broad population debate the war issue and infuse it into the political process, violent defiance of the law and left-wing counterforce generally decrease. Violence in relation to the law can more readily be diminished, not by the suppression of discussion but rather by its promulgation. For in a very real sense the legitimation of democracy entails the conversion of the antiwar movement into a specialized group.

In that sense, the radical wing of the antiwar protest movement—thermonuclear pacifists and issue-oriented politicos alike—is subject to what might be called the iron law of defeat through victory. The broadening involvement of mass numbers in intensive discussions on the nature of the war tends to subvert violent response. Thus the presidential campaign of Eugene McCarthy was, in the main, disparaged by the SDS leadership, who did not participate in the primary campaign struggles. The McCarthy organization and the SDS were antagonists, vying for the same constituency.

The antiwar movement, through the very intensification of its polemics and the very magnitude of its organization (even apart from the orthodox party system), is a potential source for reducing rather than stimulating violence. This is the intent, if not always the result, of peace. For what one commentator has recently noted about the young is equally true for the antiwar movement as a whole:

> The primary task is to develop new psychological, political and international controls on violence. Indeed, many of the dilemmas of today's young radicals seem related to their extraordinarily zealous efforts to avoid any action or relationship in which inner or outer violence might be evoked. Distaste for violence animates the profound revulsion many of today's youth feel toward the war in Southeast Asia, just as it underlies a similar revulsion against the exploitation or control of man by man. . . . Even the search for forms of mass political action that avoid physical violence—a preference severely tested and somewhat undermined by the events of recent months—points to a considerable distaste for the direct expression of aggression (Keniston, 1968b:243).

The involvement of masses in the political process, by affecting major decisions, reduces the possibility of violence so long as there is a reasonable chance that the normal political process might yield an end to the war.

In these terms, the future behavior of young politically minded people is central. If they feel that the political system cheated them out of a legitimate victory, that it is not representative of the American people, and that it can only be sustained in its present form by police tactics, then the chances for escalated violence are high. If, on the other hand, they accept the legitimacy of their defeat and feel that they had a chance to present their case to the American people and the people decided against their position, then mass mobilization will have helped to reduce the potential for violence.

Since leaders in both major parties have adopted roughly similar positions, the Vietnam War will probably not be a viable issue in party politics, despite its centrality to American political and social life. Thus, the chances of mass participation by the antiwar movement in the legitimate political process are slight. A political program that directly confronts the inability of the political party system to offer a real alternative to the war has now been developed by the radical arm of the antiwar movement. This even includes plans for disruption of the election mechanism. It is impossible to determine yet whether this will materialize, but if it does, high levels of violence on both sides can be predicted. But violence is often neither the goal nor the essential tactic of the movement. Too often it is the byproduct of the conduct of political struggle by other means.

Violence is such a tough-sounding and ultimate word that it is easy to overlook the simplest point of all: violence is often a surrogate for revolution. As Barrington Moore (1968:11) so aptly noted: "It is untrue that violence settles nothing. It would be closer to the mark to assert that violence has settled all historical issues so far, and most of them in the wrong way." The revolutionary process begins with seemingly spontaneous violence on the part of formerly inchoate groups in society. Translating violence into the antiwar movement requires two parallel phenomena: there must be a felt need on the part of large, unsponsored groups to participate in the decision-making process, and, at the same time, there must be enough closure in the political order to prevent the absorption of such groups into the customary structure of decision-making. We can hardly do better than to conclude this chapter with a remarkable quote by Staughton Lynd (1968:172) on the alienated nature of protest politics in the United States:

All that had been closed and mysterious in the procedure of the parent institution becomes open and visible in the workings of its counterpart. Decision-makers, appointed to the former, are elected to the latter. Parallel bodies in different places begin to communicate, to devise means of coordination: a new structure of representation develops out of direct democracy and is controlled by it. Suddenly, in whole parts of the country and in entire areas of daily life, it becomes apparent that people are obeying the new organs of authority rather than the old ones. Finally, an act or a series of acts of legitimation occur. . . . The task becomes building into the new society something of that sense of shared purpose and tangibly shaping a common destiny which characterized the revolution at its most intense.

One difficulty is that this new source of legitimation remains highly restricted to a small segment of society. As Kenneth Boulding (1965:18–

20) indicates, when a nation provides even a minimum rhetorical respect to a value, such as racial integration, protest movements can afford to be disruptive. But without widespread commitment to a value, such as pacifism, successful protest movements must be calm, educational, and basically respectable. Otherwise the protest itself becomes the object of controversy, which creates a strong backlash. Thus, whether protest brings a new legitimation or a new backlash depends, in part at least, on public priorities.

1968

20

Bilateralism, Multilateralism, and the Politics of Détente

There is a persistent current of opinion amongst a number of people researching the problems of war and peace that the fundamental flaw in the present negotiation process is a breakdown in moral principles. In earlier chapters I have taken issue with the position that there is an immediate need to close the breach between politics and ethics if we are to gain a true understanding of Soviet Russia. There is a far more immediate need to close the rupture between concrete politics and abstract policy-making.

Quite a number of researches into peace problems have suggested that morality is not some nonnegotiable set of strategies, but rather a goal direction that gives meaning and point to many different kinds of specific actions. And in fact, there can be no doubt that the New Civilian Militarists, (NCM) among others, are suffering from too little moral concern and too much policy concern. Since this problem has general implications for future strategies of the disarmament approach to world peace, I should like to clarify my views on the priority of political open-endedness over moral principles.

To begin with, morals are only effective when embodied in a set of operational political guides rather than the other way around. We can introduce this notion directly by indicating six related proposals for tension reduction and tactical initiatives. Briefly restated, they are: (1) a shift from a policy based on the morality of anticommunism to a policy based on common survival and the popular right of free choice in matters of social systems; (2) a recognition that the policy of deterrence is at best a halfway house in a disarmament policy and, at worst, a halfway house for those moving in the opposite direction, toward full rearmament and a first-strike posture; (3) an attempt to refocus and rechannel energies toward solving the problems of underdevelopment, development, and overdevelopment, and away from inherited postures of either promilitarism or antimilitarism; (4) the development of a method of showdown postponement to replace the present precarious notion of instantaneous retaliation; (5) the introduction of some mechanism for ensuring the "circulation and replenishment of elites" to insure political responsiveness by decision-makers; (6) the juridical securing of the concept of "veto-groups," and following this, the working out of a pattern of departmental interdependence at the governmental level to replace the present drift toward departmental "autonomy" in which the branches of the administration compete with and contradict one another, thereby increasing the possibilities of an endless number of political miscalculations and military calamities.

Admittedly, such political-organizational proposals do not have the attractiveness of a universalist ethical doctrine of peace, but neither do they have the deficits of such ethical absolutes. The call for morality is too frequently a disguised form for expressing one's displeasure with the creaky machinery of the negotiation process. It is, to be blunt, a fanciful and embroidered impulse toward fanaticism. Given the present preponderant fanaticism of the political right vis-à-vis the articulate left, a restoration of a morally centered policy approach could only have dire international consequences. The more rigidly more commitments are fixed, the narrower is the range of political negotiations; while the more open moral postures are, the wider is the range for political settlement. Peace researchers ought not to forget that it is precisely grandiose moral poses that characterize the propaganda barrage intended to obscure the functional similarities between the United States and the Soviet Union (Riesman, 1963).

In the present situation, morality has too often degenerated into ideology. It has functioned to obscure the possibility of practical settlement by effectively narrowing the range of the negotiable, not on the basis of authentic political requirements, but on discredited "face-saving" premises. Not that moral judgment ought to be suspended. Rather our definition of moral judgment, as something transcending political decision, needs serious analysis. Emmet John Hughes' book, *The Ordeal of Power,* forcefully illumines the point that those who urge a morally centered policy often do so at the expense of a politically centered policy.

In this connection, Hughes' description of the rigid and irrelevant moralizing of the late John Foster Dulles makes clear that it is not a question of "our" morality versus "their" immorality, but an absolutist notion of morality itself that is, and has been, so damaging to political settlements. "Through all the years ruled by the taut doctrines of John Foster Dulles, the national policy had decreed an almost religious kind of commitment to a moralistic definition of the relations between nations. By the terms of this orthodoxy, the promise of salvation lay in a kind of political excommunication of Soviet power. The means of grace, moreover, were assured: the political weakness of Soviet power was ultimately guaranteed by its moral wickedness" (Hughes, 1961). This is precisely the sense in which the late Joseph Stalin was also a "moral" man. Indeed, the present conflict between the Soviet and Chinese parties can be summed up at a more generic level as a conflict between political pragmatism (of a Marxian variety) and moral communism (of a Lenin-Stalin variety).

The fault with a morally centered policy is that when we descend from the lofty heights of peace platitudes about the goodness of man and the rightness of cause—the minute one forces separatist moral judgments upon social interests—the very intrusion of such an interest-ideology complex tends to burden and obscure the practice of the political arts, which must be specific as to the content of settlement.

Morality has been "Christianized" once again. It has become another word for unconditional: for the cold warriors, "victory" without conditions. What is entailed is a surrender of reason, of decision-making within a concrete political setting. The cry of morality is a call for an ideologically centered policy. The fact that the American policy elite call our ideology a morality, while our Soviet counterparts call their moral principles an ideology, does not alter the drift toward totalism, toward a fanatical vision of the future. High-minded talk about "liberation" and "rollback" only disguises an impatience with the ambiguities of the present historical epoch, ambiguities, I might add, that in some circumstances go far in preventing an all-out nuclear blast-off. "Police actions" in Korea, "paramilitary aid" in South Vietnam, and "blockades" in Cuba are assuredly dreadful facts to contemplate. Ambiguous conflict both raises the military ante and increases the possibility of "unintended war." Nonetheless, the very ambiguity of such military behavior indicates an unwillingness to cross the thermonuclear threshold.

Undoubtedly the international situation is fraught with the gravest dangers. The question, however, is whether a firm moral posture will ease the pressure and alleviate the dangers. Here I think the answer must be a categorical no: at least not the kind of moralities presently bandied about. Cuba has become "nonnegotiable" on moral grounds, thus expanding the danger, if not of World War III directly then at least of a World War in consequence of a probable attempt by the United States to block the inevitable revolutionary surge throughout the rest of Latin America. East Germany has become "nonnegotiable" on moral grounds. The Russians have their Berlin Wall, while we have pushed the outer perimeter of NATO defenses right up to that Wall. In such a context, the concept of an American Peace Movement as a moral alternative (which we are assured will have democratic political consequences) is only a reflection of the serious desperation of the situation, not a resolution.

The year 1963 witnessed the culmination of an amazing degree of disintegration of old political alliances. The structural similarities of socialism did not prevent a deepening of the political rift between the Soviet Union and China. The realignment of Communist Parties has qualities of a *Rassenkampf* in the making—with racial composition, ethnic loyalties, and continental ambitions overshadowing economic structures and moral strictures alike. The fact that the Soviet Union and China both have "public-sector" economies with a heavy premium on "forced savings" has not been a sufficient deterrent to the widening breach. The same can be said in the West. The DeGaulle position is not simply an aberrant French attitude but rather strongly reflects a new stage of development of European capitalism—a stage in which competition rather than cooperation with the United States is extremely likely. We are witnesses to the new resistance, to resolution of economic differences through imagined political loyalties of the democracies. The Kissinger nuclear-spread thesis—that the United States has "allies" while the Soviets have "captives," and therefore we can afford to share the bomb—has proved bankrupt less than a year after its initial enunciation (Kissinger, 1962). And his recent "second thoughts on flexible response" demonstrate that Kissinger would prefer to keep old "allies," however decadent the regime, than make the effort to win new "friends," however dynamic the regime (Kissinger, 1963).

We ought not to ignore the fact that political events have outstripped moral postures at every turn in the cold war from 1948 to 1962. We should thus be most cautious before insisting on absolutist ethics simply because old political definitions of the Western alliance are vanishing. We are entering a period in which new, exciting, and even embarrassing questions are being asked on both sides of the Curtain. Is the conflict between the United States and the Soviet Union losing its steam? And if it is, can the reasons be traced to a positive functional identity between "state capitalism" and "state socialism" or to a common front against other dangers? Will the adventurist Gaullist search for an independent nuclear deterrent compel the United States and Russia to arrive at an international settlement earlier than one might have anticipated? Will the military belligerence of China have the same catalytic effects? These are surely not unusual questions. Indeed, they are being seriously studied in military quarters. Power respects nothing less than equal power. The United States' military Establishment respects nothing less than the Soviet military Establishment. If the means to the maintenance of international power is great power cooperation, then one can expect that the rhetoric of cold war, which has so beclouded our political thinking from 1948-62, will finally give way to a new era of good feelings among the bipolar nations.

Once cold-war hostilities recede, and I for one have no doubt that in their present form (US-USSR) they will come to an end, then we might encourage the kind of responsible moral dialogue possible in a condition of relative nuclear monopolization. There is already a common consensus that the ultimate moral goals of the United States and the Soviet Union are roughly parallel. The "American Way" and the "Communist Victory" have few moral differences. They are, after all, both extensions of Enlightenment and Christian rationalism despite their once irreconcilable opposition. In the realm of instrumentalities, however, very sharp differences do obtain: the questions of how much coercion, how much individual expression for desired ends, etc. But the dialectic of the Anarch on one side and the Behemoth on the other is hardly unique or limited to the great powers. Nor is it an opposition to be settled by moralistic demands for doctrinal purity or for unconditional victories. The days of pure ideologies and total military solutions are over.

This in itself constitutes a moral premise, to wit, that human life and survival is worth preserving and extending above all other loyalties. I do not doubt this. On the other hand, neither does anyone else. It is the political premises that need sharper edges. Simple survival ethics cannot withstand absolute competition between sociopolitical systems seen as moral entities. When the political premises are themselves seen as capable of being bridged, turned toward and tuned into each other, then will the striving for peace register itself as a moral-political voice.

We may well be witnessing the beginning of a "big-power" settlement ment of the cold war—of an "immoral" bilateral agreement rather than the multilateral "moral" agreement many peace researchers formerly anticipated. India may not be "the hope of the world." The "third way" countries may have little to do with a negotiated settlement. What we must therefore come to terms with is an inventory of values: Is big-power settlement "bad" by virtue of its retention of a status quo situation; or is any settlement (no matter how high-handed and undemocratic in form) "good" by virtue of its promise of an extended period of peace? There are unpleasant aspects to a peace settlement. The cost factor may have to be reckoned with if we are to gain the benefit factor—a durable peace and an end to at least that form of the cold war that puts the two nuclear protagonists in menacing deadlock.

Chinese revolutions and French reactionaries alike will probably be unhappy at the "immoral" peace resolution. The revolutionary will point to the slow rate of material change in the social system (particularly in the developing nations of Latin America, Asia, and Africa), while reactionaries will weep at the end of all theories of roll-back and anticommunist victories (particularly in the overdeveloped Western European nations). From Mao Tse-tung to Charles De Gaulle one can expect to hear the cry: *trahison*. And they will be right—from a moral point of view. But from the political point of view, from the requirements of peaceful development of nuclear power, they will be wrong. We cannot even here be spared the agonies of trying decisions. The politics of peace may well turn out to be the enemy of an absolute morality of social development or economic *laissez-faire*. But if that is the case, it is all the more imperative to distinguish the political requirements of peaceful coexistence from the moral requirements of either capitalism or socialism. Perhaps we may put it another way: that a new moral dimension of common survival may enrich the political practicalities of both thereafter. Let the paradox be stated candidly. And then we shall see just who stands for what. To argue for *both* peace and morality is simple, as simple as the social-democratic argument for *both* liberty and social revolution. But in both cases, the *real* issues are joined only when the contradictory nature of the ends sought is taken into account. The soothing thoughts of many "peaceniks" is that peace is a prelude to socialism. The consoling thought of many "nudniks" who want war now is that conflict is a prelude to "modern" capitalism. Let both sides come to the realization that peace may have as its asking price the suspension of utopian dreams and restorationist phantasies, and we will arrive at a more sober kind of analysis of the "morality" of peace politics than has heretofore been the case.

While in London, I took the opportunity to listen nightly to short-wave programs emanating from Eastern Europe. (Interestingly enough, virtually all short-wave broadcasting seemed to originate in the Communist bloc nations late at night). One rather elaborate discussion concerned the statements made by President Kennedy in his inaugural address emphasizing the need for a revaluation of cold-war postures and a general reassessment of Soviet-American relations; and the follow-up remarks by Premier Khrushchev calling for more American deeds and less rhetoric. The analysis over the radio was carried on at a very worthy level. There was a noticeable absence of news slanting or mud slinging, with perfect parity given to the statements made by the two heads of state. I recollect thinking that this must be Radio Belgrade, since the absence of vituperation or bias in reporting events is uniquely characteristic of the Yugoslavs. To my surprise, it was Radio Prague speaking. I mention this simply to underscore the point that the easing of East-West tensions entails a more sympathetic rendering of what the "other side" is thinking and saying. A widespread feeling of guardianship for the fate of universal peace looms at least as large in Soviet policy-making as it does in that of the United States.

Does this simple incident imply or entail a *Pax Russo-Americana?* I should answer in two parts: yes, in terms of the *prima facie* responsibility of the two major powers to reach a general arms-control accord; no, in terms of any agreement to curb the competition between social systems.

The maturation of the Soviet economy, of a *socialist* system of production, whatever may be its deformities—particularly with its past merging of coercion with terrorism—only intensifies the will to social victory. But at the same time it provides the Russian leadership with a cushion upon which to fall back in negotiating outstanding problems of foreign affairs. Only now are the Soviets beginning to take for granted their great-power status. Thus, only now are they capable of long-range estimates and analysis. On the other side, there is a general consensus that the United States is not necessarily bound by Marxian predictions on the demise of the capitalist economic order. This is reflected not only in the continuing buoyancy of the American economy, again whatever its deformities with respect to the "other America," but also in its capacity to absorb the political fanaticism of the extreme right. Both Americans and Russians feel keenly that history is on their side, that is, that a long-run victory is possible. Given this parallel optimism, the possibility of a bilateral arms agreement with inspection apparatus and machinery for minimizing accidental warfare cannot be ruled out, whatever sort of tactical "hardening" or "softening" there is at any given moment.

Beyond this general and mutual change in social estimates for the future, the problem of cheating has finally been solved. As Franklin A. Long, Assistant Director of the Arms Control and Disarmament Agency, has indicated:

Whereas the original Geneva system discussions were based on the most tentative estimates of the numbers of earthquakes and system detection capabilities, which often changed, our current understanding of these items is based on extensive knowledge. In other words, the days when great technical uncertainties kept test-ban negotiators off balance probably are over (Long, 1963).

The prime point of my analysis is that a complete nuclear test-ban treaty, while technically quite feasible, is politically unfeasible as long as no provisions are made for a lessening of tensions across the cold-war board. Lessening of such tensions may well turn on the ability of both the United States and the Soviet Union to maintain some sort of sociopolitical equilibrium at the pressure points around the globe. The United States can scarcely attempt a full-scale attack on Cuba and still hope for an arms agreement any more than the Soviet Union can support a Chinese attack on India in the name of world pacification. The basic weakness in equilibrium models is the assumption that radical social change is an enemy to world peace. And here my position is vulnerable in placing too much faith in a bilateral settlement in a multinational world. However, the biggest single task before disarmament commissions is not the regulation of nuclear tests, but rather the formation of rules governing each side in the event (really the likelihood) of radical upheavals in the world balance of social systems.

The Chinese Communist position is clearly that such inhibiting rules would be arbitrary, too high a price to pay for securing peace. Their view is predicated on the belief that the American imperialists can never be trusted to maintain peace in the face of national liberation efforts, and hence they conclude that peace is a consequence of the victory of socialism, not its cause (cf. *Peking Review,* 1963). Just as clearly, our cold warriors argue the immorality of peace precisely on the same grounds: Communists are "by nature" expansionist, and since they can never be trusted to maintain peace, the security of the world can only be guaranteed by American vigilance and armed strength (Teller, 1962). The "legacy of Hiroshima" for civilian militarists like Wohlstetter and Teller is that while a few agreed-upon arrangements might add a little more security to our present uneasy peace, any full-scale disarmament program could make the "balance" precarious to an even greater degree.

It is such moralizing postures that the leadership of both the Soviet Union and the United States must contend with. What makes a bilateral settlement feasible is simply that people desire a test-ban agreement. As John Maddox recently noted: "Even if it did not turn out to be a panacea, it would remove the cruelest edge from the universal anxiety over nuclear war, and it could lead to more far-reaching agreements with some real promise of security (Maddox, 1963). The dilemma is ideological. Each side must produce "victories" to maintain a peace posture. Curiously, each side *has* manufactured such victories. Note how each side "won" its point in the Cuban crisis of 1962.

The rhetoric of liberalism is a needed response, not only for the "millions of Americans whose style of life, whose sense of meaning, and whose manner of economic endeavor and personal encounter have come to depend upon being publicly patriotic and firm," as Roger Hagan (1963) so rightly notes, but also for the foreign governments who even more desperately require anticommunism as a way of life in order to stave off revolutionary change. On the Russian side, the need for ideology is built into the history of Bolshevism. The myth of the "unity of theory and practice" requires doctrinal support for *every* policy decision or else the communist state runs the constant risk of a *coup d'état* (Horowitz, 1964). For that reason we can hardly expect an end to ideological competition; and for these rationalizations "victories" will have to be conjured up in support of the "free world" or in support of the "anti-colonial peoples' struggle."

A central question is: How seriously ought we to take the ideological posturing on both sides? How can the fog of ideological inheritance be lifted without revealing the internal sores of both the United States and the Soviet Union? This question has been hesitantly faced by both Moscow and Washington. The wide dissemination of the writings of Ehrenburg, Solzhenitsyn, Yevtuschenko, among others, reveals a critical cutting edge that can only mean that Khrushchev is interested not simply in eliminating the "Stalin cult"—a mission already accomplished—but also in providing the intellectual groundwork for a reappraisal of Soviet foreign policy as a whole. The mood of American intellectuals is clearly moving along similar trajectories. The refusal of scientists to participate in or countenance a cold-war debate over travel visas for East German scientists is one among many indications that conventional lines of division separating the two major thermonuclear powers are beginning to disappear—and with a good deal more official support than anyone would have thought possible in the last decade. These changes in ideological climate permit a confident prediction that a test-ban treaty is possible and that such a treaty could pave the way for an overall settlement. In short, bilateral cooperation might open the path for a future multilateral disarmament system. This may offend purists and irrationalists within both the capitalist and the communist blocs, but it is a prospect far superior to one of second-rate military powers barking over the arrogance and conceit of the major powers.

While neither side in the cold war is prepared to face the consequences of a warless world, this is really not at issue. *Both nations now seem prepared to face the catastrophic consequences of World War Three.* We cannot resolve the sociological issues until we have solved the military issues. And since they are clearly interrelated, it is best not to confuse the requirement of one with our desires for the other.

We are on the high road to new sophistication in arms-control thinking. People have begun to understand that the elimination of the short-run danger of a thermonuclear war does not require the sort of ambitious comprehensiveness, such as limitations to sovereignty, that are needed to achieve a world government. To eliminate the threat of World War III we need the following: (a) machinery (perhaps of a military type) to prevent the spread of nuclear and perhaps conventional weapons beyond present boundaries—something that the Soviet government is doing in relation to East Germany and China, and something that the "mixed manned" approach is designed to achieve by maintaining effective control by the United States; (b) the end of foreign territories as nuclear missile outposts. This use has the political effect of lining up the smaller nations into "camps" and severely limits their mediative effectiveness. The growth of Polaris soft-bases has just about made most hard missile sites technically obsolete; hence, the way is open to a general agreement on nuclear-free zones not only in Africa and Latin America but more decisively in Europe and Asia as well; (c) a mutual pact to reduce arms spending by set amounts each year until full disarmament is reached. This long-range process could also include measures for the joint use of USA-USSR funds to aid developing regions; (d) a nonaggression treaty between the NATO countries and the Warsaw Pact nations as part of any meaningful bilateral settlement. United States' disarmament director William C. Foster has predicted safe passage through Congress for such a treaty if negotiators can agree in principle to its need, while the Soviet Union's interest in such a treaty is well known; (e) an accord on measures reducing the threat of accidental war between the nuclear powers. The signing of the "hot-wire" measure, which creates for the first time a direct communications link between Washington and Moscow, has come as a genuine shock to certain pacifist elements—more perhaps because of its initial sponsorship by the Hudson Institute than because of any weakness in the proposal itself; (f) cooperation at the scientific and social levels, involving joint research and study of *peacetime* problems: i.e., teams of lawyers to study arrangements concerning property rights and air-space rights vis-à-vis interplanetary travel, the pooling of medical information on radiation hazards, joint research on communications systems in the nuclear era, the development of educational programs to make both countries bilingual in Russian and English.

These and many other moves in the direction of preventing World War III can be institutionalized rapidly and without impinging on some of the more ticklish long-range dilemmas. We should not be caught putting the cart before the horse, that is, predicating disarmament negotiations on lofty federalist premises. In the first place, to predicate a peace settlement on an expanded peace force that would exclude the Great Powers is utopianism in the negative sense, since the present conflict is of direct concern precisely to the Great Powers. And in the second place, there are few signs, if any, that national sovereignty is less valued now than it was a century ago. Indeed, at no earlier period has the national unit been a more powerful inspiration to social and political action. Nor, one might add, is nationalism a proved foe of world peace. The type of nationalism employed by the developing nations has proved to be of inestimable value in the forging of a "one world" attitude.

The evidence that world federalism and world peace are inseparable has not as yet been presented. Those who blithely talk of "limited world government" might do well to spell out just what these "limits" are before urging their purified, and yes, moralistic-totalistic solutions on social scientists. And if the acceptance of such a world government involves "dragging many kicking and screaming social scientists into a disarmed world," I for one fail to appreciate the bizarre humor of a pacifist dragging anyone, anywhere, at any time.

The "contradiction" posed by Raymond Aron (1954, 1959) between the "nation-state basis of politics" and "long term peace" is misleading. The nation-state is not uniquely an enemy to peace; reactionary social systems, backward political and military elites are. The idea of nation-hood has given a sense of independence and courage to people in the developing areas. Perhaps this nationalism will tend to frustrate the achievement of a homogeneous world, but at the same time, the new nationalism confronts the major nuclear powers as a revolutionizing force: as a peace-making force. It is the younger nations, liberated from colonialism, that have been in the forefront of the struggle for denucle-arized zones.

The contradiction belongs to Aron. He alone must square a belief in a "greater French community" with the struggle of the former colonies for national independence and national identity. It is he who must explain how France expects to be taken into the comity of nations while at the same time brandishing atomic weapons in defiance of previous test-ban agreements. It would be most unfortunate if we were to deny the possibility of a bilateral arms ban and resurrect the carcass of world federalism as a means of appeasing French pride and prejudice. The slogan of limited sovereignty will not only undermine direct negotiations, but, ironically, will sabotage the efforts of the developing nations for a greater role in the pacification of the world precisely through the emergence of independent sovereignty. Clearly, any bilateral arms agreement will be confronted with the reluctance of certain European and Asian states to curb their own nuclear ambitions. Nostalgia dies hard. The fiction of an independent nuclear deterrent—a fiction already recognized by the Labour leadership in England—may complicate an overall East-West settlement. But these are at least bearable complications, if for no other reason than that they are real. Such problems as the kind of apparatus needed to prevent a nuclear spread are surely more significant than are scenarios designed to prove that a world without war entails a world without nations.

My root contention is that conflict may prove as valuable a tool for conflict-resolution as is consensus, and that as a matter of fact, conflict patterns are more fruitful to examine than are consensual models since they square better with issues related to social development and interpersonal relations. In this, my position differs from those who tend to conceive of conflict as an interruption in the natural conditions of harmony. It is precisely the advocates of world federalism who demand a consensus of interests as a prelude to peace. It is they who speak of the "discredited" notions of self-determination, collective security, internationalism—all in the name of world government, no less! This is precisely what I mean by fanaticism. If "utopianism" signifies a mad rush to do away with the instruments of national independence in the post-World War II world, then I certainly am "profoundly antiutopian."

This in no way entails "extended arms race" as a guarantee of peace. Contrary to the beliefs of the New Civilian Militarists, disarmament and not deterrence is the fundamental need and task of our generation. However, it is important to realize that disarmament is a process not an event. The forces working to secure a durable peace must start modestly by mutual consent to establish an apparatus to prevent accidental wars, then move forward to work out a moratorium on nuclear testing, and move from that point to the establishment of a ceiling on the production of certain types of (if not all) nuclear weapons. If we can get to this dizzying height, then such matters as the sale of arms to "neutral nations" and transferring military power perhaps to the United Nations can be soberly entertained. Those who wish to see nuclear weapons phased out and conventional weapons and armies take their place if necessary do so not in any belief that conventional war is necessarily less lethal, ugly, or unjust, but because it allows for far more individual and group initiative along the way. Such a position has nothing in common with extending the arms race.

The functional convergence of the Soviet Union and the United States on a wide gamut of social, cultural, and political traits has become unmistakable (Sorokin, 1960). It is one of the fine ironies of the cold war that the Soviet Union, along with the United States, now shares the "onus" of being a "have" nation—and a selfish one that hardly contributes more than a fraction of its GNP to Third World growth. It is precisely these convergency sets that put into perspective the differences between the two powers.

There is a definite need to see the things that bind, no less than those that divide the two powers. This does not mean that the lines between democratic and totalitarian politics should be blurred. But it does mean that the issue of world peace may be viewed as operating on a level apart from such considerations. To use the racial issue as an example of American democracy and Soviet totalitarianism is surely one of the fine ironies of cold-war rhetoric. Nor would things be righted by "proving" American totalitarianism by pointing to the cold-blooded murder of Medgar Evers and William Moore in the same America. This line of reasoning is no better than that line employed by Soviet propagandists of the Hungarian uprising of 1956 as proof that American imperialism "fomented" fascist counterrevolution. Rhetoric about "our" democracy and "their" totalitarianism is precisely the kind of ideological irrelevancy that acts to prolong mutual hostilities and suspicions. The question of world annihilation is not a question of political interests—democratic or otherwise. It is not even a question of conventional warfare. It is a question of the right to maintain differences and even the right to do battle on behalf of felt interests. A bilateral settlement of the use of nuclear weapons only makes possible a continuation of differences. Bilateralism is programmed conflict—nothing more and nothing less. This loose talk about democracy and autocracy makes suspect federalist schemes for limiting sovereignty—the sovereignty of others.

Although France and China constitute their own threat to the U.S. and the U.S.S.R., this threat in itself is not sufficient to produce an American-Soviet alliance. The bilateral agreement on arms testing is something considerably less ambitious than would be an American-Soviet alliance. However, it is clear that France and China, each in its own way, are contributing to those pressures making for an arms agreement. We will omit reference to the Sino-Soviet schism, since I have taken this up elsewhere in a different connection (Horowitz, 1963). Let us concentrate on the effects of Chinese "hard-line" policies on the United States. It has been authoritatively reported that a policy paradox concerning Communist China is haunting American policy-makers. The report indicates that "administration leaders are saying that Communist China will be the nation's number one foreign affairs problem over the next decade." The State Department indicates that the dimension of the problem, if not the character, will change dramatically when the Chinese explode their first nuclear device. The new belligerence of the Chinese, whatever its causal base, will put just as much pressure on the United States as it will on Soviet Russia. Indeed, the pressure on SEATO nations aligned to the United States will probably be greater by far than anything the Soviet Union has had to endure, militarily at least. The support in underdeveloped regions for the hard Maoist position thus opens up dangerous possibilities for both the United States and the Soviet Union. If this is so, the need for a test-ban treaty is made more urgent than it was even two years ago (*The New York Times,* May 1963).

The French insistence on an independent nuclear deterrent has caused no end of anxiety to the United States. The recent statement by French Defense Minister Pierre Messmer that his government will pursue a policy of targeting enemy cities rather than military sites, what Messmer quaintly called a "demographic approach," points up most vividly the dangers of the nuclear spread (*The New York Times,* April 1963). The essential uncontrollable nature of nuclear politics, even of tactical matters within the NATO alliance, points up just the sort of risks entailed in a policy of drift. The problem of the nuclear spread may be manageable in 1963 without a test ban, but it would take an incorrigible optimist to assert that things would be no worse by 1973, or sooner if France and China harvest a sizable independent arsenal. Both the United States and the Soviet Union have much to answer for by making their respective nuclear stockpiles a matter of national prestige and national honor. But it is only they who can break this false standard of power and security. The absence of an American-Soviet arms agreement, in light of the steady rise of nth-power weapons systems, compounds the problem of disarmament qualitatively as well as quantitatively, since a multilateral settlement in the future would be much more difficult to execute than a bilateral settlement at present.

So intent are some on blueprinting unilateralism and federalism that the major events of the present period tend to be overlooked: the breakdown of cold-war alliances, and the redefinition of relations between nations that is its inevitable consequence. As D.F. Fleming (1963) has summarized:

> The recent challenges by Mao of Kremlin leadership in the Soviet bloc and by De Gaulle of American leadership in the Western bloc have made the foundations of the Cold War unstable. China defied all the rules of the nuclear club, until she could get into it; France accepted the new principle

that national sovereignty now resides in obliterative capacity and that prestige depends upon it. De Gaulle's design for Europe calls for forbidding all peace-making until the Americans no longer need their land bases in Europe and leave and until the New Europe is strong enough to deal with a Soviet Union which, eventually weakened by conflict with China, will have no choice but to join the great Gaullist European family. The prospect of a European power independent of the United States and unchecked by Great Britain drew protest from Moscow. In view of these circumstances, making peace in cooperation with Russia is not out of the question. The United States and the Soviet Union, the two great powers, have been drifting toward a common ground.

Some peace researchers seem to feel that preventing war is not feasible, since without a curb on national sovereignty wars cannot be eliminated. This seems to me a case of moralizing politics *in extremis*. The insistence on measures to eliminate war always seems to involve extraordinary means. Some federalists have actually argued the case for a war to end all wars, a war on sovereignty (Reves, 1945; see also Horowitz, 1957). Others propose an expanded peace force under United Nations supervision, excluding the Great Powers (Sohn, 1962; see also Clark and Sohn, 1958). In both systems, there is a metaphysical predisposition to consider the elimination of war as something radically distinct from the prevention of war. Here again, when peace is viewed as an event rather than a process, certain insolubles arise.

The world federalist position conveniently overlooks the fact that the distribution of United Nations voting strength is considerably different from the distribution of political and military power. If the big powers tolerate and even support a United Nations resolution on Suez or on Israeli-Arab differences, it is because a tolerance for juridical settlement exists when major-power interests are *not* involved. It would be a dangerous illusion to expect a United Nations settlement where conflict arises between the major powers. The Korean conflict of 1950-53 showed the relative impotence of the United Nations to function as a peace-making agency without a bilateral consensus. The Korean conflict was finally settled because the Soviet Union and the United States were both unprepared to escalate the conflict to nuclear proportions. The war had become risky, costly, and essentially pointless. The peace-making capacity of the United Nations was seriously compromised by the prolongation of hostilities, and the goals of the Soviet Union and the United States alike were waylaid in the process. The lesson of that conflict ought not to be forgotten: the option, the *best* alternative to disarmament and arms-limitation agreements, is not "victory" but stalemate; not the preservation of democracy, but the extension of tyranny. Likewise, the China-India border dispute was not settled by any rarified world court, but by the Soviet Union's unwillingness to supply China with petroleum supplies, its unwillingness to suspend the sale of MIG fighters to India, and even its unwillingness to allocate blame or responsibility for the disputed territory. It is just as clear that the resolution of the Cuban missile crisis was bilateral in character. The United States and the Soviet Union reached an informal accord: remove Soviet missile sites in Cuba, and the United States would move toward a pacific settlement of problems with the Castro government.

All this is not to deny the value and the validity of the United Nations as the basic instrument available for the elimination of future wars. But it should be quite clear that the central task at present is the prevention of future wars. And this task remains, not for too much longer perhaps, in the hands of Russia and the United States. If there can be a general accord on the rules for preventing World War Three perhaps it will then be possible to establish a machinery for the elimination of war as such. But first things first.

It is not that one must naturally assume that peace is only realistic within the present structure of international relations. It is the other way around. Given the present international military and political alignments, what kind of negotiations at a disarmament conference are likely to produce a new comity of nations? My position derives from that tradition in political theory (Hobbes, Rousseau, and Hegel) that holds that sovereignty is by nature and definition unlimited. As Hobbes said, the very meaning of *civitas* implies "that great Leviathan, or mortal god, to which we owe under the immortal God, our peace and defense." To speak of limited sovereignty is thus a contradiction in terms. One might speak of the displacement of one sovereignty by another, of one juridical apparatus by another, and in this special sense there are limits to sovereign power. Perhaps the best gauge of national sovereignty is how little effect "proletarian internationalism" has in regulating the relations between socialist Leviathans like the Soviet Union and China; or the "Western Alliance" has in curbing French military aspirations vis-a-vis the United States. Thus, socialism has disturbed the national basis of power and rule no more than has capitalism.

But to speak of unlimited sovereignty as if it were the mortal foe of world peace is to ignore the essential task of sovereignty, the very reason for nationhood, for *civitas:* the preservation of peace. It is only under conditions of war, of anarchy, that the "rule of law" and the "security of men" dissolve. How would a struggle to limit sovereignty aid in settling outstanding issues that divide major and minor powers alike? The argument against nationalism often spills over into a form of misanthropic Ludditism. At this level, it is no better and no worse than the argument for world peace through the liquidation of technological innovation.

If I remain unconvinced that peace necessitates a radical overhauling of the social system and unintimidated by a warrior pacifism, it is not without an appreciation of the complexities of the relation between political and moral dimensions of the peace question. Political morality dictates that a peace settlement between the major thermonuclear powers be given top priority. Moralizing politics is something else again. For it is precisely in the name of irreducible *interests* that modern wars are fought. It is not cynicism that motivates my belief that a big-power bilateral settlement is in the offing, but a shared conviction that this is the best kind of settlement possible in the immediate future.

That a bilateral arms agreement may employ "undemocratic" methods in limiting the size of the nuclear club and the number of nuclear weapons, that such a peace may restrict even legitimate aspirations of developing states, that such a peace may bridle the restorationist phantasies of a De Gaulle and lead Mao Tse-tung to vituperative condemnations of Soviet "right opportunism" is perhaps the *price* of peace. Even peace has a price. For some, this may prove to be an expensive proposition. However, it is my belief that barring a major social change in the world alignment of capitalist and socialist states, peace is worth twice the price! That the citizenry of a developing area might not come to the same conclusion underscores the strength of interest thinking and sectional morality. But this only emphasizes once more the relativity of value judgments even as they relate to the goodness of peace on one side and the goodness of social development on the other. Permit me to conclude with a reminder from Dostoyevsky's *The Brothers Karamazov:* "But after all, what is goodness? Answer me that, Alexey. Goodness is one thing with me and another with a Chinaman, so it's a relative thing. Or isn't it? Is it not relative? A treacherous question! You won't laugh if I tell you it's kept me awake two nights. I only wonder how people can live and think nothing of it. Vanity!"

1965

VI

THE END
OF
POLITICS?

21

Social Deviance
and
Political Marginality

The Welfare Model of Social Problems

The study of social deviance within American sociology has traditionally been based on a model that views delinquent behavior as a problem best handled by social-welfare instruments in the society. Those who accept this model have sought to humanize the visible agencies of social control (the police, judiciary, and welfare agents) by converting them from punitive instruments into rehabilitative instruments. This underlying premise that punishment and rehabilitation are the only two possible responses to deviance is responsible for the current tendency to evaluate deviant behavior in *therapeutic* rather than *political* terms (Nettler, 1958–59:203–212).

The rehabilitation model seeks as its long-range goal a more human redefinition of the moral code. Its short-range goal is to indicate that in ascribing subordinate status to deviants, agencies of social control adopt a superordinate role. Coser (1965:145) recognized this role conflict in the welfare orientation to *poverty* when he indicated that "in the very process of being helped and assisted, the poor are assigned to a special career that impairs their identity and becomes a stigma which marks their intercourse with others."

However serviceable this model of social deviance has been in the past, and notwithstanding its use in resisting encroachments on the civil liberties of accused deviants, the social-welfare model does not exhaust present options—either on logical or pragmatic grounds. A relationship

377

of equals is possible only in democratic politics, where conflicts are resolved by power rather than a priori considerations of ascribed status. Only in such politics can deviants attain the status of legitimate combatants in social conflict.

Political Requisites of Social Problems

In the traditional welfare model, deviant behavior is defined as a social problem. This definition stands on several important assumptions about the nature of deviance. First, it takes for granted that deviance is a problem about which something should be done. Second, it assumes that deviance is a *public* problem, which means that social agencies have the right to intervene. Finally, deviance is treated as a social problem in contradistinction to a political issue. Decisions concerning it are relegated to administrative policy rather than the political arena. As a result, deviance is handled by experts instead of being debated by the publics who are supposedly menaced.

These beliefs about the nature of deviance have scant empirical justification. They do not derive from recognized characteristics of deviance. Rather, they are normative statements about how deviant behavior should be treated. Bernard (1958–59:213) has shown a singular appreciation of this:

> Values are inherent in the very concept of social problems. The conditions that are viewed as social problems are evaluated by the decision-maker as bad, as requiring change or reform. Something must be done about them. The reason for coming to the conclusion may be humanitarian, utilitarian, or functional. In any case, a system of values is always implicit, and usually quite explicit.

In this framework, identification of the values of the decision-makers is crucial. If we take the above seriously, the selection of decision-makers who define deviance as a social problem is as Becker indicates (1963:7), a *political* process, not just a value problem.

> The question of what the purpose or goal of a group is, and, consequently, what things will help or hinder the achievement of that purpose, is very often a political question. Factions within the group disagree and maneuver to have their own definition of the group's function accepted. The function of the group or organization, then, is decided in political conflict, not given in the nature of the organization. If this is true, then it is likewise true that the questions of what rules are to be enforced, what behavior regarded as deviant and what people labeled as outsiders must also be regarded as political.

The decision to treat deviance as a social problem is itself a political decision. It represents the political ability of one group of decision-makers to impose on the society those decisions concerning deviance that reflect their particular value sentiments. The anomaly is that although the political decision has been to treat deviance as a nonpolitical problem, deviance persists as a political problem. A comprehensive analysis of deviance must determine which decision-makers define deviance as a social problem and their reasons for doing so. Lemert (1951:4) was almost alone among the sociologists of the past decade in contending that deviance does not pose an objectively serious problem:

> In studying the problem-defining reactions of a community, it can be shown that public consciousness of "problems" and aggregate moral reactions frequently center around forms of behavior which on closer analysis often prove to be of minor importance in the social system. Conversely, community members not infrequently ignore behavior which is a major disruptive influence on their lives. We are all too familiar with the way in which populations in various cities and states have been aroused to frenzied punitive action against sex offenders. Nevertheless, in these same areas the people as a whole often are indifferent toward crimes committed by businessmen or corporations—crimes which affect far more people and which may be far more serious over a period of time.

A Conflict Model of Deviance

Deviance is a conflict between at least two parties: superordinates who make and enforce rules and subordinates whose behavior violates those rules. Lemert (1967: v) noted the implications of this conflict for those trying to isolate the sources of deviance: "Their common concern is with social control and its consequences for deviance. This is a large turn away from older sociology which tended to rest heavily upon the idea that deviance leads to social control. I have come to believe that the reverse idea, i.e., social control leads to deviance, is equally tenable and the potentially richer premise for studying deviance in modern society."

The conflict model implies alternative definitions of deviance as a problem: the deviant behavior itself, and the actions of rule-makers to prevent such behavior. The political climate prescribes both the conflicts that will occur between deviants and nondeviants and the rules by which such conflicts will be resolved. The struggle of groups for legitimation thus constitutes an integral part of deviant behavior.

Deviance has been studied by employing a consensus welfare model rather than a conflict model because, for the most part, decision-making concerning deviance has been one-sided: the superordinate parties who regulate deviance have developed measures of control, while the subordinate parties, the deviants themselves, have not entered the political arena. The conflict, though existent, has remained hidden. As Becker (1967: 240–241) correctly notes, this leads to a nonpolitical treatment of deviance.

> It is a situation in which, while conflict and tension exist in the hierarchy, the conflict has not become openly political. The conflicting segments or ranks are not organized for conflict; no one attempts to alter the shape of the hierarchy. While subordinates may complain about the treatment they receive from those above them, they do not propose to move to a position of equality with them or to reverse positions in the hierarchy. Thus, no one proposes that addicts should make and enforce laws for policemen, that patients should prescribe for doctors, or that adolescents should give orders to adults. We call this the *apolitical* case.

As the politicalization of deviance develops, this apolitical case will become atypical—the hidden conflict will become visible and deviants can be expected to demand changes in the configuration of the social hierarchy.

Although there has been scattered intellectual opposition to asylums in the past, patients have as yet not been organized to eliminate or radically alter mental hospitals; or addicts to legalize drug use; or criminals to abolish prisons. Synanon, a center formed by addicts to treat drug addiction, is a striking exception to this pattern. Staffed completely by former addicts, it has no professional therapists. Thus, it represents those who argue that deviants themselves are best able to define their own problems and deal with them. Ironically, while Synanon challenges both the right and competence of professional therapists to intervene in the lives of addicts, it has not discarded the value premises of an adjustment therapy. Nonetheless, as Yablonsky (1965: 368) indicates, this marks a departure from the conventional welfare model:

> Over the past fifty years, the treatment of social problems has been dropped into the professional lap and has been held onto tightly. The propaganda about the professional's exclusive right to treat social problems has reached its high mark. The professionals, the public, and even patients are firmly convinced that the only "bona fide" treatments and "cures" available come from "legitimate professionals" with the right set of degrees.

Even where deviant social movements have become powerful, they have avoided political participation as special interest groups. For instance, Synanon has acted politically only when new zoning codes threatened its very existence. The politicalization of deviance is occurring, as groups like homosexuals and drug addicts pioneer the development of organizational responses to harassment. A broad base for the legitimation of deviant behavior will increasingly be made.

The political questions inherent in a conflict model of deviance focus on the use of social control in society. What behavior is forbidden? How is this behavior controlled? At issue is a conflict between individual freedom and social restraint, with social disorder (anarchy) and authoritarian social control (Leviathan) as the polar expressions. The resolution of this conflict entails a political decision about how much social disorder will be tolerated at the expense of how much social control. This choice cannot be confronted as long as deviance is relegated to the arena of administrative policy-making. For example, public school education is considered to be repressive by many black youths, yet black youths do not have the political option of refusing to attend school or radically altering public school education. This problem is now being politicalized by Black Power advocates who demand indigenous control over schools in black ghettos despite the citywide taxation network.

Political Marginality and Social Deviance: An Obsolete Distinction

Conventional wisdom about deviance is reinforced by the highly formalistic vision of politics held by many social workers and sociological theorists. This view confines politics to the formal juridical aspects of social life, such as the electoral process, and to the maintenance of a party apparatus through procedural norms. In this view, only behavior within the electoral process is defined as political in character, thus excluding acts of social deviance from the area of legitimacy (Campbell, et al., 1960; Key, 1961; Lipset, 1960; Lubell, 1952).

In its liberal form—the form most readily adopted by social pathologists—the majoritarian formulation of politics prevails. This is a framework limited to the political strategies available to majorities or to powerful minorities having access to elite groups (Mills, 1963: 525–552). The strategies available to disenfranchised minorities are largely ignored, and thus the politics of deviance also goes unexamined. The behavior of rule makers and law enforcers is treated as a policy decision rather than a political phenomenon, while a needlessly severe distinction is made between law and politics. Analyses of political reality at the level of electoral results help foster this limited conception of politics. Consequently, sociologists have placed the study of deviant behavior at one end of the spectrum and the study of political behavior at the other.

Conventional nonpolitical responses on the part of sociologists were possible largely because the political world itself has encouraged this kind of crisp differentiation between personal deviance and public dissent. Political deviance is a concept rarely invoked by politicians because the notion of politics implies the right of dissent. Lemert points out that this right has not always been respected for radical political deviants (Lemert, 1951: 203–209). There is a history of punitive response to political deviants in this country, involving repression of anarchists, communists, socialists, and labor organizers. This has spread at times to a persecution of liberal groups as well. What characterized the "McCarthy Era" was not the hunt for radicals, but rather a broadening of the definition of radicals to include all sorts of mild dissenters. Only on rare occasions has political deviance been defined as a major social problem requiring severe repression. Thus, with the possible exception of anarchists, communists, and socialists (and sometimes even including these groups in the political spectrum normally defined as legitimate), there is no way of dealing with political life as a deviant area. The nature of American political pluralism itself promotes dissent, at least in the ideal version of the American political system. The onus of responsibility in the castigation of a political victim is upon the victimizer. Rights and guarantees are often marshaled on behalf of a widening of the political dialogue. Indeed, the definition of American democracy has often been in terms of minority supports rather than majority victories.

The area of personal deviance is not covered by the same set of norms governing minority political life. Responsibility for deviant behavior, whether it be drug addiction, homosexuality, alcoholism, or prostitution, is not borne by the person making the charges, but rather is attached to the victims of such charges. The widespread recognition of the juridical shakiness of the deviant's position serves to privatize the deviant and embolden those who press for the legal prosecution of deviance. While the right to dissent politically is guaranteed (within certain limits), the right to dissent socially is almost totally denied those without high social status.

One simple test of society's "double standard" might be the examination of society's perceived reactions to political radicalism in contrast to its response to social deviance. If a person is accused of being an anarchist, a certain "halo effect" may actually be perceived. Perhaps a charge of naiveté or ignorance will be made against the politically marginal man, but not a censorious response demanding nonpolitical behavior.

In the area of deviance, however, if there is a self-proclamation of drug addiction or alcoholism, the demand for therapeutic or punitive action follows very quickly. If one admits to being a drug addict, society's response is to remove the curse from everyday life by the incarceration of the "patient" in a total institution, so that at least the visibility of deviance is diminished.

The line between the social deviant and the political marginal is fading. It is rapidly becoming an obsolete distinction. As this happens, political dissent by deviant means will become subject to the types of repression that have been traditional to social deviance. This development compels social scientists to reconsider their definitions of the entire range of social phenomena—from deviance to politics. Wolfgang and Ferracuti have taken an important first step toward an interdisciplinary study of social violence (Wolfgang and Ferracuti, 1967: 1–14).

This viewpoint implies a new connection between social problems and political action. The old division between the two can no longer be sustained. In terms of theory, the new conditions throw into doubt the entire history of political science as an examination of the electoral situation and of social problems research as a study of personal welfare. If politics is amplified to incorporate all forms of pressure, whether by deviants or orthodox pressure groups, to change the established social order and if sociology is redefined to include pressure by deviants to redesign the social system so that they can be accepted by the general society on their own terms, then there is a common fusion, a common drive, and a common necessity between sociology and political science, not only on the level of empirical facts, but also on the level of scientific interpretation.

Some sociologists have already adapted to this new situation. Cloward's work in organizing welfare recipients is a particularly striking effort, although an outrageous breach of both classical capitalist and socialist ideologies (Cloward and Elman, 1966: 27–35). This marks the first time that a sociologist has been involved in organizing welfare recipients. This enlargement of roles demonstrates that changes are occurring in what constitutes political life and social work—even if such efforts might properly be characterized as naive or premature.

There are several other important directions that applied sociologists might follow: drug addicts might be organized to alter laws concerning drug use, students might be organized to change the conditions of schools, and mental patients might be organized to change the way they are treated. In each of these cases, change would be initiated from below by members of subordinate marginal groups. This would be in sharp contrast to the conventional elitist pattern of politics, where decisions are made from above by members of the prevailing majority. This is the primary distinction between the existing political party style and the political outsider style that is currently emerging.

The Politicized Social Deviant

A serious dilemma for many deviant and marginal groups alike is their failure to find any main-line organizations (either overtly political or social) that can provide them with the sort of universal legitimation that governed an earlier, more tranquil period in American history. All formal and informal organizations seem arrayed against the kind of deviant particularisms expressed by freaks, Hell's Angels, or druggies. Thus the subgroups, whether of deviant lower-class origins or marginal middle-class origins, begin to align themselves with each other and against the mainstream of American life per se. A new set of cultural heroes, dance forms, and art forms coalesce to define not just a classical generational revolt, but a particularistic expression of immediate personal liberation as a prelude to a distant public egalitarianism.

That such particularistic responses may prove to be extremely effective, even if they involve small numbers, is effectively and graphically illustrated by the rise of guerilla insurgency as a military style in the underdeveloped areas. If "colored people" can conduct protracted struggles in Asia and in Africa, why can't the same sorts of struggles be conducted from the rooftops of Watts and Newark? Indeed, the expanding internationalization of the deviant and marginal groups can best be appreciated in cultural heroes such as Franz Fanon, Malcolm X, and others connected with the demimonde of the Black Power movement. The seeds of this movement were sown long ago in the works of Padmore and DuBois, who suggested precisely such ideological linkages with revolutionary forces elsewhere in the world—particularly in PanAfricanism. What was absent before was the mechanism for success. In the guerilla response to the power of the establishments, this mechanism, this critical missing ingredient, was finally supplied—and the linkage made complete.

The area of black affairs is particularly fertile ground for a revaluation of the relationship between deviance and politics. Originally, there was a clear distinction between vandalism for personal gain and acts of organization for political gain. When the political life of blacks was circumscribed by the NAACP, it became clear that political life entailed normative behavior within the formal civic culture. Similarly, it was clear that acts of personal deviance fell outside the realm of politics. Indeed, there was little contact between black deviants and participants in the civil rights protest.

The rise of civil disobedience as a mass strategy has blurred this distinction. Such disobedience entails personal deviance to attain political ends. Regardless of the political goals involved, it is a conscious violation of the law. The treatment of civil disobedience in the courts has therefore been marked by ambiguity. It is difficult to predict whether it will be treated as a political act of insurrection or a simple personal violation of the law. Many law-enforcement officials see no distinction between civil disobedience and crime, and they therefore blame the ideology of lawbreaking inherent in civil disobedience for rising crime rates and the occurrence of race riots (Lieberson, 1966:371–378).

In turn, these officials may be responding to the large-scale denials by blacks of the traditional role of the police as keepers of social order. This can be gauged not only directly, through the expressed attitudes of political leaders—from governors on down to sheriffs—but indirectly as well—that is, in the inability of local police forces to cope with black mass rioting. The Watts riots of August 1965 were, in this connection, symptomatic of the breakdown in traditional forms of police legitimacy. In that riot, which lasted four days, caused 34 deaths and 1,032 injuries, and ended in 4,000 arrests, the key fact was the role of the National Guard in quelling the riot. The Los Angeles police were unable to cope with the situation once the riot achieved paramilitary proportions. Clearly, this lesson has not been lost on black ghetto communities elsewhere in the United States.

Confining ourselves to the cluster of race riots that took place in June and July of 1967, we can see how the events in Watts heralded a new set of conditions in the relationship between deviance and politics. In the main riot areas of Chicago, Detroit, Cleveland, Cincinnati, Buffalo, and Newark (we will disregard for present purposes the satellite riots that took place in the smaller centers of Plainfield, Louisville, Hartford, Prattville, and Jackson), the following characteristics were prevalent in each community for the duration of the riot:

1. Each city requested and received National Guardsmen to restore social order. Correspondingly, in each city, the police proved to be ineffectual in coping with the riots once the shield of legitimation was removed.

2. In each city, there were deaths and serious injuries not only to the rioters but to the established police and invading guardsmen as well.

3. In each city, the riots lasted more than one day, the duration being from two to seven days, which indicates the guerilla-like nature of the struggle.

4. In each case, the triggering mechanism for the riot was an altercation involving police officials (usually traffic patrolmen) and blacks accused of reckless driving, driving without a license, or driving under the influence of alcohol.

5. In each case, the major rioting took place during summer months, when the normal load of black male unemployed is swelled by students and teenage former students not yet relocated.

6. In each city, property damage was extensive, with the sort of sniper tactics and "scorched earth" policies usually associated with so-called wars of national liberation.

7. In each case, the major rioting seemed to lack official civil rights organization sponsorship; however, participation in the protests did not take place on an individual basis.

The extent to which a conflict model dominates current black deviance and marginality alike can be gauged by the parallels with what has been called internal violence (Eckstein, 1964; Black and Labes, 1967: 555–570), and what is more customarily referred to as guerrilla warfare (Horowitz, 1967). The major riots of Los Angeles, Newark, and Detroit shared in the high number of injured and arrested, the high degree of property damage, and the massive number of national and state guardsmen used to quell the riots. One striking difference with overt guerrilla warfare is the low number of people killed—and this difference might be crucial in explaining the transitory and limited nature of the conflict; why rioting never quite resulted in armed insurrection.

What this amounts to is a military rather than a civil definition of the situation in racial ghettos. The essential deterrent was the raw firepower of the combatants rather than the legitimated authority of the police uniform. Under such circumstances, the established welfare distinction between juvenile delinquency and guerilla warfare means very little.

The rapidly rising crime rates indicate a further ambiguity in the traditional formulation of social deviance. It is of decreasing *sociological* importance whether "crime" is perceived as an act of politics or of deviance. The consequences are the same in either case: cities are becoming increasingly unsafe for whites, and white-owned businesses are suffering mounting losses. Whether it is political insurgency or traditional crime, the consequences remain the same—a disruption in the legitimation system of American society.

The Deviant Political Marginal

At the opposite pole—minoritarian politics—a similar set of ambiguities plagues those in search of precise boundary lines. An example is the behavioral pattern of the left wing. Among the radical youth of the 1930s certain characteristics emerged: a relatively straitlaced "puritan" ethos concerning sexual mores; a clear priority of politics over personal life— what might be called the ascetic purification of self; and a concern for a relatively well-defined ideology, combined with the encouragement for all to participate in the life of the working classes. The radical Left of an earlier generation shared with the dominant cultural milieu a distinct, even intense, disaffiliation from deviant patterns. Indeed, the old Left pointed to social deviance as illustrative of the moral degeneration of bourgeois society. The need for social revolution came about precisely because the existing social order was considered incapable of controlling social deviance. Thus, the demands of the traditional Left with respect to social deviance were not very different from Establishment demands.

This contrasts markedly with the response of the New Left on conventional indicators of deviance. First, the New Left exhibits substantial positive affect toward an extreme and libertarian ethos in place of puritanism. Second, there is an identification with deviant forms, stemming from a continued affiliation with the "beatnik" movement of the 1950s. (There was considerable absorption of the Beat generation of the 1950s into the activist generation of the 1960s.) The ideology of the New Left, insofar as it has clear guidelines, is based on freedom from repression. It has both political and social components: freedom for the black from the effects of racial discrimination; freedom for the student from the constraints of university regulations; freedom for the young generation from the demands of their elders; and freedom of politically powerless groups from the growing authority of the centralized state. In this sense, Freud feeds the ideology of the New Left at least as much as Marx defined the ideology of the old Left.

The traditional notion of a noble affiliation of radical youth with the working class has already been abandoned in favor of a highly positive response to deviant and marginal groups in American society. There is relative lack of concern for the traditional class alliances emerging from the common struggle for upward mobility. If there is a hero, it is the alienated man who understands what is wrong and seeks escape. Often, escape takes the form of social deviance, which is considered to be no worse than the forms of behavior traditionally defiend as normative. The traditional hero has been supplanted by the antihero, who wins and attains heroic proportions by not getting involved in the political process. This antihero is defined by what he is against as much as by what he is for; he is for a world of his own, free from outside constraints, in which he is free to experiment and experience.

What this means operationally is that the line between left-wing political behavior and personal deviance has been largely obliterated. Nowhere has this been more obvious than in the student protest movement, where it is impossible to separate the deviant student subculture from the substantive demands of the student revolt. Spence (1965: 217) accurately describes the significance of this student movement at the University of California at Berkeley:

> This was the first successful student strike at a major university in the United States. But more important, this was the first significant white-collar rebellion of our time. These sons and daughters of the middle class demonstrated and walked picket lines, not behind the moral banner of the oppressed Negro, but on the basis of their own grievances against a system that had deprived them of their rights of responsibility and self-expression.

The student rebellion underlies a major thesis herein proposed, since it led not to organized political responses of a conventional variety, but rather to a celebration of deviance itself as the ultimate response to orthodox politics. Stopping "the operation of the machine," which for Mario Savio "becomes so odious, makes you sick at heart that you can't take part; can't even tactically take part," led to only one conclusion: "The machine must be prevented from running at all" (Newfield, 1966: 27; Horowitz, 1965: 15–18).

It is interesting that victory was not defined as taking over the operations of the machine, not the classic capture of organized political power, but rather as nonparticipation and nonacceptance. Savio himself, as if in conscious defiance of Michels' "iron law of oligarchies" governing the performance of organizations, simply refused to participate in any leadership functions in the Berkeley postrebellion period. The definition of victory, then, is in the ability of marginal groups to disrupt the operations of political power either in its direct parliamentary form or in surrogate forms.

Among young members of the New Left, draft evasion has become an important form of deviance. The number of people who adopt the traditional political path by refusing to serve and going to jail as political prisoners is small compared with the number who adopt the deviant path, using mental illness, homosexuality, or drug addiction (whether these be real or feigned) to avoid serving. In effect, they are taking advantage of the prevailing established norms toward deviants. However, this path is made much more accessible with the merger of leftist politics and social deviance, since only politics can transform private desires into public principles.

An important social characteristic of the New Left is its self-definition as culturally *avant garde,* or conversely, not behind the times. This new goal of·leftism is also a central goal of the deviant subculture. So it is that Berkeley and Watts became the symbols of the twin arms of radical politics: the university campus and the black ghetto. Even in terms of social-psychological definitions of friends and foes, the line between the political Left and social deviance is now largely transcended. Thus, there is a deep distrust of formal politics and of the people who operate within the bureaucratic channels of the political apparatus. This definition of friends and foes is obvious at Berkeley, where many students feel that they cannot trust their elders.

The right-wing movement in America also illustrates this perspective. The old Right was characterized by extreme antipathy for any kind of promiscuous or overtly immoral behavior. The American Right viewed with alarm attacks upon law-enforcement officials. The old Right perceived itself conventionally as a paragon of law enforcement. This is the core around which the right wing has traditionally been established. But a phenomenon such as the Minutemen reveals the ease with which the Right accepted a spin-off from law-abiding to direct-action approaches to politics. The Minutemen, for example, are encouraged to acquire fully automatic weapons. Through organizations such as the National Rifle Association many become eligible to receive rifles and handguns at cost as well as free ammunition. The Minutemen *Handbook* contains lessons on such subjects as "Booby Traps," "Anti-Vehicular Mines," and "Incendiary Weapons Composition." The self-made saboteur is encouraged to improvise lethal weapons. Espionage and infiltration of established political groupings are also encouraged. A subunit called the Minuteman Intelligence Organization possesses a fairly sophisticated organization, not unlike those of paramilitary units (Turner, 1967: 69-76).

Breakaway segments of the New Right, like their opposite numbers in the New Left, are concerned with redefining the relationship of the person to legal code in very loose terms. The appeals to youth are in terms of training in weaponry rather than in law. When confronted by the law, for instance, the Minutemen dissolved their public leadership and created a new undergroup leadership. This phenomenon could become a more serious threat in American life, because so many armed forces veterans may be attracted to such a combination of politics and deviance. At the same time, similar military experiences may result in a Left turn, as with disillusioned veterans returning from Vietnam. A situation is arising where the line between the deviant act of gun-toting in an undisciplined way for personal (or political) ends and the use of "hardware" for the purpose of maintaining law and order is largely disappearing. Political conflict may become marked by armed confrontations between opposing marginal political groups, with the legitimate state agencies of power the enemy of both.

The Politics of Defiant Violence

Attention should now be drawn to the growing Latinization of black riots and student revolts in the present period. This is done in terms of rough macroscopic data. Here we wish to underscore this point by taking closer note of the workings of the new style of subculture in America. The largest black gang in Chicago during the 1960s was the Blackstone Rangers. This quasipolitical organization represents a clear example of the marked distinctions between criminal groups and marginal political groups, as well as the course the politics of marginality is likely to follow. The Rangers acted as an autonomous group, in conflict with both the local residents and the political powers. The gang entered into negotiations with the Chicago police and reached a satisfactory (if temporary) settlement: they agreed to surrender their weapons and stop fighting other gangs if the police would drop certain charges against their leaders and disarm a rival gang. The negotiations thus served to "keep the peace," but only at the expense of enhancing the credibility of the gang networks.

Negotiation of this sort is a major strategy of international politics, although it has seldom been used to resolve conflicts involving marginal domestic groups. The negotiation process itself entails the recognition that marginal groups represent legitimate political interests. So far, the art of negotiation has not been adequately developed for dealing with unconventional international conflicts.

The problem posed by marginal groups like the Rangers is not yet viewed as a political problem to be solved by political strategies. When police violated the negotiated settlement, the Blackstone Rangers made plans to file suit in the federal courts to prohibit a pattern of harassment. It is novel for such deviant groups to engage in political conflict with legitimate agencies like the police, but it does indicate a step beyond the "good-bad boy" approach of social welfare.

There is a growing impulse to develop political means of resolving conflicts involving marginal groups as an alternative to the military means that have thus far prevailed. The Woodlawn Organization, composed of local residents, received a federal grant of $927,341 to work with gangs like the Rangers and the Disciples. The Chicago police raided the first meeting between the gang leaders and leaders of The Woodlawn Organization, demonstrating a conflict between advocates of a political solution and proponents of what amounts to a military solution to the gang problem (Evans and Novak, 1967). In the absence of acceptable political solutions, it is probable that increasing reliance upon domestic military solutions will be sought—just as the failure of political solutions internationally often leads to pressure for quick military solutions.

This trend toward marginal politics reflects a rejection of conventional political styles that have proved to be unsuited to the needs of marginal groups. In the past, the powerless had recourse to two choices for political action: legitimate means, to which they did not have sufficient access to be influential; or accessible but ineffective illegitimate means that brought about few structural changes. Marginal minorities are now trying to develop political means that are both accessible and effective. It is probable that these new styles will be illegitimate rather than legitimate and that the distinction between social deviance and political insurgency will be further reduced.

Race riots differ from orthodox political maneuvers and acts of personal delinquency. They offer some important insights into what those seeking out new styles are aiming for. Race riots have an ideological core, while many other forms of collective behavior do not. They are avowedly political, organized, and purposeful. Typically, deviant acts such as theft, assault, and homicide have none of these attributes. For these reasons, race riots may be closer to organized unconventional warfare than to conventional crime. Once perceived in this way, they constitute a powerful if latent political weapon.

At present, in most American cities a relatively small police force can effectively control the populace. But this is true only as long as police are accorded legitimacy. When conflicts are defined totally in terms of power and force rather than authority and legitimacy, as is the case during race riots, the police cannot effectively maintain control. For this reason, riots constitute a major departure from established patterns of interaction between police and deviants. Deviants are not organized to battle police, and they have no ideology that labels police as enemies to be attacked and destroyed. Police have legitimacy as long as deviants avoid rather than attack them. However, police traditionally mount an organized collective effort against deviants, who typically respond only as unorganized individuals. The existing conflict is a one-sided war. The emergence of a bilateral conflict situation promises to be a major development in the link between politics and deviance. Race riots are the first indication of this emergence (Cray, 1967: 121).

This conflict can assume several alternative forms: on a *minimax* scale, there could be de-escalation to an equivalent of the English system, in which both black militants (or deviants in general) and police do not carry arms; at the other end, there could be escalation to race riots, which are sporadic and constitute a relatively unorganized set of events. Beyond sporadic racial strife lies the possibility of sustained conventional war. This is most closely approximated in American history by the Indian Wars and the Civil War. Presently, unconventional warfare is coming into focus. The latter two possibilities indicate how social deviance could spill over into insurrectionary politics, given both the peculiar racial division that exists in American society and the consistent exclusion of marginal groups from political and social legitimacy.

This marginal style of politics is being adopted by groups of all "extreme" ideological persuasions. Marginals of both the Left and the Right fear the growing power of the centralized government; that bureaucratic stratum which seemingly grows far beyond other social classes. This commonality is demonstrated by the high degree of social interaction that occurs, in places like Greenwich Village and Berkeley, between politically opposed deviant groups. Even such political opposites as the Hell's Angels and the opponents of the Vietnam War shared a common social network in California. Their political enmity was balanced by their similar enjoyment of deviant social patterns (Thompson, 1966: 231–257).

The clearest example of this movement toward violence, and one easily overlooked, is the reappearance of assassination as a political style, coupled with the inability to know whether "Left," "Right," or "Deviant" is spearheading this style. It is almost impossible to say whether the assassination of John F. Kennedy, Malcolm X, or Martin Luther King was a deviant act or a political act. No group took responsibility for the assassinations as overt political acts, and the assassins did not link the deaths to ideological demands. Without taking into account the breakdown in the distinction between politics and deviance, the meaningfulness of both sociology and political science is seriously compromised.

Marginal Sectors and Deviant Values

Applied social science must take account of this new view of marginality in American life. If any group has emerged as the human carrier of newly allied political and private deviance, it has been the *lumpenproletariat*, or the nonworking class. This group has replaced the established working and middle classes as the deciding political force in America. Lang and Lang (1961: 18) point out in their discussion of collective dynamics that this is precisely the condition that breeds collective deviance. Ordinarily the cleavages within a society are between clearly constituted social strata or between parties whose special interests seek recognition within a broader framework of order. When cleavages occur between the representatives of constituted authority and those who challenge that authority, or those who feel unable to share in the established authority systems, we can refer to the condition as one of widespread and general alienation.

The army of marginally employed comprises a significant segment of *both* politically radical and socially deviant cultures. While in Western Europe the bureaucracy grew disproportionately to all other classes, the disproportionate rise of the marginally employed characterizes contemporary America. This group, rather than disappearing—or, as Marx would have it, becoming a social scum to be wiped out by revolution— grows even larger. At a practical level, there is now a new and powerful intermediary class that performs vital roles in the authoritarian political system while at the same time setting the style for a new libertarian morality.

The boundaries of American politics reflect the growing affluence that typifies the American social structure. However, a significant minority of disaffected marginals exists in the midst of this affluence. It is becoming increasingly clear that these marginals threaten to destroy the fruits of general affluence and, indeed, to disrupt the entire situation. Race riots are a more serious indicator of the inability of the political system to maintain its equilibrium despite the general affluence.

The overlap of deviance and marginality is well captured in a book on the Hell's Angels (Thompson, 1966). The Hell's Angels—with the Swastika, German helmet, and Iron Cross as their main symbols—differ but slightly from the pseudo-Maoist organizations of the Left. Without wishing to equate Maoists with either Minutemen or Hell's Angels, it is clear that each of these groups is marginal and deviant with respect to established political norms. Further, it is difficult to give conventional definitions to those holding a gun in one hand and a flower in the other.

The Angels have given up hope that the world is going to change for them. They assume, on good evidence, that the people who run the social machinery have little use for outlaw motorcyclists, and they are reconciled to being losers. But instead of losing quietly, one by one, they have banded together with a mindless kind of loyalty and moved outside the framework, for good or ill. They may not have the answer; but at least they are still on their feet. It is safe to say that no Hell's Angel has ever heard of Joe Hill or would know a Wobbly from a bushmaster, but there is something very similar about their attitudes. The Industrial Workers of the World had serious blueprints for society, while the Hell's Angels mean only to defy the social machinery. There is no talk among the Angels of building a better world, yet their reactions to the world they live in are rooted in the same kind of anarchic, para-legal sense of conviction that brought the armed wrath of the Establishment down on the Wobblies. There is the same kind of suicidal loyalty, the same kind of in-group rituals and nicknames, and above all, the same feelings of constant warfare with an unjust world (Thompson, 1966:265–266).

The policy response to this dilemma has been the Welfare State—an attempt to "cool out" the marginal underclass and minimize the potential danger it poses. It is an attempt to avoid the consequences of large-scale marginality without making any social structural changes. Schatzman and Strauss (1966: 12) contend that this welfare style deals with the problem by avoiding its political implications:

> America pours its wealth into vast numbers of opportunity programs to achieve its goals and names almost any conceivable group, event, or thing a social problem if it can be seen as threatening the achievement of these goals. Hence its concern for the culturally deprived, the under-achievers, the school dropouts, the job displaced, the aged, the ill, the retarded, and the mentally disturbed. This concern goes beyond that of the nineteenth-century humanitarians who involved themselves with the underprivileged outgroups on moral grounds. Now all these aggregates are seen as special groups whose conditions are intolerable to society, if not actually threatening, in light of today's social and economic requirements.

The logic by which efforts were made to handle a highly political problem by depoliticizing it has proved inadequate. The welfare solution has not eliminated the consequences of having a growing number of disaffected people in the midst of general affluence. Indeed, the very existence of affluence on so wide a scale creates demands that parallel those made by the "poor nations" on the "rich nations." Because of this, a political attempt to solve the problem is bound to emerge. If this attempt is not initiated from above within the legitimate political or electoral apparatus, it will be generated from below and probably take illegitimate, paramilitary forms.

The implicit exchange system that formerly existed between the very poor and the very rich in American society was simple: Don't bother us and we won't bother you." In exchange for the poor not disturbing the rich, the wealthy provided just enough money for the poor to live at Ricardian subsistence levels. This exchange has been the basis of American social work and continues to define the boundaries of the welfare system. The rich have only vaguely appreciated the magnitude of the poor's potential power and their ability to disrupt the entire system. For their part, the poor only vaguely appreciate the power at the disposal of the rich, which accounts for the suicidal characteristics of many race riots.

This interchange system is now being threatened. The poor are gradually developing an appreciation of their own power, while at the same time they have greater appreciation of the power held by the rich. For their part, the rich are becoming more aware of the power available to the poor, as seen in the generalized fear created by rising crime rates and race riots. In short, there is a greater polarization of conflict between the two classes.

The primary political problem of deviance can be framed as a Hobbesian dilemma. Hobbes sought the creation of the state as a solution to the problem of social disorder in which individuals war with each other in pursuit of their individual interests. The dilemma is that the creation of the state creates a problem of social control. The solution to the problem of chaos, or the Anarch, is the Leviathan. But the Leviathan is the *totalitarian* state. Indeed, totalitarianism is the perfect solution to the problem of disorder. The dilemma for those who consider social problems as obstacles to be overcome is that any true overcoming of social problems implies a perfect social system. And this entails several goals: first, the total institutionalization of all people; second, thoroughgoing equilibrium between the parts of a system with respect to their functioning and the functioning of other sectors; and third, the elimination of social change as either a fact or value. Thus, the resolution of social problems from the point of view of the social system would signify the totalitarian resolution of social life.

The political problem posed by deviance is how to avoid social disorder while at the same time avoiding the problem of total social control. It is a dilemma precisely because of the impossibility of solving both problems simultaneously. Political decisions about deviance must reflect judgments about the relative dangers of these two problems and must constitute a weighing process based on ethical no less than empirical considerations.

Connections between deviance and politics take place most often when a society does not satisfactorily manage its affairs. For better or worse, a well-ordered society is one that can maintain a distinction in its responses to deviance, on the one hand, and to marginality, on the other. Antecedents for the linkage of deviance and marginality exist in two "conflict societies." In the 1890s in Russia, the *Narodnik* movement was directly linked to the movement toward personal liberation. In Germany of the 1920s, the "underground" movement, aptly summed up by the Brecht theater, nihilism, and amoralism, gave rise to both Nazi and Bolshevik political tendencies. The merger of the Beat generation and the radical student movements reveals this same pattern of connecting political revolution with demands for personal liberation.

These examples indicate how the fusion between deviant behavior and political processes is a prelude to radical change. If the fusion of politics and deviance is the herald of revolution, or at least the indicator of a high degree of dissociation and disorganization within the society, then radical changes in the structure of American social and political life are imminent.

What takes place in the individual's life has major political ramifications in contemporary society. Until now, American life has been resilient enough to forestall a crisis in treating marginality. This is a testimonial to the flexibility of the American system of political legitimation. But it might well be that the extent of deviance in the past was not sufficient to cause more than a ripple in the political system (Hopper, 1964:313–330). In the emerging system, with automation and cybernation creating greater dislocation and marginal employment, personal deviance may generate a distinct transformation in normal political functions; it marks the point at which the political system cannot cope with deviant expressions of discontent.

A political description of this condition begins with the inability of American society to resolve political problems that are important to *marginal* people. Almost one-third of the potential voting population does not vote and is therefore without even the most minimal political representation. The fact that these disenfranchised people have important problems in common that cannot be managed within existing arrangements creates a volatile situation (Schattschneider, 1960).

Political styles evolve that are not presently labeled as political behavior, much as race riots are not now generally considered as political behavior. These new styles are characterized, first, by a rejection of the legitimacy of the existing political system (the challenge to the rules by which the game is now played); second, by a rejection of compromise as a political style; and third, by a willingness to oppose established authority with illicit power in order to change not merely the rules but the game itself. Ends will attain a primacy over means, whereas a concern with the legitimacy of means has traditionally characterized American politics. Direct expressions of power might assume more important roles than legitimate authority in resolving important conflicts.

Political legitimacy is itself subject to change in order to meet the demands of a society in which social deviants and political marginals have become more, rather than less, important in determining the structure of American society.

1968

22

The New Unholy Alliance:
Social Science
and
Policy-Makers

How do politicians judge and assess social scientists, especially those social scientists in the academic community most intimately involved in the affairs of the political domain? The answer lies in the degree to which there exists a mutuality or incompatibility of interests between the two sectors.

Problems and Prospects in the Interaction
of Social Scientists and Federal Administrators

To construct a satisfactory framework we should focus on problem areas that are decisive for both groups: initially, how the interaction is perceived by the social scientists to be followed by a presentation of problem areas perceived by politicians. There is also the shadowy area of the consequences of the interaction of social scientists and administrators for the network of proposals and responses resulting from their relationship. Social scientists and politicians do not just interact with one another; the professional ideologies they arrive at and the norms they establish also guide present and future interactions.

One of the most serious and, at the same time, difficult to resolve aspects of the relationship of social scientists to politicians is determining at what point normative behavior leaves off and conflictual behavior starts. Only with the latter sort of interaction does a true problem-solving situation exist. For example, the norm of secrecy that guides bureaucratic behavior contrasts markedly with the norm of publicity governing most forms of academic behavior. There is little question that this normative distinction leads to a considerable amount of exacerbated sentiment. Yet, the differences between the two groups at this level are intrinsic to the nature of sovereignty and the nature of science. Such differences can hardly be "ironed out" or "smoothed over" simply because we would have a nicer world if they were. Thus, at best, an explication of the issues can permit an intellectual and ideological climate to unfold in which differences may be recognized and in this way come to be lived with. This must be stated explicitly. Those who expect a set of recommendations for the governance of relations between social scientists and politicians should be dissuaded from such an approach, lest we find ourselves manufacturing perfect doctrinal formulas and juridical restraints that prove to be far worse than the initial problem being considered.

Problem Areas Perceived by Social Scientists

The first and perhaps most immediate experience the social scientists have with politicians or their counterparts on various federal granting agencies relates to the financial structure of contracts and grants. First, the difference between contracts and grants should be explained. As an operational definition we can speak of contracts as those agreements made with social scientists that originate in a federal bureaucracy. Most research on Thailand and Southeast Asia or on Pax Americana is contract work. Grants can be considered as those projects initiated by the social scientists. Nonetheless, the distinction between contracts and grants should not be drawn too sharply, in fact if not in law, many contracts do originate with social scientists. Such agreements may be structured broadly to give the researcher a vast range of freedom or they may be narrowly conceived to produce a project tailored to an agency's "needs." The entrepreneurial spirit of social scientists, particularly those working in nonacademic research centers, makes them ingeniously adept at discovering what a government administrator is ready to pay for. Thus, while a *de jure* distinction between contracts and grants is useful, it is limited on *de facto* grounds by a subsequent inability to track down who originates a proposal and also who really shapes the final project.

Perhaps more important than the formal distinction between contracts and grants is the disproportionate amount of funds made available by various federal agencies for social-scientific purposes. The Department of Defense in the fiscal year 1967 budgeted 21.7 percent of its research funds for the social sciences. The Department of State budgeted only 1.6 percent of its funds for the social sciences, and most of this was in the separately administered Agency for International Development. This disparity indicates that the "modern" Department of Defense (DoD) is far readier to make use of social science results than is the "traditional" Department of State. A related complaint is that most contracts issued, in contrast to grants awarded by agencies such as the U.S. Department of Health, Education, and Welfare (HEW) or the National Institutes of Health (NIH), allocate little money for free-floating research. Funds are targeted so directly and budgeted so carefully that, with the exception of the overhead portion, which is controlled by administrators rather than scholars, little elasticity is permitted for work that may be allied to but not directly connected with the specific purpose of the contract itself. This contrasts markedly with contracts made with many physical scientists and even with researchers in the field of mental health, who are often able to set aside a portion of their funds for innovative purposes. Even so-called "kept" organizations such as the Institute for Defense Analysis (IDA), System Development Corporation (SDC), or RAND enjoy more latitude in developing their work programs than do the usual "free" university researchers.

Related to this matter of financial reward for "hardware" and "high-payoff" research is the funding available for social-science research as a whole. Social scientists often claim that the funding structure is irrational. Government funds are available for individual scholarly efforts. The government reinforces big-team research by encouraging large-scale grants administered by agencies and institutes and by its stubborn unwillingness to contribute to individual scholarly enterprise. The assumption is made that large-scale ideas can be executed only by large-scale spending—a fallacy in logic, if not in plain fact. Large-scale grants are also made because they minimize bureaucratic opposition within the government and eliminate specific responsibility for research failures. At the same time, this approach contributes to the dilemma of the scholar who is concerned with research at modest "retail" levels that may be far more limited than the grant proposal itself indicates. The present contract structure encourages a degree of entrepreneurial hypocrisy that is often alien to the spirit of the individual researcher and costly to the purchaser of ideas and plans. And while individual agency efforts, notably by the National Science Foundation, have moved counter to this bureaucratic trend, the bulk of funds continues to be made available without much regard for the persons actually engaged in the researches.

Social scientists have become increasingly critical of the government's established norms of secrecy. The professional orientation of social scientists has normally been directed toward publicity rather than secrecy. This fosters sharp differences in opinion and attitudes between the polity and the academy since their reward systems for career advancement are so clearly polarized. The question of secrecy is intimately connected with matters of policy because the standing rule of policy-makers (particularly in the field of foreign affairs) is not to reveal themselves entirely. No government in the game of international politics feels that its policies can be candidly revealed for full public review; therefore, operational research done in connection with policy considerations is customarily bound by the canons of government privacy. While social scientists have a fetish for publicizing their information, in part as a mechanism for professional advancement no less than a definition of their essential role in the society, the political branches of society have as their fetish the protection of private documents and privileged information. Therefore, the polity places a premium not only on acquiring vital information but also on maintaining silence about such information precisely to the degree that the data might be of high decisional value. This norm leads to differing premiums between analysts and policy-makers and to tensions between them.

Social scientists complain that the norm of secrecy often demands that they sacrifice their own essential work premises. A critical factor reinforcing the unwilling acceptance of the norm of secrecy by social scientists is that a great deal of the funds set aside for research are allocated for military or semimilitary purposes. U.S. Senate testimony has shown that approximately 50 percent of federal funds targeted for the social sciences is subject to some sort of federal review check. The real wonder turns out to be not the existence of restrictions on the use of social-science findings but the relative availability of large chunks of information.

A question arising with greater frequency now that many social scientists are conducting federally sponsored research concerns the relationship between heuristic and valuative aspects of work. Put plainly, should the social scientist not only supply an operational framework of information but also assist in the creation of a viable ideological framework? Does he have the right to discuss, examine, and prescribe the goals of social research for social science? Whether social scientists in government service ever raise such issues is less important than the fact that some might refuse any connection with the federal bureaucracy for this reason. Many social scientists, especially those working on foreign-area research, bitterly complain that government policy-makers envision social science to be limited to heuristics, to supplying operational code books and facts about our own and other societies, and that the social scientist is supposed to perform maintenance services for military missions. Social scientists, however, also consider their work in terms of its normative function, in terms of the principles and goals of foreign and domestic policy. Given their small tolerance for error, policy-makers cannot absorb mistaken evaluations. This inhibits the social scientist's long-range evaluations and renders empiricism the common denominator of investigation. Factual presentations become not only "value free" but "trouble free."

This is indicative not so much of a choice between pure and applied social-science research as of a consequence of differing perspectives on the character of application. Social scientists working for the political establishment realize that applied research is clearly here to stay. They are the first to announce that it is probably the most novel element in American—in contrast to European—social science. But federal bureaucrats operate with a concept of application that often removes theoretical considerations from research. By designing the future out of present-day hard facts, rather than analyzing types of action and interests and their relations in the present, the government comes to stand for a limited administrative Utopianism, and this creates the illusion that demands for theory and candid ideological commitment have been met.

The social world is constructed like a behavioral field, the dynamics and manipulation of which are reserved for policy-makers, upon which the future is designed. But social scientists are aware that "interests" and their representative values are contending for influence on that field and that social planning is often a matter of choosing among these values for the sake of political goals. Thus, tension arises between social scientists, who consider their work set in highly political terms, and federal bureaucrats, who prefer to consider the work of the social scientists in non-political terms. Indeed, federal administrators particularly go out of their way to depoliticize the results of potentially volatile social research so as to render it a better legitimizing device for their own bureaucratic activities. Social scientists come to suspect that their work is weighed for efficiency and applicability to an immediate and limited situation. The ability of the social system to confront large-scale and long-standing problems is left out of reckoning.

Federal bureaucrats measure the rewards of social-science involvement in the government in terms of payoffs generated. These are conceived to be the results of "big-team" research involving heavy funding (like the Model Cities Program). Moreover, the high status of individuals is appreciated when they are at the center rather than the periphery of policy performance, having an opportunity to influence policy at high levels, to secure valuable information, and to lend prestige to projects in which they participate. And, it might be added, many social scientists who contract research from the government seek just such power rewards.

Even those social scientists most involved with the government—as employees rather than marginal consultants—express profound reservations about the reward system. First, as we have noted, social scientists operate under various degrees of secrecy that stifle their urge to seek publicity for the work they do. Recognition goes instead to the men they work for. Second, social scientists must share responsibility for policy mistakes. Thus, they may be targeted for public criticism under difficult conditions more frequently than they are praised when they perform their duties well. Finally, those social scientists closest to policy agencies are most subject to congressional inquiry and to forms of harassment and investigation unlike anything that may befall strictly academic men.

The government-employed social scientist runs risks to which his colleagues at universities are not subject. He often contends that these risks are neither properly understood by academics nor sufficiently rewarded by policy-makers. (Salary scales, for example, are adequate in federal work but not noticeably higher than academic salaries.) Marginal financial payoffs resulting from publication are often denied the federally sponsored social scientists. Publication is a sensitive area for other reasons. Social scientists' fears concerning their removal from channels of professional respectability and visibility seem to increase proportionately with their distance from the academy. Few of those in federal work receive recognition from their own professional societies and few gain influential positions within these professional establishments. The marginality produced by federal work means that scholars willing to be funded through government agencies, or even to accept consultantships, will reject primary association with a federal administration. For this reason the list of high-quality social scientists who choose to remain in the government as professional civil servants remains low.

While outsiders may accuse federally sponsored social scientists of "selling out," the latter defend themselves by pointing out that they make sacrifices for the sake of positively influencing social change. This self-defense, however, is often received skeptically by their colleagues in the academic arena (as well as by their would-be supporters in the federal bureaucracy), who regard such hypersensitive moralism with suspicion. The upshot of this matter of "rewards" is then that status derived from proximity to sources of power is offset by isolation from the actual wielders of power—academic no less than political.

Problem Areas Perceived by the Politicians

Social scientists' complaints about their difficulties with government-sponsored research have received more attention than administrative complaints against social scientists simply because social scientists tend to be more articulate in examining their feelings and registering their complaints about the work they do. Also, the relationship of the social scientist to the bureaucrat has a greater import for the social scientist than for the bureaucrat. It is small wonder that government complaints about social scientists have been poorly understood.

Federal agencies and their bureaucratic leaderships remain skeptical about the necessity for employing basic social-science data in their own formulations. Among traditionally appointed officials the local lawyer or party worker is the key means for transmitting information upward. For many sectors of the military, expertise comes mainly from military personnel performing military functions and does not require outside social-science validation. As we witnessed in the military response to the Department of Defense "Whiz Kids," outside efforts may be considered intrusions. High military brass (as well as a number of politicians) "sounded off" hotly against the Defense Department and echoed in their critiques a traditional posture that pits military intuition and empirical proximity to the real world against mathematical techniques and "ivory-tower" orientations.

When social scientists attempt to combat these doubts and suspicions by preparing memoranda and documents to prove the efficacy of social science for direct political and military use, they may do more to reinforce negative sentiments than to overcome them. When the academy responds that way to the polity (as it did in its recommendations to the Defense Science Board), then it underwrites its own lack of autonomy, if not its own ineptitude. It cannot prove its worth by moral declarations and public offerings to bureaucratic agencies. The total service orientation of social research is one that breeds contempt for the performer of such services and a lack of faith in the results. This helps to explain the resentment for social-science research extending from the Joint Chiefs of Staff to the Senate Foreign Relations Committee. Suppliers of intellectual labor are well paid if they have a powerful union or guild—as many social sciences have—but they hardly command high status in a political atmosphere straining toward quick and inexpensive solutions.

The first and perhaps most significant criticism made by administrators against the academy is that social scientists make excessive demands for funds and special treatment while working on projects that frequently have little tactical value. This is translated into a charge of impracticality. Typical is the critique made by the General Accounting Office against the Hudson Institute, headed by defense strategist Herman Kahn. Underlining charges made by the Office of Civil Defense, the G.A.O. charged that the work of the Hudson Institute in the area of the behavioral sciences was "less useful than had been expected" and cited as unacceptable without "major revision." Various social-science reports, particularly those prepared by semiprivate agencies, have been criticized for their superficiality, for their "tired" thinking, for their sensationalism, and, above all, for their lack of immediate relevance. In response, social researchers claim that the purpose of a good report is imaginative effort rather than practical settlement of all outstanding issues. Government agencies should not expect a high rate of success on every research attempt, they argue. One reason for the persistence of this line of criticism is that demands for high-payoff utilitarian research are rarely contested. The questionable practicality of much social-science research remains a sore point in the relationship, which cannot be resolved until and unless social scientists themselves work out a comfortable formula governing the worth of relevance in contrast to the demand for relevance.

Another criticism leveled at academics by federal sponsors issues from the first: namely, that there are no systems for ensuring that results obtained in research be usable. A gap exists between the proposal and fulfillment stages of a research undertaking and there is an equally wide gap between the results obtained and the processes involved in grappling with problems. Proposals that are handsomely drawn up and attractively packaged often have disappointing results. And while many sophisticated agencies, such as NIH (National Institutes of Health), NSF (National Science Foundation), or OEO (Office of Economic Opportunity), are aware of the need for permissiveness in research design, those agencies more firmly rooted in hard science and engineering traditions are not so tolerant of such experimentations. Moreover, it is charged that academics engaged in government research "overconservatize" their responses to placate a federal bureaucracy. This may come, however, at the very point when the administrator is trying to establish some liberal policy departures. The chore of the federal agency becomes much more difficult since it must cope not only with bureaucratic sloth and the conservative bias of top officials but also with reinforcements for it in research reports by the social scientists from whom more liberal formulations might have been expected. Thus, not only is there a gap between proposal stage and fulfillment stage in the research enterprise, but some reports may also structure conservative biases into the programs assigned to the federal bureaucracy by congressional committees or by executive branch leadership.

The charge of inutility is often related to a differential intellectual style or culture. The government-versus-academy cleavage is largely a consequence of intellectual specialization of a kind that makes it difficult for the typical bureaucrat to talk meaningfully with the typical "modern" behavioral scientists. Most government officers in the Department of State, for example, are trained either in history or in a political science of a normative sort. International relations taught in the descriptive traditions of the twenties or, at the latest, in the style of a Morgenthau or a Schuman, continue to prevail. Whatever difficulties may exist between the academy and the polity at the level of role performance, these can at least be overcome by those who share a common intellectual formation. But often communication cannot be achieved with those behaviorists whose vocabulary, methods, and even concepts seem esoteric, irrelevant, occasionally trivial, and not rarely fraudulent. Thus, at the root of the charge of inutility is a conflict of intellectual cultures that negatively affects the relations between the academics and the politicians.

Federal administrators point out that academic men often demand deferential treatment, contrary to the norms that govern other federal employees. They charge that social-science personnel do not really accept their role as government employees but rather see themselves as transiently or marginally connected to the government. Particularly in areas of foreign affairs, the academic appears to want the advantages of being privy to all kinds of quasisecret information and of being involved in decision-making, yet avoids normal responsibilities that are accepted by other government employees.

Such attitudes smack of elitism to federal officials, an elitism built into the structure of social-scientific thinking. Trained to analyze problems rather than convince constituencies, social scientists become impatient with the vagaries of politics, preferring the challenge of policy. One reason adduced by elected officials for preferring legal rather than social-scientific advisers is that the former have a far keener appreciation of mechanisms for governing people and being governed by them. The legal culture breeds a respect for the "popular will" rarely found among social scientists attached to government agencies. Indeed, the resentment expressed by many House and Senate committees against Defense Department and State Department social scientists is a direct response to the elitist streak that seems to characterize social scientists in government.

This is the reverse side of the "involvement-autonomy" debate. The government pushes for total involvement and participation while the social scientist presses for autonomy and limited responsibility in decisions directly affecting policy. Elitism rationalizes the performance of important service while enabling the social scientist to maintain the appearance of detachment. Although social scientists view their own federal involvement as marginal, at the same time they demand access to top elites so that they may be assured their recommendations will be implemented or at least seriously considered. But access at this level entails bypassing the standard bureaucratic channels through which other federal employees must go.

The social scientist's demand for elite accessibility, though said to be inspired by noble purpose, tends to set him apart from other employees of the federal government. He sees himself as an advising expert instead of an employee. The social scientist takes himself seriously as an appointed official playing a political role in a way that most other federal workers do not. The federal bureaucracy finds that the social scientist has come to Washington to "set the world on fire," unmindful of the flame that may also burn in the heart of the staff administrator.

The question of ready access to leadership rests on notions of the superior wisdom of the social scientist; however, it is precisely this claim that is most sharply contested by federal administrators. Reflecting popular biases, administrators claim that the easy admission of social scientists to the halls of power presumes a correctness in their policy judgments not supported by historical events and not warranted by mass support from popular sectors. The separation of scientist and citizen roles often justifies the lack of citizen participation. The scientific ethos thus serves as a basis for admission into a system of power by circumventing the civic culture. This precisely is why federal bureaucrats feel that they are defending their political constituencies (and not, incidentally, their own bailiwicks) by limiting social-science participation in the decision-making process.

If social scientists chafe at being outside the mainstream of academic life during their period of involvement with the political system, the federal bureaucrats are themselves highly piqued by the degree of supplemental employment enjoyed and desired by the social scientists. Also, in clear contrast with other federal governmental personnel, social scientists are able to locate supplemental positions in the Washington, D.C. area. They work as teachers and professors; they write for newspapers and magazines; they edit books and monographs; they offer themselves as specialist consultants, capitalizing on their government involvement. They become active in self-promotion to a degree far beyond the reasons for their being hired.

In the more loosely structured world of the academy, such self-promotion not only goes uncriticized but is rewarded. Royalty payments for textbook writing, involvement with publishing firms in editorial capacities, honoraria connected with membership in granting agencies and payments for lectures on American campuses are all highly respected forms of supplemental "employment." But federal-government employment involves 12 months a year and 24 hours a day. This condition and its demands are far different from the nine months a year and fluid scheduling endemic to most social-scientist relations with academic institutions. Federal agencies disdain the marginal aspects of the academics' involvement in political life, and their awareness that men involved in government effort are often enough not representative of the most outstanding talent available in the social sciences also disturbs them, particularly because they traffic in the status spinoff of both the academy and the polity. The anomaly exists that men who may not have been especially successful in academic life make demands upon the federal bureaucracy as if in fact they were the most outstanding representatives of their fields. The same problems might well arise in connection with outstanding representatives from the social sciences, but the situation becomes exacerbated precisely because the federal bureaucrats know they are dealing with—at least in many instances—second- or even third-echelon federally employed social scientists.

Improving Interaction

In this profile, academics and federal administrators alike have been presented as more uniform in their responses to each other than is actually the case. It should not be imagined that the two groups spend all their time in bickering criticism of each other, for then certainly no stable relationship worth speaking of could exist. Still, the roles acted out by both parties make it clear that we are in a period of extensive redefinition. The criticisms that academics and politicos have of each other often have a mirror-image effect, each side sharply focusing on the least commendable features of the other. Significantly, the political context and content of this issue has in the main been unconsciously suppressed by both sides. The academics have preferred to emphasize their scientific activities in objective and neutral terminology while the politicos express their interests in organizational and bureaucratic terms. The strangest aspect of this interaction, then, is that in the world of politics it seems that nothing is more embarrassing than political analysis and synthesis. As if by common consent, social scientists and policy-makers have agreed to conduct their relations by a code of genteel disdain rather than open confrontation. The gulf between the two groups requires political distance as an operational equivalent to the social distance between competing tribal villagers.

There may be cause for concern that federal-government sponsorship corrupts the character of social-science output because it emphasizes big money, an overly practical orientation, and limited dissemination of information, and because it fails to accept the possibility that some of the research it funds may turn out to be potentially subversive. But, ironically, timid or opportunistic social-scientific personnel are not recruited by the government. Most often the social scientist seeks the federal sponsor and becomes overly ambitious in the process of pressing exaggerated claims for unique research designs and high-payoff potential. The chief danger for the academic who has come to depend on the federal bureaucracy for research funds and its variety of career satisfactions is not more financial dependence; rather, it is that he may begin to develop the loyalties and cautionary temperament of the opportunistic civil servant per se.

Many interlocking appointments between the academy and the polity have occurred at the organizational level without resolving persistent questions as to what constitutes legitimate interaction between social science and public policy. This indicates that the line between the academy and the polity is blurred enough to require precise determination of exactly who is stimulating what kind of research and under what conditions. As it becomes increasingly clear that social scientists are the stimulants and administrators the respondents in a majority of instances, it becomes obvious also that criticism must be leveled at social-science participation rather than federal practice. To understand fully the sources of tension in the interaction between academics and administrators it is necessary to illuminate the range of attitudes on the proper links between the government and the academy, which extends from calls for complete integration of administrators and academics to calls for the complete rupture of the two groups. A spectrum of positions is presented on this matter.

The quarter-century from 1945 to 1970 has seen the rise of the full range. From World War II, and even prior to that during the era of the New Deal, optimism prevailed about an integrated relationship between academics and administrators. This was perhaps best expressed by the "policy-science" approach frequently associated with the work of Harold Lasswell (1951). In his view, the relationship between social science and the political networks would be an internal affair, with political men involved in scientific affairs just as frequently and as fully as scientific men would be involved in political affairs. The policy-science approach was a noble effort to redefine familiar departmental divisions of labor. Sociology, political science, economics, and the other social sciences would be absorbed by a unified policy science that involved a common methodological core. The problem with this exchange network, as Lasswell himself well understood in later years, is that federal administrators spoke with the presumed authority of the "garrison state," while academics (even those temporarily in government service) spoke with the presumed impracticality of the "ivory tower."

The policy-science approach did in fact have direct policy consequences. The end of World War II and the fifties saw the rise of new forms of institutional arrangements for housing social science. But more than organization was involved. A new emphasis cut across disciplinary boundaries. Area studies emerged in every major university. Communism was studied as part of the more general problem of the role of ideology in social change. This was followed by centers for urban studies and the study of industrial and labor relations. But despite the rise of institutionalized methods for uniting specialities, university department structures had a strange way of persisting, not just as lingering fossils but as expanding spheres of influence. It soon became apparent that in the struggle to influence the graduate student world and to decide who should or should not be appointed and promoted in university positions the "department" held final authority. The separate departments of social sciences enabled the disciplines to retain their vitality. At the same time that the policy-science approach was confronting departmentalism, disciplinary specialization was increasing. During the postwar period, anthropology insisted on departmental arrangements distinguishing it from sociology and theology, while other areas such as political science and social work become more sharply delineated than ever before. The policy-science approach was able to institutionalize all sorts of aggressive and, at times, even progressive reorderings of available information, but failed to establish the existence of a policy-science organization. And this proved to be fatal to its claims for operational primacy.

The policy-science approach of the fifties was supplanted by the "handmaiden" approach of the early sixties in which social science was to supply the necessary ingredients to make the political world function smoothly. The reasoning was that the social sciences were uniquely qualified to instill styles in federal decision-making based on confirmed data. But this was not to entail complete integration of services and functions. This handmaiden approach was considered more suitable to the nature of both the sciences and the policy-making aspects of government and was materially assisted by a rising emphasis on applied social research. The new emphasis on application and on large-scale research provided the theoretical rationale for janitorial "mop-up" services. Applied research was to make the search for the big news, for the vital thrust; participation in this intimate consensual arrangement would deprive the social sciences of their freedom but would guarantee relevance. The "theoryless" service approach was thus wedded to an action orientation.

Advocates of the handmaiden approach such as Ithiel de Sola Pool (1967) vigorously defended the social scientists' obligation to do meaningful research for government. It was noted that an organization like the Department of Defense has manifold needs for the tools of social-science analysis as a means for better understanding its world. It was pointed out that the intelligence test had been an operational instrument in manpower management since World War I and that the Defense Department and other federal agencies had become major users of social psychology in military and sensitive areas. As the world's largest training and educational institution, the U.S. government had to acquire exact knowledge for the selection and training of an enormous number of human subjects. Equally significant was the federal government's need for exact foreign-area information. This thirst for knowledge of the particular cultural values and social and political structures of foreign countries increased as the world was carved up into potential enemies or potential allies of the United States.

The ironic aspect of this support for useful research is that although the handmaiden approach ostensibly left social-science autonomy intact, it reduced that autonomy in fact by establishing criteria for federal rather than social science "payoff." High-yield research areas uniformly involved what the social sciences could do for the political structures and not necessarily the other way around. Thus, while the policy-science approach gave way to the service-industry orientation of the handmaiden approach, the latter, too, was not based on any real parity between the academy and the polity.

A new approach, considerably removed from both the policy-science and handmaiden approaches, has been finely articulated by David B. Truman (1968). As theory, it expresses a renewed sense of equity and parity between social scientists and administrators. Under Truman's arrangement there would be frequent but largely unplanned interchanges between federal bureaucratic positions and university positions. This exchange of roles would prove valuable and could eventually be explored and encouraged on a systematic basis. Meanwhile, the selective-participation approach advocates minimal formal structure in the system.

The most important aspect of the selective-participation approach is that it is based on a norm of reciprocity. A partial interchange of personnel could be accomplished primarily through regular seminars and conferences mutually attended by social scientists and government administrators, each cluster of individuals representing carefully designed combinations. Another method might be alternating presentations of scientific development and policy problems at these meetings. Unlike the normal consultant relationship of the handmaiden style, this would guarantee some kind of equity between the academy and the polity. Selective participation would include securing grants and promoting federal research for multidisciplinary teams of academics working on political problems, instead of the usual outright political employment of individual social scientists or academic talent. This, it was hoped, would provide a flexible arrangement of specialties that would fill the gap between scientific knowledge and public purpose without detriment to either social scientists or political policymakers. Operationally, it meant a greater flow of funds from government agencies to research institutes housed on university campuses, a not inconsequential changeover from the policy-science approach, which projected a much more intimate ecological as well as ideological network.

The dilemma was that the selective-participation approach implicitly assumed an exchange network with a parity of strength between political decision-makers and academics. The approach failed to demonstrate that the academic would be on a par with the administrator, for the latter had financial inputs while the former had informational outputs. In point of fact the government agency still does the hiring, even in the selective-participation approach; and the academics participate in a policy-making role without much expectation of a payoff for social-science theory or methodology.

This has given rise to what might be called the principle of non-participation" that is increasingly being adopted. Social scientists continue to write and publish in areas of foreign research or in sectors vital to the national political arena but do not do so under government contract or as a direct response to a federal agency. It was felt that if the autonomy of the social sciences means anything at all, uses and findings legitimately arrived at will be incorporated into federal policy-making whether or not social scientists participate actively or critically. The principle of nonparticipation tended to be adopted by many conservative as well as radical social scientists who saw in the growth of federal social research a threat to the standard forms of status advancement in the professions and also a movement toward applied social planning that violated their own feeling for the generalizing nature of social science. On organizational and intellectual grounds, the principle of nonparticipation served as an effective response to the policy-science approach. The underlying assumption of the notion of nonparticipation is that the federal government has more to gain than does the social scientist by the interaction between them. Although interaction would be maintained, the order of priorities would be changed so that social scientists no longer would have the onerous task of providing high-payoff research for others with low yields to themselves.

In many ways the principle of nonparticipation suggested that the university department remain the primary agency in the organization of social science instead of the federal research bureau. The nonparticipant in federal programs often found himself to be the critic of bureaucratic research in general and of bureaucratic agencies attached to universities in particular. He did not want to have his research controlled by federal decision-making; more importantly, he did not want a federal agency to usurp what was properly a judgment in the domain of a university department. At the same time, the principle of nonparticipation spilled over into the principle of active opposition. This opposition was registered in the main by younger scholars in areas such as history and by graduate students in the social sciences; that is, among those often involved in student protest movements. From their point of view the matter could not be resolved on the essentially conservative grounds of selective use by the government of the best of social science. A conscious attempt must be made to utilize scholarship for partisan or revolutionary goals, which could under no circumstances be employed by the establishments linked to government agencies. As Hans Morgenthau indicated, this represented a movement away from the belief that the social scientist and the federal administrator inhabited mutually exclusive institutions to a belief in a more active opposition because they occupied mutually hostile positions with antithetical goals.

In one sense, the radical posture accepts the policy-science appraisal of a political world dominated by the "garrison state" but rejects its remedy of social-science immersion to reorient government away from its predatory world missions. The policy-science view assumed the educability of military-minded rulers. The antiparticipation view assumes the reverse, namely, the ease with which social scientists become incorporated into the military and political goals of men of power.

Radical critics like John McDermott assert that in practice the goals of the academy and the polity have become antithetical. Furthermore, they say that, theoretically, they ought to be antithetical. A transformation of the dream of action into the nightmare of federal participation, in which the academy became in effect an adjunct of the federal establishment, has been brought about. Academic social scientists' dream of position and prestige has in some sense been realized by their transformation into men of action: academic men have become high priests of social change. The desire for social change has, in effect, overwhelmed the goals toward which such change was directed.

The move toward active opposition is a critique of the way in which the university, no less than the government, is structured. Those who moved away from federal participation simultaneously turned their energies on the university system. They hold that the academy itself, as beneficiary of federal funds, has become the political party of the academic man. The rash of student attacks against the university must be considered as, in part at least, symbolic attacks against the notion of integration of policy-making and academic performance. The most well-guarded nonsecret of the present era of university relations to the government, at least insofar as these ties bear upon the notion of active opposition, concerns the general political and ideological climate that now prevails. Surrogate politics has now become a rooted pattern in American academic affairs, partly because academics come to politics by way of political participation. Surrogate politics is also a reflex action of the expanding articulate but impotent social sectors against what have become the dominant political trends of the United States at this time.

Surrogate politics has its place in national affairs. Indeed, the question of the relationship between the academy and the polity is precisely a question of surrogate politics. A common undercurrent of moral revulsion for professional hucksterism and amateur gamesmanship has forced a collective review of the standpoint of social scientists and policy-makers. This same reexamination should have taken place a quarter-century ago, despite the difficulties of the situaton. But precisely because of the optimal consensus that existed in the past concerning the political climate, the issues now being discussed were considered improper topics for social scientists in pursuit of truth.

During the 1941-45 period, when the United States was engaged in a world conflict in which the overwhelming number of citizens felt involved in the very survival of civilization itself, there were no pained expressions about government recruiting on campuses. There was no resentment toward the retooling of universities to satisfy military requirements related to psychological warfare, propaganda research, or conventional bombing surveys. Nor were any scholarly panels held at professional meetings concerning the propriety of social scientists who accepted appointments under the Roosevelt administration in the Office of War Information or in the Office of Strategic Services, such as those panels that now discuss the propriety of relationships between social scientists and the Federal Bureau of Investigation or the Central Intelligence Agency.

Between 1946 and 1960, or the end of World War II and the beginning of the Kennedy era, the United States was involved in a cold war with the Soviet Union as its primary protagonist. We obviously are not here concerned with either the origins or the sources of the cold war but with the fact of its existence. It was during this period that social science was perhaps most partisan in its commitment to the American foreign-policy posture. This partisanship was manifested in many ways: the rise of think-tanks with direct federal sponsorship for applied social-science research; the emergence of specialized centers such as Russian centers, Southeast Asian centers, Latin American research councils, that once more were harnessed to the tasks of American foreign policy. Beyond that was the automatic assumption that social science did indeed have values, the values of the American century. The fanciful illusion that this did not constitute an ideology was nothing more than a chimera behind which the values of social science have never meshed more perfectly, either before or since, with the tasks of American foreign policy.

This same era was not so much one of transition from wartime to peacetime, but rather a movement from an overt world struggle between democracy (then defined as both capitalist and socialist in character) and fascism to one between capitalism and communism. As a result, this specific era witnessed in the West a growing resurgence of private enterprise. But in the United States, at least, this resurgence was more ideological than organizational. The bulk of funding for research and development continued to flow in ever-increasing amounts from public government sources. As a result, the real gap between state capitalism and state communism was far narrower in practice than in theory. It has been noted that this was also the period in which the real gap between scientific disciplines diminished to a commensurate degree (Price, 1965; Salomon, 1973). This ambiguous line between disciplines reflected itself specifically in the emergence of task-oriented social research. The rise of "team" efforts oriented toward predetermined "projects" resulted in a centralization of policy. The scientific background of key personnel mattered far less than did the social (or, as it sometimes turned out, antisocial) goals of the research design.

Between 1960 (the beginning of the thaw) and 1972 (the end of the Vietnamese conflict) controversy over the relationship between social science and political performance increased in both intensity and quantity. The breakdown of the consensus was made evident within the social-scientific communities by a series of surrogate discussions over the legitimacy of the war in Vietnam, Latin American self-determination, and civil strife in American ghettos. Unable to address such issues directly and unprepared to design structures for future alleviation of such world and national pressures, social scientists exaggerate the politics of inner organizational life. Professional societies engage in mimetic reproduction of central social concerns on a low-risk and probably a low-yield basis.

Organizational struggles also received, during this period, the encouragement and support of corresponding professional people and societies from the Third World and from minority groups. It is no accident that federal projects that had Latin American targets have come under particularly severe assault. The existence of a countersocial-science establishment in countries such as Mexico, Chile, Argentina, and Brazil provides vocal support for domestic United States academic opposition and for firming up such opposition by posing the threat of total isolation from foreign-area research for a failure to heed the dangers of certain kinds of political research. Increasingly, black militants in this country have adopted a similar posture of nonparticipation in social science projects without clearly stating preconditions for protection of the "rights" of the subjects of sovereigns.

Since 1972 the fervor over heedless involvement in policy has eased considerably. However, the feeling that social science should remain a respectable distance from policy has had a residual impact. The emergence of a détente between the United States and the Soviet Union and the reestablishment of diplomatic relationships between the United States and China, coupled internally with a growing conservatism with respect to the rights of the poor and the need for further welfare measures, has led to a situation in which social scientists have become increasingly aware of the commodity value of their researches and the mandarin effects of their findings. Thus, while the amount of social-science activity increased between 1941 and 1969 almost as a constant, the character of the associaton between the social scientists and the political establishment has been tremendously altered over time. The likelihood is that this pattern will continue into the foreseeable future. The emergence of the game theory as a concept replacing organicism subjects the social scientists themselves to the very analysis they have applied to the political actors. As a result, the line between social science and political action may have blurred, while at the same time the worth of each to the other has never been more intensely felt.

The demand for social-science research findings among government agencies continues unabated, despite reluctance on the part of some sectors of the social-science community to supply such information, and beyond that, the relatively desultory results thus far obtained in the areas of applied social research. In a recent report before the American Association for Public Opinion Research, Nathan Caplan noted the following: (1) There is a need felt among most federal officials to find better ways of plugging research into the decision-making process. (2) Top officials get most of their social-science news from newspapers. (3) Policy-makers see the need for more large-scale, community-based social experiments, such as the negative income tax study, along with a widening interest in developing noneconomic measures of social well-being (Caplan, 1974). Social-science research is used about as much as hard science data. Problems of utilization are generic and cut across the board, but top bureaucrats may be more suspicious about the validity and reliability of social-science data. Even when policy-makers cite physical-science research, they are likely to notice social consequences first. For the money, the government probably gets its best utilization payoff from social-science research. While there is a "motherhood" effect in support for getting information about noneconomic social indicators (94 percent of the respondents said it was needed) policy-makers make a distinction between survey research (valuable) and public opinion (not reliable). Survey research was the third most frequently mentioned area of information needed from social science, following social experiments and quality of life. In terms of usefulness of science input, physics is at the top of the scale and psychiatry at the bottom. Economics, psychology, and sociology share the middle ground. When asked: "Is it necessary to be familiar with the scientist in order to evaluate a set of findings?" almost half the users said yes for social science. The family is gaining importance as a research area as policy-makers become more concerned about family-life alternatives, family arrangements, effects of family on child development. Despite this increased demand for policy-related social science, the teaching and learning of social science (both inside and outside the university) and its relationship to public policy is still drastically underdeveloped and in need of further large-scale efforts among government and university structures alike.

One might say of social science what Walter Lippmann long ago said of democracy: it is not a very good instrument for the making of public policy but it is about the best one available. This does seem to be the case with the social sciences although on a less philosophical, more pragmatic basis than Lippmann initially had in mind. In the absence of a mass outpouring of democratic persuasion, and in the presence of political corruption in high office and political apathy among ordinary citizens, the social sciences essentially perform the role of cementing American goals and presenting them in such a manner that, at the very least, if it does not provide a rational solution to social problems it does prevent an irrational solution from being adopted. This may not be saying much for the social sciences but it holds out considerably more promise than is offered by any other method of political participation by the social-science community under present conditions in American life.

1969

23

Ecological Movements
vs.
Economic Necessities

Contrary to the customary view that the ecology movement is a response to dirt, filth, sex, and sin, it is my belief that the ecology movement is basically a product of traditional social sentiments that lurk deeply in the minds of many Americans—especially those who still harbor faith in rural ideals and troglodyte values. Indeed it is probable that these rural ideals are more firmly and fervently held by those who have never been on a farm and never encountered an honest-to-goodness farmer. The present mood was well summed up by the quasihero of *Easy Rider*, who said to the Arizona farmer with a wife and nine children, "You have quite a stake here—quite a spread—you have everything together, man, and if I had it, I would stay here too." The ecology movement is, in part at least, indicative of a fundamental retreat from the problems of technological development and urbanization.

It is an open secret that the ecology movement has as its core an essentially middle-class constituency. "Environmental politics" has rapidly become an electoral pressure group (DeBell, 1970). It emerged as a "movement" out of the efforts in the early sixties to "keep America beautiful" and before that, from nature-loving conservation organizations such as the Sierra Club that saw in the establishment of every factory, jetport, or trailer court an affront to the American myth of rurality (Swatek, 1970). The middle classes changed from rural to urban styles between 1860 and 1920, and from 1920 to 1970 they increasingly moved to suburban styles; but the problem at this point is that the lines of communication and transportation have become overextended. Lacking adequate mass transportation networks to the major urban centers, city residents cannot move further out. Thus the move is back toward center cities, but with a new twist: having them cleaned up for proper bourgeois reentry—and that means urban relocation and industrial renovation.

So pronounced has been the trend of a middle-class suburbia surrounding a working-class inner city that the emergence of the new trend of to the inner city is perhaps not yet as noticeable as it might otherwise be. The culprits in this urban dramaturgy are both the indolent factory owners and the indifferent factory workers; in short, the keys to the industrial system itself. Further, as the middle classes increasingly are linked to service-sector activities rather than productive-sector activities, the tempo and the tide of the assault upon economic development increases. When the middle classes were pushed out of urban secors by the polarized expressions of wealth and poverty that have come to characterize our major cities, the resentment over environmental pollution seemed to quicken. Now that the reverse migration has begun, this resentment has become a veritable cascade of ideological assault.

We have come to identify Ludditism with the machine breakers of proletarian origin. In fact, it has become increasingly evident that the new enemies of industrial expansion are the middle sectors revealing the above characteristics. This bourgeois Ludditism, resting as it does on a wide network of ideologists, politicians, intellectuals, lawyers, and people occupying middle ranges of power, has thrown up the challenge to the pollutists; but thus far the challenge has taken a specifically middle-class twist: namely, consumerism (Shepard, 1971). And what one finds is a linkage between consumer needs, clean products, and a healthy environment. This very linkage to the consumer sector, however, reveals the essentially middle-class characteristics of the ecological movement.

The ecological movement is not only middle class in character; more, it is a kind of Protestant drive toward hygiene and cleanliness in which every home becomes a Howard Johnson's replica; and in which cleanliness is not only next to Godliness, but often indistinguishable from it. The religious variable and the class variable often overlap. This convergence of class and religion ought not to escape our attention. The working class is in large measure populated by ethnics and Roman Catholics. Therefore the matter of life style intersects with the matter of work style to make the ecology movement something less than a universally regarded activity; in fact, for most people it scores far less in importance than unemployment in the factories and crime in the streets.

The ecology movement is also a suburban movement. The ideological explanation of a demand for cleanliness in the inner city lest the foul air waft its way into suburban American homes has become a central city concern. Of course the high cost of environmental reform often involves severe dislocation within the inner city and even the dismemberment of factory life in the inner city. The anomaly is that those who presumably suffer most from pollution are least involved in its reform, while those least directly affected are demanding changes in the nature of factory management and control.

The most pronounced aspect of the literature on the ecology movement is that assaults from Left and Right are equally plausible and made with equal ferocity. Consider the following passages from a recent paper by Lee Thayer (1971), Professor of Communication and Director of the Center for the Advanced Study of Communication at the University of Iowa, on the subject of "Man's Ecology, Ecology's Man."

Our social policies move steadily in the direction of survival of the unfittest. We have confused freedom with self-indulgence. We have martyred the ill-formed, polarized mind. We have put mere existence before living to some end. We have enthroned tastelessness. We have mocked greatness and deified the put-on. We have made anything but short-sightedness appear "too philosophical." We have substituted the capacity to talk for the ability to say something worthwhile. We have made irresponsibility over into a state religion. We have outlawed success, made failure illegal. God is a piece of technology, like a light switch. Love is an illicit or novel orgasm. Mediocrity has become a socially-sanctioned and government-subsidized life's work. Perhaps most insidiously, our social ideologies and policies increasingly penalize competence and reward incompetence. We take from the capable and diligent student to give to the incapable or indifferent student. Our popular movies lionize the inept, the ignorant, the incapable, the purposeless (e.g., "The Graduate"). Competence and purposefulness are the butt of jokes; they are fit themes only for farce or satire. Excellence is rapidly becoming unconstitutional. "Security" is our social-policy answer to incompetence, incapacity and indolence. We have made a tacit choice between being exploited by competence and being exploited by incompetence, and have chosen the latter. . . . Humanity will not expire in a noble fight against extinction by its natural environment. With but a whimper, humanity will simply grind to a halt, ignominiously, having ingeniously created and nurtured, in its man-made environment, the seeds of its ultimate irrelevence. That is the ecological crisis we must eventually face. The diminishing of man by his own hand is the greater cause, just as it is the surer end.

It is quite obvious that social ecology for Thayer is but a stepping stone to biological eugenics. Of course the history of eugenic movements in the twentieth century, particularly in its pristine Nazi variety, should caution anyone on this course of action.

Now let us turn to the left-wing critic writing on "The Ecological Crisis." Professor Barry Commoner (1971) of Washington University, one of the most distinguished biologists and physical scientists in the United States, writes as follows:

> I believe that the system of science and technology, as practiced in the United States and in all other developed countries, is in many ways unsound and unfit as a guide to the nature of man and the world in which he lives. We live in nature; society operates in nature, and our ability to exist in the natural world depends on our knowledge of it. Science should provide that knowledge and technology guide our application of it. But we are failing in these aims. In New York harbor the sewage bacterial count has risen a hundredfold in the last decade, even though marked improvements in the extent of sewage treatment have been made. Apparently there is something wrong with the technology of sewage treatment, which after all was designed to get *rid* of bacteria. . . . Increasing environmental pollution is evidence that our technology is, in important ways, incompetent. Behind this incompetence is an intrinsic weakness in science.

It is evident that Commoner believes the culprit to be science and not, as in the case of Thayer, society. But here a dilemma arises: If the problems are scientific in nature, should not the resolutions be scientific in nature? The social control that many ecologists insist upon seems to blunt, rather than enhance, scientific efforts to resolve the problem of environmental and atmospheric pollution.

I am not suggesting that there is no ecological problem or that the environment is as clean as it should be, or that any of the many studies conducted showing the damage from water, air, and soil pollution are in any way improperly worked or improperly diagnosed; rather, that the ideology that has come to be identified with this ecology movement has ignored the general context of economic development within which problems of pollution have been generated.

The ecology movement can be viewed as a coalition of economic conservatism and scientific narrowness that is often masked by radical slogans and by a secularized vision of the religious life. At every period economic progress reveals social chaos and negative consequences usually unforeseen. The more rapid the rate of change, the more monumental and even monstrous some of these developmental consequences appear to be. But if in fact the levels of pollution in the United States are much higher, so too are the comforts and life style superior to anything known in the past. It seems fruitless to enter into a metaphysical debate over the nature of progress. For example, how does one measure the worth of automobile transportation to the urban-industrial complex in contrast to the polluted atmosphere created by poorly designed engines and high-lead fuels? While the answer may be theoretically ambiguous and open to discourse from the practical point of view, there are few people who would give up a single jetport and fewer people still who would give up their family automobile for the sake of cleansing the atmosphere.

The fact that the ecology movement has spawned an enormous indus-try of scientific byproducts—from clean detergents to clean gasoline to nontoxic soft beverages—indicates that a kind of American shrewdness has taken hold of the movement and has capitalized on its fears. That it has been able to do so is a consequence of a sophisticated awareness that any ecological improvement must take place within the framework of developmental ambitions and economic expectations. It is well known that no people will endure for long lower standards of income or a return to more primitive economic forms in exchange for either a clean atmo-sphere or clean water. Cleanliness may be next to Godliness, but it is not next to industrialism.

The conflict between ecological and developmental modes is not simply a matter of ideology. It has been incorporated into the structure of legal relations affecting environmental pollution. Nearly every recent state statute claims, as does Missouri, that its intent and purpose is "to maintain purity of the air resources of the state, to protect the health, general welfare and physical property of the people, maximum employ-ment and full industrial development of the state." A similar statute in the State of Illinois claims that the pollution law requires the board governing such matters "to consider technical feasibility and economic reasonableness" in making its rules and recommendations (Porter, Jr., 1971). The law commands both an ecological solution and an unimpeded, highly developmental economy. As a result, environmentalists claim that the laws as written have loopholes, while developmentalists claim that the laws enacted pave the way for court challenges of pollution-control rules that they feel are too restrictive or severe.

State laws for fostering economic development have long been on the books, but with the challenge of environmentalists, officials of the state political network could make rules so harsh that they would put many companies out of business. Some corporate lawyers have argued that the environmentalists must be curbed, since otherwise they could ultimately argue for confiscation of industrial property and thus create a basis for riot and rebellion. Even the federal government has taken an ambiguous tack on the relationship of ecology to economy. President Nixon in his new water-quality legislation spoke of "taking into account the practicability of compliance." This phrase did not occur in the legislation as originally drafted by the Environmental Protection Agency. But by the time the measure was sent to Congress for approval in 1971, this Executive phrase had been inserted into the bill in three places. The modifying phrase indicates that the developmentalists are mustering considerable opposition to the environmentalists—and with great effect.

What people in this country want and feel entitled to is having their cake and eating it at the same time. That has always been a seminal genius of the American conscience and it has uniformly been the source of frustration of most protest movements, whatever their class origins. What the ecologists condemn, the economists celebrate. It may have taken a year, but calorie-free soft drinks are back on the market; and this time without cyclamates. High-test gasoline is now lead free, and plans for an electric automobile, noiseless jets, and other major technological innovations have as their starting points the existing levels of technology, not a retreat from them.

It is hard to avoid sounding a celebrationist note on this matter; quite the contrary. The problem with developmental programming is its utter disregard of social needs in its linear pursuit of technological goals. As Frank M. Coffin (1971) points out:

> Aid has been administered as if there were only one objective—measurable economic gain in the foreseeable future. Projects were evaluated largely from a single-purposed point of view. Housing was financed in overcrowded areas. Saw mills were aided with no thought of the wisdom of cutting down the forest. Ports were exploited with no thought given to the ruin of nearby recreation areas. Steel mills were erected with no consideraton given to the discharge of wastes or accumulation of slum areas. Fishing industries were promoted without asking whether overexploitation was being encouraged. Pesticides were made available for crops with no thought of their effect on insects, animals, birds, or humans. Highways were planned for the shortest route from here to there without considering what this would to to the pattern of life on the land in between. Dams were built to produce a certain power capacity on the strength of a cost-benefit analysis which left out the costs to fish in the river, human beings in the valley, communities in the area. To take the planning of the Aswan Dam as an example—and it could have happened to a U.S. project—the cost analysis was limited to the cost of a concrete dam.

There was no study of the costs of a new fertilizer industry needed to desalinate the soil, of a massive medical program needed to combat the new diseases, of a soil reclamation program, of relocating displaced fishermen, or of fighting widespread community problems. In short, we have all too often wrongfully assumed that we could do merely one thing, without affecting a multitude of other things.

To avoid this kind of misplanning, we should search out the contents of an ideology, especially when it is so easily embraced by many diverse sectors which otherwise have very little in common with each other. Therefore, if the ecology movement is to have a positive payoff, it can no longer be perceived as a movement against the city or as a movement against technology, but rather as a protest against exaggerations, excesses, and absurdities within urban living and technological society.

The essential need is not for a restricted and restrained ecological movement, but rather a movement that once and for all recognizes the need for planning in American society as a global need. This means getting beyond the present consumerist stage, in which a box of low-enzyme soapsuds is equated with ecological reform. The historic animosity in America for planning, the irrational linkage of any attempt at the regulation of people with a communist conspiracy, or, at the very least, with an affront on the free-enterprise system, has resulted in the special American problem of overdevelopment—which is often equated with the ecology crisis, but is rather a function of an economic system which still has not resolved the poles of wealth and poverty, overproduction and underconsumption, too little work for too many people.

The problems of American society are linked to issues of too much rather than too little, of allocational decisions rather than production norms. The issue of the quality of product, while real, is less significant by far than is the problem of the distribution of already available goods in the society. And the careful delineation among environmentalists of the quality of life to read like a series of consumer reports would indicate a failure of nerve on their part to face up to the heavy burdens of wealth in American society and the need to break the economic cleavages which still exist; and which, in some measure, account for the sharpened struggle of races, ethnic minorities, and outsiders to participate.

From a technical point of view, the distinct advantage of urging sound principles of planning and regulation is the restoration of confidence in the full development of American society, a development that accounts for an optimal ration of ecological and environmental conditions, but within the larger context of the quantity of available goods and not simply the quality of the environment. Unless it is possible to get beyond a piecemeal attack on problems of pollution, the environmental movement must fail in its noble goals, since solutions based on sentiment must yield to those based on economics; the demand for atmospheric and oceanic cleanliness must yield to the more urgent demands of full employment and maximum production. The *laissez-faire* approach encourages an almost irreconcilable contradiction between costs and prices, quantity production and quality control. As Lewis M. Branscomb pointed out in a recent (1971) article:

> Market forces are not satisfactory to allocate these secondary costs. We can't sell air, we don't sell frequencies, and we shouldn't sell the citizen's right to peace and quiet. Only recently have we begun to face this problem of the allocation and regulation of the environment through public stewardship. The individual wants good transportation and clean environment. But when the benefit (clean air) only follows from everyone assuming the cost (a more expensive car), a collective market decision or a social decision is required. The individual's market behavior will not justify any manufacturer's effort to make a more expensive nonpolluting car. The chemical manufacturer is in the same boat. If he makes a unilateral effort to take care of the problem of wastes in the public interest, he has no protection from his less civic-minded competition. Thus, uniform standards are required.

The purpose of planning is both to assign a meaningful ordering of priorities and to develop a two-pronged attack on social inequality and ecological destruction. Obviously, the physical environment cannot be ignored or abused in the distant expectation of a resolution of social inequality. But just as certainly, the physical improvement of the quality of life will mean precious little if it assists only the precious few. In short, the ecology movement, for its own survival, must become more than posturing. If it fails to recognize the general context in which ecological issues arise, and more specifically, if it fails to appreciate the primacy of industry over ideas, then it could well displace single-taxers, vegetarians, and snake-handlers as the most impressive fossil of twentieth-century movements in the United States.

1973

24

The Revolution
of
Falling Expectations

The Stevensonian call of the midfifties for a "revolution of rising expectations" is now resolving itself as an equally urgent appeal for a "revolution of falling expectations." Universal boosterism has yielded to particularist cynicism. Time does indeed march on, but in directions so diverse and disarrayed that charting the marchers, much less participating in the events, has become a major undertaking whose outcome is highly uncertain. Nothing is more dangerous than the presumption that the models of the world that we create are either better or cruder than the natural configurations we find in nature and society.

This Polonian observation is prompted by dismay at how thoroughly unprepared the social sciences were to receive the so-called "energy crisis" of the 1970s. Less prepared yet were we to cope with the consequences of this new state of affairs. American social science has grown up in a neo-Keynesian (better, Galbraithian) world of abundance. The only admissible problem was the allocation of resources, not the availability. But the hoary demons of neo-Malthusianism have struck back, and the shared contempt that orthodox Keynesians and orthodox Marxists alike held for the Malthusian scenario of war, famine, and plague as a "solution" to poverty and population has turned upon them.

Industrial societies in general, and American society in particular, have fed the hopes and illusions of millions concerning the royal road to upward social mobility. Equity is a right guaranteed to all by democratic constitutions, but underwritten by an economic apparatus which, from nursery school to graduate school, assumes that the path to success is work, occupation, and specialization. The road to failure is any departure from this well-trodden formula. At this point in time, many themes in American culture have conspired to shake loose inherited enlightenment assumptions that social welfare and economic mobility march into the future lock-step and hand in hand. Work and welfare have become opposite expressions of the American ethos. Energy and equity have both been subject to cost-benefit analysis that all but cancels out moral visions of the good society. We are confronted by new forms of social relations and hence new forms of social antagonisms. This study is a first effort to come to terms with what is new and old in society, and, by extension, what is living and dying in social science.

The first point that strikes a novel chord about the 1970s is that in the ebb and flow of cost-benefit analysis, the present tilt clearly favors costs (and work) rather than benefits (and welfare). The concern is currently with the economy as a whole, and not just federal budgetary processes (Mishan, 1976). There has been a precipitous shift from a sociological and social welfare orientation to what might be termed an econometric and accountability model. The most pervasive fact of the United States at every level, in every sphere, is the establishment of systems of measurement to evaluate the cost and quality of performance. Questions are raised about productivity of labor, and only secondarily about welfare benefits for those who do not toil. This represents a profound shift in American society. It is a more sober and modest estimate of potentials for growth through public or governmental sectors, and a marked return to potentials for growth through production or private sector modalities.

What might be considered a derivative of this changed American view is the further recognition that this is a decade of finite resources. In several dramatic forms, heightened to a fine point by the domestic energy crisis and foreign oil embargo, a new awareness took root that resources are limited and therefore growth is limited. This is no mere ideological preference for a zero growth model in either the economy or the demography, but a response to the limits of natural wealth of any country. An acute awareness now exists that without mineral resources the entire concept of economic growth is menaced. Beyond that, the "dependency model" applies not only to the less developed nations of the Third World, but also to the more developed nations of the capitalist and socialist worlds.

To indicate the novelty of this shift, as late as 1972, reports were being issued by leading economists that by 1980 Japan would be the world's first or second leading industrial power in the capitalist orbit. There was slender awareness among most forecasters that there are major problems of scarce resources, not just routine problems of allocating abundance. Our economic obtuseness largely derived from an inherited worldview, both Marxian and Keynesian, or sometimes a combination of the two, which persists in assuming that the central problem is product allocation rather than resource availability. We are living through the shock of a change in economic paradigms in which resource availabilities once again become significant in our collective cogitations. We have come to rediscover a Malthusian-Ricardian world in which problems of famine, pestilence, shortages, and subsistence, all become mechanisms to stabilize and rationalize economic systems through gradual population reduction, if not outright military competition for dominating such scarce resources.

These developments represent the end of what might be called the optative mood Americans have imbibed. Progress has become problematic. "Built-in controls," "the search for control in the face of license," and "prudent restraint" have become familiar refrains cautioning those who simply identify progress with freedom (Bennett, 1976:852). The exceedingly high pessimism is a result, in part at least, of the recognition that resources are finite. With this has come a growing polarization within each of the dominant structures of the world economic system.

Within the capitalist world system the contradictions between the United States and Western Europe have become intense, heightened by different political and military strategies to gain necessary resources for continued high industrial and consummatory growth. Within the Socialist bloc there is intense rivalry between the Soviet Union and China, propelled by similar drives to maximize production outputs. Within the Third World there is a growing divergence among nations with oil and food resources that allows them to penetrate the advanced economies, at least as junior partners, and those nations in a Fourth World which remain poor in both food and energy resources. There is a geographic component to this Malthusian drive that intensified the polarization and breakup of world systems and empires. Not only do we witness a divergence between colonies and empires, but between empires and nations which presumably share similar economic and cultural systems.

The redistribution of wealth leads to a different image of the world. In the past it took international warfare to bring about major redistribution of wealth. World War One and World War Two both produced dramatic shifts in power and economy—but did so amongst those established European and Asian nations that by the turn of the twentieth century had already achieved high levels of productivity. While warfare remains a ceaseless problem, armed conflict has mainly been conducted at subnational and regional levels. Hence the process of redistribution of wealth has changed from military to diplomatic struggle. Such game-oriented decisions have been employed to bring about wider redistribution of wealth, but with a more telling effect than the moral persuasion arguments of earlier decades were able to achieve.

Nations such as the Middle Eastern cluster, as well as select nations within Latin America and Asia, have managed to participate in the market economy as recipients no less than donors of real wealth. As a result, there is a shrinkage of resources among the wealthy industrial countries. Making do with less has become a way of life in Western Europe, and now North America is compelled to follow suit—against its cultural will, as it were. New slogans bombard us on all sides: small is beautiful; growth is limited; resources are finite. Instead of an unreflective appeal to giganticism, there is the emergence of a miniaturization process most notable in relation to automobiles, housing, and other aspects of social life in the advanced nations.

Changing attitudes toward size, greater utilization of commodities already available, is a function of the redistribution of wealth. Such redistribution occurs without the warfares usually accompanying massive changes in ownership of wealth. As a result of these tendencies within the American economy, there have been corresponding rebellions against big government—reputed to be the source of inflated budgets and systems of welfare established without a recognition of the high cost factors involved. More specifically, the charge is made that a level of government expenditures has been reached which assumed continuing levels of economic growth that can no longer be either sustained or realistically forecast.

An essential way in which this redistribution process has manifested itself is the sharpening gap between the private and public sectors. Although the private sector has recovered from the depression of 1973–75, the public sector clearly has not. As a result, those involved in the public sector end of the economy continue to feel the burden of the recent recession—perhaps even in fuller measure than when it was underway. Almost every major indicator of economic growth—housing, new private starts, automotive production, consumer durable expenditures, number of people employed, corporate profits after taxes—would indicate that the recovery of the private sector has been fulsome, whereas the illness of the public sector has remained severe, even chronic (cf. Juster, 1976:3–5). In consequence, the politics of this period reflect a genuine belief that if a choice has to be made between lower profitability and continuing measures to insure the welfare of the citizenry, it is the latter that will have to be sacrificed rather than the former.

What lends weight to this decision of the private sector elites to weaken the public sector is its support by the proletarian cluster employed in the private sector; particularly the trade union movement. What sometimes is euphemistically referred to as a taxpayer's rebellion is in fact a working-class discontent with a system of federal expenditures that equalizes the high end of the welfare package and the low end of the working package. This rebellion from below, whether it takes the form of a taxpayer's rebellion or a trade union discontent with government schemes for increasing the welfare package, is reflected in the virtually instinctual patterns of negative voting with respect to any increase in taxation that would raise levels of federal expenditures or bureaucratic management. As a result, various programs of affirmative action, whether in education or other areas of the public sector, come hard upon tenure and seniority systems that cannot be overcome in a situation of relative economic stagnation.

American society provides a spectacle of a Pincer movement: an industrial rebellion against the public sector from above and below. Commercial elites and proletarian unions join together in negating any effort on the part of the government to increase the welfare package for marginal and under classes. Such changes have served to accommodate the new era of energy shortages with a minimal disruption to the private sectors. They may have created the conditions for new types of upward mobility in the form of demands for higher levels of participation in the work force and lower levels of tax payouts to the welfare rolls. There is no mistaking the harshness and bluntness of this antagonism: Neo-Malthusianism joins forces with Neo-Darwinianism to satisfy the claims of proletarian and bourgeoisie against the marginal underclasses. Work versus welfare becomes more critical than inherited class and race antagonisms.

Paul Neurath (1975:296–297) calls attention to this return of Malthus and Darwin. He gives a pessimistic reading of energy and food shortages. His own call for a serious standpoint somewhere between pessimism and optimism while well taken remains to be worked out in practice. For the issues are quantitative at one level: how much of a reduction in living standards advanced social sectors can accept; and qualitative at another: how much growth an American public is willing to forego to retain present standards of liberty and equity.

The velocity with which the new realities have emerged can perhaps be gauged by the fact that only a decade ago the phrase "Third World" was considered innovative and idiosyncratic. It has now become a commonplace, and, in fact, a new paradigm has come into being, the "Fourth World." Now a nation may be rich in energy/rich in food; rich in energy/poor in food; poor in energy/rich in food; or, lo and behold, poor in energy/poor in food. While the United States numbers itself among the more fortunate nations on earth, being in the first category and still very much the center of the First World, it too has had to cope with the shock of recognition that resources are finite and that problems of allocation are more nasty and brutish when one allocates from a limited versus limitless supply.

Simple aggregate data themselves reveal the implausibility of continuing the present scenario into the future. In the First World, some 20 percent of the world's inhabitants concentrated on 10 percent of the world's land mass currently absorb 80 percent of the world's resources (van Dam, 1975:11). Under such circumstances, the question of diminishing natural resources must take on a grim aspect even for the most affluent country in the world. Especially telling is the fact that although resources are reduced or withheld, as in the case of oil, American expectations continue unabated, and interest-group politics becomes the operational guideline for all citizens on the margins of society. Appeals for government relief of inequities continue at a heated pace. Statistical measures of inequality—whether by blacks in relation to life expectations, women in relation to occupational mobility, youth in relation to quality of life, the aged in relation to security and health measures—are often pressed by subgroups and crosscuttings. Whenever resources shrink, demands increase. The ideology of equality becomes more pronounced as the capability of American society to fulfill demands for equality becomes strained.

It would be profoundly erroneous to assume that such demands for equity are without merit. A recent report issued by the Council of Economic Advisors (Shanahan, 1974:10) noted that the bottom 20 percent of all families had 5.1 percent of the nations *income* in 1947 and almost the same amount, 5.4 percent, in 1972. At the top of the economic ladder there was a similar absence of significant change. The richest 20 percent had 43.3 percent of the *income* in 1947 and 41.4 percent in 1972. Thus, while the incremental wealth of Americans continued to rise during the post-World War II economic cycle, the ratio of wealth to poverty hardly budged. This is not to deny that notable gains were made on a sectoral basis: for example, the median income of black families increased from 57 percent of that of white families in 1959 to 76 percent in 1972. Yet, on the darker side, people who are defined as poor are now poorer in absolute terms when compared with the rest of the American population. In 1959, those defined as poor had about half as much income as the typical family; in 1972 they had only a little more than one-third as much. And these statistics were compiled prior to the recession that shook the United States between 1973 and 1975. Even were we to accept the premise that American society can fulfill the main prerequisites of the drive toward equality for large population clusters such as working women, black males, or minorities whose native language is not English, there remains a darker side to equity demands: they are unending and ubiquitous. As David Donnison reminds us (1975:424):

> There are in fact so many different patterns of inequity in a complex urban society that to call for more (or less) equality without specifying which pattern concerns you is a pretty vacuous appeal. The main patterns are as follows: *The time-life cycle of incomes* producing for all social classes, successive periods of relative poverty and affluence during childhood, early adult life, early parenthood, middle age, and retirement. *Spatial inequalities,* due to (a) interregional, (b) urban-rural and (c) intra-urban differences in opportunities and living standards. The patterns of *social stratification* within urban, industrial, bureaucratic societies which produce social classes with differing bargaining strengths and differing inheritances (material, cultural, physical and intellectual). Social *discrimination* which benefits or handicaps particular groups on grounds of sex, religion, ethnic origin, accent or other characteristics.

The demands for parity by short people, fat people, handicapped people, or whomever, all become increasingly plugged into the general interest-group models that American society has substituted for older class models. Demands for black psychiatrists raise counterdemands for Italian psychiatrists. Research into cancer brings forth appeals for basic research into the causes of diabetes. All these demands are perfectly reasonable none save those without compassion could deny the legitimacy of such demands. All utilize the very model American society has held out for political participation, namely, articulating interests in a legal manner and withholding political support if necessary to achieve such interests.

When one measures this cacophony of equity demands against the shrinking resources base, the problem of the American Commonwealth as it moves toward the twenty-first century becomes increasingly apparent. For it is no longer reasonable to expect other nations to permit the United States of America to dominate and prevail in the world with resources supplied by them. The demands for a New Economic Order must be taken seriously. Even if one could muster a philosophical argument along the lines of Rudyard Kipling, that along with the white man's burdens come the white man's prerequisites, no one out there is listening anymore; as well, few whites care to make such arguments. Thus, the deadly combination of shrinking resources and rising expectations must unquestionably create an explosion that will test the mettle of American society as never before in a peacetime context.

Addressing himself to the central issue, the relationship between continued inequality and a limited growth model, Karl W. Deutsch asks, somewhat rhetorically: "What is the probable effect if the world is now told to expect more scarcity, not less, and not for a short period but for a long one, and perhaps even in permanence?" His answer essentially is that a revolution of falling expectations "risks a new age of international conflicts that in the end may prove fatal to all of us." Indeed, he urges us to make a real attempt to prevent "a drift toward catastrophe." Among the mechanisms recommended are:

> National and international stockpiling, an international system of reserves of food and fuel, the opening up of new agricultural acreages and mineral deposits, the improvement of technologies, the development of substitute materials and energy sources, the transition to less heavy but more sophisticated equipment (e.g., to transistors and printed electronic microcircuits) —all these may help to stave off a "revolution of falling expectations" and thus to buy more time for mankind to become truly joined "for better or worse, for richer or poorer" in the unity of the human race (Deutsch, 1975:381–398).

But these are by all odds meliorative measures that at best "buy time" to stave off disaster by rationing available resources and suggest no alteration in essential current inequalities. The question remains just why a revolution in falling expectations cannot, or even ought not, to take place. Indeed one must argue, to the contrary of Deutsch, that persistent and increasing inflation and unemployment within industrialized nations serve precisely to accelerate a revolution of falling, or at least stable, expectations, and provide mechanisms for accommodation to lower or "sustainable" standards of living that will insure the survival of the larger political and social system as a whole.

Early efforts at futurology, based as they were on mechanistic frameworks and models that simply assumed the continuance and extension of current ratios of international resources, make no sense. If social research has proved to be so inept at anticipating the current energy crisis, even though initiated as a boycott inspired by political considerations, what is one to make of research estimates predicated on events a quarter-century in the future? To deal with the future implies an understanding of the present and that also signifies a sense of how current dilemmas can be resolved with currently available techniques. It is more than tautology to assert that problems of resources can only be resolved at this point by technology, whether it be harnessing atomic energy for industrial use or a countercultural countertechnology based on harnessing bigger and better windmills. Energy resources and their discovery is after all a problem for physical science, engineering, and technology generally. At this level we are not dealing so much with whether resources can be expanded but whether it can be done within a time frame that realistically can continue to satisfy rising social expectations. If the problem of technology is the allocation of resources, the problem of bureaucracy becomes allocating scarce resources. The bureaucratic prerequisites of the moment are to harness available resources and allocate them in such a way as to prevent an explosive civil war, race war, class war, or wars generally. Thus, in point of fact, the bureaucratic problem has little to do with the limits of growth because to talk in such terms is simply to freeze present inequities into the social system.

Those such as Jay W. Forrester (1971) urging a position based upon the "limits to growth" have argued that the question is not: "Can science remove the physical limits to growth?" Rather we should ask: "Do we want science to remove the physical limits?" Forrester observes that to assert an argument in favor of continued growth "is equivalent to saying we want growth to be arrested by social stress alone" (Forrester, 1975: 110–111). Nowhere in this position is the thought entertained that corking scientific and technological mechanisms of expansion might actually cause social stress. In this framework, stress is caused by growth; whereas tranquility is insured through stagnation. But surely one might at least raise serious objections to this reversal of independent and dependent variables, this unexamined assumption that growth causes stress rather than that social stress may result from increased demands for a technological halt. The recognition that stress may increase from a zero-growth policy has led to the emergence of a middle-ground view based on slow growth. But the question still remains how slow—and who must slow down most and/or least.

To freeze the developmental process at this point in time is equally intolerable to each of the marginal groups currently making their equity demands upon the society as a whole. The issue in bureaucratic terms, and human terms as well, is not freezing growth at present levels to create a new stasis, but rather reallocating whatever wealth and resources are available, whatever their absolute size, so that the pie is distributed in a more equitable manner. The American people have proven to be quite capable of accepting a smaller pie. They are probably not capable of accepting a smaller pie in terms of present ratios of haves and have-nots (Curtin, 1976). The present imbalance of earnings and incomes characteristic of social classes in twentieth-century America as a whole will only exacerbate questions of redistributive justice, since the total pie will clearly be reduced by virtue of international factors beyond the control even of the wealthy. The data on redistribution that would open the stratification and participation networks are not encouraging to those who want both economic change and political order.

To enter a world of technology and bureaucracy, however, is also to face a world of technocrats and bureaucrats. It is to leave behind old formulas based on class struggle along conventional bourgeois versus proletarian lines. Old classes attached to economic production shrink, whereas new classes attached directly to the state apparatus grow exponentially. Nor do technocrats and bureaucrats simply grow; they *become* each other, not just resemble each other. They often represent interchangeable parts in a commodities culture that serves to keep the system intact. This introduces yet a more advanced problem: not only that of responding to a world of shrinking resources and rising expectations, but one in which the success of these tasks may imply a curb, if not an end, to the democratic political and social structure that Americans have been used to. As unpalatable as Huntington's thesis on this might appear, his challenge is at the least one that has to be met with candor rather than rancor:

> The vulnerability of democratic government in the United States thus comes not primarily from external threats, though such threats are real, nor from internal subversion from the left or the right, although both possibilities could exist, but rather from the internal dynamics of democracy itself in a highly educated, mobilized, and participant society (Huntington, 1975:37)

Whatever else democracy is, whatever arguments can be mustered in its behalf, and there are many, it is an expensive system. It involves a great deal of deliberation, competition, conflict over goals and methods, decision-making upon humane considerations that are more political than economical. And such decisions require high growth to cover new demands.

Here we come to the ultimate problem of the last portion of our century. The issue is not only can the Republic survive: but can it survive in terms of a democratic framework that has become an extraordinary luxury in many other societies. It might well be that the allocation system will work its magic ways. Technocrats and bureaucrats alike will attempt to solve problems of shrinking resources and rising expectations respectively. However, they do so increasingly at the cost of democratic politics, by resorting to a policy-making apparatus that is effective, efficient, and highly centralized. We may be faced with a devil's dilemma: to save the Republic and lose its democratic essence, or to continue preserving democracy and seriously jeopardize the Republic as it now exists.

This is hardly a pleasant choice, but neither can the issue posed in this way be reduced to a bit of reified nonsense. Similar polarities are taking place in the world at large. Those who urge world peace, for example, often do so at the cost of continued world development; while on the other hand, those urging world development oftentimes do so without much regard for the tranquility of the world as a whole. The proliferation of atomic capability is clearly only the most important and apparent of these dichotomies. Whatever the resolution, we can expect that the new revolution in American society will be one of falling, not rising expectations. Or, put in a more optimistic manner, as the United States becomes part of the world community, it must share the burdens of others. It must become more like the rest of that world in its life styles, consumption levels, and in the productivity of its citizens. This is both for better and for worse.

It might well be that more sophisticated technology is related to decreases in productivity; and that the current malaise in worker output, variously described as alienation and anomie in the work force, is little more than an early warning that advanced industrial societies like the United States are indeed drawing closer to the rest of the world. But there is a larger sense in which this growing similitude has dire potential consequences. At the level of political organization, only a few countries in the world—two dozen at the most—can still manage the luxury of democracy. To become part of that larger world may be to lose the luxury of democracy as well, unless it can be demonstrated once and for all that democracy and development go together, and not at the expense of the permanently poor. There are no cheap victories, no scenarios for a year 2000 that can spare us the tragedy of choice.

When one views future international relations as characterized by options based on interdependence, independence, or isolation, perhaps the most persuasive, if most evasive, answer is: all of them. There is always a combination of confrontation, subordination, and superordination in the affairs of states. The question at all times is the mix. Beyond that, whether such relationships are based on superordination, equality, or subordination depends on which national, subnational, or supranational units we refer to. My own position is that the demands for economic equity and social parity that have pushed their way forward within the United States are now at work at the international level. Every person and each nation seemingly must take seriously the idea that all people (and all peoples) are created equal or risk the perils of rebellion. The concomitant approach that nations, no less than people, can only count as one will be a harder lesson for the powerful of the earth to absorb.

Equity has become the fundamental spinal cord organizing the relations of the smallest units with the largest units: Albania with the Soviet Union, Puerto Rico with the United States, and, for that matter, Nicaragua with Mexico. "Sovereignty," like "the person" in Anglo-Saxon jurisprudence, is a legal entity. It demands equity in relationships based on rather powerful constraints of law. This serves to underwrite and underscore a continuing trend toward nationalism. On the other hand, equity demands also compel a powerful drive toward various types of redistributive mechanisms that may or may not be democratic. Thus the dealings of nations with each other have increasingly been characterized by a cautionary spirit. These impulses may in part be thwarted by other phenomena such as militarism—the *prima facie* strength of powerful nations with respect to weak nations. But if there are to be a future international relations without war, then certainly equity is the touchstone and the hallmark of such a future. For the first time, the revolution of rising expectations in the Third World has been understood to entail a revolution in falling profits in the advanced nations of the First and Second Worlds. This shock of recognition that benefits for some involve costs for others is a mark of maturation in American affairs, even though it may involve potential confrontations with other nations. But as Arnold Toynbee long ago reminded us, the capacity to absorb new challenges and creatively resolve old dilemmas is the benchmark of surviving civilizations.

1976

References

5. Race, Class, and the New Ethnicity

Berger, Peter. "The Blueing of America." *The New Republic*, vol. 164 (April 1971), pp. 20–23.

Brooks, Thomas R. "Black Upsurge in the Unions," *Dissent*, whole no. 75, vol. 17 (March–April 1970), pp. 125–138.

Campbell, Angus. *White Attitudes Toward Black People*. Ann Arbor: Institute for Social Research, University of Michigan, 1971.

Centers, Richard. *The Psychology of Social Classes*. Princeton, N.J.: Princeton University Press, 1949.

Coles, Robert. *The Middle Americans: Proud and Uncertain*. Boston: Little, Brown, 1971.

Cottle, Thomas J. "The Non-Elite Student: Billy Kowalski Goes to College." *Change*, vol. 3, no. 2 (March/April 1971a), pp. 36–42.

———. *Time's Children, Impressions of Youth*. Boston: Little, Brown, 1971b.

Friedman, Milton. "Kensington, U.S.A." *La Salle College Magazine*, vol. 11, no. 4 (Fall 1967). Reprinted and distributed by the American Jewish Committee.

Greeley, Andrew M. *Why Can't They Be Like Us? Facts and Fallacies About Ethnic Differences and Group Conflicts in America*. New York: Institute of Human Relations Press, 1969.

Greer, Colin. *Divided Society: The Ethnic Experience in America*. New York: Basic Books, 1974.

Hamill, Pete. "The Revolt of the White Lower Middle Class." *New York (April 14), 1969.*

Hamilton, Richard F. "Black Demands, White Reactions, and Liberal Alarms." In *Blue Collar Workers*, edited by Sar Levitan, New York: McGraw-Hill, 1971.

Handlin, Oscar. *Race and Nationality in American Life.* Boston: Little, Brown, 1957.

Hill, Herbert. "Racism and Organized Labor," *New School Bulletin,* vol. 28, no. 6 (February 8, 1971).

Hodges, Harold M. *Social Stratification: Class in America.* Cambridge, Mass.: Schenkman Publishing Co., 1964.

Howard, John. "Public Policy and the White Working Class." In *The Use and Abuse of Social Science,* edited by I. L. Horowitz. New Brunswick: Transaction Books/E. P. Dutton, 1971.

Krickus, Richard J. "Forty Million Ethnics Rate More Than Bromides," *The Washington Post* (August 31, 1969).

———. "The White Ethnics: Who Are They and Where Are They Going?" *City,* vol. 5, no. 3 (May/June 1971), pp.23–31.

Leggett, John C. *Class, Race, and Labor: Working Class Consciousness in Detroit.* New York: Oxford University Press, 1968.

Levine, Naomi M., and Judith M. Herman. "The Ethnic Factor in Blue Collar Life." National Project on Ethnic America, American Jewish Committee (mimeograph), 1971.

Levitan, Sar. *Blue-Collar Workers: A Symposium on Middle America.* New York: McGraw-Hill, 1971.

Mikulski, Barbara. "Who Speaks for Ethnic America." In *Divided Society: The Ethnic Experience in America,* edited by Colin Greer. New York: Basic Books, 1974.

Morsell, John A. "Ethnic Relations of the Future." *Annals of the American Academy of Political and Social Science,* vol. 408 (July 1973), pp. 83–93.

Myrdal, Gunnar. "The Case Against Romantic Ethnicity." *The Center Magazine,* vol. 7, no. 4 (July/August 1974), pp. 26–30.

Novak, Michael. "White Ethnic." *Harper's Magazine,* vol. 243 (September 1971), pp. 44–50.

———. "The New Ethnicity." *The Center Magazine,* vol. 7, no. 4 (July/August 1974), pp. 18–25.

Rainwater, Lee. "Crucible of Identity: The Negro Lower Class Family." *Daedalus,* whole no. 95 (1966), pp. 172–216.

———. *Behind Ghetto Walls: Black Family Life in a Federal Slum.* Chicago: Aldine-Atherton, 1970.

Reich, Charles A. *The Greening of America: How the Youth Revolution Is Trying to Make America Livable.* New York: Random House, 1970.

Rustin, Bayard. "The Blacks and the Unions." *Harper's Magazine,* vol. 242 (May 1971).

6. Revolution and Counterrevolution in American Cities

Abrams, Charles. *Man's Struggle for Shelter in an Urbanizing World.* Cambridge, Mass.: MIT Press, 1964.

———. *The City Is the Frontier.* New York: Harper & Row, 1965.

Beck, Bertram M. "Community control: A distraction, not an answer." *Social Work,* vol. 14 (October 1969), pp. 14–20.

Bollens, John C., and Henry J. Schmandt. *The Metropolis: Its People, Politics and Economic Life.* New York: Harper & Row, 1965.

Boulding, Kenneth. "The death of the city: A frightened look at post civilization." *The Historian and the City,* edited by Oscar Handlin and John Burchard. Cambridge, Mass.: MIT Press, 1963, pp. 133–145.

Campbell, Alan K. *The States and the Urban Crisis.* Englewood Cliffs, N.J.: Prentice-Hall, 1970.

Community Relations Service. Mimeographed Reports on Urban Population. Washington, D.C.: United States Department of Justice, 1969.

Dahl, Robert. *Who Governs? Democracy and Power in an American City.* New Haven: Yale University Press, 1961.

Davidson, Robert H. "The war on poverty: Experiment in federalism." *Annals of the American Academy of Political and Social Science,* vol. 385 (September 1969), pp. 1–13.

Downes, Bryan T. "Social and political characteristics of riot cities: A comparative study." *Social Science Quarterly,* vol 49 (December 1968), pp. 504–520.

Frady, Marshall. "Gary, Indiana." *Harper's Magazine,* vol. 239 (August 1969), pp. 35–45.

Gans, Herbert J. *The Urban Villagers: Group and Class in the Life of Italian Americans.* New York: Free Press, 1962.

———. "The future of the suburbs." *Political Power and the Urban Crisis,* edited by Alan Shank. Boston: Holbrook Press, 1969, pp. 282–295.

Gittell, Marilyn. "Community control of education." *Proceeding of the Academy of Political Science,* vol. 29, no. 1 (July 1968), pp. 60–71.

Greenstone, J. David, and Paul E. Peterson. "Reformers, machines, and the war on poverty." In *City Politics and Public Policy,* edited by James Q. Wilson. New York: John Wiley & Sons, 1968, pp. 267–292.

Greer, Scott, and Davie W. Minar. "The political side of urban development and redevelopment." In *The New Urbanization,* edited by Scott Greer, Dennis L. McElrath, David W. Minar, and Peter Orleans. New York: St. Martin's Press, 1968, pp. 301–314.

Hamilton, Charles, and Stokely Carmichael. *Black Power.* New York: Random House, 1967.

Hare, Nathan. "The case for separatism: Black perspective." In *Black Power and Student Rebellion: Conflict on the American Campus,* edited by James McEvoy and Abraham Miller. Belmont, Cal.: Wadsworth Publishing Co., 1969, pp. 233–234.

Hartman, Charles W. "The politics of housing." *Dissent,* vol. 14 (November-December 1967), pp. 701–714.

Heilburn, James, and Stanislaw Wellisz. "An economic program for the ghetto." *Proceedings of the Academy of Political Science,* vol. 29 (July 1968), pp. 72–85.

Laumann, Edward O. *Prestige and Association in an Urban Community: An Analysis of an Urban Stratification System.* Indianapolis-New York: Bobbs-Merrill Co., 1966.

Levitan, Sar A. "The community action program: A strategy to fight poverty." *Annals of the American Academy of Political and Social Science,* vol. 385 (September 1969), pp. 63–75.

Lockard, Duane. *Toward Equal Opportunity: A Study of State and Local Anti-discrimination Laws.* New York: Macmillan, 1968.

Lurie, Ellen. "Community action in East Harlem." In *The Urban Condition: People and Policy in the Metropolis,* edited by Leonard J. Duhl. New York: Basic Books, 1963, pp. 246–258.

Manso, Peter, ed. *Running Against the Machine: The Mailer-Breslin Campaign.* Garden City, N.Y.: Doubleday, 1969.

National Resources Committee. *Our Cities.* Washington, D.C.: U.S. Government Printing Office, 1937.

Olson, Mancur, et al. *Toward a Social Report (U.S. Department of Health, Education, and Welfare).* Washington, D.C.: U.S. Government Printing Office, 1969.

Oppenheimer, Martin. *The Urban Guerrilla.* Chicago: Quadrangle Books, 1969.

Piven, Frances Fox, and Richard A. Cloward. "Black control of cities." *The New Republic,* vol. 157 (September 30 and October 7, 1967), pp. 19–21, 15–19.

Polsby, Nelson. *Community Power and Political Theory.* New Haven: Yale University Press, 1963.

Rainwater, Lee. "Open letter on white justice and the riots." *Trans-action,* vol. 4 (September 1967), pp. 22–32.

Saarinen, Eliel. *The City: Its Growth, Its Decay, Its Future.* New York: Reinholdt Publishing Co., 1943.

Schrag, Peter. "The forgotten American." *Harper's Magazine,* vol. 239 (August 1969), pp. 27–34.

Seligman, Ben B., ed. *Poverty as a Public Issue.* New York: Free Press, Macmillan, 1965.

Slayton, William L. "A national urbanization policy." In *Federalism Today,* edited by Jean Brand and Lowell H. Watts. Washington, D.C.: Graduate School Press, U.S. Department of Agriculture, 1969, pp. 71–80.

Smith, David Horton, and Richard F. McGrail. "Community control of schools: a review of issues and options." *Urban and Social Change Review,* vol. 3 (Fall 1969), pp. 2–9.

U.S. Department of Commerce. *Americans at Mid-Decade.* Series P-23, no. 16. Washington, D.C.: U.S. Government Printing Office, March 1966.

———. *Provisional Estimates of the Population of the Largest Metropolitan Areas. July 1, 1966.* Series P-25, no. 378. Washington, D.C.: U.S. Government Printing Office, November 1967.

U.S. Department of Labor. *The Negroes in the United States: Their Economic and Social Situation,* Bulletin 511. Washington, D.C.: U.S. Government Printing Office, June 1967.

Wilson, James Q. "The mayors vs. the cities." *The Public Interest,* vol. 16 (Summer 1969), pp. 25-40.

7. The Present Condition of the American Working Class

Adorno, T. N. *The Authoritarian Personality: Studies in Prejudice.* New York: Harper & Row, 1950.

Blauner, R. *Alienation and Freedom.* Chicago: University of Chicago Press, 1964.

Burnham, W. D. "Political Immunization and Political Confessionalism: Some Comparative Inquiries" (mimeograph). 1970.

Chinoy, E. *Automobile Workers and the American Dream.* Garden City, N.Y.: Doubleday, 1955.

Denitch, B. "Is There a 'New Working Class'?" *Dissent,* vol. 17, no. 40 (July/August 1970), pp. 351–355.

Hill, H. "Racial Practices of Organized Labor." *New Politics,* whole no. 14, vol. 4, no. 2 (Spring 1965), pp. 26–46.

———. "Black Protest and the Struggle for Union Democracy." *Issues in Industrial Society,* vol. 1, no. 1 (Spring 1969), pp. 19–29.

Horowitz, I.L. "The Trade-Unionization of the Student Seventies." *New Society* (July 1970), pp. 70–71.

Jacobson, J., ed. Special issue on "The American Labor Movement." *New Politics,* whole no. 27, vol. 7, no. 3 (Summer 1968).

Laslett, J. H. M. *Labor and the Left: A Study of Socialist and Radical Influences in the American Labor Movement, 1881–1924.* New York: Basic Books, 1970.

Leggett, J. C. *Class, Race and Labor: Working Class Consciousness in Detroit.* New York: Oxford University Press, 1968.

Lipset, S. M. *Political Man: The Social Bases of Politics.* Garden City, N.Y.: Doubleday, 1960.

Mandel, E. "Workers Under Neo-Capitalism." *International Socialist Review* (November-December 1968). Reprinted in *Economics: Mainstream Readings and Radical Critiques,* edited by David Mermelstein. New York: Random House, 1970.

Meany, G. Interview with Neil Gilbride of the Associated Press. *The Washington Post,* August 31, 1970.

Oppenheimer, M. "White Collar Revisited: The Making of a New York Class." *Social Policy,* vol. 1, no. 2 (July-August 1970), pp. 27–32.

Stouffer, S. A. *Communism, Conformity and Civil Liberties.* New York: Doubleday, 1955.

8. American Futurology and the Pursuit of the Millennium

Bell, Daniel. "The End of Scarcity." *Saturday Review of the Society,* vol. 49 (May 1973), pp. 49–52.

Cherne, Leo. "State of the Nation." *Perspectives in Defense Management* (Winter 1972), pp. 1–10.

Cohn, Norman. *The Pursuit of the Millennium.* New York: Oxford University Press, 1970.

Dahl, Robert A., and Edward R. Tufte. *Size and Democracy.* Stanford, Cal.: Stanford University Press, Politics of the Smaller European Democracies Series, 1973.

Flacks, Richard. "Making History vs. Making Life: Dilemmas of an American Left." *Working Papers for a New Society,* vol. 2, no. 2 (Summer 1974), pp. 56–71.

Harris, George T. "Era of Conscious Action." In *Britannica Book of the Year. Chicago: Encyclopedia Britannica, 1973, pp. 6–14.*

Moynihan, Daniel P. "Peace—Some Thoughts on the 1960's and 1970's." *The Public Interest,* vol. 32 (Summer 1973), pp. 3–12.

Thomas, Lowell. "What About the Future." *Mainliner,* vol. 12, no. 1 (January 1974), pp. 30–33.

Tuchman, Barbara. "History as Mirror." *The Atlantic* (September 1973), pp. 39–46.

Wattenberg, Ben J., and Richard M. Scammon. "Black Progress and Liberal Rhetoric." *Commentary,* vol. 55, no. 4 (April 1973), pp. 35–44.

Weisband, Edward, and Thomas Franck. "The Brezhnev-Johnson Two World Doctrine." *Transaction/Society,* vol. 8 no. 12 (October 1971), pp. 36–44.

9. New Conservatism in America

Adams, H. *Mont-Saint-Michel and Chartres.* New York: Heritage Press, 1957.

Adams, J. "Discourses on Davila." In *Works,* vol. 6. Boston: Little, Brown, 1850–56.

Anderson, T. *Brook Adams, Constructive Conservative.* Ithaca, N.Y.: Cornell University Press, 1951.

Berle, A. *The Twentieth-Century Capitalist Revolution.* New York: Harcourt Brace Jovanovich, 1954.

Burke, E. "Appeal from the New Whigs." In his *Works,* vol. 3. London: Bohn, 1854–57a.

———. "Reflections on the Revolution in France." In his *Works,* vol. 2. London: Bohn, 1854–57b.

Crick, B. *In Defense of Politics.* Chicago: University of Chicago Press, 1962.

Demant, V. A. *Our Culture: Its Christian Roots and Present Crisis.* London: Society for Promoting Christian Knowledge, 1947.

Hallowell, J. H. *The Moral Foundation of Democracy.* Chicago: University of Chicago Press, 1954.

Handlin, O. Preface to R. W. Leopold, *Elihu Root and the Conservative Tradition.* Boston: Little, Brown, 1954.

Hegel, G. W. F. "Phenomenology of Mind." In *Selections,* edited by J. Loewenberg. New York: Scribner, 1929.

Hogg, Q. *The Case of Conservatism.* Baltimore, Md.: Penguin Books, 1947.

Inge, W. R. "The State, Visible and Invisible." In *Leviathan in Crisis,* edited by W. R. Browne. New York: Viking Press, 1946.

Kirk, R. *The Conservative Mind: From Burke to Santayana.* Chicago: Regnery, 1953.

Lecky, W. E. H. *Democracy and Liberty,* vol. 2. London: Longmans, 1896.

Levinson, R. B. *In Defense of Plato.* Cambridge, Mass.: Harvard University Press, 1953.

Magid, H. M. "An Approach to the Nature of Political Philosophy." *Journal of Philosophy,* vol. 52, no. 2 (January 20, 1955), pp. 37–42.

Maritain, J. *Man and the State.* Chicago: University of Chicago Press, 1951.

Nevins, A. *Study in Power: John D. Rockefeller, Industrialist and Philanthropist.* New York: Scribner, 1953.

———. "Should American History Be Rewritten?" *Saturday Review,* vol. 37, no. 6 (February 6, 1954).

Newman, J. H. *Discussions and Arguments on Various Subjects,* 3rd ed. London: Pickering Co., 1878 (originally published in 1827).

Rossiter, C. "Toward an American Conservatism." *Yale Review,* vol. 44 (March 1955), pp. 354–372.

Santayana, G. *Dominations and Powers.* New York: Scribner, 1951.

———. *The Life of Reason; or The Phases of Human Progress,* rev. ed. New York: Scribner, 1953.

Strauss, L. *Natural Right and History.* Chicago: University of Chicago Press, 1953.

Tannenbaum, F. *A Philosophy of Labor.* New York: Knopf, 1951.

Tocqueville, A. de. *Democracy in America,* rev. ed., translated by H. Reeve. New York: Colonial Press, 1900.

Viereck, P. *Conservatism Revisited: The Revolt Against Revolt.* New York: Scribner, 1949.

Vivas, E. *The Moral Life and the Ethical Life.* Chicago: University of Chicago Press, 1950.

Wild, J. *Plato's Modern Enemies and the Theory of Natural Law.* Chicago: University of Chicago Press, 1953.

10. The Pluralistic Bases of Modern American Liberalism

Berlin, I. *Two Essays on Liberty.* New York and London: Oxford University Press, 1954.

Frankel, C. "Liberalism and the Imagination of Disaster." In his *The Case for Modern Man.* New York: Harper & Row, 1956.

Hartz, L. *The Liberal Tradition in America: An Interpretation of American Political Thought Since the Revolution.* New York: Harcourt Brace Jovanovich, 1955.

Lippmann, W. *Public Opinion.* New York: Macmillan, 1922.

Lowi, T. J. *The End of Liberalism: Ideology, Policy and The Crisis of Public Authority.* New York: Norton, 1969.

McClosky, R. G. *American Conservatism in the Age of Enterprise.* Cambridge, Mass.: Harvard University Press, 1969.

Mills, C. W. "Liberal Values in the Modern World." In *Power Politics and People: The Collected Essays of C. Wright Mills,* edited by I. L. Horowitz. New York: Oxford University Press, 1963.

Wolff, R. P. *The Poverty of Liberalism.* Boston: Beacon Press, 1968.

12. Capitalism, Communism, and Multinationalism

Adam, Gyorgy. *The World Corporation: Problematics, Apologetics and Critique.* Budapest: Hungarian Scientific Council for World Economy, 1971.

Adelman, M. A. "The Multinational Corporation in World Petroleum." *The International Corporation,* edited by Charles P. Kindleberger. Cambridge: MIT Press, 1970.

Barnet, Richard J. *Roots of War.* New York: Atheneum Publishers, 1972.

Blake, David H., ed. "The Multinational Corporation." *Annals of the American Academy of Political and Social Science* (September 1972), pp. 1–247.

Bock, P. G., and Vincent J. Fuccillo. "The Transitional Corporation as an International Political Actor" (mimeograph). 1972.

Boddewyn, Jean, and Etienne F. Cracco. "The Political Game in World Business." *Harvard Business Review,* January–February 1972.

Brown, Lester R. *World Without Borders.* New York: Random House, 1972.

Bruyn, Severyn T. "Notes on the Contradictions of Modern Business." *Sociological Inquiry,* vol. 42, no. 2 (Spring 1972), pp. 123–139.

Brzezinski, Zbigniew, and Samuel P. Huntington. *Political Power: USA/USSR.* New York: Viking Press, 1964.

Burtis, David, Farid Lavipour, Steven Ricciardi, and Karl P. Sauvant. *Multinational Corporation–Nation State Interaction.* Philadelphia: Foreign Policy Research Institute, 1971.

Eisenhower, David, and Henry Frundt. "A Proposal to Study the Impact of Multinational Corporations on American Foreign Policy" (mimeograph). New Brunswick: The Rutgers Multinational Research Group, 1972.

Gennard, John. "British Trade Union Response to the Multinational Corporation." *Looking Ahead,* vol. 20, no. 2 (March 1972), pp. 1–8.

Harrington, Michael. "The Anatomy of Nixonism." *Dissent,* vol. 19, no. 4 (Fall 1972), pp. 563–578.

Horowitz, Irving Louis. *Three Worlds of Development: The Theory and Practice of International Stratification,* sec. ed. New York and London: Oxford University Press, 1972.

Kennan, George F. "Interview with George F. Kennan." *Foreign Policy,* no. 7 (Summer 1972), pp. 5–21.

Kindleberger, Charles. *American Business Abroad.* New Haven, Conn.: Yale University Press, 1969.

Levinson, Charles. *Capital, Inflation and the Multinationals.* London: George Allen & Unwin, 1971.

New York Times (The). April 17, 1972.

New York Times (The). August 25, 1972.

New York Times (The). October 1, 1972.

New York Times (The). October 2, 1972.

New York Times (The). October 5, 1972.

Pisar, Samuel. *Coexistence and Commerce: Guidelines for Transactions Between East and West*. New York: McGraw-Hill, 1970.

Ray, Dennis M. "Corporations and American Foreign Relations." *Annals of the American Academy of Political and Social Science*, no. 403 (September 1972), pp. 80–92.

Science. "East-West Think Tank Born." (October 13, 1972).

Tanzer, Michael. *The Political Economy of International Oil and the Underdeveloped Countries*. Boston: Beacon Press, 1969.

Thornton, Thomas Perry, ed. *The Third World in Soviet Perspective*. Princeton: Princeton University Press, 1964.

Turner, Louis. *Invisible Empires*. New York: Harcourt Brace Jovanovich, 1971.

Tyler, Gus. "Multinational Corporations vs. Nations." *Current*, no. 143 (September 1972), pp. 54–62.

U.S. News and World Report. October 10, 1972.

Vernon, Raymond. *Sovereignty at Bay: The Multinational Spread of U.S. Enterprises*. New York: Basic Books, 1971.

Vinnedge, Harlan H. "Another Rum Deal with Russia." *The Nation*, vol. 215, no. 18 (December 4, 1972), pp. 558–559.

Weisband, Edward, and Thomas M. Franck. *World Politics: Verbal Strategy Among the Superpowers*. New York and London: Oxford University Press, 1971.

16. The American Way of Spying

Borosage, Robert L., and John Marks, eds. *The CIA File*. New York: Grossman/Viking, 1976.

U.S. Senate Select Committee to Study Governmental Operations with Respect to Intelligence Activities. *Alleged Assassination Plots Involving Foreign Leaders*, Interim Report. Washington, D.C.: U.S. Government Printing Office, November 18, 1975.

———. *Covert Action in Chile: 1963-1973*, Staff Report. Washington, D.C.: U.S. Government Printing Office, December 18, 1975.

17. Arms, Policies, and War Games

Beecher, William. "Army Uses Computers to Stage War Games for Developing Tactics." *The Wall Street Journal*, December 11, 1963.

Business Week. "Planners for the Pentagon." July 13, 1963.

Enthoven, Alain C., et al. "The Pentagon's Whiz Kids." *Time: The Weekly Newsmagazine*, August 3, 1962.

Garthoff, Raymond L. "A Manual of Soviet Strategy." *The Reporter*, vol. 28, no. 4, February 14, 1963.

Hughes, H. Stuart. "The Strategy of Deterrence." *Commentary*, vol. 31, no. 3 (March 1961), pp. 185–192.

Kennedy, John F. Quoted in *Philadelphia Evening Bulletin*. October 23, 1962.

Laski, Harold J. "The Limitations of the Expert." In *The Intellectuals*, edited by G. B. deHuszar. Glencoe: Free Press, 1960.

Newman, James R. *The Rule of Folly*. New York: Simon & Schuster, 1962.

Sokolovskii, V. D., ed. *Soviet Military Strategy*. New York: Prentice-Hall, 1963.

White, Gen. Thomas D. "What's Wrong with Civil-Military Relations." *Newsweek* (May 27, 1963), p. 30.

Wilhelm, Sidney M. "Scientific Unaccountability and Moral Accountability." In *The New Sociology*, edited by Irving L. Horowitz. New York and London: Oxford University Press, 1964.

18. Noneconomic Factors in the Institutionalization of War

Benoit, Emile. "Economic Adjustments to Disarmament." In *Economic Factors Bearing upon the Maintenance of Peace*. New York: Institute for International Order, 1960.

————. "Alternatives to Defense Production." In *Disarmament and the Economy*, edited by Emile Benoit and Kenneth E. Boulding. New York: Harper & Row, 1963, pp. 203–220.

Bergson, Abram. *The Real National Income of Soviet Russia Since 1928*. Cambridge, Mass.: Harvard University Press, 1961, p. 362.

Childs, Marquis. *St. Louis Post-Dispatch*. September 18, 1963.

Economist Intelligence Unit. *The Economic Effects of Disarmament*. Toronto: University of Toronto Press, 1963.

Galbraith, John Kenneth. *The Affluent Society*. Boston: Houghton Mifflin, 1958, pp. 349–356.

Hagan, Roger. "Reciprocal Hardening." *Council for Correspondence Newsletter*, no. 26 (May 1963), p. 7.

Henry, Jules. *Culture Against Man*. New York: Random House, 1963, p. 110.

Horowitz, Irving Louis. "Consensus, Conflict, and Cooperation." *Social Forces*, vol. 41, no. 2 (December 1962), pp. 177–188.

————. *The War Game: Studies of the New Civilian Militarists*. New York: Ballantine Books, 1963a.

————. *Games, Strategies and Peace*. Philadelphia: American Friends Service Committee, 1963b.

————. "Political Morality and Immoral Politics." *Council for Correspondence Newsletter*, no. 25, April 1963c.

————. "On the Morality of Detente." *The Correspondent*, no. 28, July–August 1963d.

Kissinger, Henry A. "The Unsolved Problems of European Defense." *Foreign Affairs*, vol. 40, no. 4 (July 1962), pp. 515–541.

————. "Nato's Nuclear Dilemma." *The Reporter*, March 1963.

Osgood, Charles E. "Questioning Some Unquestioned Assumptions about National Defense." *Journal of Arms Control*, vol. 1, no. 1 (January 1963), p. 11.

Raymond, Richard C. "Problems of Industrial Conversion." In *Disarmament: Its Politics and Economics*, edited by Seymour Melman. Boston: American Academy of Arts and Sciences, 1962, pp. 158–159.

Riesman, David. "The Concept of National Purpose." *Council for Correspondence Newsletter*, no. 27 (June 1963), p. 11.

Royce, William S. "Economics of Disarmament." *The Nation*, vol. 195, no. 6 (September 1962), pp. 105–109.

Schelling, Thomas C. "American Aid and Economic Development: Some Critical Issues." In *International Stability and Progress*. New York: Columbia University Press, 1957, pp. 127 ff.

————, and Morton H. Halperin. "Arms Control Will Not Cut Defense Cost." In *Arms and Arms Control*, edited by E. W. Lefever. New York: Praeger, 1962, pp. 287–297.

Shabecoff, Philip, and Joseph Lelyveld. "Defense Industry Shuns Plans for Possible Arms Ban." *The New York Times* (August 16, 1963), pp. 31, 37.

Sorokin, Pitirim A. "Mutual Convergence of the United States and the U.S.S.R. to the Mixed Sociocultural Type." *International Journal of Comparative Sociology*, vol. 1, no. 2 (September 1960), pp. 143–176.

United Nations. *Economic and Social Consequences of Disarmament: Report of the Secretary General Transmitting the Study of his Consultative Group*. New York: U.N. Dept. of Economic and Social Affairs, 1962, pp. 45–46.

U.S. Arms Control and Disarmament Agency. *The Economic and Social Consequences of Disarmament*. Washington, D.C. (March 1962), p. 35.

Vickrey, William. "Fiscal Strategies for Shifting $22 Billions to the Civilian Economy." In *A Strategy for American Security*, edited by Seymour Melman. New York: Lee Offset—Distributors, 1963, pp. 21–25.

Widenbaum, Murray L. "Problems of Adjustment for Defense Industries." In *Disarmament and the Economy*, edited by Emile Benoit and Kenneth E. Boulding. New York: Harper & Row, 1963, p. 67.

19. Organization and Ideology in the Antiwar Movement

Boulding, Kenneth E. "Reflections on Protest." *Bulletin of the Atomic Scientists*, vol. 21 (October 1965), pp. 18–20.

Dellinger, David. "Resistance: Vietnam and America." *Liberation*, vol. 12 (November 1967), pp. 3–7.

Flacks, Richard. "The Liberated Generation: An Exploration of the Roots of Student Protest." *Journal of Social Issues*, vol. 23 (July 1967), pp. 52–75.

Keniston, Kenneth. *Young Radicals: Notes on Committed Youth*. New York: Harcourt, Brace & World, 1968a, pp. 247–256.

————. "Youth, Change and Violence." *The American Scholar*, vol. 37 (Spring 1968b), p. 243.

Kifner, John. "Protestors Meet in Small Groups." *The New Times,* August 28, 1968.

Little, Arthur D. *Outlook for Defense Programs: 1965-1972.* Privately printed, 1965, pp. 7-9.

Luce, Phillip A. *The New Left.* New York: David McKay Publishers, 1966.

Lynd, Staughton, *Nonviolence in America: A Documentary History.* Indianapolis: Bobbs-Merrill Co., 1966, pp. 310-376.

——. *Intellectual Origins of American Radicalism.* New York: Pantheon Books, 1968, p. 172.

Marx, Gary T. *Protest and Prejudice: A Study of Belief in the Black Community.* New York: Harper & Row, 1967, pp. 170-177.

Menashe, Louis, and Ronald Radosh. *Teach-Ins: USA—Reports, Opinions, Documents.* New York: Praeger Publishers, 1967.

Moore, Barrington Jr. "Thoughts on Violence and Democracy." *Proceedings of the Academy of Political Science,* vol. 29 (July 1968), p. 11.

Weidenbaum, Murray L. *Impact of the Vietnam War on the American Economy.* Washington, D.C.: Georgetown University (The Center for Strategic Studies), 1967, pp. 60-75.

20. Bilateralism, Multilateralism, and the Politics of Détente

Aron, Raymond. *The Century of Total War.* Garden City, N.Y.: Doubleday, 1954.

——. *La societe industrielle et la guerre,* 2nd ed., revised and augmented. Paris: Plon, 1959.

Clark, Grenville, and Louis B. Sohn. *World Peace Through World Law.* Cambridge, Mass.: Harvard University Press, 1958.

Fleming, D. F. "The New Europe and the Cold War." *Annals,* no. 347, July 1963.

Hagan, Roger. "Reciprocal Hardening." *Council for Correspondence Newsletter,* no. 26 (May 1963), p. 7.

Horowitz, Irving L. "The Effects of the Sino-Soviet Split on Latin America." *Liberation,* vol. 8, no. 3, May 1963.

——. "The Political Sociology of Soviet Development." In *Il Politico* (publication pending), 1964.

Hughes, Emmet John. *The Ordeal of Power.* New York: Harper & Row, 1961.

Kissinger, Henry A. "The Unsolved Problems of European Defense." *Foreign Affairs,* vol. 40, no. 4 (July 1962), pp. 515-541.

——. "NATO's Nuclear Dilemma." *The Reporter,* March 1963.

Long, Franklin A. Quoted in *The Christian Science Monitor,* June 17, 1963.

Maddox, John. *Commentary,* vol. 35, no. 6, June 1963.

New York Times (The). April 30, 1963.

New York Times (The). May 31, 1963.

Peking Review. "A Proposal Concerning the General Line of the International Communist Movement." June 21, 1963.

Reves, Emery. *The Anatomy of Peace.* New York: Harper Bros., 1945.

Riesman, David. "Reflections on Containment and Initiatives." *Council for Correspondence Newsletter,* February 1963.

Sohn, Louis. "Progressive Zonal Inspection: Basic Issues." In *Disarmament: Its Politics and Economics,* edited by Seymour Melman. Boston: American Academy of Arts and Sciences, 1962, pp. 121–133.

Sorokin, Pitirim. "Mutual Convergence of the United States and the U.S.S.R. to the Mixed Sociocultural Type." *International Journal of Comparative Sociology,* vol. 1, no. 2, September 1960.

Teller, Edward A. (with Allen Brown). *The Legacy of Hiroshima.* London: Macmillan, 1962, especially pp. 299–315.

21. Social Deviance and Political Marginality

Becker, H.S. *The Outsiders.* New York: Free Press, 1963.

———. "Whose Side Are We On?" *Social Problems,* vol. 14, no. 3 (Winter 1967), pp. 239–247.

Bernard, J. "Social Problems as Problems of Decision." *Social Problems,* vol. 6, no. 3 (Winter 1958–59), pp. 204–213.

Black, H., and M. J. Labes. "Guerrilla Warfare: An Analogy to Police-Criminal Interaction." *American Journal of Orthopsychiatry,* vol. 37 (July 1967), pp. 666–670.

Campbell, A., et al. *The American Voter.* New York: John Wiley, 1960.

Cloward, R. A., and R. M. Elman. "Advocacy in the Ghetto." *transaction,* vol. 4 (December 1966), pp. 27–35.

Coser, L. A. "The Sociology of Poverty." *Social Problems,* vol. 13, no. 2 (Fall 1965), pp. 140–148.

Cray, E. *The Big Blue Line: Police Power vs. Human Rights.* New York: Coward-McCann, 1967.

Eckstein, H. *Internal War.* New York: Free Press, 1964.

Evans, R., and R. Novack. "The Ghetto Gangs." *Herald Tribune* (International Edition), July 5, 1967.

Hopper, B. "Cybernation, Marginality, and Revolution." In *The New Sociology,* edited by I. L. Horowitz. New York: Oxford University Press, 1964.

Horowitz, I. L. "Radicalism and Contemporary American Society." *Liberation,* vol. 10 (May 1965), pp. 15–18.

———. "The Military Elite." In *Elites of Latin America,* edited by S. M. Lipset and A. Solari. New York: Oxford University Press, 1967.

Key, V. O., Jr. *Public Opinion and American Democracy.* New York: Knopf, 1961.

Lang, K., and G. E. Lang. *Collective Dynamics.* New York: T.Y. Crowell, 1961.

Lemert, E. M. *Social Pathology.* New York: McGraw Hill, 1951.

———. *Human Deviance, Social Problems, and Social Control.* Englewood Cliffs, N.J.: Prentice-Hall, 1967.

Lieberson, S. "The Meaning of Race Riots." *Race,* vol. 7, no. 4. (1966), pp. 371–378.

Lipset, S. M. *Political Man.* Garden City, N.Y.: Doubleday, 1960.

Lubell, S. *The Future of American Politics.* New York: Harper & Row, 1952.

Mills, C. W. "The Professional Ideology of Social Pathologists." *Power, Politics and People,* edited by I. L. Horowitz. New York: Oxford University Press, 1963, pp. 525–552.

Nettler, G. "Ideology and Welfare Policy." *Social Problems,* vol. 6 (Winter 1958–59), pp. 203–212.

Newfield, J. *A Prophetic Minority.* New York: New American Library, 1966.

Schattschneider, E. E. *The Semi-Sovereign People.* New York: Holt, Rinehart & Winston, 1960.

Schatzman, L., and A. Strauss. "A Sociology of Psychiatry." *Social Problems,* vol. 14, no. 1 (Summer 1966), pp. 3–15.

Spence, L. D. "Berkeley: What It Demonstrates." In *Revolution at Berkeley,* edited by Michael V. Miller and Susan Gilmore. New York: Dell, 1965.

Thompson, H. S. *Hell's Angels: The Strange and Terrible Saga of the Outlaw Motorcycle Gangs.* New York: Random House, 1966.

Turner, W. W. "The Minutemen: The Spirit of '66." *Ramparts,* vol. 5 (January 1967), pp. 69–76.

Wolfgang, M. E., and F. Ferracuti. *The Subculture of Violence.* London and New York: Tavistock, 1967.

Yablonsky, L. *The Tunnel Back: Synanon.* New York: Macmillan, 1965.

22. The New Unholy Alliance: Social Science and Policy-Makers

Caplan, Nathan. Research cited in *Behavior Today,* vol. 5, no. 24 (June 17, 1974), pp. 172–173.

Lasswell, Harold D. "The Policy Orientation." In *The Policy Sciences,* edited by H. D. Lasswell and D. Lerner. Stanford, Cal.: Stanford University Press, 1951.

Price, Don K. *The Scientific Estate.* Cambridge, Mass.: Harvard University Press, 1965.

Salomon, Jean-Jacques. *Science and Politics.* Cambridge, Mass.: MIT Press, 1973, pp. 46–48.

Sola Pool, Ithiel de. "The Necessity for Social Scientists Doing Research for Governments." In *The Rise and Fall of Project Camelot: Studies in the Relationship Between Social Science and Practical Politics,* edited by I. L. Horowitz. Cambridge, Mass.: MIT Press, 1967, pp. 267–280.

Truman, David B. "The Social Sciences and Public Policy." *Science,* vol. 160, no. 3827 (May 3, 1968), pp. 508–512.

23. Ecological Movements vs. Economic Necessities

Lewis M. Branscomb. "Taming Technology: A Plea for National Regulation in a Social Context." *Science,* vol. 171 (March 12, 1971), pp. 972–977.

Frank M. Coffin. *Moment of Totality (Development in the Decade of Ecology).* Development Paper IV, Washington D.C.: Overseas Development Council, January 1971.

Barry Commoner. "The Ecological Crisis." In *Social Responsibility of the Scientist,* edited by Martin Brown. New York: Free Press, 1971, pp. 174–175.

Garrett DeBell. *The Voter's Guide to Environmental Politics: Before, During, and After the Election.* New York: Ballantine Books, 1970.

E. F. Porter, Jr. "Built-in Loopholes for Pollution Laws." *St. Louis Post Dispatch,* March 7, 1971.

Thomas R. Shepard, Jr. "We're Going Too Far on Consumerism." *The Reader's Digest,* vol. 50 (February 1971), pp. 147–150.

Paul Swatek. *The User's Guide to the Protection of the Environment.* New York: Ballantine Books, 1970.

Lee Thayer. "Man's Ecology, Ecology's Man." *Main Currents in Modern Thought,* vol. 27 (January–February 1971), pp. 76–77.

24. The Revolution of Falling Expectations

Bennett, John W. "Anticipation, Adaptation, and the Concept of Culture in Anthropology." *Science,* vol. 192, no. 4242 (May 1976), pp. 847–853.

Curtin, Richard I. *Perceptions of Distributional Equity: Their Economic Bases and Consequences.* Unpublished dissertation, University of Michigan, 1976.

Deutsch, Karl W. "On Inequality and Limited Growth: Some World Political Effects." *International Studies Quarterly,* vol. 19, no. 4 (December 1975), pp. 381–398.

Donnison, David. "Equality." *New Society,* vol. 34, whole no. 685 (November 20, 1975), pp. 422–424.

Forrester, Jay W. *World Dynamics.* Cambridge, Mass.: Wright-Allen, 1971.

———. "Limits to Growth Revisited." *Journal of the Franklin Institute,* vol. 300, no. 2 (August 1975), pp. 107–111.

Huntington, Samuel P. "The Democratic Distemper." *The Public Interest,* whole no. 41 (Fall 1975), pp. 9–38.

Juster, F. Thomas. "The Recovery Gains Momentum." *Economic Outlook,* vol. 3, no. 2 (Spring 1976), pp. 23–25.

Mishan, E. J. *Cost-Benefit Analysis.* New York: Praeger Publishers (second edition), 1976.

Neurath, Paul. "Zwischen Pessimismus und Optimismus." In *Wissenschaft und Weltbild (Festschrift für Hertha Firnberg),* edited by Wolf Frühauf. Vienna: Europaverlag, 1975, pp. 289–312.

Shanahan, Eileen. "Income Distribution Found Little Changed Since War." *The New York Times* (February 2, 1974), p. 10.

van Dam, Andre. "A Simpler Life for the Advanced Countries." *Progress International,* vol. 2 (November 1975), pp. 10–12.

Name Index

Subject Index